D0261124

CP/494

000000773498

CRICKET

THE GAME OF LIFE

CRICKET

THE GAME OF LIFE

Every reason to celebrate

Scyld Berry

HODDER &
STOUGHTON

First published in Great Britain in 2015 by Hodder & Stoughton
An Hachette UK company

1

Copyright © Scyld Berry 2015

The right of Scyld Berry to be identified as the Author of the Work
has been asserted by him in accordance with the Copyright,
Designs and Patents Act 1988.

A CIP catalogue record for this title is available from the British Library

Hardback ISBN: 978 1 473 61858 9
Trade Paperback ISBN: 978 1 473 61859 6
Ebook ISBN: 978 1 473 61857 2

Typeset in Minion by Hewer Text Uk Ltd, Edinburgh
Printed and bound by CPI Group (UK) Ltd, Croydon, CR0 4YY

Hodder & Stoughton policy is to use papers that are natural, renewable
and recyclable products and made from wood grown in sustainable
forests. The logging and manufacturing processes are expected to
conform to the environmental regulations of the country of origin.

Hodder & Stoughton Ltd
Carmelite House
50 Victoria Embankment
London EC4Y 0DZ

www.hodder.co.uk

To the members of Hinton Charterhouse Cricket Club,
especially those who have made catches and stumpings off my bowling,
but above all the groundsmen.

CONTENTS

A NET

OUT OF THE SHIPPING CONTAINER in Basra came a succession of strange noises. *Thud. Thud. Thud.* It had been converted into makeshift quarters for a British Army officer after the invasion of Iraq in 2003. To be more serviceable, if not homely, the container's steel walls had been plastered on the inside.

Nobody had heard this thudding through the night of shelling, when rocket-propelled grenades and screaming mortars tore into buildings and vehicles. It had been one of those intensely humid nights beside the Shatt al-Arab, the confluence of the Tigris and the Euphrates, when the moment you walk outside an air-conditioned room, a skein of sweat covers your skin. In the morning, in any event, the officer was absent from his desk at headquarters.

When his colleagues and the Military Police went to see why the officer was not on duty, and heard this thudding coming from the container, they found it locked on the inside. They had to break the steel door.

Inside, the officer was wide awake. He was not wearing the khaki helmet that was mandatory for officers when they were out of bed, in case of sudden attack by a Shi'ite militia. He was wearing a pair of underpants. On his head. Nothing else.

The thudding, they soon established, was intended to drown out the explosions. The officer had succumbed to post-traumatic stress disorder. To cope with a war remote from home, and reason, he had sought solace in the pastime of his childhood. Naked except for his improvised helmet, he was hitting a ball against the inside wall of the container with his cricket bat.*

‖

I came from Sheffield. 'Somebody had to,' as Bill Bryson said of his birthplace, Des Moines. But in terms of watching cricket I was very lucky to be born less than a mile from Bramall Lane. It was the best ground in the world according to some cricketers, and not only those from Yorkshire.

Jack Fingleton, who opened the batting at Bramall Lane for the Australians in 1938 and became an eminent journalist, declared it had 'the keenest cricketing crowd in England'. Jeff Stollmeyer of Trinidad, who captained West Indies, observed: 'There is more atmosphere at Bramall Lane than at any other cricket ground on which I have played, except Lord's. It was an atmosphere vastly different to Lord's, tense and full of the spirit of combat, accentuated as it was by the squat chimneys looming black outside the ground.' When the West Indians of 1950, including Stollmeyer, narrowly won their match against Yorkshire, the crowd of 30,000 threw their seat cushions on to the field in disgust. The ground had drawn crowds of double that size for England football internationals and for an FA Cup final replay, when everybody stood.

Bramall Lane's colours were primary bright. As Stollmeyer saw, the Lane itself was as black as the soot from steel factories and foundries that rained on the city. 'Stoke up the boilers, lads!' was reputed to be the cry when word went round that Yorkshire were bowling, to hamper the batsmen's vision.

St Mary's church, at the head of the Lane, was coal-black from

---

* Personal interview with a relative of the SAS officer sent to investigate. The army officer who had PTSD was medically evacuated to the UK, and recovered.

the tip of its spire down to the smashed windows. Whenever my mother and I walked to a match, we never went inside the church. That awe which every child is said to need could be found at Bramall Lane.

As we passed St Mary's, and the terraces of two-up two-downs, with corner shops advertising Craven "A" and Tizer, the blue lettering of Yorkshire became clearer on the posters on the blackened stone walls of the ground – the red of their opponents in smaller lettering below. Clutching my two shillings and sixpence, I might have run ahead to the turnstiles. Yorkshire staged four first-class matches a season at Bramall Lane, often three in the Championship and one against the touring team.

After pushing through the turnstiles, I rush up the steps to the top of the terraces and down the other side to get below the roof-line of the stand.

The crash barriers, after the football season, are freshly painted red.

The sightscreens are bright white, like few things in Sheffield before the Clean Air Act.

The field is luscious green, especially where the cricket outfield overlaps the football pitch.

'Scoring card, get the official card!' shout men in coats that once might have been white as they stride up and down the terraces – not that I ever see a rival selling unofficial cards. 'Cards at sixpence each!' They record the ascendancy of a county that has never been equalled. In the 1960s, not only were Yorkshire county champions for seven years; they also beat the Australians by an innings, the Indians by an innings and the New Zealanders by an innings, all at Bramall Lane, and the West Indians by 111 runs at Middlesbrough.*

---

* While Surrey were county champions seven times in the 1950s, they lost to the Indian tourists of 1952, the Australians of 1953 and the South Africans of 1955.

Australian tourists called their match against Yorkshire 'the sixth Test'. During the 1960s, so I believed, Yorkshire at home were the strongest cricket team in the world.

Brian Close is Yorkshire's captain and man-manager, and perhaps the bravest man who ever faced fast bowling or stood unhelmeted at short-leg. Raymond Illingworth, soon to become England's foxiest captain, is in charge of tactics. (Not for another 40 years, until the Ashes series of 2005, did I see such error-free cricket from an English team again.)

Fred Trueman opens the bowling with a perfect side-on action; Jimmy Binks keeps wicket as a butler takes care of the silver; Phil Sharpe conjures at first slip; Ken Taylor is swift or Geoffrey Boycott safe in the covers; John Hampshire bends at short-leg to scoop up catches with a blacksmith's forearms. Bramall Lane's pitches are ideal for three-day cricket: damp and seaming on the first morning, excellent for batting on the second day, spinning on the third afternoon.

The only fly in the ointment is the yeasty smell from Ward's brewery beside St Mary's if the wind blows in the wrong direction. Nothing else detracts from the raw drama on this green ground in the heart of an industrial city.

After tea, a waterfall flows down the terraces when the gates are opened and spectators are allowed in for free, mixing with the thousands intent on the action. The Grinders' Stand, its back to the Lane, is renowned as the most knowledgeable stand in cricket. Not that we dare to sit on those wooden benches: my mother and I sit on the terraces on the opposite side, on cushions hired for twopence, without throwing them.

On these summer afternoons when Yorkshire move towards another Championship, generators hum in the factories outside the ground. The only time I am nearly so happy is when my mother takes me to pick bilberries on the moors above Sheffield and we have a picnic beside a stream. But Bramall Lane is where I am most alive. This hum is the hum of my universe.

|||

The closest I can come to an average day of county cricket, to see why people in England now watch the sport, is a Championship match between Gloucestershire and Glamorgan at Bristol.

Nevil Road is like a number of county cricket grounds left over from the Victorian era. Only a few thousand permanent seats; a small area for net practice, as spare land has long since been sold to keep the club solvent; little space for parking in the ground or the surrounding streets on the rare days when a crowd attends. The truth is that the ground is there because the weight of the past is too heavy for it to be moved.

On this sunny morning in early September, the schools have yet to go back, so one might have expected to see a cluster of boys, watching the game or playing with bat and tennis ball: entry to Nevil Road is £15 for adults, £5 for under-16s. But in the grim grey-stoned building which used to be the Muller Orphanage, housing two thousand inmates, the ghost of the beadle must be on the prowl. The handful of autograph-hunters at the foot of the steel steps leading up to the dressing rooms, who had their books signed before the start of play, are middle-aged or old, not young truants. No security officials are needed to stop intruders; the only bouncer is on the pitch. Championship cricket is self-policing, like most communities in Britain before the social weave unravelled.

Were this professional sport in the United States, spectators would be bombarded with brochures, burgers, memorabilia and promotion deals. Nevil Road's biggest advertisement is a poster fading on the side of the press box: 'BRISTOL'S BIG CRICKET NIGHT OUT: Gloucestershire Gladiators v Somerset'. Inside are two journalists; in the radio commentary box a reporter from BBC Wales.

English cricket can outstrip American sport, however, when it comes to memorabilia. A marquee, erected for the summer, sells new and second-hand books; and cricket has produced more books and pamphlets in English, about 20,000, than any other sport in any language. Those who drift into the marquee seem more interested in the past than the current match, especially in biographies of Gloucestershire heroes whose names are perpetuated by the main buildings: the Grace Suite, the Jessop Pavilion, the Hammond Suite. The first a Victorian hero, the second Edwardian, while the most recent dates from between the two World Wars.

The largest scattering of spectators, in a crowd of about three hundred, sits atop the Hammond Suite on terraced rows of benches, while underneath lunch is prepared. The days when every county was linked by an umbilical cord to the community it represented, and when a hard core of several thousands – often football supporters out of season – would turn up for knockout ties, or a Lord's cup final, are gone.

Some spectators sit in pairs, others three or four to a bench. Everybody seems to feel free to speak to those around him. A conversation continues while the ball is bowled; laughter ripples. The talk is of how Gloucestershire's campaign for promotion from the second division had faltered at the Cheltenham Festival, as it has done for the last decade; or not of cricket at all but of City, or Rovers, or the government. Never does this morning murmur escalate into loudness.

On the field, the dominant colours are the cricketers' white – this is the old-fashioned Championship, not Twenty20 – and the green of the turf. Beyond the boundary, beige and fawn predominate: not so much the colours of autumn, Nevil Road being short of trees and hedges, as of spectators' clothing. The majority of spectators – barely a handful of women – wear light-coloured shirts and maybe a light brown jacket. Those feeling young at heart might wear an England replica shirt.

Another group characteristic is the absence of audible interest in money. Conversations are not about stocks and shares, equities and annuities. This may be related to the fact that the overall sums do not add up: the action on the field is subsidised by the broadcasting deal for covering England's international matches. Gloucestershire's gate receipts, membership fees and other sources of income make up around one-quarter of the county's revenue.

One colour arrests the eye: a dozen or more streaks of electric blue dotted around the pavilion. Today, 1 September, happens to be the 35th anniversary of a characteristically English institution. Alan Gibson, a former president of the Oxford Union, used his talents to best effect when writing about county cricket for *The Times*. He aggrandised journeymen into lovable personalities: above all, Colin Dredge of Somerset as 'the demon of Frome', and Jack Davey of Gloucestershire, originally from Devon. Whether Dredge could be ranked among Somerset's all-time top 100 cricketers, or Davey among Gloucestershire's, would prompt a prolonged debate on the roof of the Hammond Suite. What mattered, though, was that Gibson welcomed his readers into a warm world of West Country characters.

In a book for sale in the marquee, *Growing Up With Cricket*, Gibson had written of Davey:

Jack has only one Christian name. One day his captain, Tony Brown, felt that this was a little unfair on him, as everybody else had two initials. So they popped in an extra J. This was repeated on scorecards up and down the country for some time. Speculation grew, encouraged I fear by a mischievous journalist, as to what the extra J stood for. Jolly Jack? Jocose Jack? Jovial Jack? Jubilee Jack? Jocund Jack? Jesting Jack? Jabbering Jack? Jaunty Jack? Jumping Jack? Hence the query on the tie of his fan club.

About two dozen members have turned up for the lunch to celebrate the 35th anniversary of the JJ? Club. Arthur Anderson, the genial chairman and a retired accountant, explains that he had bought an electric-blue suit in 1971 and had chosen the tie to match it. Our eponymous hero, Jack Davey, has turned 66 and remains jolly, jovial, even jaunty. He is glad to be alive after dying twice, from heart and renal failure, when he was 50. The cardiac specialist subsequently told Jack that he normally stopped trying to restart a heart after 24 attempts with the 'jump leads' but, as Jack was a non-smoker, he was planning to give him a couple of extra shocks – just as he came back to life at the 23rd attempt. Jack was still unconscious for two weeks, and when he looked in the mirror after losing three stone did not recognise himself.

Over the wine of 'luncheon', anecdotes are told, or rather retold. Jack recalls the most famous game in Gloucestershire's history: their Gillette Cup semi-final at Old Trafford in 1971, in front of a 30,000 crowd and probably the largest television audience ever to see a county game. So important was a county semi-final, and so thrilling the climax in Manchester's twilight, that the BBC delayed the start of the Nine O'Clock News. 'And our appearance fee for that game from the BBC was five pounds fifty!' said Jack, without any trace of bitterness or envy of today's players. He admits himself: 'I wouldn't get through the warm-ups now.'

A collection is made during lunch for a charity, launched in memory of another Devonian cricketer who represented Gloucestershire, although David Shepherd was to become famous as an umpire. This charity funds cricket coaching for youngsters in the West Country. It is hard to think of a gathering of men in suits and ties that could be less materialistic or less intent on self-promotion. Jack, living in Exeter, is content with driving a hire car for three or four days a week 'to pay the golf club fees'.

Of the club named after him, Jack says: 'It's lovely, and it's great to think it's still going on after all these years. But it is a bit eccentric.' When luncheon finishes, just before tea, a large electric-blue banner is unfurled and paraded very slowly around the boundary, again without a security man in sight. While the four or five members show their flag, the public-address system announces that Hampshire have scored 373 for one wicket against Somerset, prompting a few mild laughs at Gloucestershire's neighbours. Somerset have never won the Championship; Gloucestershire can claim a title or two, in the 1870s, under Grace.

Before the members of the JJ? Club disperse for the winter, they kindly fill out a questionnaire in which I ask several questions, including 'What do you like most about cricket?' The majority had played the game in their youth, usually inspired by seeing their father do so. But what three-quarters of them liked most was 'the friendship', or 'camaraderie', or 'social life'.

England, fundamentally an Anglo-Saxon country, values privacy more than most societies; and the other side of this coin is loneliness. If you want other people to keep their distance, they are going to do that even when you feel like some company. Surveys say that more than one-third of the UK's population over 65 is lonely from 'sometimes' to 'always'; one-fifth of those between the ages of 35 and 44 feel lonely a lot of the time.

At any county cricket ground from April to September, however, anybody can go and sit beside a stranger and talk without a formal introduction: about Grace or Hammond, cricket or football, politics or people. Behaviour which would be regarded as weird or antisocial in a public park or cinema or train becomes acceptable in a public house or an English cricket ground. This sport promotes socialisation among those who watch it. It offers friendship in a society which can value privacy too highly.

I was the same. I clung to cricket as an emotional surrogate, before discovering its other pleasures.

On the morning of Thursday, 27 July 1967, I was leaning out of the train window with a transistor radio, trying to listen to the Test match commentary. My mother had driven my father and me to Sheffield station, near Bramall Lane, to put us on the train to Liverpool, from where we were going to take a ferry to the Isle of Man for a week's holiday.

It was the first day of England's Test series against Pakistan at Lord's. Transmission was intermittent as we went over and through the Pennines, and on the ferry. After England had made a large total, Pakistan collapsed at the start of their first innings. On the third day, they began to rally, led by Hanif Mohammad. On the Sunday morning, a rest day in the Test, my father and I were having breakfast at a small hotel in Laxey when he was called to the phone in Reception. My sister Melloney was ringing from home: my mother, while decorating a bedroom, had suffered a brain haemorrhage.

I cannot remember how we returned to the mainland, whether by ferry or plane. My next memory is stopping in a taxi past midnight – it must have been too late for a train back to Sheffield – on the Snake Pass. My father rang from a telephone kiosk and spoke to the Sheffield Royal Infirmary. The latest news was that my mother had suffered a second, far more serious, haemorrhage.

We reached the hospital about dawn. I was not allowed into the intensive care unit. So I never saw my mother again. Melloney took me home, to wait. A kind neighbour came round and found something to keep me occupied: to continue decorating the spare bedroom. While I scraped away at wallpaper, the radio was on, and Hanif was still batting. He batted for more than nine hours, long enough to take my mind away from the impending reality for the odd moment.

Early on the morning of 1 August 1967, my mother died. She had never regained consciousness after the first haemorrhage. The second, I was told, had been so severe she would never have been able to lead a normal life. I do not remember crying much, or feeling angry or bitter, or even talking. I suppose I carried on decorating, and listening to the radio, just infinitely sad.

My father sold our house and moved into a hall of residence at Sheffield University. He was a professor of English who used to proclaim: 'The two greatest men who ever lived – and you cannot say that Jesus was only a man – are Hammond and Shakespeare. Or rather Shakespeare and Hammond, in that order.' Having lost his mother in childbirth, and been caned frequently at school, he sought refuge in English literature and Cheltenham festivals – not the literary ones but those dominated by Wally Hammond. He was there for the week in 1928 when Hammond made a century in each innings and took ten catches against Surrey; then he scored 80, took 15 wickets and bowled unchanged throughout both innings against Worcestershire.

My father was an archetypally English professor, the most impractical of men, through a combination of accident and design. One day, my mother and I had gone out, maybe to Bramall Lane, leaving his lunch in the oven. When we came home, he had not eaten it: he had been unable to work out how the oven opened.

My father had served in the army in Malta in the Second World War, during the Siege. He would have been dangerous with a gun in his hand, though not to the enemy. From the army, he was seconded to teach English at a school in the medieval hilltop town of Mdina, from where he watched German planes swooping over the Mediterranean from their bases in Italy to bomb the island into submission. We were never close, because he never removed the mask of Victorian fatherhood; but when I took him back to Malta for his 90th birthday, I met several of his former pupils who were overwhelmed by their memories of the animation with which my father had staged their performances of *Hamlet* and *Macbeth* amid Mdina's battlements. He had escaped from the practical world and thrown himself into English literature as the antidote to his childhood.

So my father went into a hall of residence, my sister to university, and the contents of our house were sold. Even our cat had to be given away; a few months later, a letter came from her new home to say she had died of flu. On a similar basis, it was decided I should be sent to boarding school. My father had read that the school which sent the highest proportion of pupils to Oxbridge was Ampleforth College (he might have missed the small print saying that Ampleforth, as a religious foundation, had its own Oxford college to train Catholic priests and swell the numbers). He had longed to go to Oxford himself, but did not have the money and had to train as a solicitor's clerk.

After boarding for a year or two, I would sometimes lie in bed in the dormitory after the lights had been turned out and count, not sheep, but the number of adults I had spoken to in my life. I had entered Ampleforth in the January term, after everyone else in my year had joined in September and made friends. Excluding people at school, I can remember the total at some counts amounting to fewer than 20.

Sunday evenings were worst. From the cold supper, I would escape early and run to queue for the school's only public telephone. When my father answered, I pushed Button A and we had a few shillings' worth of 'How are you?' and 'Oh, I'm all right.' Neither of us began to say how we felt.

Cricket kept me going – firstly reading about it, then writing about it, before I ever had the chance to play. One day, after going to the dentist's in York, I found in a second-hand bookshop a complete run of Yorkshire CCC yearbooks from 1898 to 1940. Here was a world I could enter, inhabited by Wilfred Rhodes, Roy Kilner, Herbert Sutcliffe, George Macaulay, Emmott Robinson, Hedley Verity . . . Here was camaraderie, of a vicarious kind.

If I appeared diligent in the school library, it was because it contained several books by Len Hutton and Neville Cardus. By the time I was supposed to be studying for A levels, I felt I knew enough about the Yorkshire cricketers of 1925 – never has a county won more Championship matches in a season without defeat – to try and write a book about them. Only Sutcliffe was still alive, in a nursing home, but I did what research I could – at school, if not at home, which was now in London. My father had remarried hastily; and my stepmother was prone to hit the bottle and wreck her/our house.

A piece of fortune was that Yorkshire's captain from 1927 to 1929, Sir William Worsley, lived a few miles away at Hovingham Hall. After I had laboriously typed eleven chapters of juvenilia, he penned the kindest of forewords: 'It was a team of infinite cricket ability and strong character: seven of its members played for England and all the others achieved distinction in the game. Berry has analysed their ability and their personality with devoted atten- tion. I understand he would like to become a writer on cricket and this volume gives clear evidence to me that this may well be a very successful line for him. I do wish him luck.'

By now I was 17 years old, and I still had not played a single game of cricket – not one proper match other than pick-up games. It was partly my fault, for being truthful. On arriving at Ampleforth, when asked by the games master if I had been in the first team at my previous school, I said I had been in the first-team squad, but not in the first XI.

Cricket at Westbourne preparatory school in Sheffield had been dominated by William Ward – not the one who scored 278 for MCC at Lord's in 1820, but another who may have been almost as good. He would make a century out of a total of 138 or so, and went on to break the record for most runs in a season at Uppingham. The cover drives of Boycott at Bramall Lane and Ward at Westbourne – his front foot pointing towards where I sat beside the boundary – are the first strokes I still recall. When given a chance, I bowled leg-breaks that were very slow but turned a long way, and added a googly; but even after Ward had left, I was not selected for the first XI for their few matches. Instead, I reasoned I would be chosen for the second XI's match at Bakewell. It was logical: I was in the first-team squad of 14, so the two others and I who were not in the first XI would be chosen for the second team. I set my heart on it. My parents then happened to invite the headmaster to our house, and he asked me if I would be scorer for the second XI. I ran out of the room, into the kitchen, and burned. It was the most embarrassing, disappointing and frustrating moment of my life. It still is.

The drawback to living in Sheffield was that Bramall Lane and the university were the only cricket grounds anywhere near the centre. The city had produced plenty of cricketers in the nineteenth century – George Ulyett, the Ian Botham of his day, grew up in Sheffield, as well as the county's first captain, Roger Iddison – because they had space in which to play. Thereafter factories and terraced houses expanded down Bramall Lane, leaving no flat land for a boy to play, without going to the leafy suburbs.

For my first two summers at boarding school, aged 14 and 15, I was condemned to cross-country and tennis. Aged 16, I broke my collarbone playing football, so another summer passed without a game. And how do you get selected for a match if you have never played one? Even Don Bradman might have had a problem. 'How about reviving the Optimists, old chap?' my housemaster, Fr Edward, said one day. 'We used to have a school team that played against the local villages. That's why we were called the Optimists – we didn't stand much chance of winning.'

So one summer evening, when I was 17, the team I had assembled poured out of a school minibus to play a 20-over game at and against Rievaulx Abbey. The ruins were magnificent, but when we looked for a cricket ground, we found arrangements were almost as medieval: a field of sheep with a roped-off square. After chasing them away, and at the end of the first over of my first cricket match, Rievaulx had scored four runs for the loss of three wickets. Having arranged the fixture and collected the team, I thought I deserved to be captain, and drew on my observations of Brian Close.

Faced with a bunch of schoolboys, however, Rievaulx had reversed their batting order and given their younger lads a chance. As the Reformation cast its shadow, the home side won easily enough. We then persuaded the master-in-charge that, having missed school supper, we needed to stop at a pub in Scawton on the way back. The Hare claimed to be the smallest pub in England, but it was large enough for us to eat ham, egg and chips, and drink to excess and the success of our new cricket team. I had a strange feeling. I realised I was happy for the first time in years.

We played four or five games that summer, and the following, although the rationale for the team's name was soon manifest, no matter how many of the school's first XI I persuaded to play. Every village team in Yorkshire contains canny cricketers. Our most one-sided game was at Newburgh Priory, where Oliver Cromwell's head is reputed to be buried. Our batsmen lost theirs when we chased Newburgh's 170 off 20 overs. At number ten I was the highest scorer, with 11 not out in a total of 28 for nine. I did not dare bat any higher, and it was only later when I took my driving test that I found I needed glasses. I never had the confidence to bowl a single ball.

I was 18 years old, therefore, when I bowled my first over in a proper match. Fr Edward chose me for a side he had assembled to play against the Under-16 first XI, whom he coached. I began quite tidily, bowling with a windmill action which a few years later Jack Fingleton, who was umpiring, said was like that of his Australian teammate Bill O'Reilly: he was not obviously joking, bless him. I started to take some wickets. The Under-16s were not bad – one went on to play a few first-class games for Oxford University – but they could not spot a googly. In my first 11 overs of formal cricket, I took six wickets for 24 runs, and led the side off to tea.

Only there was no tea, no interval, no time to savour the elation after waiting so long. 'You'd better come and have a bowl,' said the school coach. A first XI trial was in progress so, without a break, I went out and took off my sweater to bowl again. The umpire was Brian Statham. Me, who had never bowled until that afternoon, handing my sweater to Brian Statham, the taker of 242 Test wickets for England. He was known as 'Gentleman George', one of nature's finest, and he neither said nor did anything to increase my discomfort. But it still seemed sacrilege. It would have been more appropriate if I had spread my sweater on the ground for him to walk on.

I ran in and bowled straight away. Out came a googly. I ran in again, intent on a leg-break, and out came a googly. And another. Every ball was turning in to the right-hander. I had no idea what was happening. The pitch was slower, more puddingy, than the one I had just been bowling on further up the hill, but that did not account for this sudden reversal. The batsman could predict which way the ball was going to turn.

In the afternoons following this trial, I went back to the nets and still the same thing happened. Only googlies, no leg-break. Nobody offered a word of advice. It was years before I worked out that, because I had tired after my first spell of 11 overs and all the nervous excitement, I was no longer turning side-on but bowling increasingly chest-on. My wrist had consequently 'collapsed' – instead of pointing my palm at the batsman – so only googlies came out.

I was still chosen for Ampleforth's next second XI game against Durham School Seconds. I took four wickets for eight runs as we dismissed them for 50. Having waited throughout my childhood for a game, I had taken my first ten wickets for 32 runs. But my leg-break had not returned – that took a couple of years – and I was soon dropped, or 'allowed to concentrate on my A levels'. That was not undeserved, but I was subsequently written out of the school magazine. The master-in-charge awarded my wickets to the bowler at the other end, who had taken four wickets for nine.

In the following year, 1973, Bramall Lane was closed as a cricket ground. It had been discussed in the local newspapers for years. Sheffield United wanted their ground exclusively for football, even though they did not attract the crowds to fill the stand that was going to be built on the fourth side across the cricket square. Yorkshire had declined drastically since 1968: Close, Illingworth, Binks and Trueman gone, with all their knowledge and winning habits, through bad management more than age. Closure, nevertheless, felt like a gratuitous wound.

I went to the last game of cricket at Bramall Lane, the Roses Match against Lancashire, which was ruined by rain. Supporters were invited at the close to dig up the turf and take a piece home. That, for me, would have been desecrating a cemetery; but maybe it was better that the place where my childhood was happiest should be closed. Had I kept returning to Bramall Lane every summer, in pursuit of memories of my mother, I might not have moved on.

'Tis little I repair to the matches of the South'ron folk,
    Though my own red roses there may blow;
'Tis little I repair to the matches of the South'ron folk,
    Though the red roses crest their caps, I know.

Seldom did the late Victorian poet Francis Thompson revisit Lord's after the heroes of his youth, Hornby and Barlow, had ceased to play for Lancashire and 'flicker to and fro, to and fro': he could not afford to watch his old county, having drifted south to the streets of London, where he wrote his poetry and sold newspapers and became an opium addict. I never went to Bramall Lane again, after my own white roses there had blown.

But at least during my childhood I had watched cricket being played at its best, and had tasted the briefest success as a player. Before the door of the steel container slammed, I had seen the happiness that could lie beyond.

1

LOVE'S LABOUR
NOT LOST

What mighty Contests rise from trivial Things.
Alexander Pope, *The Rape of the Lock*

A S AN INNKEEPER, George Smith knows everything there is to know about the morning after. But when he stirs on 19 June 1744, he senses something different.

First light is filtering through his garret window. The hour is being chimed at St Mary-le-Bow, although he is not alert enough to count the exact number. Down below, in Chiswell Street, a cart rumbles over the cobbles. In the courtyard of his inn, the Pyed Horse, he hears a barrel being rolled. Good, young William must be already astir.

When George stretches, a stream of recollections is undammed. Apart from his head, his right shoulder is a bit sore, but he does not feel bad, considering . . . Considering what a long, hot day in the City of London it had been . . . Considering what a cricket match it had been . . . Considering what his profits would be!

Thousands upon thousands of folk poured through his inn yesterday, to buy tickets for the Kent v England match and enter the ground of the Honourable Artillery Company next door. Members of the august Company have their own entrance, and do not have to pay for entry.

Thinking of the tickets makes George smile. It was a clever idea, when sketching a few players on the face of the ticket, to give them all shadows. Roll up, roll up – it's going to be a sunny day!

George remembers why his shoulder is sore, and it's not from batting or bowling. He had to send William to the inn's stables to fetch a whip when the crowd spilled on to the field of play. He cracked the whip to force the spectators back over the rope. There *was* some disorder – and the HAC committee are bound to haul him in and tell him it must never be allowed to happen again, forsooth. But it is not as if the Riot Act had to be read.

A pity Kent won – so narrowly, too. It was hardly George's fault. It is true he scored only nought and eight runs for England, but he was so busy all day in supplying fine wines, victuals and viands to the gentle-folk, ales and pies for the rest, not to mention cracking the whip.

Then, as if ten thousand spectators were not enough, he had to cater for royalty. If the HAC committee knew that His Royal Highness Frederick, the Prince of Wales, was going to attend, and his younger brother, the Duke of Cumberland, why did they not let George put up a special tent? He could also have increased the price of a ticket from twopence to threepence, or more, because spectators had these royal personages to view into the bargain.

What a finish, too! If only Thomas Waymark had held on . . .

George sees again the ball hit up into the sky, when Kent's last pair had three runs still to make for victory. What steadier man in the whole realm to take that catch? Poor old Tom. He had been the groom for the Duke of Richmond. This morning he might be sleeping in the kennels.

The Bow bells chime the half-hour.* George opens his eyes,

---

* Sorry, but one of cricket's finest witticisms cannot be allowed to pass: it is based on the Yorkshire and England bowler who dismissed Don Bradman for nought at the height of his powers. If a Cockney is someone born within the sound of Bow bells, what is the definition of a Yorkshireman? So asked Michael Carey, the cricket correspondent of the *Daily Telegraph* in the 1980s. The answer: someone born within the sound of Bill Bowes.

stares at the ceiling – and sees the future of cricket at the Artillery Ground. Matches of three or five players a side are all very well, but they do not last the whole day, as Kent v England had. Teams must be eleven a side in future. Matches must also consist of two innings per side when there is sufficient time and daylight at the height of summer. Besides, it is in the spirit of Englishmen, fair and true, that a fellow should be given a second chance, as he was after scoring nought.

And if he could fill the Artillery Ground with ten thousand folk for one grand match, he can do it again. Since the Great Plague, and the improvements in clearing the streets of rubbish and beggars and ne'er-do-wells, many men have moved to live in London. They have money to spend, too: some are making handsome profits out of trade with France and the West Indies – 'the middling sort', as they are called. Royalty, gentlefolk and this new middling sort, they all want entertainment, and they are prepared to pay good money to watch cricket. Boxing, bear-baiting, cock-fighting and horse-racing do not have a venue to accommodate ten thousand people and charge them as they enter, like he does.

George sits up in bed. If he increases the cost of admission from twopence to sixpence, and ten thousand folk buy a ticket – or eight thousand, because Company members have to be admitted free – then sixpence multiplied by eight thousand equals . . . equals . . .

'William! Come hither, boy! And bring pen and paper, prithee!'

Kent v England at the Artillery Ground on 18 June 1744 is the first cricket match for which an entrance ticket survives; and the first for which a match report survives; and the second for which we have a scorecard. This evidence, together, gives us a detailed picture of why the playing and watching of cricket was so attractive, even in its infancy, to English people.

While the first surviving ticket was printed for George Smith, his age unknown, the first match report was written by James Dance, when he was 23. At the same age, I covered my first Test series, the Ashes of 1977, and my first England tour. One is eager to play shots at 23, and see how far one can push irreverent wit.

The parallels, I should add, do not extend much further. His father, George Dance the Elder, was the architect who at that time was designing the new Mansion House as the Lord Mayor of London's residence. At 18, James Dance had achieved a precocious hat-trick. He had gone up to St John's, Oxford, and a few months later down again; he had joined Lincoln's Inn; and he had married Elizabeth Hooper, daughter of a customs officer. While none of those ventures quite worked out, Dance had shown an early sign of finding his niche when he had defended the prime minister with what the *Oxford Dictionary of National Biography* calls 'a smart poem'. Sir Robert Walpole, Britain's first prime minister, had been ridiculed in anonymous verse, which was suspected of being composed by Alexander Pope, the most acerbic of satirists, and Dance had come up with a witty riposte. It did not lead to a career in Downing Street, where Walpole had been granted a residence at Number Ten by King George II, but it had marked him as a young man of promise.

Having been one of the ten thousand spectators at the Artillery Ground that day – did he ask George Smith for a free press pass? – Dance was inspired to write a poem of three hundred lines. Unlike most match reports, which have to be finished a few minutes after the close of play, Dance had several months for composition, and he made the most of the extra time to give full rein to his irreverent wit. He chose the mock-heroic style, along the lines of Pope's two famous poems, *The Rape of the Lock* and *The Dunciad*, which had people rolling in the aisles – provided they were not the butts. The barbs Pope hurled in *The Dunciad* at the

House of Hanover were more vicious than anything published about the royal family in our litigious age.

Dance was also a player himself, in more than one sense. He played cricket for the Richmond club, although none of his scores survives. At the Richmond Theatre, he worked as an actor, playwright and manager; David Garrick, most celebrated of actors and known to watch cricket, was to invite Dance to Drury Lane to play Falstaff in what was considered his finest role. Dance also acquired a mistress: the actress known as Catherine de l'Amour. And while living up to his real surname by leading his wife and children a merry dance, he took the pseudonym of James Love, presumably to identify with his mistress. It was under this name that his *Cricket: An Heroic Poem* was published in 1745.

We do not know whether Catherine was French or if she simply adopted 'de l'Amour' as an exotic stage name. Either way, I suspect James Love is teasing her in his poem when he launches into ridicule and takes his first potshot at France, as one of those European countries which do not play cricket. He calls the games that French people play 'Eunuch Sports', a barb worthy of Pope. Primarily, Love has billiards and bowls in mind.* In a footnote, Love says that billiards is 'Frenchifi'd' and played by 'Beaus of the first Magnitude, dress'd in the Quintessence of the Fashion' – veritable fops! In the eyes of Love, the only proper sport apart from cricket is tennis: real tennis, the sport of kings, as lawn tennis was not invented until the nineteenth century.

Remember that what Smith is introducing is nothing less than the commercialisation of leisure, an historic moment in the western world; whenever we buy a ticket to watch sport, we are following in

---

* Love could not know that Dr W.G. Grace would represent England not only at cricket but also, in his dotage, at bowls.

the footsteps of Smith's customers who went through his Pyed Horse into the Artillery Ground. In 1744 the parameters of formal sport are only just being explored. Military fighting is still on the agenda – the last battle on British soil was to take place the following year, never mind excursions overseas – so what form should peaceful sport take in developing manly prowess? Love is defining the parameters, or trying to, when he scorns 'puny' billiards and bowls.

Love next takes aim at the Honourable Artillery Company – always safer to ridicule institutions or foreign countries, rather than individuals who can jeopardise one's career prospects. King Henry VIII had founded it for the defence of the realm, and even today the HAC is the City headquarters for the British Army Reserve, or Territorial Army formerly. But in the two centuries following its foundation, the members of the Company seem to have become less than fit for purpose. Their records for February 1744 mention a procession to celebrate the 17th anniversary of the accession of King George II, and even though war was in the air and austerity the order of the day, each member afterwards was still entitled to 'a pint of wine'. Love takes aim at these fat-cat city-slickers who have let their military training lapse, and fires:

> A Place there is, where City-Warriors meet,
> Wisely determin'd not to fight, but eat.
> Where harmless Thunder rattles to the Skies,
> While the plump Buff-coat fires, and shuts his Eyes.

A hit, a veritable hit! These 'warriors' are intent on feeding, not fighting. They are 'plump' and close their eyes – even though their ordnance is composed of blanks.

More ridicule comes when Love dedicates his poem to Lord Sandwich. He bows and scrapes so obsequiously, and lavishes so much mock-heroic praise on him, the effect is absurd: 'With the greatest Diffidence I presume to lay this imperfect Poem at your Lordship's Feet.' After expressing nothing less than 'Veneration', Love goes on: 'Far be it from me . . . to attempt a Description of your Lordship's exalted Qualifications: Those Excellences which every Englishman is sensible of, but no one can express.' Come on! This is the Lord Sandwich whose claim to fame is inventing a snack. After his death, and a long ministerial career, this epitaph was proposed: 'Seldom has any man held so many offices and accomplished so little.' (The Sandwich Islands ceased to be named after him and were instead called Hawaii.)

Love was impecunious – he had a wife, children and mistress to support – so I suspect he wrote this grovelling dedication to wheedle a few guineas out of his lordship. Modern naval historians claim that Sandwich was not entirely useless, and reformed the Admiralty to some effect, but Love goes so far overboard as to hail him as 'the Cicero of the Age'. He signs himself at the end of this dedication as 'Your Lordship's Most Devoted, Most Obedient, and Most Humble Servant.' You would have thought Sandwich would have splashed out and ordered a few extra copies. Had his lordship bought one for each of the children of his mistress, never mind his other relatives, he would have swelled sales of the book by at least nine.

As Love loves a lord more than most, for sound financial reasons, another peer to receive his utmost deference is Lord John Sackville, who played for Kent in this match. Sackville had issued the original challenge: Kent would play the best cricketers in the rest of England in two fixtures, home and away. Sackville was the son of the first Duke of Dorset and had therefore grown up playing cricket on the ground in the family estate at Knole Park, near Sevenoaks. His elder brother, the Earl of Middlesex, played cricket too, but he was not involved in this game, because he had more pressing duties as Master of the Horse for the Prince of Wales.

Mistresses were commonplace in Georgian society, and Sackville was not to be left out. On the last day of 1743, he had had a son by Lady Frances Leveson-Gower, sister of the Duchess of Bedford, out of wedlock. Two days later, however, on 1 January 1744, Sackville had been compelled to marry the mother of his child.

Sackville, now 30, held several offices of state, but without the income to match. He was an equerry to George II's wife, Queen Caroline; and Lieutenant of Dover Castle (his father was Lord Warden of the Cinque Ports); and he had been the MP for Tamworth since the age of 21. To his partial rescue came Frederick, the Prince of Wales, granting him an annuity of £800 a year. But Sackville needed more besides: hence, perhaps, the challenge of these two cricket matches for a stake of one thousand guineas a side.

Of Sackville's scandal, Love breathes not a word. An explanation could be that he feared his own mistress would be exposed by a reviewer in the public prints. Instead, he lays on flattery like clotted cream whenever he mentions Sackville. He is not only 'Illustrious', he is 'Swift as the *Falcon*, darting on its Prey' and 'pants for mighty Honours, yet to come.' Such deference must have resulted in a few more sales.

George Smith, as a commoner, does not receive quite the same veneration. But when Love pokes fun at him, he does so fairly gently. In one of his witty footnotes, Love refers to him as: 'Mr *Smith*, the Master of the Ground, who, to his *immortal Honour*, and *no inconsiderable* Advantage, has made great Improvements, and been perhaps a principal Cause of the high Light in which CRICKET at this Time flourishes.'

Smith was therefore the major figure in cricket's infancy. He was in charge of the best ground in England, and the ticketing, and the catering, and the security; and he was a player selected for England, or 'the Counties', as Love called them. They sure don't make all-rounders like Smith any more.

Love records for us one of the 'great Improvements' which Smith made. The Artillery Ground was the first cricket ground known to have its playing area marked out by a boundary rope. (An advertisement of 1731 advertises a cricket match on Kennington Common that will be 'roped out', but no report has been discovered to confirm that it happened.) Smith seems to have started doing so before 1744, his invention stemming from the necessity of containing a large crowd in a small space. The contemporaneous painting of a cricket match at 'the Mary-le-bone Fields' depicts spectators scattered over a wide plain – the area that became Lord's being then open country. Where did Smith get several hundred yards of rope? Living close to the Thames, he would not have had far to go to a chandler's. In any event, Smith was so ahead of his time that a boundary rope was not used at Lord's until the second half of the nineteenth century.

> Wide o'er th' extended Plain, the circling String
> Restrains th' impatient Throng, and marks a Ring.

Another Improvement which Smith made – another first at any rate – was to charge for admission. The Artillery Ground was the first sports ground in post-Roman Britain to do so. It was surrounded by streets, buildings and the graveyard where Daniel Defoe and John Bunyan are buried, so by restricting public access to it through the courtyard of the Pyed Horse, Smith could charge twopence a head. Or maybe more . . .

Love does not ridicule the other cricketers in this match. Thereby he set a fine example as the first cricket correspondent. Being a player himself, he must have known just how sodding difficult the game can be at times.

And because Love played the game himself, his enthusiasm when he describes the start of a cricket season is palpable almost three centuries later:

> When the returning Sun begins to smile,
> And shed its Glories round this sea-girt Isle;
> When new-born Nature deck'd in vivid Green,
> Chaces dull Winter from the charming Scene:
> High panting with Delight, the jovial Swain
> Trips it exulting o'er the Flow'r-strew'd Plain;
> Thy Pleasures, CRICKET! all his Heart controul;
> Thy eager Transports dwell upon his Soul.

So here we are, close to the summer solstice, the perfect time of year for a long day's cricket. The stage is perfect, too, or at any rate the best in existence, as Thomas Lord has yet to be born. Let the cricketers enter – and what a fine sight they make, especially when compared with the normal denizens of the Artillery Ground, those members 'plump' and cowardly:

> The Stumps are pitch'd. Each Hero now is seen,
> Springs o'er the Fence, and bounds along the Green,
> In decent White, most gracefully array'd,
> Each strong-built Limb in all its Pride display'd.

'Fence' may be poetic licence for the rope. Or it may be that the cricketers changed in the main building of Armoury House, then jumped over a wooden fence in front of it, while the rope restrained spectators on the other three sides of the ground.*

Here we also have cricket's first reference to costume. The players in this match dressed in white, and it was a bit of a trend-setter, for the next 233 years, until the advent of World Series Cricket. Ladies

---

* It is not just the sight of cricketers taking the field, as a white waterfall flowing down the pavilion steps, which excites us; it is the sound, too. One follower of the game, blind since childhood, told me his favourite cricket sound is that made by studded boots as the players leave their dressing-room and clatter down steps on to the grass.

dressed the same: on 26 July of the following year, when XI Maids of Bramley played against XI Maids of Hambledon (the Hambledon in Surrey near Godalming), they all dressed in white, augmented by blue ribbons in the hair of the Bramley players and red ribbons for the Hambledon team. Stripes have come, been, gone and returned, on shirts and caps, but white was the dominant colour from the outset – a decision that could only have been made in an era of many servants to do the laundry.

The consequences have been unquantifiable yet, I would argue, considerable. White clothes do make a man, or woman, more 'gracefully array'd' than he or she would be in clothes or uniform of another colour. White suggests purity, too; or so the priesthood thinks. This has shaped our image of cricketers. I believe we have come to expect them to behave better on and off the field, if only slightly, than players in other team sports who do not wear white. I suspect, too, that more match-fixing and spot-fixing have been perpetrated in coloured uniform, in limited-overs cricket, than when the clothing has been white.

As informatively as a match brochure, Love proceeds to talk us through the stars of the forthcoming show, starting with the England captain, Richard Newland. Love, in a footnote, calls him 'a famous *Batsman*': so, as another first, Newland inaugurates the sequence of players who have been hailed as the best batsman in England. The same footnote says that Newland comes from Slindon in Sussex and is a farmer by profession, although he used the money he made out of cricket to train as a surgeon and practise a different kind of cut. Aided by two of his brothers, Newland was the pillar of the Slindon team that lost only one of more than 40 matches in the 1740s.

In his poem, Love tells us that Newland is left-handed – and by my reckoning, if we take into account the players of the Hambledon era portrayed by John Nyren in *The Cricketers of My Time*, about a third of the known batsmen in the eighteenth century were left-handers. I can only deduce that they enjoyed the same advantage – of having a right-arm bowler bowling the ball across them, rather than at the stumps – as left-handers now. But stern and inflexible Victorian mores set in, demanding conformity, so that *Baily's Magazine* observed in 1870: 'There is not now a first-class left-handed batsman in England.' Hence the first left-hander to score a century for England, Frank Woolley, did not do so until 1911–12 in Australia. The same conventions shackled Asian batsmen until the professional, post-Packer era.

The second cricketer Love introduces is Bryan, his first name unrecorded. Bryan comes from London and is a bricklayer by trade: a strong fellow, as we shall later see. In mock-heroic vein, echoing Homer, Love imagines Newland and Bryan hearing about the challenge issued by Lord Sackville, on behalf of Kent, to the rest of England – and laughing as they carouse. How dare these cricketers of Kent issue such a challenge, which reaches 'Great Newland's Ear':

> Where, with his Friend, all negligent he laugh'd,
> And threatened future Glories, as they quaff'd.

If this seems a far cry from the modern team talk in a huddle, with the captain stressing the importance of bowling in the right areas and fighting together, Newland does exhort Bryan before the start:

> Let Us with Care, each hardy Friend inspire!
> And fill their Souls with emulating Fire!

The match commences at noon – or so it was scheduled, and wealthy patrons who came to bet did not expect to be made to hang around. Kent take the field, led out by their captain. (Love makes no mention of a toss, or of a bell, a feature of Christian culture, so one would have been ready to hand.)

And here comes what is, to my mind, the most amazing fact in the history of English cricket.

Bear in mind this is the mid-eighteenth century. Oliver Cromwell's revolution was less than a century before, and few people wish to return to a republic, provided the monarch is bound to some extent by Parliament. In general, therefore, the social hierarchy is strict. If you are an aristocrat, you command; if a commoner, you obey. This applies in the army, the navy, the government, the Church – and in cricket. The captains chronicled to this date have been dukes, nobles, knights. (When the first Laws were drawn up, for the match in 1727 between the Duke of Richmond's team and Mr Alan Brodrick's team, the latter was the heir to Viscount Midleton.)

Yet, when Kent take the field, their captain is revealed to be not Lord Sackville at all. It is the Duke of Dorset's gardener.

Love does not explain the rationale behind this decision. But he implicitly approves it, because he describes this gardener, Val Romney, in most eloquent terms as an outstanding physical specimen, with almost divine attributes. Yes, cricket's first poser comes from Kent:

> Bold Romney first, before the *Kentish* Hand
> God-like appear'd, and seiz'd the chief Command.
> Judicious Swain! Whose quick-discerning Soul
> Observes the various Seasons as they roll.
> Well-skill'd to spread the thriving Plant around,
> And paint with fragrant Flow'rs th' enamell'd Ground.
> Conscious of Worth, with Front erect he moves,
> And poises in his Hand the *Bat* he loves.

Romney was employed as the head gardener at Knole Park ('Well-skill'd to spread the thriving Plant around'), and combined this work with playing cricket when the Duke desired: he was one of the first semi-professionals. The year before this match he had represented Three of Kent against Three of All-England at the Artillery Ground, and although he had not been captain, Kent had won by two runs: so he had experience as well.

Above all, however, the captaincy was awarded – surely by Sackville, who had captained Kent previously and had issued the challenge – to Romney *on merit*. We can surmise that it was because Sackville was desperate to win the game and the stakes, and thereby fund his domestic life. But the fact remains that the social hierarchy was overturned at this early point in cricket's evolution, and while there were interregna when amateurs of little merit captained county teams, including Kent, the principle was established in the sport as a whole that the best man to be captain should and would be captain. It may be an exaggeration to think so, or maybe not, but it is at least conceivable that cricket might have been no more than a niche sport in upper-class English life, like polo or fives, but for this decision and the precedent it set.

This match was the second of the two fixtures: it was Kent's away match, after the home leg had been staged at Coxheath three days earlier, on the Friday. The result of this first leg is unrecorded. We could guess that Kent had lost, under Sackville's captaincy, and it was as a reaction that Romney was promoted. It matters not. Romney was now in command, Sackville under him; and Love gives us the impression that Sackville was happy with this appointment, because he 'Attends with ardent Glee the mighty Play'r', i.e. Romney.*

---

* In literary terms, a trend is at work here: the author, Love, comes from 'the middling sort', to use the new phrase, and likes to think that an elite member of society, like Sackville, can admire someone from the lower orders like Romney. (George Eliot does the same in *Adam Bede.*) It creates a warm feeling, in writer and reader: we English people are all the same at heart, patricians and plebs. Or, as a modern politician might try to persuade us, 'We are all in it together.'

Love next introduces us to Kent's opening bowler, William Hodsoll.* Look, dear reader, at how tough and strong this fellow is – and be amazed at the speed he bowls! It is such an attractive theme for any cricket correspondent: all hail this new bowler, arguably the fastest on earth. In a footnote – straight up, no mockery – Love informs us that Hodsoll is a tanner by trade, from Dartford in Kent, as well as a formidable bowler:

> Brisk *Hodsoll* next strides on with comely Pride,
> Tough as the subject of his Trade, the *Hide*.
> In his firm Palm, the hard-bound Ball he bears,
> And mixes joyous with his pleas'd Compeers.

Love describes Hodsoll's bowling action when he delivers the first ball of the match: 'then pois'd, and rising as he threw,/ Swift from his Arm the fatal Missive flew.' What sounds like a bending of the knees would have given Hodsoll some momentum for his forward thrust in delivery. Love does not say whether he had a run-up, but the implication is not, because of an earlier couplet about Hodsoll and his opening partner John Mills, a gamekeeper from Bromley:

> *Hodsoll* and *Mills* behind the *Wickets* stand,
> And each by Turns, the flying Ball command;

Of Hodsoll's pace, Love gives a vivid impression. Remember that nothing in Georgian London was faster than a runaway horse. Even from a standing position, Hodsoll – tough as a tanner – bowls with startling speed, which Love embellishes with all the hyperbole he can command:

* Also found as 'Hodswell' and 'Hadswell'.

Nor with more Force the Death conveying Ball,

Springs from the Cannon to the batter'd Wall;

Nor swifter yet the pointed Arrows go,

Launch'd from the Vigour of the *Parthian* Bow.

It whizz'd along, with unimagin'd Force,

And bore down all, resistless in its Course.

To such impetuous Might compell'd to yield

The *Bail*, and mangled *Stumps* bestrew the Field.

Let us suppose Hodsoll could bowl at 60 mph: even though under-arm, such bowling on a rough pitch would have been a test of physical bravery.* David Harris, the finest bowler of the Hambledon era at the end of the eighteenth century, was known to grind a batsman's unprotected fingers against the bat: 'Many a time have I seen the blood drawn in this way from a batter,' wrote John Nyren in *The Cricketers of My Time*. But whether it is Hodsoll or Dennis Lillee, Malcolm Marshall or Dale Steyn, who knocks 'mangled' stumps out of the ground, the sight is cricket's most dramatic.

The ball, then as now, weighed between five and six ounces. The ones used in this match might even have been manufactured by the Duke family, and therefore the make England still use in Tests at home: we know that in 1780 Duke's supplied cricket balls to the Prince of Wales, who became King George IV. 'The great secret of it is to wind the thread round an *octagon* piece of cork,' wrote the diarist Joseph Farington after seeing the Duke's cottage industry in Penshurst in 1811. 'When the Ball is perfectly formed

---

* My guess, in the absence of any scientific evidence, is that bowling reached 70 mph after the legalisation of round-arm in 1828; passed 80 mph when Harold Larwood reached his prime; and touched 90 mph with Frank Tyson in 1954–55.

with Cork and thread . . . they put on the Leather cover which is made of Bull Hide."

In no other English sport is a ball put into play more quickly by a human being, without the aid of an implement, than it is by the pace bowler. (In baseball, the fastest pitchers have historically delivered the ball 5 to 10 per cent more quickly than the fastest bowlers.) Love contrasts this speed of action with 'puny *Billiards*, where, with sluggish Pace,/ The dull *Ball trails* . . .' Bowls is equally dull, in Love's opinion, because the bowl 'wanders to the Goal'.

The colour of the ball was red, or 'crimson' in Love's more flowery vocabulary. It remained so until the late 1970s and the introduction of floodlit cricket, when white balls were tried, and orange, and pink. On my visit to the Duke's cottages in Penshurst, shortly before it moved to modern premises and mechanisation, the handful of remaining craftsmen said a cricket ball was red simply because that was the colour of one of the few natural dyes to which their predecessors had access in the eighteenth century: no reason other than that. (Artificial dyes were largely the invention of the chemist William Perkin in the 1850s.) Aesthetic considerations, however, have surely contributed to keeping the ball red for the best part of three centuries: against a green background, the 'crimson rambler' has inspired many a poet apart from Love.

But the length of a cricket pitch has not changed one inch since 1744. It remains 22 yards, or one chain, which points to the sport's agricultural origins: a chain is said to be the shortest distance in

---

* Cricket balls were first manufactured in Australia by A.G. Thompson's in Melbourne. When I visited their factory in 1986, a senior member of the firm told me, off the record, that when they started production just after the Second World War, their Kookaburra balls were made without a prominent seam, and were therefore easier to bat against, on the unofficial instructions of Don Bradman. The first Test series in which their machine-made balls were used was the one against England in 1978–79, very low-scoring because of the proud seams, but that did not last.

which a horse pulling a plough can turn around. The weight and size of the cricket ball have also stayed the same, while the width of the bat has not altered since 1771. Yet male human beings in England and elsewhere have grown taller. The first national census was not until 1801, but the HAC's minutes for 1744 record their committee's decision that all sergeants in future must be at least five feet six inches tall, which suggests the average height of the time. Nowadays an international bowler below six feet is rare. Cricket's measurements have not changed, yet the height of cricketers and their bowling speeds have increased considerably.

The effect of never having had to alter these basic measurements of pitch, bat and ball has surely been considerable, albeit at a subconscious level. Cricket is known as a conservative sport, reluctant to change. To some extent, this must be the consequence of there having been no need to alter the essential elements, and the mindset it breeds.

Hodsoll's first over consists of four balls, as laid down in the Laws of 1744. The over was increased to five balls in the 1880s, and six in the 1890s, and grew to eight in Australia in the twentieth century. My interpretation is that four balls made for sufficient interest for one over when pitches were bad, before they were prepared by rolling and mowing. It was excitement enough if two balls shot along the ground, another hit a bump and went over the two stumps, and the next passed between them (the third stump was not added until the Hambledon club legislated in 1776). After four such balls, the striker, umpires and spectators must have felt it was time for a breather.

Once the mechanical mower had been invented in the 1840s, four balls could be blocked, and the average over would have come to seem rather dull and abrupt. Furthermore, the bowler was forced to use his wits, and needed more scope to bait his trap. He might want to set a batsman up with four or five quicker balls, then a slower one, or by spinning five balls one way and the sixth the other.*

Mills bowls the second over of this match, from the opposite end to Hodsoll. This simple act of routine, of switching ends after each over, has given cricket an essential variety which baseball has never enjoyed. Fielders, in moving from end to end or side to side, are given a change of scene. Spectators have to shift their focus every few minutes when the bowling switches to the other end and is directed at the other batsman. It was a brilliant invention, and not only for reducing the wear and tear on parts of the pitch by half. It saved a cricket match from the ever-increasing dullness of middle practice. It promoted variety and the scope for drama: how much excitement has been generated simply by the batsman trying to take a single off the last ball of an over to keep the strike? We would have missed all such action if Mills had bowled from the same end as Hodsoll, at the same striker.

Hodsoll takes three quick wickets and Mills two, all of them bowled, to make their opponents reel. England have lost their first five wickets for only three runs, or as Love reports: 'three *Notches* only gain'd, five *Leaders* out.' I estimate we have to multiply by four or five to get the equivalent number of runs in today's terms. Even by this reckoning, though, a score of 15 for five wickets was the worst of starts. (The first surviving scorecard, of Slindon v London a few days earlier, also records bad starts, with most of the runs scored by the middle order.) Love adds the gloss: '*The Odds run high on the Side of* KENT.' In the poem itself, he mentions the

---

* After the eight-ball over had been abolished in Australia in 1979, to allow more advertisement breaks per hour on television, Ian Brayshaw, who represented Western Australia, told me how the state's left-arm spinner Tony Lock – of Lock and Laker fame – would fire through six balls at a tailender, then toss up the seventh, tempting a wild mis-hit. The case against the eight-ball over was that a bowler took extra time in walking back to his mark, conserving his energies. After England's 1950–51 series in Australia, E.W. Swanton, in *Elusive Victory*, estimated that the eight-ball over 'cost the best part of an hour's play per day'.

betting which went on around the field or 'the Plain', a term connoting that of Troy, where the Greeks had heroically fought:

> But while the drooping *Play'r* invokes the Gods,
> The busy *Better* calculates his *Odds*,
> Swift round the Plain, in buzzing Murmurs run,
> *I'll hold you Ten to Four*, Kent.—*Done Sir.—Done.*

Hereabouts Richard Newland comes to the wicket. In a prosaic note, Love writes: 'Bryan and Newland go in; they help the Game greatly.' In verse, he sings that Bryan and Newland 'pant to redeem the Fame their Fellows lost./ Eager for Glory . . .'

During his innings, Newland, we are told, displays his 'Prowess' and his 'strenuous Arm'. Even against under-arm bowling, batting appears to have had aesthetic possibilities.

Bryan, meanwhile, winds up and hits five runs with one shot: perhaps our equivalent of 20 off a single ball! He uses arms made powerful by bricklaying: physical strength, even in cricket's infancy, was an influential factor.* We can almost hear the bedlam as Bryan sends the ball flying into the crowd:

> . . . he wav'd his *Bat* with forceful Swing,
> And drove the batter'd Pellet o'er the Ring.
> Then rapid *five Times* cross'd the shining Plain,
> E'er the departed Ball return'd again.

This rallying stand for England between Newland and Bryan is ended straight after Bryan's shot for five, when we have the first recorded instance of a big hit going to a batsman's head.

---

* Len Hutton told me, more than once, but not for publication: 'You can go a long way in cricket [pause] – with brute force and ignorance.' He was referring, ruefully, to fast bowlers.

Beware, unhappy *Bryan!* oh beware!
Too heedless Swain, when such a Foe is near.
Fir'd with Success, elated with his Luck,
He glow'd with Rage, regardless how he struck,

Here we have the first recorded stumping or, as Love phrases it in a note: 'Bryan *is unfortunately put out by* Kips'. Love adds: '*Kips* is particularly remarkable for *handing* the Ball at the *Wicket,* and knocking up the *Stumps* instantly, if the *Batsman* is not extremely cautious.' Thus we are in at the start of cricket's longest-running tradition: excellent wicketkeeper/batsmen from Kent. Ned Wenman, in the Kent side of the 1840s, was the first keeper to cope with round-arm bowling; Edward Tylecote, in the 1880s, was the first keeper to score 50 in a Test; Les Ames was the prototype of the modern keeper/bat, in that he scored more than 100 first-class hundreds; Godfrey Evans was a prototype, too, in bouncing around, being vocal and keeping his fielders energetic; Alan Knott still wins votes as the best wicketkeeper of all time, and popularised the sweep in England; Paul Downton and Geraint Jones maintained the lineage, although the first left Kent and the second went there; and Sam Billings assumed their mantle. Another Kent keeper, Derek Ufton, told me he was watched at Canterbury by Fred Huish, who was the first to make 100 first-class dismissals in a season (he did it twice just before the First World War). Huish and Hopper Levett, another fine keeper, offered advice to their successors, so there was a degree of mentoring;* and the pitches in Kent are true enough for batsmen and keepers to perfect their craft. But I can offer no further explanation for why Kent should have

---

* Levett cheerfully shouted to Paul Farbrace, who kept wicket for Kent before coaching Sri Lanka and England, after he had dropped a skyer: 'I'd've caught that between the cheeks of my arse, old boy!'

produced this unique sequence, rather than a neighbouring county like Essex, Surrey or Sussex, other than this mentoring and a snow-balling sense of tradition.

After Bryan's dismissal, England collapse again; the harassed Smith is dismissed for nought. They are all out for 40, the equivalent of 160 or so, with their captain Newland left stranded on 18 not out. Now, all stand please, ladies and gentlemen, for His Royal Highness Frederick, the Prince of Wales, fashionably late, and his younger brother, very soon to be nicknamed 'Butcher Cumberland'.

‖

'Keep politics out of sport' was the cry of those who supported South Africa's apartheid government and cricket team in the 1970s. Irrespective of the ethics involved, if any, the cry itself was irrational. Politics are by definition the affairs of the city, literally, or the community; and the cricket match on 18 June 1744 was part of the affairs of London, or even the country, and the politics of the day.

What Frederick did at this cricket match was to set an example which was to be copied, unwittingly, over the coming centuries. After the CIA and MI6 combined to rig the general election in British Guiana in 1953, to stop Cheddi Jagan becoming prime minister, those wanting to protest went to the Test match between West Indies and England at Bourda to demonstrate in February 1954. When Benazir Bhutto went to the Gaddafi Stadium in Lahore during the first Test between Pakistan and England in 1977, she was there to protest against the imprisonment of her father; and most of the 50,000 spectators did not attend in order to see Mudassar Nazar score the slowest Test century. When Sri Lanka played their first Test in England, in 1984, Tamil spectators ran on to the field to bring their cause to the attention of the British public. All were following in Frederick's footsteps.

Frederick went to watch the Kent v England match to demonstrate his Anglophilia and his credentials as a man of the people. He was, by birth and upbringing, German. So what better way to make himself popular than to commission Thomas Arne to write an opera including the song that has been number one among English patriots ever since, 'Rule, Britannia', and to patronise the quintessentially English sport?

The first Fred to use cricket to spread his popularity nationwide, but not the last,* had grown up in Hanover. His father, the Elector of Hanover, was German, which did not matter in English eyes until he became King George II as well in 1727. Many of his new subjects were appalled by his boorishness: the king seemed to be interested only in fighting and hunting. His court spoke French. Worse still, he began to use the taxes he raised from the British people to finance the European wars in which he had become involved as the Elector of Hanover. He was the last British monarch to lead his or her army into battle, at the Battle of Dettingen in 1743.

Fred was left alone in Hanover after his father and mother had gone to London to manoeuvre their way towards the throne. Nothing of the original Herrenhausen Palace remains, as the RAF did a thorough job in the Second World War, but we can see where Fred first played cricket. As a boy he had cricket bats sent from England, but there was nowhere for him and his brother to play in front of the palace: the Grosser Garten – 'the greatest treasure that the city possesses', according to a local guidebook – had been laid out in the seventeenth century by the Electress Sophia, after she had visited Versailles. This Baroque garden is so filled with flowers, fountains, statues and mazes of hedge that 22 yards of unadorned turf do not exist.

* Andrew Flintoff, hero of the 2005 Ashes series, did so in a chip van.

Turning left out of the Herrenhausen, however, Fred would have entered a different, more natural world where, after a few trees had been cut down, there would have been open space for the boys to run around. We might even regard Fred as the first person to have used cricket as an emotional surrogate. As one might guess, George and Queen Caroline were not a touchy-feely couple. The Georgians, indeed, have been called the most dysfunctional of Britain's royal families. If Caroline had more social accomplishments than her husband, she was still ridiculed by Alexander Pope as a dunce. And the extent of her maternal instincts can be judged from her opinion of Fred: 'My first born is the greatest ass, and the greatest liar, and the greatest canaille*, and the greatest beast, in the whole world, and I heartily wish he was out of it.' (To which Fred, no doubt, replied: 'Love you too, Mumsy.')

By the time he arrived in England in 1728, aged 21, Fred seems to have been pretty damaged and manipulative. If his mother's verdict sounds harsh, we have the testimony of Lord Hervey, who recalled Fred as 'never having the least hesitation in telling any lie that served his present purpose.' This tribute, however, followed their falling out over a mistress they had shared. On the humanitarian side, Fred was to visit the woman who had rowed Bonnie Prince Charlie over the sea from Skye, Flora MacDonald, after she had been imprisoned in the Tower of London, and he obtained her release from his younger brother's clutches.

England in the 1740s, as always, was divided between being European and insular. Italian opera had been the fashion; now the growing taste was for Handel and songs in English. The father was frittering away taxpayers' money on fighting in the War of the Austrian Succession. The son allied himself with William Pitt the

* French for 'blackguard'.

Elder, Paymaster-General and the most popular politician in the land after his attacks on George II.

Fred is the first person known to have presented a prize to the winners of a cricket match: all those who hold the World Cup aloft can thank him for the trend he set. He was a poor cricketer himself, but that did not stop him becoming one of the first county captains when he led 'Surry' against a team from Kent on Kennington Common in 1732, next to what has become the Oval. He was the first royal to understand the advantage of seeing, and being seen, at a cricket match – an endorsement that can only have added to cricket's popularity, for if royalty was going to take an interest in this new sport, so would the newspapers and their readers.

In reply to England's total of 40, Kent in their first innings score 53. For their lead they have to thank their captain Romney, who leads from the front by scoring 11, and Kips, who top-scores with 12. Just as Richard Newland is the only batsman to reach double figures in both innings for England, so is Kips for Kent. In addition, he does not concede a bye in the match, whereas in the other surviving scorecard from 1744 byes were quite numerous – unsurprisingly, as keepers before Wenman wore no gloves. If Love had written his match report for a newspaper and I had been subbing, I would have been tempted to go for the headline: 'No byes, Mr Kips'.

After seven of England's batsmen made a duck in their first innings, every one gets off the mark in their second. The deficit of 13 is cleared and England go into credit as Waymark scores nine notches, and Newland holds the middle order together again with 15. Even Smith finds time to contribute eight runs to England's growing lead. 'The *Strokes* re-eccho o'er the spacious Ground,' Love reports.

Here we have the first reference to the game's most enduring sound, that of bat on ball. In those days it was not always leather on willow, because hard wood was originally used for bats: a single piece, perhaps with some form of strapping like leather around the rough-hewn handle. It was not until the nineteenth century that willow was universally preferred for being lighter, if less durable. Yet Love was clearly delighted with the sound, as generations have been ever since. The sound of bat on ball, however, is not inherently euphonious: no single sound is, until placed in the context of other notes. Thus willow on leather has become delightful to us by association – with cucumber sand-wiches, pastoral settings and memories of summers past.

For the batsman, another sensation is involved: that of touch. This pleasure in timing the ball – hitting it with the meatiest part of the bat – is unappreciated by those who have not played the game (it never ceases to please me on the rare occasions I middle one). In 1728, a Swiss French traveller, César de Saussure, visited England and observed the game in *A Foreign View of England in the Reigns of George I and George II*: 'The English are very fond of a game they call cricket . . . They go into a large open field, and knock a small ball about with a piece of wood. I will not attempt to describe this game to you, it is too complicated; but it requires agility and skill, and everyone plays it, the common people and also men of rank.' It is a fair summary, except that 'knock' does not begin to convey the sensory pleasure of batting – unlike 'stroke', a term used by Love and all subsequent reporters.*

* A stroke like a well-timed cover drive is so satisfying primarily because an enormous number of muscles are involved, especially in the arms, wrists and hands. In neuro-logical terms, the ball is first tracked by the eyes and motor cortex, and compared with similar balls the batsman has seen in the past. His brain then makes calculations about the pace of the ball and its trajectory, and about the state of the pitch. Bursts of

Now comes some shameless grovelling by Love. Richard Newland hits a ball in the air, and who should be underneath it but Lord John Sackville? Sackville does not simply catch it like a normal fielder (or 'Seeker-out' in Love's terminology). Oh no. Sackville, as we have already been informed, is not only 'Illustrious' and 'Sure of Success' but also 'Swift as the *Falcon*, darting on its Prey'. At least Love has the decency to admit in a fawning footnote: 'It is hop'd that tho' this Description may a little exceed the real Fact, it may be excus'd, especially as there is a great deal of Foundation for it.'

In the event, after all Love's bombast, Sackville secures this crucial catch to dismiss Newland, who has top-scored again. Of England's 110 runs in the match, Newland scores 33 for once out. In front of the huge crowd, Sackville has held his nerve (something he would fail to do a couple of years later).

England are thus dismissed for 70. Hodsoll has taken a minimum of eight wickets in the game and probably more: in the scorecard, if a batsman is out caught, only the fielder's name is recorded, not the bowler's. Kent are left to score 58 to win the match, the honours, the stakes and any bets their players may have laid.

It might be anachronistic to use the word 'pressure' in describing Kent's second innings, as the analogy with physics had yet to be made. But the same phenomenon that we know today was at work. Love testifies that Kent's batsmen 'wildly pant, and *almost own* they fear'; that is, they almost admit or acknowledge the fact that they fear.

A close run-chase was therefore just as exciting in cricket's infancy as now. These are the moments when spectators watch

---

nervous impulses then go from the brain of an experienced batsman, who has played the stroke many times before, to the correct muscles (the energy is more diffused in an inexperienced batsman). If the ball is hit in the middle of the bat and dispatched to the boundary, a mass of sensory receptors send a message to the brain, from which it takes great satisfaction, such has been the complexity of the task achieved.

most closely – even if some members of the batting side cannot – and a player's mental fibre is thoroughly examined. More than two centuries ago, the psychology of cricket was studied, especially that involved in the run-chase. When John Nyren – the son of Richard Newland's nephew – wrote *The Young Cricketer's Tutor*, he advised: 'If your party go in the last innings for a certain number of runs, always keep back two or three of your safest batsmen for the last wickets. Timid or hazardous hitters seldom do so well when the game is desperate, as those who, from safe play, are more confident.' Nyren offered his old Hambledon team-mate Tom Walker as an exemplar of the right temperament: 'his skin was like the rind of an old oak, and as sapless' and he was 'the coolest, the most imperturbable fellow in existence'. (Walker, Nyren added, was also the first to try bowling with his arm at shoulder-height.)

So many of Kent's batsmen succumb to fear as they chase that, when their last pair come together, they still need at least five runs to win and maybe more (the scorecard does not record the score at the fall of wickets). One batsman is Hodsoll, who has enjoyed a grand day with his eight or more wickets, and must have had an all-rounder's confidence. His partner in this tenth-wicket stand is John Cutbush, exact age unknown, but older than the 26-year-old Hodsoll.

And the pressure is not only on Kent's last pair; it is also on mine host, George Smith. Thousands of spectators, not all sober, are surging forward to gain a closer look. Already, Love has told us:

> But if encroaching on forbidden Ground,
> The heedless Croud o'erleaps the proper Bound;
> *Smith* plies, with strenuous Arm, the smacking Whip,
> Back to the Line th' affrighted Rebels skip.

Can we see Smith dashing to the boundary's edge at the end of an over, grabbing the whip from young William and plying it again to force the spectators back over the rope? Smith may not have middled many shots when he batted, but he's making up for it now.

When Kent's score reaches 55 for nine, with three more runs wanted for victory, a catch goes up. It is Hodsoll, I suspect, who goes for glory; Cutbush is a clockmaker from Maidstone and knows a bit more about timing. Or in Love's felicitous phrase:

> The mounting Ball, again obliquely driv'n,
> Cuts the pure *Æther*, soaring up to Heav'n.

After a very long day, of four innings, we have arrived at the climax. The England fielder underneath this ball soaring up to heaven is Waymark. He has a reputation for being excellent in this department, an athlete who had won purses of fifty guineas in single-wicket and double-wicket matches, to supplement his earnings from the Duke of Richmond. As Love tells us:

> *Waymark* was ready; *Waymark*, all must own,
> As sure a Swain to catch as e'er was known . . .

At this moment, the lesson is proved that in sport uncertainty is all – and what more agonising uncertainty than a cricket match which boils down to the last pair in a nip-and-tuck run-chase? Finally, after Waymark has waited and waited, Love keeps us in suspense no longer:

> The erring Ball, amazing to be told!
> Slip'd thro' his out-stretch'd Hand, and mock'd his Hold.

Waymark drops it.

Does one of the England fielders go up to Waymark, put an arm round his shoulder and console him? 'Never mind, Tom, just concentrate on the next ball.'

Or does one of the Kent batsmen have a go at him? 'Don't worry, mate – they'll still be talking about your mistake in three hundred years.'

Hodsoll and Cutbush, in any event, knock off the last three runs to win the match for Kent by one wicket. Or, in the words of Love:

> And now the Sons of *Kent* compleat the Game,
> And firmly fix their everlasting Fame.

Sure enough, George Smith was hauled in front of the HAC committee. He was admonished for the 'great disorder', and doubt-less reminded that any repetition might lead to the loss of his lease at the Artillery Ground.

But Smith had seen the possibilities for cricket and its future growth as a mass spectator sport. He bounced back and offered another of cricket's firsts: 'a ring of benches that will hold at least 800 persons'. This was the first stand at a cricket ground.

In 1747, Smith was allowed to increase his price of admission to sixpence. Rumours abounded that Smith was promoting the sport to his not 'inconsiderable Advantage', as Love had phrased it. But he responded warmly by offering to open up his accounts to prove he was not cashing in extortionately: 'The Town may be certain that the taking Six-pence Admittance is out of no avaricious Temper. Two-pence being greatly insufficient to the Charge that attends the Matches, which Mr Smith is ready and willing to make appear to any Gentleman.'

Smith had a point about not being avaricious. In the

following year, 1748, he was declared bankrupt. The HAC committee was listening, however, and must have appreciated his worth: Smith kept going at the Artillery Ground until 1752, when William Sharpe took on the lease. Smith headed west, to take over the Castle Inn in Marlborough. He is not known to have played any more cricket. He died in 1761, age unrecorded, his epitaph to be written in *Start of Play* by David Underdown, Emeritus Professor of History at Yale: 'George Smith was the indispensable middleman in the organization of London cricket at mid-century.'

Smith's legacy was that the connection between cricket and publicans was established. As landlord of the Bat and Ball Inn, and captain, Richard Nyren was the most important person in the Hambledon club in the 1780s, organising everything. Thomas Lord, prominent in the wine trade, found that building his own ground was an inspired way of finding customers for his wines. In Australia, as we shall see, a landlord was at the heart of the first cricket club for native-born Australians. In the Anglo-Saxon world, publicans enabled the sport to grow by providing a changing area, a venue for selection and committee meetings, and above all perhaps food and drink. Because cricket consumes the longest time of any team sport, refuelling is essential in the course of all but the shortest matches – and mine host can do that as part of his job, profitably.

A year after this historic match, the country did not have much time for sport. War had been in the air throughout 1744, and not just war but invasion. Bonnie Prince Charlie had been raising troops on the continent, and the threat from the exiled claimant to the throne may have been underestimated. When he was in Rome in 1743, *Read's Weekly Journal* had used cricket imagery in its report: the Bonnie Prince had been practising his batting 'but the Chevalier being of a weakly Constitution soon gave it over and contented himself with being a Seeker-out [i.e. fielder]; which an arch wag was heard to say was the fittest for him, he having been a Runner from his Cradle.' Ouch.

When the Bonnie Prince invaded England in 1745, King George II chose his younger son to lead the army, not Fred. Their relationship had broken down. Fred had not only Pitt the Elder on his side, but Lord Sandwich and popular opinion. George had been increasingly hated for wasting taxpayers' money, but the threat of invasion rallied people around him. On 16 April 1746, the Duke of Cumberland won the Battle of Culloden. Scots prisoners, tried for treason, were hanged, drawn and quartered on Kennington Common.

While this war was going on, Love had *Cricket: An Heroic Poem* published by W. Bickerton of 'the Temple-Exchange in Fleet-Street' at the price of one shilling. Sales were insufficient to enrich Love and his wife, children and mistress. He went on to make his career in the theatre, as did Catherine de l'Amour, except that when she played in Edinburgh she was seduced by James Boswell, Dr Johnson's biographer. Love – loveless? – died in 1774.

The victorious captain, Val Romney, was well treated for his efforts on the cricket field. The Duke of Dorset's accounts refer to a Christmas present of two guineas for Romney in his retirement. Lord John Sackville maintained his interest in cricket for a while. His letter of September 1745 survives, when he told the Duke of Richmond that he had selected the wrong wicketkeeper: 'I wish you had let Ridgeway play instead of your stopper behind, it might have turned the match in your favour.'

Sackville had two more children; and Fred appointed him a Lord of the Bedchamber in 1745. But all was not well with Sackville: perhaps as the second son, with a long-lived father and scant prospect of inheriting the duchy, he found little to motivate him. Without a portrait to guide us, we should be wary of reading too much into his mind. For certain, his later life was shocking. In 1746, when the 2nd Foot Guards were ordered overseas, Sackville – their commander – deserted on the very day they were due to sail.

Sackville's younger brother was to have the rare distinction, for an officer, of being court-martialled for cowardice after a battle in France. So Sackville was not the only member of his family to suffer a crisis of confidence. And did this unease first manifest itself on 18 June 1744 when Romney, not Sackville, captained Kent? We know he was confident enough to take the vital catch that dismissed Richard Newland, and to score five runs in his first innings. But had the prospect of continuing to captain Kent, when so much money was at stake, been too much for his nerves?

To minimise the scandal, Sackville was declared insane. He was sent to Switzerland, where he was seen wandering around in rags, and muttering about his younger brother's cowardice, before dying in 1765. He never became the Duke of Dorset; but his son did. As the third Duke of Dorset, he became the British Ambassador to France, and introduced cricket in the Champs-Elysées in the mid-1780s. He was planning a cricket tour of France until over-taken by events beyond his control.

The growth of cricket from its base in south-east England was spasmodic. When Dr Johnson published his dictionary in 1755, he defined it vaguely as 'A sport, at which the contenders drive a ball with sticks in opposition to each other'; and he did not list such a basic term as 'wicket'. Horse-racing took over as the fashionable sport, and silks were invented to identify the owners. Most of all perhaps, cricket's first great patrons faded away, including Fred. He died in 1751, before he could succeed to the throne, from an abscess which was likely to have been caused when he was hit by a cricket ball. One proposed epitaph suggests he was not widely mourned: 'Here lies Fred, who was alive and is dead.'

The seed, however, had been planted. In the nineteenth century, cricket was to grow into England's most popular sport, with W.G. Grace the first sporting star, and it would remain so until it was surpassed by association football. Love was not wrong when he hailed cricket's place in British, or more accurately English, life:

> Hail CRICKET! Glorious, manly, *British* Game!
> First of all Sports! be first alike in Fame!

As I see it, the match between Kent and England in 1744 had appealed to every one of the five main senses – in addition to all the camaraderie that had been engendered during the day, among the players in each team, between the two sides, and in the capacity crowd.

The eye, of both player and spectator, had been delighted by the spacious setting of the Artillery Ground in the otherwise congested City of London – the *rus in urbe* – and by the athletic skills of Newland, Kips, Romney, Hodsoll and others.

The ear, of both player and spectator, had been delighted by the sound of bat on ball, and stimulated by the cheering and shouting at the climax. The batsman's sense of touch had been delighted when he had middled the ball, like Bryan; so too the fielders' tactile sense when they had caught the leather ball cleanly, unlike poor Waymark.

Everyone's sense of smell had been delighted by the fresh June grass, in contrast to the rubbish and ordure of the surrounding streets; and, no doubt, by Smith's fine victuals. The sense of taste, especially of Kent's victorious players and their supporters, would also have been delighted long into the night at the Pyed Horse.

A sport so gratifying, for those who played and those who watched it, was bound to have a future.

2

WHERE AND WHY THE GAME GREW

I'd rather be at Lascelles Hall
Ephraim Lockwood, of Yorkshire, at Niagara Falls

LASCELLES HALL is no longer renowned, let alone famous, even if you rhyme it with 'hassles' as West Riding folk do. After stopping at a pub on a moor above Huddersfield, I had to inquire of several staff and customers before getting directions to the village a couple of miles away. My satellite navigation refused to admit the very existence of Lascelles Hall.

Yet this village of fewer than one thousand souls once had the strongest cricket team in England – other than representative sides like MCC, or the Players, or the North of England – and therefore in the world. Before the 1870s, a few scattered individuals played cricket, rather than communities, so there was no single place in which the standard could advance. As analogy, individuals studied science in various Classical cities, but it was only when Greek-speaking scientists came together in Egypt's Alexandria, in buildings devoted to research, that major advances were made in astronomy, geography and physiology. One generation thereby handed on its knowledge to the next generation, who did not have to go back to square one, but raised the standard further.

Lascelles Hall was cricket's first hot spot, or nursery, or academy. The Hambledon club, in Hampshire, had been the centre of the sport in the 1780s, but few if any players came from the village: thus the club faded away when their more aristocratic members returned to London during the French Revolution. In the 1860s and 1870s, the majority of men who lived in Lascelles Hall played cricket. Thus they enabled their village to:

- defeat Yorkshire 2–1 in the three matches they contested
- defeat Surrey by an innings in their only match, in 1874
- have the better of a drawn match in 1878 against the North of England, who included the best cricketers from Lancashire, Nottinghamshire and Yorkshire other than themselves
- beat Sheffield in 1870 for a stake of £500 and the unofficial title of 'home of Yorkshire cricket'
- supply five members of the Yorkshire team for numerous matches, on one occasion six, and on another seven, except one had to stand down through injury.

Lascelles Hall used to call itself 'the happiest village in England'. Going back there helps to explain why cricket is played more in some places than in others, and to a higher standard.

The advent of the railways turned the series between Gentlemen and Players – intermittent after its inauguration in 1807 – into the focal point of the English cricket season. (A mass spectator sport needed mass communication so that the best players could move around the country.) Before international fixtures, the Gentlemen v Players match was the main test of a cricketer's calibre, given the natural rivalry between amateurs and professionals; and the first batsman to carry his bat through an innings in this series, in 1874, was not W.G. Grace, but Ephraim Lockwood of Lascelles Hall.*

As the match in question was played at the Oval, Lockwood had an advantage: it was his favourite ground. Six years earlier, in 1868, he had been summoned there by telegram to make his debut for Yorkshire against Surrey. One of Yorkshire's players had dropped out and their opening batsman, John Thewlis, who lived in Lascelles Hall, had recommended Lockwood – who happened to be his nephew. Lockwood took the train to London, where he was mystified by the Underground and refused entry by the Oval gateman because he looked so rustic. 'I'm a laiker,' Lockwood protested in his Yorkshire dialect. 'I've coom 'ere to laik.' He looked no less rustic when, having been told to open the batting with his uncle, he walked out to bat in a checked shirt, tight trousers and boots two sizes too big: the Oval crowd nicknamed him 'Mary Ann', which stuck for life.† But Lockwood scored 91 on his debut, Thewlis 108, and their partnership of 176 stood as a record for Yorkshire's first wicket for 29 years.

According to Grace, Lockwood was 'not a brilliant batsman, nor particularly free in his style; but what he lacked in that respect he made up in patience and carefulness.' Lockwood's own recipe for success was 'practice and more practice' – which is exactly what set the cricketers of Lascelles Hall apart from those in every other community in England. Grace's description makes me think Lockwood also pioneered the aerial chip shot, which the New Zealander Glenn Turner was credited with inventing a century

---

* The term dates from the time when a team would have only a couple of bats to share amongst all the players, so when a batsman was dismissed he would leave the bat at the crease for the next man. The batsman left undefeated at the end would carry his bat from the field.

† The previous year of 1873 had seen the hanging of Mary Ann Cotton, a serial murderer whose husbands and children tended to die mysteriously – until traces of arsenic were found in them.

later when batting for Worcestershire in one-day cricket: 'off slow bowling, he [Lockwood] made what seemed a half-hearted hit just over the bowler's or mid-off's head, but which did not go far enough for long-field to reach.'

At the Oval in 1874, Lockwood carried his bat for 67 out of the Players' total of 115: the Grace brothers, W.G. and Fred, were all over the professionals, taking nine wickets for 38. In the second of the two Gentlemen v Players fixtures of that year, on this occasion at Lord's, Allen Hill performed the first hat-trick in the series. Hill, too, came from Lascelles Hall. 'He was one of our very best round-arm bowlers, particularly between 1870 and 1875,' according to Grace, who had been bowled by Hill in both innings in the Oval fixture of 1874. 'He had a very easy delivery and beautiful style. He did not put much work on the ball, although now and then he would break from the off; but he bowled very straight and kept a good length.'

Hill's hat-trick was a rare one for being unassisted: one batsman was lbw, two caught-and-bowled. One victim was Albert Hornby, immortalised by Francis Thompson in his poem 'At Lord's', who became England's captain. We are told it was the talk of the Lord's pavilion that Hill and Lockwood not only came from the same Yorkshire village, but lived next door to each other. Thanks to Hill, the Players won at Lord's, their first victory in this series since 1866, when Grace had appeared and weighted the scales towards the Gentlemen.

In the first ever Test match, at Melbourne in 1877, two members of England's team came from Lascelles Hall: Hill and Andrew Greenwood (Lockwood was too much of a home-lover to want to tour). England's best all-round Test cricketer ever in statistical terms also came from Lascelles Hall: Willie Bates, whose Test batting average of 27 and bowling average of 16 gives him a differential of 11. It might have been bigger but for a tragic accident of a kind that has been remarkably and mercifully rare. Bates was practising at the Melbourne Cricket Ground, on England's 1887–88 tour, when a stray ball struck him in the eye and damaged his sight so badly it terminated his career aged 32. He tried coaching and suicide, before dying of pneumonia, caught while attending Thewlis's funeral in Lascelles Hall.*

The national census of 1841 listed the population of Lascelles Hall as 500. By 1881 it was 800, of whom we can estimate that between 120 and 150 were men of working age. In the following year of 1882, according to the club secretary, 23 players from the village were employed in cricket around the country, whether as players, coaches or groundsmen – while Luke Greenwood, Andrew's uncle, umpired the Oval Test that year, which Australia won by seven runs, when he impressed the tourists with his fair judgement. Later that decade, a Huddersfield newspaper claimed that more than 30 of the villagers were employed in cricket, without listing them. This would mean one adult male in every four was working as a professional cricketer. To me, it is inconceivable that any community of any size in the world has ever had such a high ratio of its menfolk employed in cricket.

Cricket's first hot spot was no accident, but the product of circumstances. Above the Hall, built by the Lascelles family after their arrival from Normandy, squat granite-stone cottages climb the hillside. The villagers used to make their living inside them by spinning cloth on hand-looms; and by working at home, not in factories, they could work whatever hours they liked, by candle-light if necessary, and go out to play cricket whenever they wanted and the weather allowed.

Hand-weaving has no part in training for today's cricketers, yet it was almost as beneficial as working out in a gym. The first

---

* *Cricket: A Weekly Record of the Game* records in November 1890 that Australian sympathisers donated £250 to Bates, including £147 raised by 'a football match' between Carlton and Port Melbourne. The money served to bring up his son, who also played for Yorkshire, before becoming a mainstay of Glamorgan when they joined the County Championship in 1921.

historian of Yorkshire cricket, Alfred Pullin, observed the villagers of Lascelles Hall: 'In their work as hand-loom weavers hand and eye were being constantly trained, and feet kept in active motion. Between shuttle and pick and treadle a weaver had his power of sight, smartness and endurance very considerably sharpened, and thus the groundwork was laid for that remarkable quick timing of the ball and general activity in the field for which most of the Lascelles Hall cricketers became famous.' Pullin was not exaggerating: the fielder singled out for praise by Australian newspapers after the inaugural Test of 1877 was Allen Hill.

When word that it was time for cricket spread up and down the village street, the men and boys of Lascelles Hall put on their wooden clogs and walked up the steep hill – as good a way of warming up as any – to the ground they had made themselves. The ninety or so club members had dug and flattened the field, then laid new turf of lawn seed and white clover. They must have done a fair job, because John Lockwood, Ephraim's cousin, became a groundsman at the Oval.

When the villagers practised – in the middle, not in nets – the custom was for each player to bat for 40 balls. Afterwards, when not bowling, he took a turn at every position in the field, to gain experience of it. Thus the players of Lascelles Hall practised intensely on a summer evening, enjoying the long hours of northern daylight, like no other community in England. At Lord's, the groundstaff would bowl to members who were in town, and pupils at certain public schools had nets in which to practise. Hornby, when at Harrow, even had use of one of the original bowling machines, a Catapulta. On the other side of the world, it was around this time that the Melbourne Cricket Club began to systematise training for its members. But in the northern hemisphere, the players at this Yorkshire academy had a start of several heads.

Situated at the top of a hill, the ground was naturally drained, and a club member would be paid a shilling an evening out of club funds to work on it. So the pitches were true, like almost nowhere else at this period except the Oval (stones could be found in the pitches at Lord's). When Harrow Wanderers, including Hornby, came to play Lascelles Hall on their northern tour, they complimented the villagers on their pitches but thought the boundaries were a bit short (naturally so, as there is a steep drop down the hill on one side). Harrow Wanderers may have been a little sniffy after they had lost four of their five matches there, drawing the other.

No stroke depends more on the predictable bounce of a pitch than the cut shot, and Ephraim Lockwood became renowned for it. When he scored 208 not out for Yorkshire against Kent, on a fast pitch at Gravesend, he kept cutting one of the fastest bowlers of the period until the Kent captain posted six slips. But old 'Mary Ann' still worked her thread through the eye of a needle.

Pullin, the son of a curate, could claim to be the first full-time sports journalist, as he reported on both cricket and rugby union for the *Yorkshire Post* under the pseudonym of 'Old Ebor'. He rendered the game fine service by tracking down former Yorkshire cricketers and publishing some of their hard-luck stories, shaming the club into making some provision for them, and making other counties follow suit. He found the 70-year-old Thewlis walking 20 miles a day in Manchester, collecting and delivering laundry. Lockwood was better off after he had retired from 'laiking', as he sold cricket equipment at a shop in Huddersfield. When Pullin caught up with Lockwood, he talked about his cricket and especially his favourite stroke, the cut: 'It came to me naturally. It was a hard chop, square with the face of the bat, and with full force behind it. Yet it was all from the wrist; a quick turn of the wrist on to the ball and away it used to go to the boundary . . . I never was a powerful man; it was simply a natural action.'

Lockwood can be forgiven for using a term which in cricket has seldom been used correctly. When batting, what is 'natural' is ducking or swaying the head out of the ball's path: this is instinct at work, the survival instinct. (The pull shot, whenever the batsman raises his front leg to protect his genitalia, could be included.) But no cut, clip or drive is natural or instinctive; it is the product of conditioned reflexes. Take the finest athlete in France or Russia who has never seen cricket, and give him a bat: he will not be able to play any shot naturally, without instruction, except perhaps a swing to leg. (A related myth is 'muscle memory'; muscles do not have a memory.) So Lockwood's cuts – and his chip shot, to judge from Grace's description – were the fruit of hundreds of hours spent conditioning his brain and strengthening his muscles in an environment designed for practice.

What happened next in Lascelles Hall, after the 1880s, is as revealing as what happened before: almost nothing. The villagers kept on playing cricket, and still do today, but they had lost their head start. Pullin interviewed the former club secretary, Mr Jessop, to whom public schools or clubs or wealthy landowners used to refer for a player or coach. 'Fast looms have destroyed our fast bowling,' Mr Jessop lamented. The villagers, instead of doing piece-work at home, had been forced to walk to factories and work long fixed hours, so that by the time they got home the daylight had gone. The nature of their work had altered, too: mechanisation did not develop agility of hand and foot in the way the old looms had. Lascelles Hall won the Heavy Woollen District Challenge in 1891, and that was it. The club survived, and remains in the Huddersfield League, but no more cricketers of note were born or nurtured there. Cricket's first hot spot, or academy, or nursery, was closed.

Surrounding communities, meanwhile, caught up. Look across the valley from the Lascelles Hall ground, and a couple of miles away is another hilltop ground, Kirkheaton. England's first left-arm swing bowler learned to harness the prevailing breeze there – an inswinger from George Hirst, bowling round the wicket, was said to be like a fast throw from cover. In a farm building on the outskirts of Kirkheaton, a left-arm spinner practised so assiduously one winter that he became a club professional in Scotland, before returning to Yorkshire and becoming the highest first-class wicket-taker of all time: Wilfred Rhodes. At least until the 1950s, when Keith Miller and Garfield Sobers raised the bar, the local saying was valid: 'Who is the greatest all-rounder there has ever been? Nobody knows, but he batted right and bowled left and came from Kirkheaton.'

Once the Factory Acts allowed workers their Saturday afternoon off, much of the West Riding became one big cricket hot spot. Football, having to compete with rugby league, was less prestigious. Cricket clubs and leagues proliferated in towns and villages, until almost every male child had access to a ground and a pathway to the top. In the 66 Championship seasons from 1893 to 1968, Yorkshire won the title 29 times and shared it once.[*]

Of the 665 players who had represented England at Test cricket at the time of writing, 81 were born outside England and Wales. Of the remaining 584 players, 97 – one-sixth – were born in Yorkshire, mostly the West Riding, making it the most fertile soil in the country, even allowing for its density of population. And while 14 of them were playing for another county when they were first selected to represent England, like Jim Laker of Surrey, the vast majority (83) were exercising their birthright and playing for Yorkshire.

The county where the second largest number of England Test players have been born is Lancashire with 54, and Nottinghamshire the third, with 37. Even London has produced fewer England Test cricketers than Yorkshire, depending on your definition of the city's environs: 80 by my calculation.

* Another local saying is 'If Yorkshire are strong, England are strong.' But England have been at their strongest in the periods of 1953–58, 1969–71 and 2004–12, when Yorkshire were not winning the Championship. They *were* supplying their best players to England, however, often including the country's captain.

ENGLISHMEN ABROAD

Of the 81 England Test players born outside England and Wales, 16 were born in India, 12 in the West Indies, 11 in South Africa, 10 in Australia, 8 in Scotland, 7 in Ireland, 3 in Zimbabwe, 2 in each of Germany, New Zealand, Pakistan and Zambia, and 1 in each of Denmark, Hong Kong, Italy, Kenya, Papua New Guinea and Peru. A triangular Test series could be played, in theory, between the England teams born in India, South Africa and West Indies. England-from-India, with five reserves, have the bench-strength and capacity to cope with various conditions. England-from-South Africa are astonishingly formidable in batting, so much so that Kevin Pietersen would have to revert to his original Natal persona of off-spinner, while England-from-West Indies are so stocked with pace bowling that seven of them could take the new ball.

England-from-India	England-from-South Africa	England-from-West Indies
John Jameson	Chris Smith	Wilf Slack
Douglas Jardine	Andrew Strauss	Sir Pelham Warner†
K.S. Ranjitsinhji	Jonathan Trott	Lord Harris
Colin Cowdrey	Allan Lamb	Roland Butcher
K.S. Duleepsinhji	Robin Smith	Chris Lewis
Nasser Hussain	Basil D'Oliveira	Chris Jordan
Errol Holmes	Nick Compton	Phillip DeFreitas
Bob Woolmer	Kevin Pietersen	Neil Williams
Richard Young†	Matt Prior†	Gladstone Small
Min Patel	Tony Greig	Devon Malcolm
Robin Jackman	Ian Greig	Norman Cowans
George Emmett		Joey Benjamin
Norman Mitchell-Innes		
Nawab of Pataudi Snr		
Neville Tufnell		
Edward Wynyard		

Note: Oh, to be a fly on the wall of these dressing rooms! When the players of England-from-South Africa come to elect their captain, would Kevin Pietersen have anything to say about the respective merits of Tony Greig and Andrew Strauss? A discussion between Douglas Jardine and Nasser Hussain about who should be captain – Colin Cowdrey might not get a word in – would also be worth listening to. So, too, the moment when Lord Harris breaks the news to Sir Pelham Warner that there is nobody else to keep wicket to their seven fast bowlers . . .

The 655th player illustrated the qualities of Yorkshire cricket as well as anyone. Joe Root came in to bat in the fourth Test against India in Nagpur in 2012–13 to find as big a crisis as England have faced outside an Ashes Test: England's batsmen, so desperate to win a Test series in India for the first time in 28 years, had ground almost to a standstill at 119 for four in the 61st over. Alastair Cook, the captain, had scored one run off 28 balls; so had Ian Bell. But Root walked out, smiled at his partner Kevin Pietersen and scored ten runs off his first ten balls in Test cricket. He just put the bad ball away with orthodox technique and unflappable temperament. As soon as he replaced his helmet with an England cap, he could have come from any decade of Yorkshire cricket in the previous century; but when Root bent into his forward defensive against an Indian spinner, head so low that his eyes were bail-height, really 'sniffing it', he was reminiscent in particular of Len Hutton, embodiment of the best in Yorkshire cricket through the ages.

On one visit to Lascelles Hall, I bowled a few 'walk-throughs', towards the sheep on the moor at one end, towards Kirkheaton at the other. The ground was damp and I should apologise for leaving footmarks in the creases. Twilight had set in . . . yet I could just about make out the Victorian womenfolk sitting against the granite wall with their shawls and backs to the wind: about half of the women of Lascelles Hall were said to attend a match, and highly informed their criticism was, too. I could just about make out the Thewlises and Greenwoods, Bateses and Eastwoods, packing up their kit and walking along the farm track to the lane dropping down into the village. They were talking about the tours being arranged for the forthcoming winter, to the United States and Canada or Australia, and the terms being offered to the pros. Old 'Mary Ann', looking down on the West Riding spread out below like a banquet, would have none of it. He had seen Niagara

Falls, he said, and they were all right, but 'I'd rather be at Lascelles Hall'.

Among the General Orders issued from Horse Guards Parade on 3 March 1841 was, I think, the single most important decision in the history of global cricket. The consequence was that cricket became embedded as the sport of the British army and, therefore, of the British empire.

The *Hampshire Advertiser and Salisbury Guardian* reproduced this General Order:

The Master-General and Board of Ordnance being about to form cricket grounds for the use of troops at the respective barrack stations throughout the United Kingdom, commanding officers of regiments, depots, and detachments, are to cause these grounds to be strictly preserved, and no carriages or horses to be suffered to enter them. The cricket-ground is to be considered as in the immediate charge of the barrack-master, who, however, cannot reasonably be expected to protect it effectually unless assisted in the execution of that duty by the support and authority of the commanding officer of the station, as well as by the good feeling of the troops, for whose amusement and recreation this liberal arrangement is made by the public. Lord Hill will treat as a grave offence every trespass that shall be wantonly committed by the troops, either upon the cricket ground or upon its fences. The troops will, moreover, be required, in every such case, to pay the estimated expense of repairs, as in the case of barrack damages. Special instructions have been issued to the barrack masters by the Master-General and Board of Ordnance.

By command of the Right Hon.

General Lord Hill, commanding in chief

Cricket in England was moribund by the 1840s. The Dukes of Dorset and Richmond, and royals like Frederick, Prince of Wales, had not been replaced. The Regency period was the most decadent in England's annals: nobody who was anybody got out of bed until the afternoon. The nation's resources had been drained by the war against Napoleon. MCC moved from one ground to a second, then a third: a season passed without the leading club playing a single game, let alone taking the lead. Following a volcanic eruption in Indonesia, 1816 was known as 'the year without a summer'. And when cricket was played, it was gripped by an existential crisis like never before or since: should bowling be under-arm or allowed to shoulder-height? For as many cricketers that cried 'forward', as many cried 'back' – among them the Reverend James Pycroft, who coined a phrase when he said that round-arm bowling was 'not cricket'.

Inter-city cricket had died out all too early. As the sport had spread north from the south-east of England, matches between the growing industrial cities were the natural vehicle of competition, without any need for patrons putting up stakes and purses. Nottingham v Sheffield was a crowd-puller: lacemakers v steelworkers. Coventry v Leicester was a vibrant fixture in the 1780s: 'The Leicester players were met at the entrance of their town by an incredible concourse of people . . . who took the horses from the carriage and drew it to their inn through the principal streets of the town, some of which were illumi-nated for the occasion, and the evening was spent amidst the congratulations of their friends and the satisfaction of conquest,' according to the *Northampton Mercury*. When the squirearchy took on the organisation of county cricket, from the mid-nineteenth century, it was driven by less demotic vigour than inter-city cricket.

Even the fixture which should have been the highlight of every season seemed moribund, because the Gentlemen, after the realignment of the aristocracy, could no longer give the Players a game. Absurd attempts were made to engineer a balance: nine

Players were matched against eleven Gentlemen, or eleven Players against sixteen or eighteen Gentlemen. Even more ingeniously, the size of the wicket was reduced when the Gentlemen batted: in 1832, they were given stumps five inches lower and two inches narrower. In 1837, William Ward, the city financier and MP who had bought the third Lord's ground and scored 278 on it for MCC v Norfolk, had a brainwave: when the Players batted, they would have to defend a wicket made of four stumps, three feet high and one foot wide. Yet they still won by an innings. The match came to be known as 'the Barn Door Match', or 'Ward's Folly'.

Rowland Bowen, the cricket historian who was so eccentric that he tried to amputate one of his legs in a bath, called 1820 to 1840 the era of single-wicket matches. One local champion playing another for a purse might have been interesting for the two players concerned, and gamblers, but not for anyone else, because they were representing themselves alone. A single-wicket player had up to five fielders, and no runs could be scored behind the wicket; moreover, to score a single run, the batsman had to run to the non-striker's end and back. So difficult did batting become that in 1846 Felix batted for two hours against Alfred Mynn before getting off the mark. 'The Victorian idea of team spirit had not yet been born when the period began,' Bowen noted. It was cricket without teammates, without camaraderie, without spice.

Only in one respect was cricket well resourced. Bookmakers lurked around the pavilion at Lord's, like money-changers in the Temple. In 1817 MCC banned the leading professional batsman, William Lambert, for match-fixing, but – just as in our day – some fixers were too big to touch: in this case, Lord Frederick Beauclerk. No wonder Mary Mitford, author of *Our Village*, scorned the higher echelons of the game in favour of her beloved village teams. 'I do not mean a set match at Lord's Ground for money, hard money, between a certain number of gentlemen and players, as they are called – people who make a trade of that noble sport, and degrade it into an affair of bettings, and hedgings, and cheatings, it may be, like boxing or horse-racing.' On 28 July 1827, *The Times* reported from Brighton: 'People are talking here very loudly, that the cricket match [Sussex v All England] which has just ended was a cross, and that it was lost purposely by the men of Sussex.'

In the context of this decadence, the command that every barracks in the United Kingdom should have a cricket ground was momentous. Approximately fifty regiments around the country were to benefit, and when they were posted abroad they would inevitably take the game with them: cricket became a – the – embedded sport. The *Lancaster Gazette and General Advertiser*, on 27 March 1841, was typical in voicing approbation: 'A capital thing. Cricket has long been practised in the 43rd Light Infantry, and that regiment, we all know, is a perfect model. The British army had not had a major engagement for 26 years, since the Battle of Waterloo, and it was considered to be high time for the officers and troops to have some amusement and recreation.'

Cricket was already played overseas, sometimes by soldiers, but in small pockets. Malta and Corfu had most of the ingredients: a sufficient number of Englishmen, a warm climate not disturbed by much rain, some flat open ground and a port where cricket equipment could be transported without prohibitive cost. The sport never bloomed in Malta and Corfu, however: they were naval bases.

But wherever in the empire British soldiers went thenceforth, bat and ball would go with them. The seed would be spread, and most notably to three main hot spots: one in Australia, one in India and one in the West Indies.

All three were ports, where the heat was tempered by sea breezes, and cricket could be played for most, if not all, of the year. The first was Sydney, where cricket had started to be played in the 1820s. The second was Bombay, where members of the Parsi community watched soldiers and civilians playing cricket at the Gymkhana club and decided it was fun, or more than fun: as a tiny minority in India, they thought they would be playing their economic and social cards right if they emulated Englishmen. The third hot spot was Barbados, where the garrison laid out a cricket ground beside the sea on the edge of Bridgetown.

Being a non-contact sport was essential to cricket's growth around the empire. A bowler from Barbados or the North-West Frontier Province could bowl as fast as he liked, but he could not come closer than a few feet to the batsman who represented the Raj, and certainly not touch him. If there had been any physical contact – as in football, let alone rugby – it is inconceivable that the British establishment in the colonies would have taken the field alongside their native subjects.

Who does cricket have to thank for this momentous decision? The General Order was issued 'by command of the Right Hon. General Lord Hill, commanding in chief'. He was renowned as a good egg, such a kind commander that he was affectionately known by his troops as 'Daddy Hill'. But cricket was not Hill's sport; the hunting of foxes and otters in his native Shropshire was. We should look elsewhere for the author of this command, before examining its far-reaching consequences.

As a boy, Arthur Wesley,* the future Duke of Wellington, did not play cricket at all, and certainly not on the playing fields of Eton. While attending school there, from the age of 12 to 15, Wesley spent most of his spare time in the stream near the house where he lodged; or so he recounted in later life. As a sensitive youth, and the son of the Professor of Music at Trinity, Dublin, the only thing he

---

* His surname was subsequently changed to 'Wellesley'.

played was the violin. The dictum about Waterloo being won on the playing fields of Eton was never uttered by Wellington; it appeared in an article by a French journalist who visited the school to write a profile of the Iron Duke.

On returning from Eton to his native Ireland, Wesley had few prospects. The family inheritance went to his elder brother, the Earl of Mornington. On falling in love with a girl from a neighbouring estate within the Pale, he was rejected by Kitty Pakenham because his prospects were so poor (once they improved, so did her attitude). At this juncture, he did the Georgian equivalent of 'man up'. He abandoned the violin for ever, bought a commission in the army and became aide to the Rt Hon Major Hobart, whose name is commemorated in Tasmania. Hobart had attended Westminster School and learned his cricket on the ground at Vincent Square.

On 8 August 1792, in Dublin, the Garrison played All Ireland 'for the sum of one thousand guineas, five hundred each side', according to the *Freeman's Journal*. And there can be little or no doubt that the future Duke of Wellington represented All Ireland. The only surviving scorecard, printed in the *Freeman's Journal*, lists 'Hon. A Wesby' batting at number five; but this has to be a typographical error by the Dublin printers. The reporter sent to cover this match clearly knew very little about cricket: he reported the result as a draw, whereas the Garrison actually won by an innings. Maybe the bibulous fool had a few drops of the hard stuff in the marquees before scrawling down the scores in his notebook with several misprints. In the next edition of the *Freeman's Journal* he tried to laugh off his mistake as 'rather unlucky'. In any event, the surname of 'Wesby' is not recorded anywhere else in Ireland in this period. Arthur Wesley, on the other hand, was then Honourable, and a captain. When the match report refers to 'the Hon. Captain Wesby', it has to be the future Duke of Wellington.

In this match on the Fifteen Acres, as Phoenix Park was called, the outstanding cricketer was the captain of the Garrison team, Lieutenant Colonel Charles Lennox. Even the reporter of the *Freeman's Journal* – anonymous, and thus he should remain – could see Lennox was an elite athlete. He scored 59 in the Garrison's only innings, and 'astonished the spectators with a display of agility and skill during the whole contest, which even the amateurs of the science admitted to have been without parallel in the coarse [sic] of their experience. His subtlety at bowling it was that so soon caused the event of the day to determine in favour of the Garrison; and his facility of catching the ball may be witnessed, but it cannot be described.'

This report of 'subtlety' suggests that Lennox might have been the first under-arm bowler to spin the ball both ways. Spinning the ball from leg had been the norm in under-arm bowling until the late 1770s, when a shepherd called Lamborn (first name unknown) had tried off-breaks as he whiled away his hours in meadows. In subsequent life, Lennox went on to become the fourth Duke of Richmond, and was destined to meet Wesby, or Wesley, again on the eve of Waterloo – on the same side, this time. Eventually, he was appointed Governor-General of Upper Canada, where his athleticism could not save him from being bitten in the face by a rabid fox.

Wesley – for it was surely he – was bowled by Lennox for five in his first innings, and caught for one in his second. (As in the scorecards of 1744, if the batsman was caught, only the name of the catcher was recorded, not the bowler.) Two unproductive innings did not, however, stop our foolish reporter fawning. He did not mention the lower ranks, who batted down the order in almost strict adherence to the social hierarchy. But Wesley was high enough, in the pecking and batting order at number five, to be rated 'active, and remarked for a promising player'.

Four years later, in 1796, Wesley – or Wellesley as he had now become – set sail for India as colonel of the 33rd Regiment. He is known to have taken plenty of books on the voyage, and no violin, but did he take a bat and ball as well? A tradition survives on the Malabar Coast, or Kerala as it is now, that the future Duke of Wellington introduced cricket when he set up a garrison in Thalassery, or Tellicherry; and the natives were allowed to participate when the garrison did not have sufficient soldiers to make up a game. When he reached Calcutta, he certainly found cricket being played by men of the East India Company like the diarist William Hickey and his hedonistic companions.

Having risen through the ranks, the Duke of Wellington was commander-in-chief by the Peninsular Wars, and his second-in-command was 'Daddy Hill'. Wellington remarked: 'The best of Hill is that I always know where to find him.' It was a valuable trait before the mobile phone. In the mayhem of battles like Badajoz, Salamanca and Vitoria, Wellington knew where to find his number two. But for all their victories in Spain, in the summer of 1815 the conclusive battle still lay ahead, the one on which Europe's future hinged. Napoleon Bonaparte, having escaped Elba, left Paris for Brussels with an army of 122,000 men, confident that he would be victorious and that most of Europe would be assumed into his French empire. Only if Wellington won, with the principal aid of the Prussians, would the nation-states of western Europe survive.

In the week before Waterloo, we know that Wellington, based in Brussels, was awaiting the delivery from London of the boots that he favoured. This was the calm before perhaps the greatest storm Europe had seen. Five days before Waterloo, he decided to take the afternoon off, to go and watch some of his officers playing cricket nearby at Enghien. For company, he took with him the 16-year-old Lady Jane Lennox, daughter of the captain of the Garrison team in that match of 23 years before. Lady Jane's father, by now the Duke of Richmond, was playing in the game at Enghien.

What did they talk about in the carriage? The last thing

Wellington would have mentioned – because that would have been tempting fate – was his famous record of having won more than 50 battles and only losing one, his first, in India – or his marriage to Kitty Pakenham. When he had returned from India and proposed after 12 years away, and Kitty had accepted, she turned out to be so far from what he remembered that he made overtures to the high-society courtesan Harriette Wilson. Assuming Lady Jane did not say she was bored with cricket and stamp her foot, and demand to go shopping in Brussels and drink hot choclolate, the Iron Duke may have settled for regaling the 16-year-old girl with stories of her father and the subtlety of his bowling . . .

The game was not played out: it was halted when the Prince of Orange arrived, and never resumed. According to the tutor of the Lennox girls, the Duke returned to Brussels with Jane later that evening. And maybe it was on the ride back to Brussels, if not before, that the seed was sown in Wellington's mind: that if the greatest of battles was won, and British troops had some peace to enjoy, then they too might benefit from the 'amusement and recreation' of playing cricket.

By 1841, the Duke of Wellington was both prime minister and the army's honorary commander-in-chief, and the national debt had been partly repaid. It would have taken only a few moments to summon Hill and instruct him that every barracks in the country should have its own cricket ground. It was an order obeyed so comprehensively that cricket became the only sport for which every regiment in the British army had a team.

While the villagers of Lascelles Hall in Yorkshire were looming large, so to speak, a family in Downend, Gloucestershire, was practising no less hard. The rivalry between the three Grace brothers spurred them on until they all represented England in the same

Test team at the Oval in 1880 (the only other instance of three brothers representing their country in a Test is the Mohammad brothers of Pakistan in 1969–70). Cricketers need space in which to play, which favours those who grow up with a garden, or an orchard like the Graces. They were coached by their father and more especially their mother. Their cousins joined in, and their dog fetched the balls. Given such resources, a family structure can go a long way towards producing cricketers. A family can be a miniature form of hot spot, academy or nursery. A family has the same strength in offering lots of practice, but does not eliminate failings and weaknesses so thoroughly as a hot spot would.

Almost one-quarter of the players to represent England at Test cricket have had a brother, father or uncle who represented England: 154 out of 665. In addition, another 110 England Test players have had a father, brother or half-brother who has played first-class cricket. Such is the enormous advantage at a young age of having somebody good to play with and against: somebody who will bowl at him, give him a few basic tips, perhaps buy him a bat, and start programming his brain to the paths of a cricket ball. Of England Test players, 264 out of 665 – two in every five – have benefited from beginning in the miniature form of hot spot that is the family.

Where both the father and son have played Test cricket, the son has been the better cricketer in roughly twice as many cases. This measurement cannot be made entirely objectively. If the father has played in an era of far fewer Tests, the fact that his son has scored more runs or taken more wickets does not automatically make him better. Worldwide, 33 sets of fathers and sons have played Test cricket for the same country. In nine cases, I would say, with an element of subjective judgement, the father has been distinctly better; and in 17 cases, the son has been distinctly better; while in the other seven cases, no such conclusion can be drawn.

TEST-PLAYING FATHERS AND SONS

1. The nine cases where father and son have played Test cricket for the same country, and the father has been distinctly the better cricketer, even where their Test records do not bear this out.[*]

	Tests	Runs	Average	Wickets	Average
England					
Colin Cowdrey	114	7624	44.06	0	–
Chris Cowdrey	6	101	14.42	4	77.25
Len Hutton	79	6971	56.67	3	77.33
Richard Hutton	5	219	36.50	9	28.55
C.L. Townsend	2	51	17.00	3	25.00
D.C.H. Townsend	3	77	12.83	0	–
India					
Vinoo Mankad	44	2109	31.47	162	32.32
Ashok Mankad	22	991	25.41	0	–
Pankaj Roy	43	2442	32.56	1	66.00
Pranab Roy	2	71	35.50	–	–
New Zealand					
H.G. Vivian	7	421	42.10	17	37.23
G.E. Vivian[†]	5	110	18.33	1	107.00
Pakistan					
Hanif Mohammad	55	3915	43.98	1	95.00
Shoaib Mohammad	45	2705	44.34	5	34.00
West Indies					
George Headley	22	2190	60.83	0	–
Ron Headley	2	62	15.50	–	–
Tommy Scott	8	171	17.10	22	42.04
Alfred Scott	1	5	5.00	0	–

[*] Here and throughout, statistics are correct up to the end of the 2015 World Cup.
[†] Viv Richards told me he learnt how to field by watching Graham Vivian at cover on New Zealand's tour of the West Indies in 1971–72, but this does not tip the balance.

2. The 17 cases where father and son have played Test cricket for the same country, and the son has been distinctly the better cricketer.

	Tests	Runs	Average	Wickets	Average
Australia					
Edward Gregory	1	11	5.50	–	–
Syd Gregory	58	2282	24.53	0	–
England					
Chris Broad	25	1661	39.54	0	–
Stuart Broad	74	2193	24.09	264	29.90
Alan Butcher	1	34	17.00	0	–
Mark Butcher	71	4288	34.58	15	36.06
Joe Hardstaff Snr	5	311	31.10	–	–
Joe Hardstaff Jnr	23	1636	46.74	–	–
Jeff Jones	15	38	4.75	44	40.20
Simon Jones	18	205	15.76	59	28.23
Jim Parks Snr	1	29	14.50	3	12.00
Jim Parks Jnr	46	1962	32.16	1	51.00
			and	ct 103	st 11
Arnold Sidebottom	1	2	2.00	1	65.00
Ryan Sidebottom	22	313	15.65	79	28.24
Micky Stewart	8	385	35.00	–	–
Alec Stewart	133	8463	39.54	0	–
			and	ct 263	st 14
Fred Tate	1	9	9.00	2	25.50
Maurice Tate	39	1198	25.48	155	26.16
India					
D.K. Gaekwad	11	350	18.42	0	–
A.D. Gaekwad	40	1985	30.07	2	93.50
Yograj Singh	1	10	5.00	1	63.00
Yuvraj Singh	40	1900	33.92	9	60.77

	Tests	Runs	Average	Wickets	Average
New Zealand					
William Anderson	1	5	2.50	–	–
Robert Anderson	9	423	23.50	–	–
Lance Cairns	43	928	16.28	130	32.92
Chris Cairns	62	3320	33.53	218	29.40
South Africa					
John Lindsay	3	21	7.00	–	–
			and	ct 4	st 1
Denis Lindsay	19	1130	37.66	–	–
			and	ct 57	st 2
Dave Nourse	45	2234	29.78	41	37.87
Dudley Nourse	34	2960	53.81	0	–
Peter Pollock	28	607	21.67	116	24.18
Shaun Pollock	108	3781	32.31	421	23.11
Len Tuckett	1	0	0.00	0	–
Lindsay Tuckett	9	131	11.90	19	51.57

3. The seven cases where father and son have played Test cricket for the same country and have to be judged more or less equal as cricketers:

	Tests	Runs	Average	Wickets	Average
England					
David Bairstow	4	125	20.83	–	–
			and	ct 12	st 1
Jonny Bairstow	14	593	26.95	–	–
			and	ct 16	st 0
Francis Mann	5	281	35.12	–	–
George Mann	7	376	37.60	–	–
India					
Hemant Kanitkar	2	111	27.75	–	–
Hrishikesh Kanitkar	2	74	18.50	0	–
Vijay Manjrekar	55	3208	39.12	1	44.00
Sanjay Manjrekar	37	2043	37.14	0	–

	Tests	Runs	Average	Wickets	Average
New Zealand					
Wynne Bradburn	2	62	15.50	–	–
Grant Bradburn	7	105	13.12	6	76.66
Zinzan Harris	9	378	22.23	0	–
Chris Harris	23	777	20.44	16	73.12
Rodney Redmond	1	163	81.50	–	–
Aaron Redmond	8	325	21.66	3	26.66

Notes: Frank Hearne of England and South Africa was roughly as good as his son George of South Africa.

George Headley of West Indies was one of the all-time greats. His son, Ron Headley of England, was neither so good as his father nor as his son, Dean Headley of England.

Nawab of Pataudi Snr of England was not so good as his son, Nawab of Pataudi Jnr of India.

Walter Hadlee of New Zealand was better than his elder son, Dayle, but not so good as his younger son, Richard.

Lala Amarnath of India was better than his elder son, Surinder, but not so good as his younger son, Mohinder.

Jahangir Khan of India was not so good as his son, Majid Khan of Pakistan, while Majid was better than his son, Bazid Khan.

Wazir Ali of India was better than his son, Khalid Wazir of Pakistan.

Or perhaps the parents have no time for, or interest in, cricket. In that case, a first-born boy may have to wait until a younger brother arrives and begins to bowl at him. The sample size in English cricket is too small to generalise: there have been ten pairs of brothers who have played Tests for England, in addition to the three Graces and three Hearnes. But, worldwide, 65 pairs of brothers have played Test cricket (excluding, for this purpose, two sets of twins).

In 17 cases, by my estimation, the elder brother has been better at Test cricket. In 32 cases, the younger brother has been better, while in 16 cases, they have been more or less equally good. This sample size is big enough to suggest it is a distinct advantage to be a younger brother, presumably because he plays and practises more at a formative age than his elder brother, who may have had to wait for someone to play with.

In addition to being the better cricketer, the younger brother is more likely to bowl. According to my estimation, in 12 cases the elder brother has been more of a bowler than his younger brother, while in 25 instances the younger brother has been more of a bowler. Anecdotal evidence suggests the elder brother has a bat first, perhaps because he owns the equipment, and the younger brother has to dismiss him before he has a turn to bat.

How many of us watching a talented boy play cricket have been told: 'Ah, but you should see his younger brother'? Thus, Martin Crowe was perceived to be more naturally gifted than his elder brother Jeff Crowe, and Robin Smith more talented than Chris Smith. But too much subjectivity is involved to prove that younger brothers as a rule have been more talented, however that term is defined: is Dwayne Bravo, the all-rounder, more talented than his younger brother Darren Bravo, the batsman? Or it may be that the younger brother is often perceived to be more talented than his elder brother because, aside from batting, he is more of a bowler.

The one exception, although again the sample size is too small to be conclusive, occurs in India: here the first-born son has in general been more successful than his younger brother or brothers who have also played Tests. This is consistent with the cultural trend in India of pouring more resources into the first-born son than any other child, in order to safeguard the family inheritance.

TEST-PLAYING BROTHERS

1. The 17 pairs of brothers of whom the elder has been better at Test cricket than the younger.

Key: * = elder brother was more of a bowler
         † = younger brother was more of a bowler
         No mark where one brother bowled as much as the other.

	Tests	Runs	Average	Wickets	Average
Australia					
Charles Bannerman	3	239	59.75	–	–
Alick Bannerman	28	1108	23.08	4	40.75
*George Giffen	31	1238	23.35	103	27.29
Walter Giffen	3	11	1.83	–	–
England					
*Arthur Gilligan	11	209	16.07	36	29.05
Harold Gilligan	4	71	17.75	–	–
Tony Greig	58	3599	40.43	141	32.20
Ian Greig	2	26	6.50	4	28.50
Peter Richardson	34	2061	37.47	3	16.00
Dick Richardson	1	33	33.00	–	–
India					
Madhavrao Apte	7	542	49.27	0	–
Arvindrao Apte	1	15	7.50	–	–
Subhash Gupte	36	183	6.31	149	29.55
Balkrishna Gupte	3	28	28.00	3	116.33
Kripal Singh	14	422	28.13	10	58.40
Milkha Singh	4	92	15.33	0	–
Cottari K Nayudu	7	350	25.00	9	42.88
†Cottari S Nayudu	11	147	9.18	2	179.50
New Zealand					
John Bracewell	41	1001	20.42	102	35.81
Brendon Bracewell	6	24	2.40	14	41.78

Pakistan

*Wasim Raja	57	2821	36.16	51	35.80
Ramiz Raja	57	2833	31.83	–	–
*Saeed Ahmed	41	2991	40.41	22	36.45
Younis Ahmed	4	177	29.50	0	–

South Africa

Tony Pithey	17	819	31.50	0	–
†David Pithey	8	138	12.54	12	48.08
Eric Rowan	26	1965	43.66	0	–
†Athol Rowan	15	290	17.05	54	38.59

West Indies

Denis Atkinson	22	922	31.79	47	35.04
†Eric Atkinson	8	126	15.75	25	23.56

Zimbabwe

Andy Flower	63	4794	51.54	0	–
†Grant Flower	67	3457	29.54	25	61.48
Paul Strang	24	839	27.06	70	36.02
Bryan Strang	26	465	12.91	56	39.33

2. The 32 pairs of brothers of whom the younger has been better at Test cricket than the older.

	Tests	Runs	Average	Wickets	Average
Australia					
Ken Archer	5	234	26.00	–	–
†Ron Archer	19	713	24.58	48	27.45
Mel Harvey	1	43	21.50	–	–
Neil Harvey	79	6149	48.41	3	40.00
Robert McLeod	6	146	13.27	12	31.83
C.E. McLeod	17	573	23.87	33	40.15
Harry Trott	24	921	21.92	29	35.13
†Albert Trott	3	205	102.50	9	21.33

John Trumble	7	243	20.25	10	22.20
†Hugh Trumble	32	851	19.79	141	21.78

Bangladesh

Nafees Iqbal	11	518	23.54	–	–
Tamim Iqbal	37	2743	38.09	0	–

England

*John Gunn	6	85	10.62	18	21.50
George Gunn	15	1120	40.00	0	–
Chris Smith	8	392	30.15	3	13.00
Robin Smith	62	4236	43.67	0	–
George Studd	4	31	4.42	–	–
†Charles Studd	5	160	20.00	3	32.66

India

Surinder Amarnath	10	550	30.55	1	5.00
†Mohinder Amarnath	69	4378	42.50	32	55.68
Ladha Ramji	1	1	0.50	0	–
†Amar Singh	7	292	22.46	28	30.64

New Zealand

Jeff Crowe	39	1601	26.24	0	–
†Martin Crowe	77	5444	45.36	14	48.28
Dayle Hadlee	26	530	14.32	71	33.64
†Richard Hadlee	86	3124	27.16	431	22.29
Phil Horne	4	71	10.14	–	–
Matthew Horne	35	1788	28.38	0	–
Murray Parker	3	89	14.83	–	–
John Parker	36	1498	24.55	1	24.00

Pakistan

Humayun Farhat	1	54	27.00	–	–
Imran Farhat	40	2400	32.00	3	94.66
*Nadeem Khan	2	34	17.00	2	115.00
Moin Khan	69	2741	28.55	–	–
			and	ct 128	st 20

South Africa

Reginald Hands	1	7	3.50	–	–
Philip Hands	7	300	25.00	0	–
Peter Kirsten	12	626	31.30	0	–
Gary Kirsten	101	7289	45.27	2	71.00
Albie Morkel	1	58	58.00	1	132.00
†Morne Morkel	62	710	12.03	217	29.35
*Peter Pollock	28	607	21.67	116	24.18
Graeme Pollock	23	2256	60.97	4	51.00
Stanley Snooke	1	0	0.00	–	–
†Sibley Snooke	26	1008	22.40	35	20.05
George Tapscott	1	5	2.50	–	–
Lionel Tapscott	2	58	29.00	0	–
Daniel Taylor	2	85	21.25	–	–
†Herbie Taylor	42	2936	40.77	5	31.20
Herbert Wade	10	327	20.43	–	–
Billy Wade	11	511	28.38	–	–
			and	ct 15	st 2

Sri Lanka

Dulip Samaraweera	7	211	15.07	–	–
†Thilan Samaraweera	81	5462	48.76	15	45.93
Mithra Wettimuny	2	28	7.00	–	–
Sidath Wettimuny	23	1221	29.07	0	–

West Indies

Cyril Christiani	4	98	19.60	–	–
			and	ct 6	st 1
Robert Christiani	22	896	26.35	3	36.00
			and	ct 19	st 2
Bryan Davis	4	245	30.62	–	–
Charlie Davis	15	1301	54.20	2	165.00
Robert Samuels	6	372	37.20	–	–
†Marlon Samuels	55	3251	35.72	36	56.41

Victor Stollmeyer	1	96	96.00	–	–
†Jeffrey Stollmeyer	32	2159	42.33	13	39.00
Zimbabwe					
*John Rennie	4	62	12.40	3	97.66
Gavin Rennie	23	1023	22.73	1	84.00

3. The 16 pairs of brothers, and half-brothers, who have been more or less equally good at Test cricket.

	Tests	Runs	Average	Wickets	Average
Australia					
Edward Gregory	1	11	5.50	–	–
Dave Gregory	3	60	20.00	0	–
England					
Adam Hollioake	4	65	10.83	2	33.50
†Ben Hollioake	2	44	11.00	4	49.75
Johnny Tyldesley	31	1661	30.75	–	–
Ernest Tyldesley	14	990	55.00	0	–
Clement Wilson	2	42	14.00	–	–
†Rockley Wilson	1	10	5.00	3	12.00
India					
Wazir Ali	7	237	16.92	0	–
†Nazir Ali	2	30	7.50	4	20.75
New Zealand					
*Matthew Hart	14	353	17.65	29	49.58
Robert Hart	11	260	16.25	–	–
			and	ct 29	st 1
*Hedley Howarth	30	291	12.12	86	36.95
Geoff Howarth	47	2531	32.44	3	90.33
Pakistan					
Waqar Hasan	21	1071	31.50	0	–
†Pervez Sajjad	19	123	13.66	59	23.89

South Africa

William Richards	1	4	2.00	–	–
Alfred Richards	1	6	3.00	–	–

Sri Lanka

Lalith Kaluperuma	2	12	4.00	0	–
Sanath Kaluperuma	4	88	11.00	2	62.00

West Indies

*Dwayne Bravo	40	2200	31.42	86	39.83
Darren Bravo	32	2311	43.60	0	–
John Cameron	2	6	2.00	3	29.33
Francis Cameron	5	151	25.16	3	92.66
Pedro Collins	32	235	5.87	106	34.63
Fidel Edwards	55	394	6.56	165	37.87
George Grant	12	413	25.81	0	–
†Rolph Grant	7	220	22.00	11	32.09
*Norman Marshall	1	8	4.00	2	31.00
Roy Marshall	4	143	20.42	0	–
Wilton St Hill	3	117	19.50	0	–
†Edwin St Hill	2	18	4.50	3	73.66

Notes: The two pairs of twins, Mark and Steve Waugh of Australia, and Hamish and Jamie Marshall of New Zealand, have been excluded from the above lists.

In addition:

Australia have produced the three Chappell brothers who have played Tests: Ian, Greg and Trevor.

In addition to his three Tests for Australia, Albert Trott played two Tests for England.

England have produced the three Grace brothers who have played Tests: Edward, William and Fred; and three Hearne brothers: Alec, Frank and George.

Pakistan have produced the three Akmal brothers who have played Tests: Kamran, Adnan and Umar; and the three Elahi brothers: Manzoor, Saleem and Zahoor; and the four Mohammad brothers: Wazir, Hanif, Mushtaq and Sadiq.

South Africa have produced the three Tancred brothers who have played Tests: Bernard, Louis and Vincent.

Sri Lanka have produced the three Ranatunga brothers who have played Tests: Dammika, Arjuna and Sanjeeva.

Schools with cricket facilities are another form of hot spot. Of England's 665 Test cricketers, 220 have either been amateurs before the distinction was abolished in 1962, and can therefore be assumed to have attended a fee-paying school; or else, since then, can be verified as having attended one. In other words, one-third of England's Test cricketers have come from fee-paying schools, whereas less than one-tenth of the population has attended them. Such a background has been, and remains, an enormous advantage, especially for batsmen.

At these fee-paying schools, normally known as public schools, a larger part of the timetable is set aside for cricket than at state schools, where in many cases there is no cricket or ground at all; and the pitches are likely to be maintained far better. The coach at a fee-paying school has often been a county cricketer himself, so he knows the network and how to put in a favourable word for a pupil. Public schoolboys who went on to Oxford or Cambridge universities have been expected to graduate into their county side and captain it, with the prospect of an even higher honour. Of England's 79 Test captains, 32 went to Oxbridge.

If one side of the coin is that England has the advantage of these mini-hot spots, the down side is far too many cold spots, notably cities in the Midlands and north of England. Not one England male Test cricketer has been born in Wolverhampton (in 2011 Rachael Heyhoe Flint was created Baroness Heyhoe Flint of Wolverhampton). One England Test cricketer has been born in each of Hull, Newcastle and Wakefield. Two England Test cricketers have been born in each of Cardiff, Plymouth, Stoke-on-Trent and Sunderland. One Test cricketer has been born in Liverpool, and one in Sheffield, since the nineteenth century. Overall, half of the 20 most populated cities in England and Wales have barely produced a Test team in the last hundred years.

This failure to maximise human resources goes a long way

towards explaining why England has not been so successful as Australia at cricket, in spite of having a population several times larger. Boys who have grown up in the state-run primary and secondary schools of England's inner cities have had a vastly reduced chance of reaching the top. The lack of cricket grounds, of time and support by teachers and families, of coaching, of networking, and of peers who also aspire to play cricket for a living, has marginalised a large section of the population of England and Wales.

An alternative pathway used to be football: 58 of England's Test players are listed in the *Who's Who of Cricketers* as having played football. Most of them represented professional league clubs, the earlier ones Corinthian Casuals. The last of this line was Arnold Sidebottom, who represented England at Test cricket in 1985. At one time a football club was a quasi-cricket academy, in that it made the cricketer fitter and probably better at fielding and more confident. A figure of 58 out of the 512 England Test cricketers who played football, up to and including Sidebottom, gives a proportion of 11.3 per cent. Since his day, it has been impossible for a boy to combine both sports after his very early teens.

Very few of the 584 England Test cricketers born in England and Wales have reached the top without the help of at least one of these four stepladders: 1. a fee-paying school; 2. a close relative who has played either Test or first-class cricket, or will do so; 3. professional football, with the benefits entailed; 4. being born in Lancashire or Yorkshire, where even small communities tend to have a cricket ground (Nottinghamshire lost more than 20 grounds when its collieries were closed and has been replaced by Durham as a source of fast bowlers). The majority of the male population of England and Wales does not fit into any of these categories. The waste has been enormous.

Nurturing, I conclude, is highly significant in the development of cricketers, and batsmen in particular, more so than in the case of most sportsmen. As one example of what is almost cause and effect: when Sir Everton Weekes grew up in Bridgetown, the ball was lost if he hit it out of his garden, so he hit no more than two sixes in his 4455 Test runs, and one of those did not clear the ropes but was all-run. There are many similar anecdotes: a batsman favours the cover drive because if he hit straight at home, the ball went down the road. The cricketers of Lascelles Hall excelled because of their nurturing – because they practised more than any other commu-nity of their time – rather than nature. If genes had been decisive, their descendants would also have excelled at cricket.

Take identical twins at birth, and bring one up as the only child of an inner-city family living in a high-rise apartment and attend-ing a state school. The other identical twin is brought up by a father who has played first-class cricket, in a house with a garden, along with several brothers, before being sent to a fee-paying school. One identical twin is far less likely to play cricket for England than the other.

Nurture, not nature, accounts for the extraordinary case of Wolmer's. This school was founded in Kingston, Jamaica, by a British merchant who made his fortune when Port Royal was infa-mous for its debauchery, and who set aside money for a school in his will, perhaps in the hope of saving his soul. It remains the oldest school in Jamaica, but not the most elite, because it has expanded so much, to the point of having more than one thousand boys and more than one thousand girls.

West Indies had played 290 Test matches to the end of the fifth Test against England in 1991 – and former pupils of Wolmer's had kept wicket in 138 of them, or 47 per cent. Karl Nunes kept wicket, and captained West Indies, in their first three Tests. Shortly after-wards, he was succeeded by Ivan Barrow, who kept wicket in ten

Tests, in addition to scoring the first Test century for West Indies in England. After the Second World War, Gerry Alexander kept wicket in 25 Tests, Jackie Hendriks in 20 Tests, then Jeffrey Dujon in 80.

Not one of these West Indian wicketkeepers who attended Wolmer's was related to another. They came from very diverse backgrounds: a mixture of German, Jewish, Scottish, English, French and African origins. What they had in common, apart from a cricket ground in the school, and a snowballing tradition of producing West Indian wicketkeepers, was a type of nurturing. A former pupil, after playing Test cricket, would return to the school, watch matches being played by the new generation and advise a wicketkeeper who was talented. This unofficial mentoring system had ceased, so I was told during my visit in 1998. But the tradition was revived when a downtown Kingston kid was sent on a scholarship to Wolmer's, and Carlton Baugh followed in Dujon's footsteps for 20 Tests.

In an area of southern Birmingham that could at best be described as tired-looking, and more accurately as run-down, lies Stoney Lane Park. It is not how many people would envisage a park. It is green only where there is neither tarmac nor concrete, and no larger than a football pitch. When a tornado ripped off surrounding roofs and they had to be replaced with new ones, it was said to have done the area a favour.

Yet here is a hot spot to compare with Lascelles Hall or anywhere else in the West Riding, or with the playing fields of Eton and Harrow. In the middle of this park, an area the size of a cricket square is surrounded by a wall about three feet high. The surface of tarmac is not perfectly flat, but at least it is not dangerous to bowl on with a taped tennis ball, as the boys do.

Like most cricketers in Pakistan, where many of their forefathers came from, or the West Indies, these boys were not coached until their teens, if then. They learned for themselves – with the odd shouted tip from their mates – while playing all day at weekends and in the holidays. They could play into the night because this cockpit, along one side, had mini-floodlights – before they were vandalised. Floodlighting was also a factor in the development of Jos Buttler into the most versatile hitter the England team had known: it enabled him to play on the verandah of the family home on winter evenings from aged three, with his elder brother. Without artificial lighting, an English batsman is less likely to practise for the ten thousand hours which have been identified as the key to genius. This does not apply to bowling: the lad who bowls pace for ten thousand hours will not be able to stand, for stress fractures.

Two England Test cricketers grew up in this cockpit: Kabir Ali and his first cousin Moeen Ali; and two county cricketers who played for several years, Kadeer Ali and Naqaash Tahir; and at least two minor county cricketers in Omar Ali and Rawait Khan. Several of them had brothers who were skilled players. From the local primary school, named after Nelson Mandela, which runs alongside one edge of this park, they moved on to Moseley School, where they were able to play some cricket, and the Moseley Ashfield club. At one stage, the club had a team that included eight members of Warwickshire Under-15s.

In 2014, Moeen Ali went on to become England's ninth Test cricketer born in Birmingham, less than a year after the eighth, Chris Woakes, whose background was not much more privileged. It is possible for anyone to reach the top, because success in sport is multifactorial. There are some advantages, too, in learning cricket in the street: such players are not over-coached; they are stretched when playing against boys older than themselves or young men; they become streetwise, if they want to survive the gang battles; they learn to fight and scrap (Kabir Ali became a death-bowling specialist); and without nets to hem them in, they can grow up scoring all round the wicket and seeing the value of their shots. (A schoolboy who plays a cover drive in the nets is likely to be told 'Good shot' with no regard to his placement of the ball.) Moeen Ali became one of the most gifted of all England's strokeplayers; when his teammates watched him in the nets, they tried to work out which balls he did *not* hit for four.

No one background for a cricketer can be considered ideal. What is essential is that a team should be composed of cricketers who think on their feet and hail from a variety of backgrounds. Bowling is the posing of problems, and batting the solving of them. You do not want all the players coming at them from the same perspective – even if they were born in Lascelles Hall, and went to school at Wolmer's.

_____3_____

AUSTRALIA'S
ARDENT DESIRE

Quickness of eye and foot, strength of arm in throwing, confidence in themselves, an ardent desire to win, and good temper under defeat.

First independent assessment of Australian-born cricketers, 1832

IT IS THE Sunday morning before Christmas. I am not at home with my wife and children, but on the other side of the world, in a four-poster bed in a country house outside Melbourne.

Thick curtains cover the tall windows of this mansion, which was the finest in Australia in the late Victorian era, but from early morning the midsummer sun pierces. In the grounds of the estate, a galah laughs, un-Englishly.

Why am I here, at Rupertswood, alone?

The answer, in large part, lies very close at hand. In this bedroom, on the Sunday before Christmas 133 years earlier, another Englishman had stayed. He was somewhat more youthful, aristocratic and eligible – and in a state of rare passion.

The Honourable Ivo Bligh had been charged by Lord Harris, ruler of MCC and English cricket, to lead a cricket team to Australia. They were to avenge England's defeat at the Oval in the sole Test of 1882 by seven runs. It was said then that the body of English cricket had been cremated, and the ashes taken to Australia; for honour's sake, and as good sport, they had to be recovered. (I do not think I am alone in ignoring the slightly macabre nature of what is involved: the symbolic contents of the urn are the remains of a cremated body, that of English cricket.)

On the voyage to Australia, Bligh had met Sir William and Lady Janet Clarke, the owners of Rupertswood, who had undertaken a European tour while a ballroom was being built. Bligh had been invited to visit once his team had arrived in Melbourne. The Clarkes slept across the stairwell from my room, which was then the main guest bedroom, where Bligh would have stayed.

Sir William Clarke, the first man born in Australia to be made a knight and baronet, was worthy of these honours, to judge by his philanthropy. His father, 'Big Clarke', had emigrated from Somerset and bought large tracts of Tasmania and Victoria. William dedicated his life to spending his inheritance wisely. Apart from building Rupertswood, which was named after his first son, William Clarke funded the first hall of residence for women at the University of Melbourne and named it after Janet, his second wife. When their servants were ill, the story goes, he and Janet would visit them with soup. In London, while receiving his knighthood, he endowed the Clarke Music Scholarship at the Royal College of Music, one of numerous grants and endowments. He was also president of the Melbourne Cricket Club.

Aboard the SS *Peshawur*, daily at 4 p.m., Lady Janet served tea on deck for Bligh and his team, mostly his Cambridge chums augmented by four northern professionals. And Janet seems to have been the first woman to whom Bligh warmed. A repressed childhood at Cobham Hall in Kent – his mother, daughter of the Earl of Chichester, was renowned in society as an icicle – was followed by Eton and Cambridge, where women continued to be conspicuously absent. Janet offered tea and sympathy. When Bligh cut his hand in a tug-of-war on board, she bandaged it. A few months later Bligh composed a long poem about Rupertswood and its inhabitants, dedicated to Janet:

What pleasant times there were upon that good old ship,
What games we played, what cosy teas at four o'clock
You did dispense so kindly to us thirsty ones.

Not inspired, yet heartfelt.

Janet had arrived at Rupertswood as the governess, from the outback, basking in the surname of Snodgrass – and had stepped into the breach in an emergency. Sir William's first wife had been driving a horse and trap down a street in Sunbury, a town less than a mile from Rupertswood, when the horse was startled by a rabbit and bolted. His wife was thrown from the trap and killed before their children's eyes. Janet seized the reins, brought the horse to a standstill and saved the children. A couple of years later, the marriage shocked Melbourne society, as she was of such lowly birth. But Janet seems to have been a strong, good woman, who embraced Sir William's philanthropy, and the children of his first marriage, as well as their own.

At the time of this voyage, Janet was 31 while Bligh was 22. He was clearly enchanted by her Aussie warmth and generosity, the like of which he had never known from his mother. Did he fall in love with her? In a sense, yes: the poem suggests some romantic yearnings. But propriety forbade anything further. In their correspondence, which has been preserved, she addressed him as Mr Bligh. Besides, Janet may have had someone else in mind for him.

Straight after his team had landed in Melbourne, Bligh took the train to Rupertswood, which had its own private station just outside Sunbury. From there, he had a short walk through the estate, past the lake which had been dug in the shape of Australia – the mainland, without Tasmania, where Big Clarke had begun to make his fortune. On arrival, Bligh was introduced to Florence Morphy, the 19-year-old piano teacher and governess of the Clarke children – and he was smitten. From her Irish parentage she had derived bright auburn hair, which in her old age was to go black, not white; she had the eyes of a tigress; and her character matched the flaming hair.

During Bligh's stay at Rupertswood before Christmas 1882, he was joined by his fellow amateurs as house guests ahead of the first Test starting on 30 December; and on Christmas Eve, Lady Janet and Florence together created something that would embody the myth of the ashes. A game had been played on the paddock, between the English amateurs and the menfolk of Rupertswood, whether members of the Clarke family or estate workers. The English amateurs, though outnumbered, had been sufficiently strong to win; and afterwards the two women put their heads together to see if they could come up with a suitable prize. They did; they surely did. The passion of these two women gave birth to the physically smallest prize in sport, yet the most coveted, given how long it has been competed for: cricket's holy grail, the Ashes urn.

My mobile rings on the bedside table. The *Telegraph*'s sports editor in London says that Graeme Swann has announced his immediate retirement in his column in a rival Sunday newspaper. A story of eight hundred words, please, to be composed and filed in half an hour.

After Swann's retirement, England's tour of 2013–14 went from bad to worse, to the worst ever. England had lost an Ashes series 5–0 twice before. Once was in 1920–21, when they had every excuse because so many of their pace bowlers had not survived the First World War. Their pace attack then might have comprised John Hitch of Surrey, who did survive the war; Major Booth of Yorkshire, who died at the Somme; and Percy Jeeves, the Warwickshire all-rounder whose name and fastidious appearance had attracted the attention of P.G. Wodehouse, before he too was killed at the Somme. The second whitewash had occurred in 2006–07, but then

England had rallied to win the one-day series that followed. In 2013–14 it was a remorseless descent into disintegration: defeat by a margin of 5–0 in the Tests, 4–1 in the one-day series, and 3–0 in the 20-over internationals.

If Australia had been ceaselessly whitewashed in England, I am confident the public would have grown weary. The essence of sport is unpredictability, and England's disintegration in Australia in 2013–14 made the outcome all too predictable. Yet the appetite of Australia's public and players for winning did not visibly diminish. If holding the Ashes is fundamental to the Australian sense of manhood, this went further, because it lasted long after the urn had been recovered. In every limited-overs game, the players went flat out to beat the Poms, and their enjoyment – their relish, their sense of fulfilment whenever they defeated England – never ebbed. It was inexplicable, except in the context of the origins of cricket in Australia.

Native-born Australians, from the outset of colonisation, grew up intensely motivated to beat the British at cricket. Their parents had been deported and often treated brutally by this British elite, both civilian and military. The native-born could not fight back physically: Sydney was still garrisoned by regiments. The alternative was to beat those regiments at their own game. The native-born were desperate to forge a new identity for themselves, by winning. So deep was this desire that it is still alive 200 years later whenever Australia's cricketers take the field against – always against, never with – England.

For the first three decades of its existence, Sydney was too preoccupied with the basics – finding fertile soil, growing crops, building and fortifying the settlement, treating diseases – to have much leisure. Before 1830 there is just one brief report of a cricket match, in Sydney's Hyde Park in 1826. We can infer, nevertheless, that the match was between the British military and the native-born.

Regiments had been posted to Sydney from the foundation in 1788, and some brought cricket implements with them, before the General Order of 1841 decreed a cricket ground in every barracks at home. According to the chief historians of early cricket in Sydney, Dr Richard Cashman and Stephen Gibbs, most of the original games took place in Barrack Square, where the regiments were quartered.

In this first recorded match of 1826, we know that one of the native-born players was Edward Flood. He performed much the same role in the growth of Australian cricket as George Smith had in London and Richard Nyren in Hambledon. Flood, the son of Irish convicts, was not only a skilled all-rounder, but also the landlord of the Australian Hotel in George Street, where the first cricket club for native-born players – the Australian Cricket Club – held their meetings. He was known to challenge to single-wicket contests players such as a soldier from the 4th Regiment, the King's Own. A man of ever-increasing substance, Flood took up umpiring after playing, and was elected to the City Council and the Legislative Assembly.

The snootiness – the sheer snottiness – of the British establishment looking down on the early efforts of Flood and his teammates is still palpable. In a report of the 1826 match, the *Monitor* derided the native-born team as 'a few mechanics of Sydney', adding that 'their mode of handling their bats and balls was most unskilful, and worse playing was never witnessed either in England or the Colony.' Flood determined to beat 'em on the field, then join 'em off it.

The British-born establishment in Sydney also looked down on the rudimentary dress and equipment of these native-born cricketers. Some used bats hewn from cedar, because equipment imported from England – via the Cape of Good Hope until the Suez Canal was opened in 1869 – was prohibitively expensive. These native-born players also had to do without shoes. So prevalent was this fashion, or absence of fashion, according to Cashman and Gibbs in *Early Cricket in Sydney*, that when the first intercolonial match was staged in 1856, the New South Wales team played 'in bare feet or in socks, which occasioned considerable surprise among the spectators.' These spectators were the free-born burghers of Melbourne, far more refined and respectable; but the lack of cricket boots did not stop NSW beating Victoria by two wickets.

Some of these native-born players were tough enough to spurn headwear as well as footwear in Sydney's summer sun. 'The military went to the wickets in black or tall hats, à la Lillywhite, and with shoes having spikes in them. The native boys, members of the Australian Club, took the field either bareheaded, with a handkerchief tied around their heads, or with the popular cabbage-tree hat encircled with its broad blue ribbon, and with long streamers floating behind.' They were very proud to be different.

This distinction between British and native-born cricketers was spelt out in the names of their clubs. The native-born represented the Australian Cricket Club. British-born players played for the Amateur Club, if they were civilians; or the Victoria Club, founded after the Queen's accession in 1837; or their regiment. The first flag of the Australian Club was the corn stalk, after the cereal which had been transported from North America to become Australia's staple (the sobriquet for the Australians who toured England in 1878 was 'the Cornstalks'). After the Australian Club* achieved an innings victory over the Amateur Club in 1833, a patriotic newspaper proclaimed: 'The Corn-stalk . . . once more towers in its native pride, triumphant over the rose, the thistle, and the shamrock.' Not only were the English put in their place, but the Scots and Irish, too.

* Native-born players gave themselves the nickname of 'Currency Lads'. As Cashman and Gibbs explain: 'Local "Currency", in the ordinary sense, referred to bills or notes which were issued by private individuals and were convertible – sometimes – into "Sterling", or English money, at a discount. The names were thus adopted to distinguish the Australian-born cricketers from the British-born.' In some fixtures, the rivalry was boiled down to the basics: Natives v Emigrants.

From these earliest beginnings, the chief characteristics of Australian cricket were manifest – in fielding, for a start, because this was something everyone could do without costly kit. 'The fielding of the [Australia] Club was unrivalled by anything ever seen before in the Colony,' reported the *Australian* after the club's defeat of the 4th Regiment in 1833, and that newspaper was disposed towards the British elite. We also have the more impartial testimony of J.R. Hardy, a Cambridge blue who had just emigrated to Sydney: 'They field beautifully – run like kangaroos – and throw to perfection.' He added that the Australian Club fielders were 'so correctly stationed in their places and kept such an eye on the game that their opponents . . . possessed no chance.'

In the same unbiased vein, 'Etonian' wrote to the *Australian* newspaper in 1832 with his assessment of native-born cricketers. In his anonymous opinion, they needed to decide upon one wicket-keeper. This, I suspect, was a function of their lack of any wicketkeeping gloves, forcing a player to take a turn as keeper until his hands hurt so much he had to swap places. Overall, though, the raw material so pleased 'Etonian' that he offered one of cricket's most perceptive insights: 'In my opinion, the native youth shew qualities of cricket-playing that I never saw surpassed. Quickness of eye and foot, strength of arm in throwing, confidence in them-selves, an ardent desire to win, and good temper under defeat.'

Almost two centuries later, what, if anything, has changed?

Thus we can see Australia's environment already exerting its beneficial effect. 'The two best cricket coaches are sunshine and space,' so the free-thinking England all-rounder Trevor Bailey told me after he had been on three tours of Australia. The native-born were growing up in sunshine and space like no cricketers before, and in the process combating two adversaries: their opponents and the conditions. It was not like England, where on the rare hot day a cricketer can usually find somewhere to hide in the field because the pitch is slow; where a batsman, after being dismissed, can find comfortable compensations in the pavilion, while his Australian counterpart returns 'to the shed'; where the overall softness is summed up in sandwiches and cake for tea, not a meat pie and water. Only those Australians who had an ardent desire were going to play cricket in heat and bare feet.

When I first sat metaphorically at Sir Leonard Hutton's feet as his ghostwriter, he leaned forward in his armchair at his home in Kingston upon Thames to make his first Delphic utterance: 'In Australia the ball is harder, and the pitches are harder.' He paused. 'And the people are harder too.'

The scoreboard at the Melbourne Cricket Ground makes grim reading for the colonials at lunch on Thursday, 15 March 1877, the first day of Test cricket: 3–1–41. Or as the Englishmen, captained by James Lillywhite, prefer to say: 41 for three wickets, last man 1.

Expecting Australian cricketers to compete on level terms with England's finest professionals was always asking a lot! So it is proving.

Only one hour of Test cricket has been played so far, because the start had to be delayed until 1 p.m. Some Melbourne newspapers had advertised the start time as 11 a.m., but the match committee decided to allow the Englishmen more time to find their land-legs. Only yesterday did they arrive from New Zealand, after crossing the Tasman.

It is the Australians, however, who have been at sea in the opening hour. Only Charles Bannerman has come to terms with the English bowling, scoring an unbeaten 27 out of the 41 runs made by the interval, and showing the benefits of almost a week of hard practice by the colonials at the MCG.

The five New South Welshmen had arrived by steamer from Sydney five days before the match and put up at the Duke of Rothesay Hotel in Elizabeth Street. There were to have been six of them, but Frederick Spofforth had refused to play if he could not have his own choice of wicketkeeper: he wanted Billy Murdoch, who kept for NSW, not Jack Blackham of Victoria, who had been selected by the match committee.

On the afternoon of their arrival, the New South Welshmen had gone to practise at the MCG, and twice Bannerman had hit the ball out of the ground. His brilliant driving set him apart from the other Sydney men, although the 18-year-old Tom Garrett was noted as a fine all-rounder in the making, and from the Victorians, too.

But at least the Victorians could claim to have the finest cricket ground in the Colonies. Soon after the foundation of Victoria in 1837, the Melbourne Cricket Club had conceived the ambition of making their ground at least the equal of MCC's back home. Sydney's cricketers had tried Hyde Park, but the 4th Regiment held their parade on it every Monday, which was practice day for the Australian Club. The Outer Domain had been tried, but it too was used by the military and their horses' hooves. Then the Military Ground had been opened at the barracks in Moore Park in 1854, with proper boundaries measured and marked. But it was still in military, not civilian, hands.

The MCC of the New World had all the space required for a cricket ground and more, once native bush had been burnt. The resources, too: Melbourne had boomed since gold had been discovered inland at Ballarat and Bendigo. Coal came up the River Yarra from the new Newcastle; bushels of hay and barley by the thousand were harvested in the Victorian outback. Bursting with railway stations, government buildings, libraries, art galleries and a university, though not yet a cathedral, Melbourne had overflowed into suburbs like St Kilda, Richmond and Prahran. 'This was the golden age of the bourgeoisie,' wrote the eminent Australian historian Manning Clark, who had kept wicket for Oxford University. He was wearing a most unacademic digger's hat when I met him in Canberra on my first tour of Australia in 1978, and recalled being bowled by Hedley Verity when he played against Yorkshire in 1939. (Well, he was a Rhodes scholar, not a Verity scholar.)

When the first match on level terms between an English touring team and a combined Australian XI had been mooted, no serious alternative to the MCG was advanced. The first permanent stand had been built in 1862 for the arrival of the first English cricket tourists, who made a satisfactory replacement for Charles Dickens after he had cancelled a lecture tour originally planned by the restaurateurs Spiers and Pond. By 1877, a ladies' stand had been constructed, and a lawn where gentlefolk could promenade.*

The MCC of the New World was so keen to be Australia's premier cricket club that, shortly before the inaugural Test, they signed three players from East Melbourne as professionals: Bransby Cooper, born in Dhaka and schooled in England, Tom Horan and Billy Midwinter, both born in the British Isles but taken to Australia at an early age, like Bannerman. These signings did not go down well with Melbourne's other clubs, until the MCC agreed to allow their opponents an extra man for each professional the MCC fielded. Thus, if they played all three professionals, their opponents could field 14 players.

Horan had shared a useful stand with Bannerman for the second wicket after Nat Thomson of NSW had been the first person to be

---

* So nice, so genteel, were the arrangements for MCC members that *The Age* informed its readers, or their servants: 'The police regulations for the traffic of licensed vehicles attending the match are as follows:– Disengaged cabs to stand on south side of Wellington-parade, to have their horses' heads towards the west, and to extend from sixty feet east of entrance to the Yarra Park, the two first cabs to stand within twenty feet of the entrance. Engaged cabs to stand along south side of the three-rail fence, and to have their horses' heads facing eastward, and to extend westward from 17 feet from corner post. Omnibuses to stand on south side of parade along the fence, to have their horses' heads towards the east, and to extend westward from twenty feet west of entrance to Yarra Park. Traffic to the ground through Jolimont will not be allowed.' Woe betide the equine head daring to point east by south-east!

dismissed in Test cricket: Thomson had been bowled by Allen Hill, the Yorkshireman from Lascelles Hall who bowled wicket to wicket. Bannerman and Horan had taken the score up to 40, when Horan had been dismissed by George Ulyett, the fastest bowler on view. A ball had landed in a heel-mark and hit Horan on the thumb. It 'thence bounded into the sure hands of Hill at short slip. 2–12–40': so the correspondent for *The Argus* recorded. Horan, Victoria's best batsman, had contributed 12 runs to the partnership of 38 with Bannerman, the New South Wales 'crack'.

Even though only an hour had been scheduled for the morning session, there was still time for a third wicket to fall before lunch, that of Australia's captain, Dave Gregory. 'Handsome Dave' had been born in New South Wales, only for his mother to die and his father to return 'home' to England after a few years of teaching at a grammar school. He abandoned David and his siblings (one, Ned, also played in this first Test) in an orphanage in Sydney. David joined the National Cricket Club, which had succeeded the Australian Cricket Club as the base for the native-born. He was not much of a batsman – an orphanage is not the best nursery – but made himself into a fine fielder and captain, and was so handsome, beard and all, that he had three wives and sixteen children. At the dawn of Test cricket, Australia's players had elected him their captain. According to *The Argus*: 'The choice lay between him [Gregory] and Mr Cooper, and there can hardly be any doubt that the Sydney man was the fittest of all the eleven for the position. They showed by the appointment that no silly rivalry between two colonies was to be allowed to interfere with prudent conduct of the match.'

Gregory had gone in to face the best bowler in England, Alfred Shaw: a length bowler, or rather *the* length bowler. For Nottinghamshire, at medium pace, he would concede one run per four-ball over. Not the most athletic of figures, he was built to bowl all day and make the most of what was in the pitch. According to the correspondent of *The Age*, Gregory 'went out to the first ball, off which he got a single to long-on.' James Lillywhite, England's captain, reacted by bringing in the fielder at long-on – Harry Jupp – to mid-on. As *The Age* reported: 'in trying a single in Shaw's next over to mid-on Gregory was run out through the splendid return of Jupp.' Gregory had set the tone for Australian Test cricket by taking these two aggressive options: he had gone after the opposition's best bowler from his first ball, and he had put pressure on the fielders, even if the second option had failed.

Such is the position confronting Bannerman as he walks to the middle with Cooper after lunch. Two and a half hours remain of this abbreviated first day of Test cricket and, as the scoreboard announces all too clearly, Australia's cricketers have yet to prove a match for the Mother Country's. One of the Melbourne newspapers goes so far as to say it is impertinent of colonial cricketers to think they can compete on level terms with those from home. The attitude of the British elite lingers on.

Bannerman alters the mood as he begins to unleash his drives on both sides of the wicket and his pulls. 'The former [Bannerman] made matters very warm for the field, and knocked the bowling about all over the ground,' reports *The Herald*. 'Cooper showed a splendid defence, but scored very slowly.' Cooper is often observed playing the ball only six inches from his stumps.

In mastering the English bowling, Bannerman is assisted by Lillywhite's captaincy. Instead of bringing back Shaw after lunch, the English captain tries Tom Armitage of Yorkshire. This is spreading the load, which day-in day-out county cricket tends to do, as opposed to flogging your four main bowlers, then resting them after the match, in the Australian style. Armitage is the least of the players in the party; he has only been selected for this match because Ted Pooley was arrested in New Zealand on a charge of damaging hotel property in Christchurch, after a dispute over betting during the game had turned nasty. What is more, Armitage tries lobs – he had bowled them successfully the previous season in taking 13 wickets against Surrey at Sheffield, but here they are greeted with amusement and derision.

Bannerman hits the four balls of Armitage's first over for four, nought, two and four: ten runs for minimal risk and effort. Any lingering sense of awe about English cricket which the crowd may be feeling is largely dispelled in this one over. The correspondent of *The Age* scoffs: 'Such rubbish as was delivered by Armitage has probably never been seen at the ground, full tosses high over the batsman's head being varied by common domestic grubbers.'

But Cooper is bowled for 15 by James Southerton: 118 for four. Bannerman meanwhile has raced to 81, turning the game in the colonials' favour. When Bannerman reaches 87, he drives Southerton to long-off, but the Australian – 13 runs short of his century – has good luck not bad. The fielder is the burly or even bulky Shaw, who is slow to the ball and lets it go for four.

In Southerton's next over, Bannerman again drives towards long-off, but he places the shot more precisely and takes his score to 95. Bannerman has never made a century in his few first-class games, but he shows no sign of seizing up in the nervous nineties. In the same Southerton over, he hits another four to square-leg, taking him to 99.

Lillywhite then bowls, Bannerman takes a single and the crowd rises to applaud the first century in international cricket.* Spectators inside the ground number only 4000 – it is a weekday and the hours of play are abbreviated – but they are augmented by those outside the MCG. 'The gum-trees in Yarra-park bore the usual number of black clusters of free onlookers,' notes the correspondent of *The Argus*.

* Cricket's first international match, between Canada and the USA in 1844, did not contain a century of any kind. The scores at the St George's Club in New York on 24–26 September were: Canada, 82 and 63, beat USA, 64 and 58, by 23 runs.

Bannerman, after reaching his hundred, does not take the safe option of playing for stumps. He keeps attacking until 5 p.m., and scores the astonishing number – for any period – of 99 runs in the session off his own bat, and against the finest bowlers England can muster apart from W.G. Grace. For readers of *The Herald*'s country edition, their correspondent writes after stumps have been drawn: 'At that time the score stood at no less than 166 for six wickets, a result mainly attributable to the splendid cricket of Bannerman, who, without giving a chance, made a total of 126. His innings will long be remembered in the colonies as about the most noteworthy exhibition of cricket ever witnessed. The 126 put together by him yesterday consisted of twelve fours, nine threes, twelve twos, and the rest in singles.'

None of Bannerman's teammates makes 20, but it takes a brilliant catch by Ulyett to dismiss Midwinter for five. Midwinter 'stepped out to Southerton, and the ball flew swiftly through the air towards the grand-stand. Ulyett, stationed at the very edge of the turf, backed across the path till pulled up by the fence; then curved his back into the form of a bow, and stretched up his hands. The ball was taken, and securely held. Had it been six inches higher Midwinter would have saved his life, and the scorers would have written down 5. Ulyett was loudly applauded.' In other words, Ulyett used what we now call the Australian method, fingers pointing upwards. Unfortunately, neither J.R. Hardy nor 'Etonian' indicate whether the original Australian fielders caught the same way.

Next morning, Friday, 16 March, the wonder increases. Bannerman not only picks up from where he left off, but his stroke-play goes from strength to strength, until it matches anything seen in the Old World. For *The Herald*, their correspondent writes at the close of day two: 'Bannerman's play yesterday was, if anything, better than it was on Thursday, and when he had to discontinue his innings he had made 165 runs – the grandest display ever seen on the Melbourne ground, and as admitted by the Englishmen themselves, equal to anything they had seen in England. His hitting, especially to the off, was perfection – clean and hard.'

The correspondent for *The Argus* adds: 'Lillywhite says he has seen as good a display in England (which may well be believed), but never better.' Grace, we should bear in mind, has just enjoyed the finest summer any batsman has ever known, hitting the first two triple centuries in first-class cricket and the enormous total of 839 runs in three consecutive innings.

All of Bannerman's practice in the week before this match is paying off, not least financially. 'Bannerman's splendid score is now certain to be recognised by a testimonial commensurate with the brilliancy of the performance,' *The Herald* reports. 'In this matter Victorians are anxious not only to recognise undoubted skill, but also to show that to them whether an Australian hails from one side or the other of the Murray it is all the same – he is still an Australian.' The rivalry between Melbourne and Sydney is serving as a creative tension.

Bannerman's innings is 'discontinued' after a ball from Ulyett hits the second finger of his right hand. Unlike Horan, Bannerman is not wearing batting gloves: he hails from rougher, tougher, less affluent Sydney. He retires with a split finger, which needs stitching. Correspondents assume he will play no further part in this match, but already Bannerman has had his impact. To this day, Bannerman's 165 out of Australia's total of 245 remains the highest percentage of runs – 67.3 per cent – scored by one batsman in a side's completed Test innings. He has emboldened the home players, pressmen and public. Before the game, the Melbourne newspapers had headlined their reports 'The Cricket Carnival: Old World v New World' or 'England v Victoria and New South Wales'. After Bannerman has shown the way with his century, the headline in *The Herald* reads simply 'England v Australia'.

SOUTH AFRICA'S FIRST TEST

In the first Test between England and South Africa, at Port Elizabeth in March 1889, there was not the same difference between 'them' and 'us' as in the first Test between England and Australia.

Australia's first captain, Dave Gregory, was a Cornstalk from Sydney. South Africa's first captain, Owen Dunell, though born in South Africa, had been educated at Eton and Oxford. Another member of their inaugural Test side, and chief organiser of the English tour, was William Milton, born in England and schooled at Marlborough College, before becoming Cecil Rhodes's private secretary. Two other members had been born and educated in England, while a fifth had been born in India and educated in England. Of the five members of the first Australian side born in Britain, four had emigrated at an early age; only Bransby Cooper had been educated there.

A cap was awarded to the members of this first South African XI, with 'SA' stitched on by Mrs Dunell, the captain's wife. But the two teams were composed of men of largely similar background. As the English captain, Aubrey Smith, said in a speech in Cape Town: 'When they come to a colony, Englishmen find brothers and cousins extending to them the right hand of welcome and they feel then that in reality they are Englishmen one and all.'

Only one member of the first South African team was an Afrikaner, Arthur or 'Okey' Ochse (at 19 years and one day, he remains South Africa's youngest Test debutant). Christian missionaries in the Eastern Cape preached cricket and rugby to divert the Xhosa elite from their tribal customs. But apart from the Cape Coloured all-rounder Charles Llewellyn, before the First World War, no non-white player was selected for South Africa until 1992.

Without an ardent desire to establish their own new identity, South Africa lost in two days by eight wickets. They had no batsman like Bannerman to spark excitement and forge a new identity. When South Africa batted first, the *Eastern Province Herald* referred to 'the batsmen seeming to confine their efforts to defending their wickets.'

By 1907, when South Africa played their first Test in England, a national style had emerged. It was not so aggressive as Australia's.

After their game against Lancashire at Old Trafford, the *Manchester Guardian* summarised on 2 August 1907: 'The South African batting, apart from its soundness, was not greatly to be admired. The men played for a long time in a depressingly grim spirit – as if they had needed, say, ten more runs to win. There was really no need for this excessive caution, especially in the case of a batsman who can hit like Nourse. But it is probably a habit with them to play in this grim fashion until their position is assured.' This tendency, to save a game before thinking about winning it, has always made South Africa hard to beat, especially at home, but not the most exciting or successful side: the desperation not to lose leads to 'choking'.

South African bowling has, overall, been more admirable. The *Manchester Guardian* in 1907 noted 'its originality and versatility', as the tourists had four wrist-spinners. A lot of South African cricket was played on matting until the 1930s, especially on the dry High Veld, where a googly could bounce chest-high. After the Second World War, a tradition of fine fast bowling emerged, reinforced when Afrikaners took up the sport in greater numbers. After apartheid, indigenous Africans – notably Makhaya Ntini – were permitted.

South Africa's hot spots have been their elite schools, originally for whites only. Durban High School has produced 27 players who have represented South Africa in one format or another. Their finest XI might be: Barry Richards, Trevor Goddard, Hashim Amla, Lee Irvine, Dennis Dyer, Lance Klusener, Dennis Gamsy, Hugh Tayfield, Geoff Griffin, Richard Dumbrill and Richard Snell. Diocesan College (aka Bishops), in Cape Town, and King Edward VII, in Johannesburg, come second equal, with 18 players. Thanks to these schools, South Africa has seldom been anything less than sturdy, competitive, and excellent at fielding. But if there was an excess of one virtue, it was of collective discipline, at the expense of individual spontaneity – before A. B. de Villiers became the world's most brilliant batsman.

The day after the first Test a match was arranged in Port Elizabeth between Married and Single, according to the *Eastern Province Herald*, 'in which several of the English cricketers will take part.' A day after the inaugural Test in Melbourne, I cannot imagine Australia's cricketers playing alongside England's.

At the start of England's first ever Test innings, on the second after-noon, an umpiring controversy arises. Jupp leg-glances a ball for two off Australia's left-arm medium-pacer, John Hodges – and a bail is seen to fall. Jupp, in this inaugural Test match, does not give himself out, or walk.

The umpire at the bowler's end is Curtis Reid, who in the termi-nology of the period is standing 'for' Australia. The one at square-leg is Richard Terry, standing 'for' England, and from there originally, although now employed by the Melbourne Cricket Club. Reid refers the appeal to Terry, who gestures that he has not seen how the bail fell from its groove. In these circumstances, the umpires have to say 'not out'. England play on, without losing a wicket, but the MCC members are none too happy, and Terry is jostled when he returns to the pavilion at stumps on the second day. In the words of *The Argus*: 'Terry was bounced at the close of play for his inability to see the bail drop from Jupp's wicket.' A bats-man not walking, members of the premier club not accepting the umpire's decision: not much sign of the Spirit of Cricket at the dawn of Tests.

Why Hodges is playing at all, let alone opening Australia's bowling, is a story in itself. Australia's bowling attack was to have consisted of Frank Allan, Edwin Evans and Spofforth. Allan, a left-arm pace bowler, was known as 'the wonder of the age' because he made the ball swerve, or swing as we would say, like no one else either side of the Equator. Several weeks before what was advertised as 'the Combination Match', Allan had agreed to participate, but the match committee received a letter from him only a day or two before the game to say he was pull-ing out: a carnival was coming up in Warrnambool, where he was working as a land commissioner, and he preferred to social-ise with his friends. Melbourne's newspapers lambasted Allan for letting the side, and the whole country, down. *The Argus* thundered:

> As the matter stands at present these bowlers appear in the most puerile light, and whatever may be their abilities, we can only regret that the colonies have to place their cricketing reputation in the hands of such weak-minded persons as Messrs Allan and Spofforth, one of whom, on his own showing, prefers the mild dissipation of a provincial carnival to the great contest in which it was hoped he would play a prominent and honourable part; while the other is content to cast public interests and the reputation of his native land overboard simply because a request of his, based on a strong vanity, is not complied with.

The only point to be made in Allan's favour is that, from what we know of his character, his dissipation at the carnival would have been very far from 'mild'.

Edwin Evans – 'certainly the best bowler on this side of the line [i.e. the Equator]', according to *The Herald* – had already declined to travel from his native New South Wales. 'Banjo' Paterson, the author of *Waltzing Matilda*, described the occasion he saw Evans: he was 'a first-class horseman. Then he astounded us by taking his rifle and killing a kangaroo that was going past at full speed . . . Evidently the keen eye that had made him a crack slip fieldsman was also useful looking along the sights of a gun.'

Allan, Evans, Spofforth: Australia's three finest bowlers all refused to play. As there was no time to summon someone from Sydney, the match committee had to resort to Melbourne grade cricket for reserves. One bowler was Hodges, a bootmaker, who had not played for Victoria but was in form for Richmond: he had taken five wickets for 16 against East Melbourne a few days before.

The second call-up was his Richmond teammate, Thomas Kendall, a left-arm spinner. Although Kendall and Hodges were to bat at ten and eleven for Australia, both had batted in the top four for Richmond and scored 30s earlier in the month, seizing their chance to play a competitive innings.

In the first of all Tests, a second controversy arises, this time concerning Ulyett, England's all-rounder and prodigious hitter. Ulyett, like Sir Ian Botham, bowled fast with lots of bouncers, hit the ball enormous distances, enjoyed life to the full and once scored 149 not out against Australia. (The parallel does not extend to Botham throwing an Arab boatman into the Red Sea at Port Suez when he demanded extra baksheesh for ferrying him back to his steamer.) In his short innings so far, Ulyett has already struck a ball into the pavilion bar, though it counted four only; and England have reached 98 for two in reply to Australia's 245 when he is given out lbw by Reid, Australia's umpire.

As the correspondent for *The Argus* sees it: 'There could be no doubt, from the way Ulyett shook his head, that he had no mind to leave.' Another report says he 'strongly expressed his dissent, and lost his temper so much as to dig his heel into the ground where he said the ball had pitched.' *The Argus* viewed Ulyett's behaviour more benignly: 'Though he undertook subsequently to prove to friends and listeners, if they would only go down to the wickets with a tape-line, that his leg could not have possibly been in the way, he did not show his disapprobation in a very open manner to the spectators.'

England end the second day on 109 for four. Apart from Jupp, who has prospered after his umpiring reprieve to reach 54 not out, only Henry Charlwood made a score: his 36 included a 'draw' between his legs. Had cricket commentary on the radio been inaugurated at this Test, rather than at Bannerman's benefit match in Sydney in 1922, we might have had the prototype of Brian

Johnston's 'leg-over' episode, for Charlwood, according to the newspapers, 'put Kendall nicely under his leg for 3.'

Although England and Australia lie at opposite ends of the earth, no difference in the Laws of Cricket or their interpretation is evident. A dispute had arisen in a game between Victoria and New South Wales about whether the ball had been dead at the end of an over, and after the matter had been referred by letter to Marylebone Cricket Club, their judgment had been enforced. But some differences in playing method are discernible in this first Test. For one, the England professionals are much better at taking quick singles, according to the Melbourne critics: in this game their batsmen have sometimes pushed the ball five yards and easily completed a run, when the Australian batsmen would never have contemplated one.

The weather for the third day, Saturday, 17 March, is perfect for cricket after Friday's cloud. The crowd is estimated at between ten and twelve thousand, the highest of the four days, in spite of all the sporting counter-attractions. A special train is leaving 'Spencer-street' at 10 a.m. to take people to Kyneton Races, which the Governor of Victoria will graciously attend. The Northern Rifle Club is staging their monthly competition at Sandridge. Sculling on the Yarra is popular too: only the previous year Edward Trickett had won the Championship of the World by rowing from Putney to Mortlake on the Thames in 24 minutes and 36 seconds and become the first Australian world champion in any sport. Furthermore, the coursing season opens with a meeting on the estate of W.J. Clarke – soon to be Sir William – at Donnybrook. On Monday morning, however, the Melbourne newspapers report that this meeting was hampered by 'the excessive warmth of the weather' and 'the scarcity of game'.

EARLY DAYS IN NEW ZEALAND

Compare these conditions with the disadvantages cricket faced when trying to get off the ground in New Zealand. On this 1876–77 tour, Lillywhite's men played several games in New Zealand, including one at Wellington which was reported by 'A Special Correspondent' for *The Australasian*: 'Considering that everything was against good play – ground, weather, and attendance – it is not so wonderful that the local twenty-two were disposed of with such ease. Rain fell heavily each day; the ground, which is in a hollow at the bottom of a gully and extremely small, was more like a sponge than anything, and the visitors did not exceed more than 1,500 during the whole time. There was nothing to remark on in the first innings of the Wellington men; they were simply so afraid of Shaw that he was able to mow them down as he pleased.'

Already a feeling of superiority over New Zealand was developing in Australia. 'The result of the English matches, so far, goes to prove that both New South Wales and Victoria are a long way in advance of their southern friends, and that a really good Australian eleven would play and defeat any fifteen the respective provinces could produce.' The Australian board did not condescend to a Test match against New Zealand until after the Second World War. New Zealand's cricketers were left in isolation, except for an occasional visit by tired England players after an Ashes tour. Anybody who wanted to be a professional cricketer had to emigrate, like Clarrie Grimmett to Australia, or Ces Dacre or Tom Pritchard to England, until Glenn Turner broke the mould in the 1970s.

New Zealand has, therefore, depended on the miniature hot spot of the family: they have had the highest proportion of Test players who have been fathers and sons, and the highest proportion of brothers. This trend includes their best batsman, Martin Crowe, and best bowler, Sir Richard Hadlee: perhaps the two cricketers who have come closest to technical perfection.

The cultural change began with versatile groundsmen who produced pacey drop-in pitches in multi-sports stadia. Brendon McCullum then turned New Zealand from the most defensive Test-playing country into the most attacking, and led his buccaneers to the World Cup final of 2015. It was the style of cricket which he and his players believed that New Zealanders wanted to see.

Saturday's crowd sees England pushed close to the indignity of following on. According to the Laws of the day, if the side batting second are 80 or more runs behind on first innings, they are forced to bat again. But after Jupp is given out lbw to Tom Garrett for 63, and England are reduced to 145 for eight, 'a free, dashing innings' of 35 not out by Hill limits Australia's lead to 49.

After Australia's first innings, the correspondent of *The Herald* had prophesied about their second attempt: 'The batting power of the colonials is so great that, under any circumstances, they are not likely to be disposed of for less than 100.' Here we have an early example of the commentator's curse. (No black magic is involved, however: the commentator is tempted to make his big statement when a cricketer is at his peak and can only decline.) Sure enough, Australia in their second innings slump to 75 for nine, only 124 runs ahead. Shaw is accuracy personified, while *The Age* reports that Ulyett bowled 'very viciously – pitching half-way and bumping.' At the close of day three, *The Herald* summarises: 'Such bowling as that of Shaw and Ulyett in the second innings of the Australians has never before been witnessed here, and the fielding was splendid.'

England's cricketers are quartered at the White Hart Hotel. Sunday is a rest day. On Saturday night, does the hotel do a roaring trade, perhaps into the early hours, behind locked doors? Australia have ended the third day on 83 for nine wickets, only 132 ahead, and the widespread assumption is that the Englishmen will win.

On Monday morning, however, Australia's last-wicket pair of Kendall and Hodges score at almost a run a ball: such is the value of grade cricket. Four byes cannot be prevented by either Selby, England's stop-gap keeper, or Armitage, his long-stop. Australia's tenth wicket adds 29, the highest stand of their second innings. England's target has been swiftly extended to 154.

Gregory had tinkered with Australia's batting order in their second innings: he promoted Tom Garrett, who scored an unbeaten 18 first time round, and demoted himself. Lillywhite, his counterpart, alters his order completely: of his first nine batsmen, only Shaw occupies the same position in both innings. Selby may have been demoted from opener to number five because he has been keeping wicket, but why has Jupp been demoted from opener to number three after his first innings of 63? Lillywhite's objective may be to hit off the runs quickly and get to the station early on Monday afternoon. Their next game is in Bendigo the following day.

England's opening batsmen in their second innings are two men from Lascelles Hall: Andrew Greenwood, normally a middle-order bat, and Hill, presumably on the strength of his hitting in the first innings, even though he has just been bowling. For once, they can do their village no credit. Confronted with Kendall's left-arm spin, Hill gives his team the worst of starts when he is caught at mid-off off the second ball of England's innings.*

England's start worsens as they collapse to 22 for four. 'The wicket had become a good deal worn from having been played on for four days, and made the ball "bite" a bit': so reports the correspondent of *The Age* with his practised eye. Buoying Australia's morale, after that last-wicket partnership, Bannerman has decided to field in spite of his stitching: 'His appearance on the ground was hailed with a hearty cheer.' Then another twist, as Selby and Ulyett raise England's total to 62 for four – halfway to their target but for Australia's last-wicket stand.

* The pair made some amends when the second Test was played a fortnight later, again at the MCG. Even though Spofforth relented and played, Greenwood scored 49 and 22, while Hill took five wickets and scored 49 run out and 17 not out, as England won by four wickets.

AUSTRALIA V ENGLAND
(1st Test)

Played at Melbourne Cricket Ground, Melbourne, on 15, 16, 17, 19 March 1877

AUSTRALIA

C. Bannerman	retired hurt	165		b Ulyett	4
N.F.D. Thomson	b Hill	1		c Emmett b Shaw	7
T.P. Horan	c Hill b Shaw	12		c Selby b Hill	20
D.W. Gregory*	run out	1	(9)	b Shaw	3
B.B. Cooper	b Southerton	15		b Shaw	3
W.E. Midwinter	c Ulyett b Southerton	5		c Southerton b Ulyett	17
E.J. Gregory	c Greenwood b Lillywhite	0		c Emmett b Ulyett	11
J.M. Blackham†	b Southerton	17		lbw b Shaw	6
T.W. Garrett	not out	18	(4)	c Emmett b Shaw	0
T.K. Kendall	c Southerton b Shaw	3		not out	17
J.R. Hodges	b Shaw	0		b Lillywhite	8
Extras	(b 4, lb 2, w 2)	8		(b 5, lb 3)	8
Total	(all out; 169.3 overs)	**245**		(all out; 68 overs)	**104**

ENGLAND

H. Jupp	lbw b Garrett	63	(3)	lbw b Midwinter	4
J. Selby†	c Cooper b Hodges	7	(5)	c Horan b Hodges	38
H.R.J. Charlwood	c Blackham b Midwinter	36	(4)	b Kendall	13
G. Ulyett	lbw b Thomson	10	(6)	b Kendall	24
A. Greenwood	c E.J. Gregory b Midwinter	1	(2)	c Midwinter b Kendall	5
T. Armitage	c Blackham b Midwinter	9	(8)	c Blackham b Kendall	3
A. Shaw	b Midwinter	10		st Blackham b Kendall	2
T. Emmett	b Midwinter	8	(9)	b Kendall	9
A. Hill	not out	35	(1)	c Thomson b Kendall	0
James Lillywhite*	c & b Kendall	10		b Hodges	4
J. Southerton	c Cooper b Garrett	6		not out	1
Extras	(lb 1)	1		(b 4, lb 1)	5
Total	(all out; 136.1 overs)	**196**		(all out; 66.1 overs)	**108**

ENGLAND	O	M	R	W		O	M	R	W
Shaw	55.3	34	51	3		34	16	38	5
Hill	23	10	42	1	(3)	14	6	18	1
Ulyett	25	12	36	0	(2)	19	7	39	3
Southerton	37	17	61	3		–	–	–	–
Armitage	3	0	15	0		–	–	–	–
James Lillywhite	14	5	19	1	(4)	1	0	1	1
Emmett	12	7	13	0		–	–	–	–

AUSTRALIA	O	M	R	W		O	M	R	W
Hodges	9	0	27	1	(5)	7	5	7	2
Garrett	18.1	10	22	2	(4)	2	0	9	0
Kendall	38	16	54	1	(1)	33.1	12	55	7
Midwinter	54	23	78	5	(2)	19	7	23	1
Thomson	17	10	14	1		–	–	–	–
Gregory	–	–	–	–	(3)	5	1	9	0

Fall of wickets:

	Aus	Eng	Aus	Eng
1st	2	23	7	0
2nd	40	79	27	7
3rd	41	98	31	20
4th	118	109	31	22
5th	142	121	35	62
6th	143	135	58	68
7th	197	145	71	92
8th	243	145	75	93
9th	245	168	75	100
10th		196	104	108

Umpires: C.A. Reid & R.B. Terry
Toss: Australia

Close of play: Day 1: Aus (1) 166–6 (C. Bannerman 126*, J.M. Blackham 3*)
Day 2: Eng (1) 109–4 (H. Jupp 54*)
Day 3: Aus (2) 83–9 (T.K. Kendall 5*, J.R. Hodges 3*)

Result: **Australia won by 45 runs**

This is as close as England come to winning the inaugural Test. They have been one step behind from the moment Bannerman raised his game. Selby is dismissed for the top score of 38, Ulyett is bowled by a 'leg shooter' for 24 and England fold for 108, to lose by 45 runs. Kendall ends the innings with seven wickets for 55.

Enthusiastic are the celebrations. According to *The Herald*, a large proportion of the 5000 spectators 'swarmed in front of the pavilion, and clamoured for the most prominent players to show themselves, each one being greeted with a round of applause as he appeared. Then someone suggested "three groans for Allan", which were given with great gusto. Then "three groans for Spofforth" also met with due attention, and the proceedings wound up with "three more for Allan". So much for refusing to represent Australia: anyone doing so in future would be pilloried in the stocks of public obloquy.

The collection made on Bannerman's behalf realises the grand sum of £83. Yet Victorian pride, while acknowledging Bannerman's prowess, cannot be entirely contained. 'If New South Wales can point to the most brilliant batting performance ever seen in the colonies, Victoria can confidently refer to wicketkeeping that has never been excelled, both for smartness and general effectiveness. Blackham's wicketkeeping has never been surpassed – even if equalled – here, and he kept without a longstop nearly the whole time without allowing a single bye.'

An editorial in *The Australasian* proclaims:

The match between a combined eleven of this colony and New South Wales and the Eleven of England will be ever memorable in the annals of cricket as the first occasion on which, meeting on even terms, the representatives of the old world have succumbed to those of the new . . . and their success must be doubly gratifying to all who have the welfare of these colonies at heart. For although cricket is, when all is said in its favour, merely an amusement and recreation, yet, nevertheless, the great proficiency attained by colonial players is a most hopeful sign, and gives us reason to believe that the same energy and determination which have led to such happy results in the cricket field will be displayed also in the more important concerns which tend to the advancement of the colonies at large.

Tangible, amidst these Australian celebrations, is relief. An earnest debate has been taking place as to whether the Englishman degenerates when transported from Anglo-Saxon soil to the heat of the colonies. Trickett's rowing victory on the Thames was the first evidence that Australia's climate was not too enervating. Here is further proof. After the game, *The Argus* proclaims: 'The event marks the great improvement which has taken place in Australian cricket and shows, also, that in bone and muscle, activity, athletic vigour, and success in field sports, the Englishmen born in Australia do not fall short of the Englishmen born in Surrey or Yorkshire . . . Here we need only to compliment the victors on their achievement, and Australia at large on the proof which the victory affords that the physical qualities of the English race show no sign of decline in these sunny southern lands.' Alert to the wider social scene, *The Herald* adds: 'For there is still a very large class of persons even in the colonies themselves who hold that anything from the old country must for that simple reason be superior to a colonial production. These were principally people who knew little or nothing of cricket . . .'

Most of England's cricketers catch the evening train to Bendigo. A few stay on at the White Hart for one more night. Do some of the Australian players join them? They have enjoyed their victory over the Englishmen, but they want their visitors to have a good time while being beaten in the colonies, otherwise they will not return.

The Australian cricketer's attitude to touring teams is a bit like a boxer's: he holds his opponent close with one hand while slugging him with the other.

The pattern of English professional cricket is already established: to play, and play. The Australians practised for five days before the game, performed and peaked, then rested. Time has proved the efficacy of their methods. English cricketers have made more money in the course of time; Australians have had more success.

The remainder of Lillywhite's men catch the train to Bendigo at seven the next morning, except for one: Armitage is seen to arrive on the platform as it steams out. He does not reach Bendigo until four that afternoon, long after the game has started. The advancement of Australian cricket has left him and his lobs behind.

'Mateship' was the supreme attribute for those living in Australia's outback. 'Ignorant of the consolations of religion, untouched by the traditions and conventions of European society, they looked for a comforter to offset the loneliness of their lives and to protect them against its dangers,' Manning Clark wrote of bushmen in *A Short History of Australia*. 'They found it in mateship.' Mateship is mutual trust and working together, without shirking, in a small, tight group. These values are also integral to a successful cricket team, and no national team has been anywhere near so successful as Australia's. They have won a higher proportion of Tests, and more one-day World Cups, than any other country.

One of Australia's original XI was soon dropped for letting his teammates down. Thomas Kendall turned up for a game in New Zealand the worse for alcohol, and was thrown out of Dave Gregory's team to tour England in 1878. Here again, the culture of

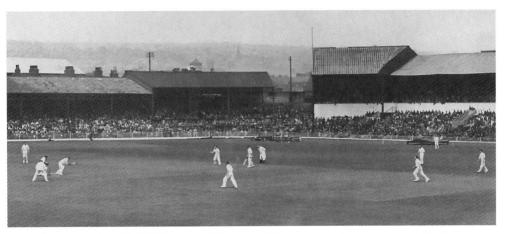

The only Test match at Sheffield, the only Test ground in England to become extinct: England v Australia in 1902. Bramall Lane runs behind the stand on the left side of the photograph.

Cricket's first major ground: the Artillery Ground, looking towards Armoury House, behind the covers at the far end. George Smith's Pyed Horse was at the opposite, nearer, end.

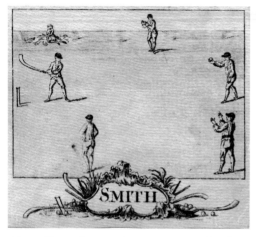

Above: The earliest surviving entrance ticket for a cricket match, Kent v England in 1744, issued by George Smith.

Right: One of the first county captains, HRH Frederick, Prince of Wales, who led Surrey in the 1730s, possibly in their T20 clothing.

Below: A reverse sweep is played at the Oval by Surrey's James Burke with the earliest surviving cricket bat, made by William Pett of Sevenoaks and belonging to John Chitty.

Cricket's first nursery, and academy, and hot spot: Lascelles Hall in the West Riding in the 1950s.

The best English cricketers of 1880, the decade when the professional sport took off. W.G. Grace, nominally an amateur, naturally dominates. Ephraim Lockwood stands third from right, while another player from Lascelles Hall, Willie Bates, sits nearest to him.

The first non-indigenous Australian team to tour England, in 1878.

Ivo Bligh, second from the left in the middle row, wearing the white hat, with the team that won the first Ashes series, in 1882–83.

Clockwise from top left: Florence Morphy; the Hon. Ivo Bligh; Rupertswood, where they courted; their metaphorical offspring, the Ashes urn.

'God no doubt could create a better batsman than Victor Trumper if He wished, but so far He hasn't' – Sir Neville Cardus.

The Melbourne Cricket Ground, looking towards the Grand Stand, in 1877, the year of the first Test match.

Could anyone now score a Test century before lunch, as Ranjitsinhji did on his Test debut against Australia in 1896, with a bat so thin?

Ranjitsinhji, as Jam Sahib of Nawanagar, with a glass eye (right) after his shooting accident.

One of the least crowded areas of Azad Maidan in Mumbai. The station originally known as Victoria Terminus is in the background.

Indigenous cricket in all its vitality at Albrecht Oval in Alice Springs: *Cricket in Alice*, January 2013, by Rooth Robertson.

Australian cricket was established, once and for all: drink as much as you like, but never turn up unfit to play. When Andrew Symonds appeared in a similar state to represent Australia against Bangladesh at Bristol in 2005, he too was dropped. It has always seemed to me that Australia's cricketers have resembled their states: autonomous, responsible for their own development, but ready to pull together in the national cause.

Gregory was captain again when the first white Australian cricketers toured England in 1878, using Lillywhite to arrange their fixtures. It turned out to be a lucrative venture – the players put up £50 each to finance the tour and received a return of £750 each – once they had beaten MCC at Lord's in a single historic day. ('The Australians came down like the wolf on the fold,' *Punch* parodied.) Gregory's men were not professional cricketers, but men of substance who made themselves even more substantial when they took time off from their jobs to play cricket. Gregory went on to become Paymaster to the Treasury in New South Wales; his brother Ned, who also played in the first Test, became the curator of the SCG, which had been demilitarised; Garrett qualified to be a clerk in the Supreme Court; Murdoch, who took over the captaincy from Dave Gregory, was a solicitor; Blackham and Spofforth worked in banks. Midwinter died in an asylum aged 39, driven mad by the sudden death of his wife and children.

The colours of the 1878 Australians were blue – the same as that of the Currency Lads – and white. Not until the twentieth century was the cap of green and gold introduced. The Australian historian Gideon Haigh has shown how a modern myth was made of 'the baggy green' when Steve Waugh became captain, and how it was monetised: Don Bradman's cap for the 1948 tour of England fetched A$402,500 at an auction in 2008. Even so, before then, the baggy green had inspired fear. The English journalist Dudley

Carew wrote of Bradman's 1938 Australians and 'those broad green caps which for so long seem to paralyse English elevens by their very presence in the field.'

In 'the baggy green', we have one facet of a cult. Then we have the communion rite of sharing a beer together in the dressing room after each day's play; and, more recently, a creed in the Australian team song that celebrates victory. Such rituals keep the desire ardent.

‖

The most widely accepted version of the Ashes legend has a bail being burnt. So it was, I believe, but not in the first instance.

While the Clarkes were on their European tour, early in 1882, they had visited the Swiss Lakes. There Lady Janet purchased, or was presented with, an urn – which subsequent analysis has shown to have been made of clay from northern Italy. It was designed to hold henna-like make-up, to adorn a woman's eyes.

But when Janet and Florence decided to fill this tiny urn with ashes on Christmas Eve – to symbolise the body of English cricket which had been cremated after the Oval Test back in the English summer – and to present it flirtatiously to Bligh, they would not have had time to burn a bail. A bail, of hard wood, could only have been incinerated as part of an elaborate fire.

Besides, the memory of Rosemary Trasenster, Florence's daughter-in-law, was crystal clear on this subject. Although she never met Bligh, she knew Florence, in England, for many years. And although Rosemary was into her nineties when I met her, she was living independently, and cooked lunch for her grand-nephew Rupert and me, and was thoroughly compos mentis. She was adamant that Florence had told her that the ashes that went into the urn were those of a veil. 'A veil, not a bail,' Rosemary insisted.

Ladies of Melbourne in the 1880s, Rosemary explained, wore chiffon scarves: such can be the winds in Victoria that a woman can easily have her hair blown around, so anybody who was anybody would have possessed several scarves, or veils. It would have been the work of a few minutes, amid the bustle of Christmas and the cricket match, to burn a veil and place the ashes in the terracotta urn, then to present the prize to Bligh – perhaps, in Florence's case, as an earnest of what was to follow.

After England had won the 1882–83 series 2–1 – it was originally scheduled to be three Tests, although a fourth was added – Bligh was presented with, or took, a pair of bails from the stumps used in the third Test at Sydney as a memento. One of these two bails was made into a holder for a knife to be used for opening letters. It is highly feasible that the other bail was burnt ceremonially at Rupertswood, and its ashes placed in the urn, being more appropriate than those of a veil.

When Bligh returned to England, with Florence, he took his urn and placed it on his mantelpiece at Cobham Hall, after he eventually inherited the title. But the contents were either diluted or completely replaced: family stories of the urn being cleaned by servants, or knocked from the mantelpiece and the contents spilled, are too numerous to be disbelieved. Marylebone Cricket Club, unsurprisingly, have declined to reveal the findings from the analysis of the ashes themselves. But no matter what they are or were made of, the ashes have fanned the flames of the contests between Australia and England. Without the Ashes being transmuted into physical form, if they had simply remained a myth, Test cricket between England and Australia would surely have survived. But it would not have reached anything like the same level in the public consciousness.

A long, grim recession struck Australia in the 1890s. Drought spread from the deserts, wool prices slumped. The Clarkes moved into their town house in Melbourne, Cliveden, and from its kitchen Janet supervised the feeding of hungry people by the hundred. Many others wandered the streets of Sydney in search of work. From his window, the poet Henry Lawson watched them, and told those who cared to listen:

> They lie, the men who tell us, for reasons of their own,
> That want is here a stranger, and that misery's unknown;
> For where the nearest suburb and the city proper meet
> My window-sill is level with the faces in the street –
> Drifting past, drifting past,
> To the beat of weary feet –
> While I sorrow for the owners of those faces in the street.
>
> And cause I have to sorrow, in a land so young and fair,
> To see upon those faces stamped the marks of Want and Care;
> I look in vain for traces of the fresh and fair and sweet
> In sallow, sunken faces that are drifting through the street –
> Drifting on, drifting on,
> To the scrape of restless feet;
> I can sorrow for the owners of the faces in the street.

In this period, about one-third of Australia's white population was of Irish descent: virtually the bottom third in socio-economic terms, except for a few achievers like Edward Flood had been. So it would be wrong to claim that cricket offered consolation to this section of society. Yet enough has been said and written for us to see that Victor Trumper, who was coached by Charles Bannerman and inherited his mantle, was something more than a sporting hero.

Trumper came from the masses in Sydney, out of wedlock as he was born six years before his parents married, and they might not have been his natural parents. He was teetotal, non-smoking, untidy, generous to a fault, pigeon-toed and superstitious: he wore the cap in which he scored his first Test century for the rest of his career. He was wirily strong from playing rugby league, and habitually shrugged his shoulders while batting in order to cool the sweat under his shirt – shoulders that could throw or hit a cricket ball prodigious distances. When he scored 335 for Paddington against Redfern in 1903, one of his on-drives was measured at 150 yards to the point where the ball hit a building. This cannot be myth or fable: the second-floor window of the boot factory could not have moved.

In addition to these physical attributes, Trumper was saint-like in his selflessness; after his death, his widow Sarah attended Mass almost every day for the rest of her 85 years. 'To those of us who were privileged to meet him during his illness, his cheerfulness under great suffering was amazing,' wrote his Australian team-mate Frank Iredale. 'Just as in his cricket, so in his illness, he refrained from choosing the middle way, but fought the foe face to face. His was a noble nature, free, unrestrained, and open. He made no foes, his opponents always recognised the fearless fighter and the generous friend.' Another teammate, Charlie Macartney, himself one of the most brilliant of all strokeplayers as one of the few to score 300 in a day, wrote: 'I say, without hesitation, that he was the best batsman I ever saw. He excelled on any wicket, and against any bowling, but beyond all his cricket he was a *man*, a fighter on the cricket field, and a thorough gentleman at all times.'

Trumper's essence, of physical prowess and spiritual softness, was best encapsulated by Arthur Mailey, of Irish descent. Mailey grew up in Sydney in the 1890s, his family so poor that he and his six siblings took it in turns at breakfast to eat the top of their father's boiled egg. When Mailey's dream was fulfilled and he bowled at Trumper in a grade match, he had him stumped off a googly. Mailey's famous reaction: 'I felt like a boy who had killed a dove.'

Trumper had a direct connection with the masses. Those who could not afford the entrance money when he represented New South Wales or Australia could watch him playing for his club, Paddington, then Gordon. He scored 36 centuries in grade cricket, in addition to 42 in first-class. His 335 was watched by a crowd estimated at between nine and ten thousand. After his death in 1915 from Bright's disease, the procession headed by Bannerman stretched for almost three miles through Sydney's streets.

Although indigenous Australia is filled with spirits, white Australia has produced relatively few religious figures. This cannot be solely a function of recentness: the United States of America, not much older, has produced several prophets, not least in Salt Lake City. Cricket has filled some of the functions of a religion in white Australia, and Trumper had some of the qualities of a saint.

In addition to the Ashes, the rivalry between New South Wales and Victoria has maintained the heat in Sydney and Melbourne. During the 1920s, Bill Ponsford twice made the world-record score for Victoria, 429 and then 437, before Don Bradman surpassed it with 452 not out for New South Wales. Bradman went on to make unprecedented Test scores against England in the 1930s, at a time when many Australians thought the tariffs and taxes imposed on them by Britain were turning a recession into depression. But this was not the source of Bradman's motivation in hitting a century once every three innings, in Tests or first-class cricket, and 12 Test double centuries – a record unequalled for almost 70 years after his retirement.

A two-hour train ride from Sydney to Bowral gave me an insight into what drove Bradman to heights never scaled before or since. Whisper it not in Bowral that Australia is egalitarian: the town is to Sydney what Windsor or Sunningdale is to London, a weekend retreat for the social elite. Sydney's establishment took to these hills to escape from the masses, and such was their abhorrence of everything wild and indigenous that Bowral's hills were planted with European trees, any trace of native bush extirpated.

Bradman entered this strict social hierarchy at the bottom. His father had moved to Bowral from Cootamundra, where he had been 'a bush carpenter': not equipped with machinery, that is, but a rough-and-ready manual labourer. The son aspired to better himself. He courted a girl attending a boarding school in Bowral and won the heart of Jessie; he joined a real estate firm at 16. On the field, he scored slightly quicker than his contemporaries, but what distinguished him was an unrelenting ambition to make bigger scores than anyone had ever done before, even – especially – the Melburnian Ponsford.

When Len Hutton visited Australia for the last time, I asked him if he wanted to see Sir Donald Bradman. As a lad in the crowd at his home ground of Headingley in 1930, Hutton had watched Bradman score 334 against England. Hutton had trumped this score at the Oval in 1938, grinding down the Australian bowling under Bradman's captaincy for more than 13 hours to score 364. The two champions, I naively thought, would want to meet one final time. 'No,' said Sir Leonard, without pausing as he used to do for a Delphic utterance, before repeating the allegations about insider-trading which were made after Bradman moved to Adelaide and joined the stock exchange. To compete with Bradman during his career, Hutton had to be obsessive, and that obsession was not going to die before he did. The hatchet, if thus it was, went unburied.

From Bannerman to Trumper, from Macartney to Bradman, the greatest of all batsmen, from Doug Walters to Mark and Steve Waugh, to Michael Clarke, David Warner and Steve Smith, the torch of Sydney batsmanship has been passed on. They have made the most of the space, and the sunshine which Sydney receives in more lavish abundance than Melbourne, where the cricket season starts a full month later. Not even Bombay's school of batsmanship can equal Sydney's.

In only one respect would I say that male Australian cricket has failed to maximise the country's resources. Given more humanity and generosity of spirit on the part of politicians and cricketers, Australia could have unleashed a counter to Harold Larwood in the Bodyline series of 1932–33.

The first of all cricket teams to tour England was the Aboriginal team of 1868. Some of them contracted European diseases, or failed to take to the game, or concentrated on the circus acts they also did, such as throwing boomerangs and running backwards. But two of them were sterling all-rounders who scored more than 1000 runs and took more than 100 wickets, Johnny Cuzens and Johnny Mullagh, as did their English captain Charles Lawrence. With this triumvirate carrying the team, they won 14 and lost 14 of their matches, taking a first-innings lead over MCC at Lord's.

It was, however, no bridgehead. When the survivors returned home, their knowledge and experience were lost. Mullagh played a couple of games for Victoria, and that was it. The opportunity to make cricket the sport of Australia's immigrant *and* indigenous people drained into the Nullarbor Plain. The two cultures remained polarised.

It could have been different. Two indigenous bowlers, though both were only five feet seven in height, bowled faster than any of their contemporary countrymen: Jack Marsh and Eddie Gilbert. On his first-class debut, for New South Wales in 1900, Marsh bowled five batsmen in South Australia's only innings while Clem Hill scored 365, the highest Sheffield Shield score to date.* In his third match, Marsh took ten wickets, six of them bowled, as NSW exacted some revenge for Hill's effort: they beat South Australia by an innings and 605 runs.

In Marsh's fourth match, he was no-balled 17 times for throwing. 'The great sensation of the day was the no balling of Marsh, the New South Wales bowler,' reported the *Sydney Morning Herald*. 'It appears that his very fast ball is fair, but that it is his slow and medium balls which are doubtful.'

Illustrating how throwing, like beauty, can be in the eye of the beholder, the umpire who no-balled Marsh was Bob Crockett, who had officiated in Marsh's second game and not called him for throwing. In Marsh's fourth game, Crockett also called another NSW bowler, Howard, for throwing three times in the same innings. Yet the umpire at the other end, Sam Jones, did not no-ball Marsh at all – and Jones had played plenty of Tests (including the one at the Oval in 1882, when he

---

* When England toured Australia in 1903–04 and played against Marsh at Bathurst, Herbert Strudwick – who went on to set a world record for the most first-class dismissals, 1495, since surpassed – thought Marsh threw, on the basis that he alone seamed the ball on a flat pitch. But not another Aboriginal fast bowler for Queensland, Albert Henry: 'He was certainly the fastest bowler I have ever seen, for a few overs,' Strudwick wrote in *Twenty-five Years Behind the Stumps*. One ball from Henry in Brisbane hit the screen 'at the second bounce . . . and came half way back to the wicket.'

had been run out by Grace), whereas Crockett never played at first-class level.

Even when Marsh subsequently put his arm in a wooden splint and bowled at the same pace, he could not exonerate himself. Less than two years after his debut, his first-class career was over, after he had taken 34 wickets in only six matches at an average of 21. He took to alcohol, and was killed in a street brawl aged 42.

Gilbert had much the same action, generating pace with exceptionally long arms and following through until his right arm almost swept the ground. Don Bradman faced him on a damp pitch at Brisbane's Gabba in 1931–32. Gilbert brushed his cap with one delivery, knocked Bradman's bat out of his hands with another and had him caught behind for nought – but it was still long enough for Bradman to say it was the fastest bowling he ever faced. Gilbert lasted a little longer than Marsh, taking 87 wickets at less than 30 runs each in the highest-scoring period that first-class cricket has known, before being no-balled out of the game. Both Marsh and Gilbert bore the mark of the fast bowler not truly assimilated: they were always made to bat at number eleven.

Not until 2001, when another quick bowler, Jason Gillespie, proclaimed he was part-Aborigine, were indigenes openly represented again on the first-class field. I played against an indigenous team once in Alice Springs, and the characteristics of their cricket were similar to those of uncoached cricketers in the West Indies, and the Cape Coloured community, and Afghanistan. They bowled as fast as they could, and hit the ball as far as they could, which is the best of starting points. Coaching, nets, bowling machines, nutrition, psychology and the rest can come later.

Australian indigenes who live in the outback, perhaps more

than any other community on earth and certainly in the English-speaking world, develop the power of throwing from an early age. They throw stones at birds or reptiles, and spears at fish or game. But without encouragement from cricket's authorities, they gravitated towards baseball, and towards Australian Rules football in the footsteps of a role-model. Doug Nicholls joined the Carlton club in Melbourne, where their members would not let him play, so he moved to struggling Northcote and helped turn them into a premiership-winning side in 1929; he went on to become a pastor; and the first indigene to be knighted, as Sir Douglas Nicholls; and the Governor of South Australia. The chance to turn those throwing arms into bowling arms was thrown away.

Aside from the indigenes, a vigorous boy was delivered into the cricket world in March 1877. He grew to excel not only at batting but every aspect of the game. Jack Blackham was agreed to be the best wicketkeeper of his time; Adam Gilchrist to be the best wicketkeeper-batsman of all time. The finest Australian spinners have learned to turn the ball on any surface: from Mailey, who strengthened his fingers as a teenage glass-blower, to Bill 'Tiger' O'Reilly* to Shane Warne, agreed to be the best

---

* Dear Tiger,

The greatest privilege of my ten England tours of Australia was to share a press box with you, and see how fearlessly you spoke the truth to power, and preached the value of wrist-spin when it was almost extinct. In 1980 I asked you about Ray Bright, who was labelled a left-arm spinner, although he didn't spin the ball much by anyone's standards let alone yours. 'Would you take Ray Bright on the tour of England next year?' I asked. Your instant reply: 'I wouldn't take him on a trip to Manly!'

P.S. Given that the 1930s was the highest-scoring era, even more so than today, and you took more than 20 wickets in four consecutive Ashes series (it

spinner of all time. Fast bowlers have run in with the whole country roaring them on, like Ray Lindwall, Dennis Lillee, Glenn McGrath and Brett Lee, men who have defined our image of what a fast bowler should be. (There has been one excess of this ardent desire: the practice of a fielder throwing the ball at the batsman as much as to the wicketkeeper, mainly during Steve Waugh's captaincy, was contemptible bullying.) And Australia's representatives have never fielded poorly, for that would be letting their country down. Even the spectators in Australia field well: from my observation, a ball hit into the crowd there is far more likely to be caught than in any other country. Good on yer, mate.

The shortest of verbs sums up all the elements which have gone into making Australia the country that has been best at cricket. 'Australia is three down for 200,' their commentators or spectators say, or 'Australia is going to win the first Test.' It is as if their crick-eters do not represent their country, they embody it. Other countries, like England or India, *have* won the toss and *are* batting. Australia, the very country, *is* playing cricket.

Does Australia's cricket contain the seeds of its own decline, if not destruction?

The MCG was not used during the winter until around 1860, when some MCC members designed a game based on Gaelic foot-ball to keep the club's cricketers in trim during the off-season. This sport grew into the Victorian Football League, part-time and amateur, then into the Australian Football League, sprouting

---

would have been more than 25 if a wash-out hadn't limited the 1938 series to four Tests), perhaps you should be bracketed with Warne as the best of all wrist-spinners.

professional clubs in every state capital on the mainland. From 2010, 'Aussie Rules' offered about 800 playing jobs around the country, on salaries from A$100,000 upwards. The back pages of newspapers nationwide feted the teenage athletes who were drafted into the clubs. Cricket offered around 100 jobs, mostly at lower salaries.

Will the offspring, more than 150 years down the line, devour the parent and replace cricket as Australia's national game? Perhaps not. Cricket's roots, in Sydney at least, are too deep.

4

BOMBAY MIX

Cricket, if I may judge from the boys I coached at Cooch Behar College, has done a little to bring friendship between races where there might otherwise have been greater bitterness.

Harry Lee, Middlesex professional

HE RESEMBLED THE Ancient Mariner in having witnessed something beyond the ken of ordinary mortals. But what this old Yorkshire villager had seen was not sailors made into skeletons by thirst in the Great Southern Ocean; he had seen one of the seven wonders of the cricket world, and bowled to him.

In the early 1900s, Kumar Shri Ranjitsinhji, long established in the England Test team, had come to spend his holidays in the North Riding. Ranji had first met the Reverend Louis Borissow, the Rector of Gilling East when he had been the chaplain of Trinity College, Cambridge, and Ranji had stayed with him before going up. A fine rectory it was too, being the castle above the village of Gilling East, and most agreeable for a holiday. We now know, however, that Ranji visited not only for the air and the view: it has emerged that he had a child by one of Mr Borissow's daughters, Edith.

This mariner's eyes may have had cataracts, as he was well into his eighties, yet there was more to the gleam than that. 'He'd come down from the castle,' said the villager. 'He'd come down in the evenings with a bat, and we'd bowl at him in the field over there . . .'

He did not have to hold me with his skinny hand. Though only 16, I had read enough about Ranji to know he had been a novelty and more. The first major sensation in cricket had been W.G. Grace in his summer of 1876. The second had been the Australian touring team of 1878, when they had beaten MCC at Lord's. The third was Ranjitsinhji.

Ranji was not only the first Indian, or non-white, to represent England at cricket; not only the first to score 3000 runs in a first-class season; not only the first to score a century before lunch in a Test match (on his debut, too, against Australia at Old Trafford in 1896, when he hit 113 runs in the morning session of 130 minutes). Ranji had also revolutionised batting by opening up the leg-side. It was there as Holy Writ in one of the first *Wisdens* I owned, that of 1896, which referred to Ranji's batting for Sussex the previous season: 'his wonderful placing on the leg side quite disheartening many of the leading professionals, who were unaccustomed to see perhaps their best ball turned to the boundary for four.'

'He said we could bowl as fast as we liked,' the villager said, 'even though he didn't wear pads or anything.' In a field, too, not on a proper pitch. 'Afterwards, he would give us sixpence each. Think of it, sixpence each – for bowling at Ranji! And sixpence meant something in them days.'

Ranji was not everything he claimed to be. Having arrived at Trinity and set himself up in a ménage as exotic as Lord Byron's – it was claimed Ranji owned the first car in Cambridge, not a mere bear – he gave the impression that he was a prince by styling himself Kumar Shri. He lived the life of royalty, and bestowed lavish gifts, but only by running up bills that often went unpaid. He was then as remote from the throne of Nawanagar in terms of lineage as mileage. It was only after he had established himself as the most famous cricketer in England, and suppressed the scandal of his illegitimate son by giving him away for adoption and cutting him off for ever, and after a palace coup, that he succeeded in claiming the throne as Jam Sahib.

In the meantime, nobody could question the authenticity of his batting: it was based on the simple premise of 'play back or drive', which is still a fitting technique against spin bowling more than a century later. Nobody could question his fielding either: his sleight of hand made him the finest slip in England, and he once wrote that he actually preferred fielding to batting. The old villager's eyes were testimony to Ranji's unprecedented brilliance. So too were the words of W.G. Grace, when he told the guests at a dinner in Cambridge in 1908: 'I assure you that you will never see a batsman to beat the Jam Sahib if you live for a hundred years.'

Was W.G.'s prophecy correct? The heights of batsmanship in England have been scaled by Jack Hobbs, Wally Hammond, Len Hutton, Denis Compton, David Gower, Graham Gooch and Kevin Pietersen, and maybe a few others on their day. But I do not think that the wonder they excited at their peak, when they made their Ashes centuries – not even Pietersen's at the Oval in 2005 – exceeded the awe Ranji generated. Equalled, perhaps, but not exceeded.

If nothing else, statistics confirm Grace's prophecy. To this day, nobody who has had a career based in England has achieved a higher first-class average than Ranji. On uncovered and sometimes minimally prepared pitches, in games that never lasted longer than three days, he averaged 56 – which would have been 57 had he not returned to play a few innings for Sussex in 1920, as the Jam Sahib of Nawanagar, with one eye. He had lost the sight of his right eye during the First World War, in an accident when shooting on the North Yorkshire moors not far from Gilling.

‖

I went to Ranji's palace in Jamnagar to research my first book, on England's 1981–82 tour of India. At university I had read Arabic Studies and thought I wanted to be the Middle East correspondent of *The Observer*, based in Beirut. But the week after I visited that city in 1975, the civil war in Lebanon began, not to cease for 25 years. After spending a couple of years in the Middle East, I considered the Foreign Office, and had an interview with MI6, but a friend who worked for the organisation said it was '90 per cent paperwork abroad'. I met Dame Freya Stark, in her eighties but still travelling intrepidly, in Sana'a, the capital of North Yemen as it was. She said discerningly: 'You are still searching, aren't you?' And it was not until I joined *The Observer* to cover cricket that I found.

The Observer's photographer, Adrian Murrell, and I flew from Bombay to Jamnagar as the Jam Sahib's guests and stayed in the biggest bedroom I have ever slept in: a cross between a baroque cathedral and a millionaire's mansion in Las Vegas. Our host did not appear on the first day, or the second. He sent a note instead about meeting the following day, which gave me the line: 'It seemed to be a case of the Jam yesterday, and the Jam tomorrow, but never the Jam today.'

Ranji's bedroom had been preserved as it was on the day he died in 1933. His spectacles lay on his dressing table along with a selection of six glass eyes. On day three, the Jam Sahib appeared and showed us around Ranji's princely state, telling us tales of intrigue in the harem or 'zenana', including a poisoning, that opened the way for Ranji to take the throne.

But the story of Indian cricket, I learnt, did not begin with Ranji. Indeed, he could be said to have played no part in it after leaving his boarding school, Rajkumar College in Rajkot; he was then taken to Cambridge by his headmaster, Chester Macnaghten, a Trinity graduate, who entrusted Ranji to Revd Borissow. Ranji may have been an Indian cricketer but he represented England, and when he returned to rule Nawanagar, he had little to do with Indian cricket except help select the All-India party to tour England in 1932. It was only after his death, to commemorate him, that the Ranji Trophy was instituted as the prize for domestic cricket.

The other Indian princes who took up cricket did not leave much of a legacy either. When the first All-India team arrived in England in 1911, the Maharajah of Patiala abandoned all thoughts of captaincy and batting. He went off to enjoy the London season, and promote his political prospects, taking the team's best batsman as his secretary: Colonel Mistri, a Parsi. When the Maharajah of Porbandar captained the second Indian team to tour England, in 1932, he was such a poor player he had to stand down for India's inaugural Test match. When the equally hopeless Maharajah of Vizianagram captained the third Indian team in 1936, his ego was such that he sent home the best all-rounder, Lala Amarnath, on an exaggerated charge of indiscipline.

India's Test cricket set off on the wrong foot, led by princes who owed their captaincy to wealth and influence. Richer maharajahs, like Patiala, would hire English cricketers as well as local ones to do the bowling and fielding for them. Their bad habits became ingrained. There was no prestige in bowling – low-caste manual labour – and less in fielding. It is tempting not to dive on a dry south Asian ground that does not have underground sprinklers,* but lordly Indian princes set the worst example. As captains, they had a sense, not of team or country, but of entitlement.

Indian cricket teams became divided between cricketers of one region and those of another, based on language. Alone of Test-playing countries, India had to build a national team out of a population that spoke 800 languages. When I was researching my first book, *Cricket Wallah*, I was told by more than one Indian Test

---

* In a press match at the Karachi Gymkhana I won the fielding prize of 800 rupees for the best catch of my life. I had to dive to my left and half-forward to catch a skimming drive. The cost of my tetanus injection was 1000 rupees.

player of the 1950s that a fielder from one region might not try to stop the ball if the bowler came from another.

By way of redemption, it was a princeling who paved the way for India to become unofficial world champions. Schooled at Winchester, the Nawab of Pataudi Jnr was brought up on a soft surface beside the River Test to give everything in the field. India's spinners of the 1960s needed the support of infielders and close catchers, and finally they were given it. The effectiveness of Bhagwat Chandrasekhar, Bishan Bedi and Erapalli Prasanna was increased by Pataudi, and his emphasis on fielding, to the extent that they shared more than 700 Test wickets in what was still, outside England, the amateur era.

Batting was the one on-field activity that interested India's princes, but again their style of batting did not set the best example. The Maharajah of Patiala had more children, 88, than his highest score, 83, his only fifty in first-class cricket; and the feature of his batting was hitting, not running between wickets or rotation of the strike.* This innings came in a match billed as 'India v England' at the Bombay Gymkhana in 1918. When the Maharajah walked in at 44 for three, Harry Lee, in *Forty Years of English Cricket*, remembered that he had been told: 'Whatever you do, don't get the Maharajah out for a duck. He doesn't like it.' The Maharajah then hit Lee 'for several sixes in the course of two or three overs'. When V.V.S. Laxman retired from Test cricket in 2012, having authored several of the greatest innings, he summed up: 'By nature Indian batsmen are aggressive and love to hit boundaries.'

These Indian princes generated colourfulness, amusement and

---

* It is surprising these maharajahs did not take a leaf out of the Sultan of Morocco's scorebook. When cricket was introduced to Morocco before the First World War by *The Times* correspondent W.B. Harris, the custom was for everyone to bat and bowl as normal, then for the Sultan to fill in the names in the scorebook afterwards. The highest score tended to be made by himself, or one of his favourites.

scandal, not heat. It was no thanks to them that India's first hot spot was Bombay.

▊

The temperature at ten o'clock on 30 January 1890 was no higher than 77 degrees Fahrenheit, according to the following day's *Bombay Gazette*. Yet this was the day when Bombay became the hot spot of Indian cricket. This was the first day of the match that anticipated the mass-hit film *Lagaan* by more than a century.

The only place where this spontaneous combustion could take place was the Bombay Gymkhana, the city's one cricket ground, lying in the Fort, a few hundred yards from where ships dock or anchor. For decades British regiments had come ashore here, bringing not only their military but their cricket equipment, and certain people had long regarded them with special interest: members of the Parsi community, whose first cricket club was founded in 1848.

The Bombay Gymkhana, however, was a club for Europeans only: native Indians were excluded. Parsis who wanted to play with bat and ball were forced to find another space, and when they did, they found themselves thwarted again. An area near the Fort was used by Parsis until a European lady (no mere 'woman') was out walking her dog and was hit by a stray cricket ball. Another open space the Parsis used was sometimes required by British polo players. 'This makes the ground so rough and bumpy that the Parsi cricketers became apprehensive of a fractured rib, or a twisted nose, a black eye or loss of teeth and avoid playing on the ground in summer until it becomes green and not so fiery in the monsoon.' So wrote Mehallasha Pavri, who had toured England with the second Parsi team of 1888, before returning to qualify as a doctor.*

* It was Pavri who slightly underestimated the age of Parsi cricket when he wrote in 1901: 'The Parsis seem to have begun the game of Cricket about fifty years ago and for

In January 1890, however, the Parsis had been granted the privilege – not given to any other native Indians – of playing against the
first English team to tour India. It was led by Lord Hawke, until he
fell ill, then by George Vernon, the Middlesex amateur who had
gone on Bligh's tour of Australia in 1882–83 and had represented
England at rugby as well as cricket. And just as the match had to be
staged at the Bombay Gymkhana, the fixture itself had to be played,
for political reasons. The British government had invited the Parsis
to send a cricket team to England in 1886, and although they had
been pretty useless – the party consisted of those wealthy enough
to pay their passage, not their best cricketers – the Parsis had
served to strengthen the bonds of empire, and their successors on
the tour of England in 1888 had improved commendably; so they
could hardly be ditched now.

'*Divide et impera*': so Julius Caesar had decreed. After the Indian
Mutiny (or National Uprising) from 1857 to 1858, when no other
community had stayed completely loyal to the British, the Raj
decided that it was in their interests to divide the Parsis from the
other communities. That was why the British government had
showered hospitality on the Parsi teams of 1886 and 1888: one
game was against MCC, captained by W.G. Grace, at Lord's;
another at Windsor Great Park against a side including two of
Queen Victoria's grandsons, Princes Victor and Christian. It would
have been impolitic to refuse the Parsis a fixture against Vernon's
XI – although club rules could not be relaxed, and no native Indian
could be allowed into the Gymkhana clubhouse, except servants
and the Parsi groundsman, Pestonjee.

---

the knowledge of the game their thanks are due to the Englishmen, chiefly the military officers of the Marine Battalion, stationed at Bombay, who inspired a love for it
among them.' Pavri, while completing his medical studies in London, played for
Middlesex against Surrey at Hove in 1895: as Sussex fielded K.S. Ranjitsinhji, this was
the first Championship match in which both counties fielded an Indian.

At least the chance of Vernon's men losing to this native team, and damaging imperial prestige, was minimal. The Parsis had arrived from Persia with some tradition of sporting and athletic prowess a millennium before, when expanding Islam had pushed out the worshippers of Zoroaster and his fire. In Persia they had played *Chugan Gui*, which translates as 'bat and ball', while Persian ladies were reputed to have played polo. But, since arriving in India, the Parsis had settled into mercantilism: they were middlemen, adept at commerce, rather than men in the middle. According to one of their founding myths, the leader of a group of Parsis who had landed in Gujarat went to the local ruler and asked permission to stay. When the ruler asked why he should let the Parsis in, when his land was already packed with people, the Parsi leader took a glass of water filled to the brim and placed a coin in it, without spilling a drop. This is how the Parsis would fit in, without disturbance.

When the Honourable East India Company arrived in the eighteenth century, Parsis transferred their loyalty to these new rulers. It was even said they revered the Englishman as a second Zoroaster. British ships brought goods to Bombay, and who was going to arrange for onward transportation into the 'mofussil' or interior? Given their knowledge of local languages and terrain, and loyalty to the British, Parsis could be trusted. In return, they began to adopt British values, study English literature as they had no secular literature of their own, and educate their girls. They had no priests imposing traditional values or taboos, thereby restricting contact with Europeans. The very surnames adopted by the Parsis illustrated their keenness to adapt to the new economic order: Doctor, Writer, Readymoney, Engineer, Warden, Merchant (not all Merchants were Parsis: for example, Vijay Merchant, a Hindu), and Contractor.

Sealing this bond of trust was the Parsis' enthusiasm for cricket: they tried tennis, football, racquets, billiards and other sports, but cricket was their game. Even in the early stages, when the British had

spurned their efforts at cricket, the Parsis had persisted. The indiffer-
ence of the British, like that of the woman beloved, was infatuating.
After watching soldiers and civilians playing at the Gymkhana, they
went away and improvised with pieces of wood as best they could.
Simultaneously, in the United States of America, the exact opposite
was happening: cricket was being rejected for being *the* English sport,
except in Anglophile Philadelphia, and destined for extinction.

A picture of the early Parsi cricketer was painted by J.M. Framji
Patel, a member of this community who had studied at Cambridge in
the 1880s and won his colours in three sports at Gonville and Caius:

> He went to the wicket with a white band around his forehead, giving
> him quite the air of the inmate of some hospital, and a still whiter
> apron dangling from his waist, which was encircled by the sacred
> thread of his faith. Thus equipped, with patent-leather boots and
> silken trousers, he was a fit study for an artist . . . Parsi cricket in its
> infancy was *sui generis* – the players had their peculiar phraseology,
> strokes, dress and nicknames.

Against such weird opponents, Vernon's men simply could not
lose – and plenty of bets were placed on them. Besides, they were a
capital team. Although Lord Hawke was indisposed, most of the
remaining tourists played first-class cricket in England. Vernon
and three others played for Middlesex, and three more for
Cambridge University. The only player not of high standard was
the Honourable A.N. Curzon, who happened to be doing a grand
tour of India, along with his elder brother Nathaniel, when he was
asked to fill in for Lord Hawke.*

Vernon's team had naturally not been beaten in any of their matches

---

* Nathaniel Curzon was not interested in games but in becoming India's Viceroy, which
he did. As Lord Curzon, he was, in the words of the limerick, 'a most superior person'.

in Oudh and Bengal against indigo planters and the military, or even looked like being so. They had one outstanding player in Hylton Philipson, universally known as 'Punch', who had won a blue at Oxford in four different sports. Now a wicketkeeper-batsman for Middlesex, he was rated the third best keeper in England behind a couple of professionals, and was soon to play five Tests against Australia. If the 1889–90 tour contained the slightest element of controversy, it involved Punch's sola topi: it was so broad-brimmed, to keep off the sun, that when he was standing up to the stumps his topi protruded in front of them. Should the square-leg umpire call no-ball?

Vernon's proclivity for drink could have been a second source of controversy – off the record of course, old boy! He had missed the start of a game on Bligh's tour of Australia after being detained by nocturnal activities in Melbourne. When Vernon's team visited Meerut, their captain socialised all too well. Bit of a rag in the mess of the 5th Lancers, so Lord Hawke later recounted in his memoirs. Vernon 'was brought on a stretcher at 3 a.m. to the house of his host, Sir George Greaves, who was in command.' Mrs Vernon was summoned from upstairs, and 'his dear, pretty little wife came down in a pink dressing-gown to receive the living remains of her husband.'

In the first of their two fixtures in Bombay, Vernon's men were far too good for the Gymkhana Club – British players – and won by an innings. John Hornsby, of Middlesex and MCC, a left-arm spinner who took over 50 first-class wickets at only 17 runs each, ran through the Gymkhana's batting, taking 13 wickets. 'Several of their batsmen played back in a weak, undecided way to balls which they could have easily smothered by playing forward,' *The Times of India* reported. Their correspondent then previewed the second game: 'The visitors, we think, should have no difficulty in keeping their laurels untarnished, but the Parsees with their well known pluck and capacity for playing an up-hill game are sure to put them on their mettle. The chances of cricket are such that if Mr Vernon's

XI take it too easy, or run away with the idea that they may hold their adversaries cheap, it is just possible that the Zoroastrians may score a victory after all. In any case the public may look forward to a capital match with good bowling and fielding on both sides. In batting the visitors are no doubt the stronger side, but the Parsees have improved much of late, and will no doubt make a good show.'

The Times of India also supplied their readers with some gossip about the wife of the next Governor of Bombay. Lord Harris, the former captain of Kent and England, had been appointed to succeed Lord Reay. Now the newspaper quoted *Vanity Fair* to say that Lady Harris, accompanied by her daughter, would go out to India ahead of her husband. She would travel 'before the end of the cold season, in order to avoid the intense heat of the Red Sea later on', and stay at Government House with Lord and Lady Reay until 'the arrival of the new Governor in March'. One for the diary, what?

On the morning of Thursday, 30 January 1890, the *Bombay Gazette* lists 'Cricket – Mr Vernon's Team v The Parsis' as the first event of the day.* Underneath this item comes the meeting of the Municipal Corporation at 3 p.m., and the Prize Distribution by Lord Reay at Lower Colaba Schools, these events listed in chronological order rather than order of social importance. Not that the Parsi community needs any reminder about the first item: they had been 'present in very large numbers' at Vernon's victory over the Gymkhana Club. And a photograph from this period of a cricket match in Bombay shows a stand full of seated Parsi women in white head-scarves, highly animated. If it was not the same as playing polo back in Persia, it was better than being confined to the house, like upper-class women of the Hindu and Muslim communities.

---

* I owe special thanks to the librarian at Bombay's Central Library for allowing me to consult the back numbers of the *Bombay Gazette*, which had been neither micro-filmed nor preserved in air-conditioned archives and were therefore on the verge of disintegration.

'So intense was the enthusiasm that merchants, bankers and all others forsook business for the day and came to see the most exciting cricket match ever played in India.' If this sounds biased, coming from Dr Pavri, a more impartial judgement is offered by Captain Philip Trevor, who attended the game and wrote about it in his book *The Lighter Side of Cricket* (he went on to become the cricket and rugby correspondent of the *Daily Telegraph*). Trevor called it 'the most famous match ever played in India' and estimated the crowd at between ten and twelve thousand on each of the two days.*

'The canvas tents pitched on the western side of the ground were closely packed with the *elite* of Bombay Society, European and Indian,' wrote Framji Patel, back home from Cambridge to captain the Parsis. 'The dark-eyed daughters of the land for the first time mustered strongly ... The Parsee priests in their white garb invoked the aid of the "Asho Frohers" to secure victory to the Zoroastrian arms. The schoolboy managed to take French Leave, and his interest in the game was so keen that he had provided himself with bits of paper on which to jot down the placing of the field by the English Captain, Mr G.F. Vernon, a thorough sportsman. The "man in the street" was out enjoying his holiday, and in tiers of five and six deep the eastern and northern boundaries of the ground were closely packed by impatient sightseers. Some perched themselves (to get a good view of the game) on the trees surrounding the enclosure.' Nowhere can there be a surer indicator of popular interest in cricket than spectators watching from trees.

||

---

* According to the census of the following year, 1891, Bombay's population was 821,764, but most inhabitants lived far from the Fort and Colaba, in outlying slums that had already grown up around the spinning and weaving mills, railway workshops and tanneries, which made Britain's wealth. By 1896 this breeding ground for bubonic plague was claiming the lives of more than 1,900 people per week.

Vernon wins the toss and decides to bat. Thereafter the match against the Parsis does not go according to his plan. One of his opening batsmen is clean-bowled for nought: James Walker, an Oxford blue who was to play 44 matches for Middlesex and represent Scotland at rugby. *The Times of India* says that Walker has 'a grand pair of wrists to make runs between cover point and third man, as well as being a first-rate point.' His opening partner, Edward Lawson-Smith, who represented Gentlemen of Yorkshire, is also clean-bowled; so too Arthur Gibson, who played a couple of games for Lancashire. The bowler in each case is R.E. Mody, fast round-arm. Framji Patel later writes of him: 'It was his terrific pace that upset me and many others. For a fast bowler his length was very good and he often shot in a yorker with deadly effect.'

It is with some consternation that the *Bombay Gazette* summarises the first innings of Vernon's team after they have been dismissed before lunch for a total of 97 off 31.4 five-ball overs. The only individual score of note was Vernon's unbeaten 45, after the captain had entered at number four and played some vigorous off-drives (his 'dear, pretty little wife' must have done her job in limiting the chota-pegs of whisky the night before):

This is the first time that our English visitors have been opposed by a purely native team, and their performance yesterday must have been rather surprising to them ... Those who had seen the immense improvement in Parsi cricket fully expected that they would give a good account of themselves but it is safe to say that the most sanguine did not expect that they would come off as well as they did yesterday. Their bowling was fine as a reference to the analysis will show, Mody's performance being particularly creditable. Gagrat is a fast underhand bowler, and the destructive effect of his delivery is a proof that a good underhand bowler is a great

acquisition in a team. The fielding of the Parsees was all but perfect
– as good at any rate as that of their opponents.

In other words, the Parsis' fielding is not remotely like that of the
Indian princes other than Ranji.

A few minutes remain before tiffin, and the Parsis' opening bats-
men survive until the interval. Both teams then adjourn, not to the
Gymkhana clubhouse because the Parsis are forbidden entry, but to
'Mr Tatta's bungalow', as the *Gazette* describes it.

At least it is no ordinary bungalow, for Jamsetji Nusserwanji Tata
(more commonly than Tatta) is no ordinary man. He is the founder
of what became India's biggest business. He is his own man, with
his own vision of what India should become. He ought to be
considered 'the most important innovator of the Indian economy',
according to the German author of *The Parsees in India*, Eckehard
Kulke (who adds that the first Muslim woman to unveil in Bombay
society did so at Tata's bungalow). Parsis had made themselves
indispensable to the British by organising their supplies in wartime,
starting in Afghanistan, and Tata had started out by supplying the
British-Indian army during their war in Abyssinia, before building
up a textile business. By 1890 he was planning an iron and steel
industry for India, instead of relying on British imports.*

Tiffin at Tata's is so prolonged that the afternoon session of play
does not begin until 3.20 p.m. Framji Patel, a member of MCC and

---

* But when Tata visited Whitehall, he was treated with disdain, and when the Viceroy
heard about his plan, he guffawed that he would eat his hat if Tata produced one ingot
of steel. Before he died in 1903, Tata went to America and met President Theodore
Roosevelt, to ask for American experts to go to India to do geological research and
identify the best location for a steel plant. Yet Roosevelt's first question to Tata was:
'How is Parsi cricket going on?' The American president also sent through Tata a
message of encouragement to Parsi cricketers. He sent the experts as well, and steel
production commenced in Jamshedpur – named after the late Tata – in 1912. The
needs of the British army in the Middle East were thus supplied in two World Wars.

Surrey, uses the occasion to deliver a welcoming speech which could be faulted for prolixity but not any lack of loyalty to the Empire (when he subsequently wrote *Stray Thoughts on Indian Cricket*, he was rather more aggrieved about the exclusiveness of Anglo-Indian clubdom):

We thoroughly appreciate your sportsmanlike spirit in coming here to play us at personal inconvenience in the home of Parsi cricket. I need not tell you that your cricketing expedition was looked forward to by us with feelings of great pleasure, because we believe that just as your real invasion a century ago had been the means of making us prosperous and loyal citizens, [so] would your cricketing invasion make us efficient and better cricketers. I for one am quite sure that you will carry pleasant recollections of your Indian tour, especially of this first meeting of the cricketers of the East and West in the first city in India, just as the Parsi cricketers have brought happy recollections of their two trips to England. I must at once tell you that the Parsi cricketers did not go to England to try conclusions with the great cricketers of your native land, but they went there as artists go to Italy in search of knowledge, or as pilgrims go to Jerusalem to pay homage at a shrine . . . In a country like India cricket is a very useful agency in bringing the rulers and the ruled together, and I am glad that the destinies of this Presidency will be in future in the hands of a famous cricketer. I have had already a long innings, but before I sit down I thank heartily once more Mr Vernon and his team for the honor [sic] they have done us to-day in coming here, and we who are brought up in your language and great and glorious traditions, have adopted your national game as our own, and I now ask you to drink to the health of the best exponents of the English game in India, and wish them long and prosperous lives and a safe journey to their native land, the land of liberty, and the land of cricket.

In reply, Vernon thanks Framji Patel for his kind words and the hospitality his team have received. Rather convivial hospitality? Parsis, unlike Muslims, have no ban on alcohol and it is possible that during luncheon Vernon and his men down a chota-peg or two. They seem a little sluggish in the field after tiffin. Twice the Parsi batsmen run five, and the Gymkhana ground is not huge.

The first occasion is when Dinshaw Kanga cuts Albert Leatham, a left-armer who played for Gloucestershire, 'very prettily for five'; the second when S.B. Doctor 'drove De Little beautifully to near the boundary for five.' A whisky-flavoured oath of 'dammit, sir!' wafts down through the ages as a well-fed fielder watches the ball pull up a few feet short of the rope and sets off in warm, if not hot, pursuit.

The Parsis, without an England batsman like Vernon to hold them together, lose wickets regularly. They also appear to be more adversely affected than the tourists by the law which limits a hit over the boundary to four runs. (Not until 1910 did a hit over the rope count as six.) As one instance, Dinshaw Kanga 'put one of Hornsby's into the tent in fine style'; Kanga 'ran up his 14 with very free hitting', according to *The Times of India*.*

In addition to Kanga's hit into the tent, Jal Morenas gets 'one of Gibson's over the tent ropes', while B.C. Machliwalla makes 'a hit over the boundary off Gibson'. Machliwalla came to be known as 'the Parsi Jessop' on account of his big hitting, often done from down the pitch, even though the keeper was standing up. From consecutive balls, Machliwalla hits 4, 3 and 4 before being caught on the off-side from the next ball.

The Parsis now have some decent bats and are no longer wielding home-made pieces of wood. One of their community leaders,

---

* However, it is the name of his younger brother, Homasji Kanga, that lives on in Bombay. The Kanga Shield was considered to be the best club competition, higher in standard than The Times of India Shield, because it used to be played in the monsoon season when pitches are livelier.

Sir Cowasji Jehangir, had donated cricket kit, which was expensive after being imported from Britain. During this prestigious week for cricket, the *Bombay Gazette* carries a front-page advertisement which lists an 'all cane bat', the finest available, at 14 rupees and 8 annas – twice as much as a set of stumps, or wicket-keeping gauntlets, or batting gloves ('best improved Vulcanised Tubular Indiarubber'). Leg guards of chamois skin are priced at 8 rupees and 4 annas, while the Duke's Treble Seam ball costs 5 rupees and 8 annas.

Lacking anyone to hold up one end, the Parsis finish the first day at 80 for nine wickets, still 17 runs behind. Almost a century and a half has elapsed since the 1744 match between Kent and England at the Artillery Ground, yet the totals have increased by only half. Pitches, rolled by hand, still begin bumpy and are liable to disintegrate. The Gymkhana pitch, according to *The Times of India*, played 'fast and true till toward the end of each innings, when the pitch towards the pavilion end, where there appeared to be a slight rise, got exceedingly bumpy'. Mouthpiece of the Raj in Bombay since 1838, *The Times of India* adds: 'The visitors appeared to recognise that they had met with a tough lot, and though it is not generally expected that the Parsi team will win, yet the day's results portend a tough contest for the morrow.'

The first day is far from over. If Vernon's men are too late to attend Lord Reay's Prize Distribution, the last of the four events listed in the *Bombay Gazette* remains for their delectation: 'Evening Entertainment, Mr Vernon's Team, Petit Hall, Malabar Hill.'

Numerous are the political nuances behind this invitation from Sir Dinshaw Petit, as behind Tata's. Petit's great-grandfather had worked for the East India Company in the opium trade, as numerous Parsis had done, before making a fortune of his own. The

relationship was cosily symbiotic: the British were the sharehold-
ers, and kept their hands and consciences clean, while the Parsis
loaded ships with opium grown in India and cut deals with Chinese
merchants in Canton. Several European powers wanted a slice of
this trade, irrespective of its illegality and immorality. It was French
traders who had dubbed Sir Dinshaw's great-grandfather 'le petit
Parsi', and the diminutive attribute had stuck.

By 1890 the Petits are moving in the more reputable spheres of
brokerage and textiles. Sir Dinshaw is a philanthropist too, and
later in this same year is upgraded to a baronet. What more generous mark of the Empress of India's favour could there be than
honouring members of the Parsi community? Not Tata (too independent) but the Petits, Jeejeebhoys and Cowasjis. The first Parsi to
be knighted, Jamsetji Jeejeebhoy, had been a well-known opium
trader; his loyalty to the Empire was deemed more significant.

Thus the Petits are 'sound' as well as wealthy. No doubt they are
Freemasons too, as Bombay is booming with Masonic halls, where
Indians were admitted long before the Gymkhana let them in. Sir
Dinshaw can therefore be trusted to give the English cricketers a
good time at his palatial residence on Malabar Hill. The *Bombay
Gazette* reports next morning, on Friday, 31 January, the second
day of this match:

> On Thursday night an entertainment was given by the Parsis at Petit
> House. The grounds were tastefully illuminated with vari-coloured
> *buttees*, and presented a beautiful appearance. At about nine o'clock
> the numerous guests who had been invited began to arrive and were
> ushered into the drawing-room, where, later on, some of the guests
> played and sang. Shortly after 10 o'clock the company adjourned to
> a mandap which had been erected in the compound. Refreshments
> were partaken of and the assembly did not disperse till a late hour.

But perhaps the ultimate accolade for the Parsi community comes in *The Times of India*, which lists the most important guests at Petit Hall in the following order: Sir Jamsetji Jeejeebhoy, Bart.; the Hon. Sir Frank Forbes Adam; the Hon. Mr Justice Bayley; and so forth. A Parsi subject tops the list, ahead of the Raj's rulers! Sir Jamsetji is the son of the first native Baronet, not an opium trader himself, and he has made it to the pinnacle of Bombay society. His community has surely pinned its colours to the right political mast.*

In the week before this match between Vernon's XI and the Parsis, the Indian National Congress held their annual meeting in Bombay. It had nearly not been held in Bombay at all, but in Poona, such was Parsi opposition to the Congress with their notions of Indian independence. When the meeting did go ahead in Bombay, the Parsis boycotted it. Native Indian women, however, attended it for the first time. Subscriptions amounting to 63,000 rupees were raised to open a permanent agency of the Congress in London. It would be close not only to Parliament but also to Ireland, where their independence movement was working with India's.

In the very same week as this match at the Gymkhana came the news that the Raj was going to use the Parsis militarily as well as politically and economically. 'Our readers will be glad to learn that the Government have at last sanctioned the enrolment of Parsis as Volunteers,' the *Bombay Gazette* proclaimed. 'We congratulate the Parsis community [sic] on this appreciation by the Viceroy of their loyalty... We are informed that his Royal Highness the Commander-in-Chief expressed himself very much in favour of it, and that the Bombay Government also supported it.' Thus, in the

---

* The majority of Parsis, however, were to find themselves on the wrong side as Indian independence dawned. Bombay saw anti-Parsi riots in 1921 when, according to Eckehard Kulke in *The Parsees in India*, 'anti-British aggressions on the part of Hindus and Muslims were diverted to the weaker Parsis'.

event of a second national uprising, Parsi militias would fight alongside the British against their fellow Indians.*

When Lord Harris arrived later in 1890 to take over as Governor of Bombay, he was to use cricket even more than Lord Reay. Back Bay, or what is now the Queen's Necklace, was claimed from the Arabian Sea so that the Parsis could have a cricket ground of their own. The Parsis were granted regular fixtures against the Presidency – a team of Europeans which the Governor of Bombay selected, and which included some notable first-class players on his staff, such as 'Jungly' Greig and Major R.M. Poore, who both played for Hampshire on home leave (Poore averaged 91 in the English first-class season of 1899). From 1892 these biannual matches were staged in Bombay and, during the Hot Weather, in Poona. This was the official seal of social and political approval for the Parsis. Framji Patel wrote, a touch fawningly, of Lord Harris: 'During his regime generally physical culture in the Western Presidency received much-needed stimulus and encouragement in many ways, and Parsi cricket particularly improved its status and position.' (The Harris Shield is still contested by Bombay schools: it was in this competition that Sachin Tendulkar shared the world record partnership of 664 with Vinod Kambli.)

In 1907, fifteen years after the first Presidency v Parsis match, the Hindu community joined in, so it became a triangular tournament in Bombay. In 1912, the Muslim community joined in, so it became a quadrangular; and, in 1936–37, a pentangular when minority

* Modern Parsi history has had to be revisionist, minimising the loyalty towards the British which the majority of their community felt before the First World War, and maximising the role the minority played in the independence movement. The Tata family was in the latter camp: not only J.N. but J.R.D., who was to start the first Indian airline and many other companies, and built up India's steel industry until it eventually took over Britain's. The Petits and Jeejeebhoys, Cowasjis and Camas, honoured and knighted, sided with the Parsi majority. Caesar, at any rate, would have approved.

communities, such as native Indian Christians, joined in as 'The
Rest'. We should not conclude, however, that social or economic or
political advancement was the primary motivation for those who
competed. It was apparent on 30 January 1890 that Indian cricketers and spectators derived much delight from playing the English
at their own game, even if there were benefits from networking off
the field. Surely the primary motivation was pleasure: to walk out
on a grassy ground in Bombay on a warm day, the humidity
tempered by a sea breeze with a salty tang, and to play a competitive game against people who were different but with whom one
nevertheless had something in common. Cricket was used as a tool
by the British Empire; but, in the process of becoming the hottest
spot in India, Bombay enjoyed fun and games along the way.

When play resumes on the second morning at 11.30, the tenth
Parsi wicket adds only a couple of runs, leaving Vernon's XI with a
lead of 15 on first innings. Now comes some clever captaincy by
Framji Patel. In the first innings of Vernon's team, the Parsi bowling
was opened by Mody, who took three wickets for 32, and Pundole,
who had toured England in 1888 but was expensive here, conceding 25 runs from 25 balls without taking a wicket. Instead, the
captain pairs Mody with Pavri, a versatile athlete. Pavri can throw
ambidextrously; and he did the double of 1000 runs and 100 wickets on the 1888 Parsi tour of England.

Pavri is a bowler of a type not uncommon in the late nineteenth
century: his pace is medium and, in the expression of the day, he
'breaks both ways'. Pavri is also a man of moods, according to
Framji Patel, and this morning he is in the mood. A band has been
advertised for the second day, and it might be their music which is
inspiring him. *The Times of India* reports:

This time the Parsi Captain put on Mr Pavri to bowl instead of Mr Pundole. His judgment proved to be perfectly correct, as Mr Pavri was in rare form, and in his first over disposed of Mr Lawson-Smith, whom he caught with one hand off his own bowling. One for two; or anything but a cheerful beginning. Mr Gibson came in and quickly got Mr Mody away for 4. A brief stand was made, but presently Mr Pavri gave fresh evidence that he was on the spot by bowling the last comer, who played on. Mr Vernon next appeared, and almost immediately cracked Pavri to the on for 4. After he had scored but one more Mr Walker called him for a run and then sent him back with the result that he was run out. It was a very near thing indeed, and a wonderful bit of luck for the Parsis. Indeed, we may say that this piece of good fortune practically determined the match in their favour. Mr Philipson was next, but he had hardly taken his place before Mr Pavri shot down Mr Walker's stumps. Three for 15 and four for 15. Mr De Little came in and started with a two to leg. He only scored one more, however, before Mr Mody bowled him clean. Five for 20, a truly wretched state of things. Mr Philipson and Mr Hornsby were now together, and for a time they raised the hopes of their side by scoring freely. Mr Hornsby made a four in the slips, upon which the grubs [i.e. the under-armers of Gagrat] were put on, but without effect. Mr Philipson then cracked Mr Pavri to the boundary three times in succession for four each time. In attempting to repeat the stroke for the fourth time he failed to get well hold of the ball, and was caught at mid-on by Mr Patel. He had made a good and plucky attempt to turn the fortune of the day by hard hitting, but luck was against him and it was not to be. Major Von Donop was well caught at short leg before he had time to score, and Mr Hornsby was bowled by Mr Pavri when his score amounted to 9.

Framji Patel, with pardonable pride, fleshes out this newspaper report with the detail that Mr Philipson was 'in fine fettle and in a smiting mood. He drove Pavri in the direction of mid-on thrice, but luckily the fourth time I managed to hold him close to the ground.' A one-handed catch, to boot. Again, not the sort of example that princely captains were to set.

The procession of Vernon's men continues unabated. Mr Hone-Goldney 'had his stumps uprooted by Mr Pavri and the innings came to an end for 61 only. There was nothing in the state of the ground to account for this very poor display of batting, and the very highest credit must be given to the Parsis for their excellent bowling and close fielding.' (Credit, too, to Tata and Petit for their lavish entertaining?)

Thus do the Parsis turn on the heat. The total is by far the lowest that Vernon's XI make on their tour of India. Pavri takes seven wickets for 34, Mody two for 18. Vernon's men, nine of whom played first-class cricket in England, are bowled out on a pitch which is 'apparently playing nearly all right again' in only 27.2 five-ball overs.

The target of 77 remains, however, before history can be made. The Parsis reach 11 without loss in their second innings, then slump to 17 for four wickets. Nerves no doubt set in at the prospect of a native team beating an English team for the first time in India. The game, and with it great prestige, is anybody's. Objectivity goes out of the flap in the press tent. *The Times of India* reports: 'Victory seemed still to hang in the balance if not to incline towards the strangers.' These 'strangers', in the reporter's eyes, are the Parsis who live down the road, not the tourists from England. His later reference to 'the strangers' allows no room for ambiguity.

But Pavri, who has opened the batting in both innings as well as the bowling second time round, is still at the crease, and he begins to turn the tide with Gagrat. Ernest de Little is bowling, an Australian pace bowler who has just won a Cambridge blue and dismissed W.G. Grace twice in one game, but his length seems variable. Against the Gymkhana Club, de Little bowled 'a head ball', and now he bowls to Gagrat 'a very long hop, which he promptly dispatched to the off for six. Had it travelled a yard or two further it would have reached the boundary and scored four only.' We can still hear ten thousand voices, male and female, roaring on Pavri and Gagrat as they turn for a fourth run, and a fifth, then a sixth, while a ruddy-faced Englishman removes his sola topi to give chase, and priests offer thanks to Zoroaster.

Gagrat is run out soon afterwards amidst the excitement, but Pavri continues 'a good sound innings. His defence was excellent, and he occasionally got the ball well away to the boundary,' according to *The Times of India*. 'In conjunction with Mr Machliwalla he raised the score rapidly. The latter played the right game for the crisis. He jumped out courageously to fast and slow bowlers alike and despatched the ball vigorously to all parts of the field. Mr Pavri was got rid of at 60 for an excellent 21, but it was of no avail. There were now too few runs to get for there to be any chance of saving the match, and Mr Dubash and Mr Machliwalla soon knocked off the required number, thus leaving the Parsis victorious by four wickets. They are heartily to be congratulated on their really splendid victory.' The *Bombay Gazette* adds the detail: 'Dubash finally hit the winning stroke with a slog into the tent for four.'

PARSIS V G.F. VERNON'S XI

Played at the Gymkhana Ground, Bombay, on 30, 31 January 1890 (two-day match)

G.F. VERNON'S XI

J.G. Walker	b Mody	0		b Pavri	2
E.M. Lawson-Smith	b Mody	17		c & b Pavri	1
A.B.E. Gibson	b Mody	0		b Pavri	6
G.F. Vernon*	not out	45		run out	5
H. Philipson	b Gagrat	0		c Patel b Pavri	14
E.R. de Little	b Gagrat	4		b Mody	3
J.H.J. Hornsby	b Gagrat	0		b Pavri	9
P.G. von Donop	run out	14		c Dubash b Pavri	0
A.E. Leatham	b Pavri	9		lbw b Mody	15
G.H. Hone-Goldney	lbw b Pavri	0		b Pavri	4
A.N. Curzon	b Gagrat	0		not out	0
Extras		8			2
Total	(all out; 31.4 overs)	**97**		(all out; 27.2 overs)	**61**

PARSIS

M.E. Pavri	c & b Leatham	6	(4)	b de Little	21
J.M. Morenas	b Hornsby	17		b de Little	4
D.D. Kanga	b de Little	14		lbw b Hornsby	2
B.D. Gagrat	lbw b de Little	0	(6)	run out	9
N.C. Bapasola	b de Little	4	(9)	did not bat	–
J.M. Patel*	run out	1	(1)	b Hornsby	9
S.B. Doctor	c von Donop b Hornsby	13	(5)	b Hornsby	0
D.F. Dubash	b Hornsby	8		not out	8
B.C. Machliwalla	c Hornsby b Gibson	14	(7)	not out	20
R.E. Mody	b de Little	0		did not bat	–
D.C. Pundole	not out	1		did not bat	–
Extras		4			4
Total	(all out; 52.2 overs)	**82**		(for 6 wickets; 41 overs)	**77**

PARSIS	O	M	R	W		O	M	R	W
Mody	13	3	32	3		10	5	18	2
Pundole	5	1	25	0		–	–	–	–
Gagrat	10.4	3	29	4	(3)	4	3	7	0
Pavri	3	1	3	2	(2)	13.2	5	34	7

VERNON'S XI	O	M	R	W		O	M	R	W
Leatham	6	3	17	1		–	–	–	–
Hornsby	21.2	12	25	3	(2)	16	9	22	3
Gibson	8	3	11	1		8	4	13	0
de Little	17	11	25	4	(1)	17	2	38	2

Fall of wickets:

	Ver	Par	Ver	Par
1st	6	8	2	11
2nd	6	25	?	14
3rd	39	29	15	17
4th	40	35	15	17
5th	54	42	20	?
6th	54	43	?	60
7th	74	59	?	
8th	92	79	?	
9th	92	80	?	
10th	97	82	61	

Toss: G.F. Vernon's XI
Close of play: Day 1: Parsis (1) 80–9 (S.B. Doctor 12*)

Result: **Parsis won by 4 wickets**

Captain Trevor, on the other hand, is appalled – utterly appalled. So is Anglo-Indian clubdom. 'I was in the tent of the Byculla Club when the end came, and the head of one of the largest firms in the city of Bombay said to me, "I know nothing of cricket and I care less, but I could have collected a lac of rupees on the ground to prevent this, if money could have prevented it."'

Captain Trevor then embarks on one of the finest paragraphs in the history of dyspepsia:

> Of that vast multitude not a thousand knew the name of the thing at which they were looking, not a hundred had even an elementary knowledge of the game of cricket. But they were dimly conscious that in some particular or another the black man had triumphed over the white man, and they ran hither and thither, gibbering and chattering and muttering vague words of ill omen.

The Parsis' victory is greeted with some official approbation, too. 'The first to congratulate the Parsi Captain on his victory were English gentlemen, Sir N.G. Lyttelton and Sir Charles Sargent, the Chief Justice of Bombay. I shall never forget the kind and encouraging words of these two sportsmen,' wrote Framji Patel.

After a weekend of reflecting upon the contest, 'A Correspondent' for *The Times of India* chivalrously concludes: 'It may fitly stand as the greatest achievement the Parsi cricketers have yet done that they should defeat a team which has beaten all the picked elevens of Bengal and Northern India . . . It was hard to see the Parsis beat our Englishmen at their own game, but all the more credit to them; they played the game right well, and fairly astonished everyone, including most of those whose money changed hands at the result! The match cannot fail to have a most stimulating effect on Parsi cricket . . . Their fielding and their fast bowling are exceptionally good, their batting improves every year, while in keenness and smartness they are second to none, and they only want at present two good slow bowlers.'

Vernon and his men have to leave for the railway station straight after this match, to take the train to Lucknow, but before doing so they are garlanded by Parsi ladies and presented with some beautiful Indian artwork, so Framji Patel related: 'The English cricketers took this solitary reverse in their Indian tour like good sportsmen.' The Parsi community turn out in force at Victoria Terminus to fare them well, and their luminaries are listed in the *Bombay Gazette* the next day. No Europeans are listed. Do they feel that Vernon's men have let the whole side down?

On Saturday morning the *Bombay Gazette*, after disposing of the cricket match, turns its sporting attention to the horse races at the Gymkhana.* The Parsis continue to celebrate. 'It is quite on the cards that the imaginative and emotional Parsi youth felt for a day or two that he was the victor of the victors of Waterloo,' Framji Patel recollected. 'Cricket was affected everywhere for some days and the Parsi Team was dined by the leading clubs in Bombay. In short, like Byron, they found themselves famous when they woke the next morning.'

There is, however, a sting in the tail. Mody, the Parsi fast bowler, is publicly accused of throwing. And it is done in the semi-official channels of *The Times of India*, by 'A Correspondent', who sounds as though he has been briefed by the departed and defeated captain, Vernon:

> Having thus given them their measure of well merited praise, we
> hope they [the Parsis] will pardon us if we allude to one defect which
> we think should be rectified at once. We are of opinion, and always
> have been, that Mr Mody is a thrower and not a bowler at all. Under

---

* On the same day, according to the *Gazette*, at the Esplanade Police Court, Mr Jardine was due to defend 'a native Engineer' on a charge of defamation. Informal charges were to be laid against his son Douglas during Bodyline.

the circumstances we think he should not be allowed to play. We have the authority of those of Mr Vernon's XI who are best qualified to express an opinion on the subject that his action is a pronounced and unmistakable throw, and if he is allowed to go on it will be all against the interests of Parsi cricket. He is certain to be no balled if he goes to England, and worse than that, as he is successful with his throws, he will have a lot of imitators among the rising generation unless he is checked, and we are sure that the Parsis themselves will realize how fatal this would be to the progress of their future bowling strength.

Framji Patel adamantly disagreed with this judgement that Mody threw. Mody was his quickest bowler one minute and gone the next, though he played a few more games as a batsman only. From this distance, without any action photographs, we cannot know what the objection was. Perhaps, being round-arm, quick, uncoached and with a fine yorker, Mody was like Sri Lanka's Lasith Malinga.

When he looked back in later life and wrote *Stray Thoughts*, Framji Patel was a successful industrialist; he had been honorary secretary as well as captain of Parsi Gymkhana; and he was to become president of the Indian Olympic Association. He cannot have had many regrets or gripes, but here was one. He mentioned that Mody was a champion swimmer and, among his feats of athletic prowess, once ran from the Parsi Gymkhana ground into the sea and swam frantically for fifteen minutes to save the lives of two drowning Hindus.

'Unfortunately, his brilliant career came to an early end, as his action was objected to,' Patel wrote. 'I think the no-balling of Mody was the tragedy of Parsi cricket.'

Had Bombay been left to set the standard without princes to interfere, and if regional differences had not intervened, Indian cricket might have fulfilled its potential sooner, on the lines of India's hockey team. (They were Olympic champions from 1928 until Pakistan displaced them in 1960.)

In an annual tournament based on sectarian divisions such as the Bombay Pentangular, heat was guaranteed, and intensity, and selection on merit. Before the First World War, the Hindus selected a net bowler from Poona, Palwankar Baloo, because he was an excellent left-arm spinner, overlooking the fact that he was an Untouchable: a unique story narrated by Ramachandra Guha in *A Corner of a Foreign Field*.

During the Second World War, when the Pentangular was augmented by British military personnel playing for the Europeans, the batting bar was progressively raised. First, in December 1941, Vijay Merchant made 243, the highest score in the tournament to date. In December 1943, in the semi-final, Vijay Hazare of The Rest topped that with 248. Then Merchant reclaimed the record in the final with 250 and, in the same game, Hazare trumped it with 309. Hazare did not live in Bombay but went there for the Pentangular, like other cricketers from the main cities such as Karachi and Madras. When these players of different religions played against each other, they set a high standard, even if they did not always pull together when they played alongside each other for India.

In every Test-playing country the top batsmen are celebrated, but even more so in India. Merchant and Hazare, then Sunil Gavaskar in the 1970s, paved the way for the mass adulation of V.V.S. Laxman, Sourav Ganguly, Rahul Dravid and, above all, Sachin Tendulkar. 'Given the rewards and associated publicity it was not surprising that cricketers in India ranked as high socially, or almost as high, as film stars,' Dr Richard Cashman wrote as long ago as 1978 in *Patrons, Players and the Crowd*. 'Cricket's prestigious status was and is sustained by the government, the media, the business community, the social elite and the spectators.' To which list I would add the army and police: nothing is more likely to reinforce the cult of a personality than hundreds of armed men surrounding him.

Bombay has long had miniature hot spots to nurture players from an early age: its schools, often founded by Christian missionaries. In the rest of India, not so well endowed, colleges of tertiary education have been the incubators. Like Pakistan's Test team in the 1950s, India's in the 1960s was filled with graduates: 'more than two-thirds' according to Cashman. Colleges offered coaches and grounds, but it was often too late for an aspiring batsman to catch up by that stage of life. The prime product of colleges were India's spin bowlers, from Prasanna and Bedi to Anil Kumble.

There is no touchier subject in Indian cricket – almost a taboo – than the down-played fact that a disproportionate number of India's international cricketers have come from one of Hinduism's four main castes: Brahmins. This trend – 'Brahmins are about four percent of the population', according to Guha, 'but perhaps thirty per cent of our cricketers' – does not sit comfortably with modern, or westernised, thinking. So it is dismissed as coincidence. But this is failing to understand the nature of hot spots, and their impact on the development of batsmen. Brahmins are the educated class; therefore they go to school and college; therefore they have access to cricket facilities; therefore they become the nation's cricketers, particularly batsmen. It is cause and effect, not directly a function of caste.

Pace bowlers are less bound by social convention than any other type of cricketer. In India, as everywhere else, they owe most to nature, least to nurture. So while middle-class players have preferred to bat – the least physically demanding activity, as those maharajahs knew – pace bowling has been left to those aspiring on the margins. The country's pace bowlers have come less from the Hindu college-educated middle-class and more from small towns and villages, and from the Muslim communities there: from Mohammad Nissar, whose new-ball burst shocked England in India's inaugural Test at Lord's in 1932, to Zaheer Khan, the single most important player – I would argue – in India's rise to number one in the Test rankings in

2010. I selected Zaheer as one of *Wisden*'s Five Cricketers of the Year because he turned the runs made by his famous teammates into victory. In the World Cup final of 2011, Zaheer's first three overs were maidens; nobody else in the match bowled one.

And there she was, skipping down the hotel steps in Poona, wearing a very tight pair of jeans and an equally mischievous smile. She jumped into a car, and was gone.

After visiting Jamnagar on my first tour of India, I had gone to Poona to reconnoitre the venue of England's opening first-class game and was staying at what was to be the team hotel. Wow, she has to be one of the top ten stunners I have ever seen. That was my immediate reaction, even though I beheld her for only a few seconds. How to see her again? This was India. She was not a girl in a million, but one in a billion.

The misfortune I had in losing my mother was made up for by the fortune in finding my wife. I saw her again the following day, in the hotel, and she gave me the phone number of the college in Bombay where she was studying. Miraculously – for this was still the age of wires and landlines, when connections were infrequent – the number worked and she came to the phone. Decades later Sunita remains, still with the most beautiful smile I have seen, the basis of my life. We named our daughter Freya.

It had all the ingredients, from the moment the Indian Premier League was launched in Bangalore on 18 April 2008. Opening ceremonies in general? No, thanks. But this one featured the captains of the eight franchises – and even if some were past their peak, Sachin Tendulkar, Virender Sehwag, Rahul Dravid and Shane Warne were still stellar names. I was sure before the start that this 20-over tournament was bound to be an instant spectacular success. It was offering the form of cricket India's people wanted to watch.

I was also at the Sydney Cricket Ground on 27 November 1979 for the first one-day international after Kerry Packer's revolution (one-day internationals had previously consisted of white clothes, a red ball, more than 50 overs per side and no razzamatazz). That format was not quite the same instant success as the IPL, in that it took several hours to get off the ground. It was early afternoon when Australia and West Indies began their 50-over international and the members, representing the establishment, had stayed away from the SCG to express their disapproval of the popularist Packer. It was when the sun went down, and lights illuminated the first floodlit international cricket, that the crowd poured in and filled the ground to bursting. This was cool cricket, the place to go and be seen, and for both genders, not just middle-aged men. It was the one-day cricket of the future.

The IPL was a brilliant concept, by the extremely controversial entrepreneur Lalit Modi. The natural vehicle for competition in India was the eight main cities, with a franchise in each, playing against each other home and away. A total of 56 games, plus the knockout stage of semis and final, made for a time span of six weeks. A team – your team – could start badly but still have time to rally and reach the knockout stage; or the reverse. It was not so short that one or two defeats would end your season, and not so long that your attention would wander.

Allowing each franchise team to play up to four overseas stars was another brilliant concept. What glamour was brought by Chris Gayle, Kevin Pietersen, Ricky Ponting, Dale Steyn – and, after he had hit 158 off 73 balls on that opening night in Bangalore, Brendon McCullum. This proportion of overseas players made the IPL seem cosmopolitan, and captured the attention of cricket followers in other countries, without alienating the home market. Each team still had its own Indian Test players – and local rookies. They might be medium-pacers scarcely above club standard, and clubbed they were, but Indian television viewers could identify with them as not being impossibly better than themselves.

If these were the chief ingredients, the cake's icing was spot-on. Dancing girls gyrated whenever a four or six was hit – and boundaries were brought in to ensure that was at least once an over – but they were not scantily clad like their American counterparts, so as not to shock local sensibilities. Fireworks: who can be so world-weary as not to enjoy fireworks in a night sky? But, above all, warmth. From March to May in India you want to be outdoors in the evening, when most IPL matches are staged. In England, there are not ten evenings a year when I want to sit out after sunset.

Bollywood had been the mass entertainment of India. The IPL offered not only escapism but the illusion of involvement. The man in the street – the man living in the street – could be swept into a stadium that was not full enough for the organisers' liking and appear on a million screens if he cheered wildly or caught a crowd catch. About one hundred million middle-class Indians had their evenings to fill, and the IPL offered plots more plausible than the soaps, and more celebrities on and off the field.

The IPL was also a return to the heyday of Parsi cricket, in that females watched. For decades, the crowds at India's international matches had consisted of young men. Only they were prepared to queue for hours to buy a ticket, scrummage to get into the ground, sit all day on concrete in the sun and endure the occasional lathi charge whenever the army or police wanted something to do. Elderly persons, women and children were never to be seen at most grounds outside the VIP enclosure and, that Indian speciality, the VVIP enclosure – until the IPL came along and welcomed spectators of all kinds, letting them in for free if necessary, so that television could display capacity crowds.

Although corruption set in, and players were found guilty of spot-fixing, and the rumours were rife, the concept was still flawless. Traditionalists in Sydney on that historic evening in 1979 lamented the World Series Cricket revolution by Packer because it changed the old, tranquil, ill-paid order for ever. I think the IPL would have happened with or without Packer. All the ingredients for its success in India were present – and simply had to be brought together.

Cricket spread to what was to become Pakistan for the same reason that it began in Bombay: in Karachi there were Parsi middlemen to incubate the game. A quadrangular tournament was set up on the same communal lines, raising the standard. But after Partition the sport's hot spot in Pakistan was Lahore, and not because of the Gymkhana ground in the Bagh-i-Jinnah, lovely though it is. It was because Lahore had parks, or maidans, like Minto Park and Zaman Park, where anybody skilled and persistent enough could get a game.

Given that it was once a single country, the styles of Indian and Pakistani cricket are remarkably dissimilar. The difference in physiques has been one factor but more important, perhaps, has been the difference in pitches. The stock description of the Pakistani cricketer is 'volatile': this fails to grasp the conditions with which they have to contend. Pakistan's pitches, if well maintained, are the most unresponsive to bowlers: they begin as concrete, and at the end of five days they remain concrete, not wearing and tearing like Indian pitches. Twice I have played at the Gaddafi Stadium in Lahore on the Test strip two days after a Test, and it was still unresponsive.

Hence the Pakistani cricketer has been conditioned to resemble a volcano: dormant most of the time, then flaring into life. If they played as England play, at the same level of intensity throughout, there would never be a result on a traditional Pakistani pitch, not in 27 and a half hours, which used to be the length of a Test match there. But by flaring into action at the right time, and busting a gut, their bowlers could force the breach on a flat pitch. One of my great privileges has been to watch Pakistan teams get a sniff, swarm through the breach and sweep aside England in a session.

PAKISTAN

Pakistan's cricket was born in austerity and run on a shoestring – a shoestring donated by the first secretary of the Pakistan board, Bobby Cornelius. He was a judge in the Lahore High Court, who lived with his wife in ground-floor rooms at Faletti's hotel, and he gave me a lengthy interview in his retirement. The stationery and stamps for communicating with MCC and other boards came out of his law firm's budget; the first Tests in Pakistan had to last only four days as an economy measure; the players could not travel first-class by train, let alone fly; and it was 1953–54 before they could afford to stage a domestic tournament.

Pakistan's cricketers of the 1950s radiated the same integrity. Not charm – match-fixers radiate charm – but decency and a quiet pride in what they had achieved. Their early Test teams consisted almost entirely of university graduates from Lahore and the Mohammad brothers from Karachi, under Abdul Hafeez Kardar, who added to his aura by being Oxford-educated and having played for Warwickshire. Kardar was soon known as the Douglas Jardine of Pakistan. I remember being woken by a phone call in Lahore one morning at 7 a.m. – not an alarm call but, far more urgent, Kardar picking on something I had written in *The Observer*.

Pakistan's tightly knit group made the strongest entry into Test cricket of any country since 1877. They had few resources, yet they won a Test match in the first series they played against every country. I am pretty sure the home umpires – both Pakistani in those days – were proud and nationalistic: they wanted Pakistan firstly to be given Test status, then to uphold the honour of this young Muslim country. When MCC toured Pakistan in 1951–52, it was to judge whether they were fit for Test status, and Tom Graveney subsequently told me that some of the umpiring was 'extremely dodgy'. Yet, I think, it was for the greater good: cricket was better served by Pakistan being given Test status than by Pakistan losing badly to MCC and being denied Test status.

Necessity being the mother of invention, Pakistan made the most of the little they had by preparing in camps. England and Australia had never seen the need for them; but Pakistan's players prepared with an intensity born of patriotism. Here they benefited from a patron: the Pir of Pagaro, the only religious leader to have had his own first-class team.

Venerated, and a powerful political influence, the Pir made available his garden in Karachi to create a very grassy cricket pitch. (It is difficult to interview someone whose father has been hanged by your countrymen, for being a terrorist/freedom-fighter, but when the Pir talked to me in Islamabad in 1987 he made no accusation of collective responsibility.) These were the conditions the Pakistan team would find in England on their inaugural tour in 1954, and there the batsmen practised as sunset approached, to simulate the light in England. Pakistan were outclassed for much of their tour, yet shared the series 1–1.

Their match-winner was Fazal Mahmood, who took 12 wickets for 99 in the Oval Test. In 1978, on the outfield at Harrogate before rain curtailed a press match, he bowled a few looseners: one ball fizzed through the air at medium pace and cut back sharply from the off, the next fizzed and cut back sharply from leg. Fazal was one of those bowlers with a vast array of theories, and wrote a book about religion, but he was of the same mould as the other Test cricketers who had put Pakistan on the map in the 1950s. Fazal was a former policeman – some were in the army – and they were all disciplined, smart and patriotically proud.

One of Pakistan's few assets at Partition was Lawrence Gardens, or the Bagh-i-Jinnah as they were renamed after Independence. The ground was presided over by Sir George Abell, on the lines of the Oxford Parks, where he had played as a student (Abell was a good enough batsman to make 210, the first double century in the Ranji Trophy, before becoming Field Marshal Wavell's private secretary). I would say the ground is even more beautiful than the Parks, because the trees are closer and more luxuriant. When England arranged a practice game there against the Gymkhana Club on my first tour in 1977, the atmosphere was so relaxed I umpired when England fielded. And such were the times that when John Lever swung a ball back into one of the club's openers, he shook his head almost imperceptibly to indicate that the batsman should be spared.

On the edge of the gardens is the museum, where John Lockwood Kipling was in charge, and his son sat astride the great gun Zam-Zammah. Laid out in the museum is some of the sumptuousness of Mughal life – clothes, Korans, calligraphy and everyday artefacts, so simple yet tasteful, even serene. It is a world of Islamic civilisation which has passed, but should never be forgotten, in the hope that one day it will be revived.

The value of the maidan has been conclusively proven since 2000. Bangladesh played their inaugural Test match then, against India, and while their limited-overs team has defeated a main country occasionally, the standard of their Test cricket has remained woeful. I ascribe this failure to improve, firstly, to the absence of maidans in their cities, notably Dhaka and Chittagong. From what I have seen in Bangladesh, any spare land in the countryside is used for food production: the changing course of the rivers of the Delta, and the growing population, force people to look for any cultivable land. In a city, any spare land is built on and inhabited. There is nowhere to play, unless you are a member of one of the few elite sports clubs. Bangladesh has sunshine but no space where youngsters can practise for ten thousand hours.

When India toured the West Indies in 1961–62, four members of their party played for a single club on Bombay's Azad Maidan. Parsi Cyclists is only a hundred metres from the Gymkhana, but three other clubs have squeezed into this gap, each with its own tent which has become a permanent pavilion. The club was founded in 1909 for cyclists who also wanted to play some cricket, and in the more demotic surroundings of the maidan, rather than at the Parsi Gymkhana which Lord Harris had built for their community.

In the second Test of the 1961–62 series in the West Indies, members of the Parsi Cyclists club batted for India at numbers two, three, five and nine. Nari Contractor opened, and captained; Rusi Surti batted at three, opened the bowling, bowled spin and came to be known as 'the poor man's Sobers'; at five came Pahlan or 'Polly' Umrigar, who was India's highest Test run-scorer by the time he retired; and at number nine was Farokh Engineer, who kept wicket in addition to being the top-scorer in India's second innings. The community was still living up to Framji Patel's prayer: 'I hope to see the industrial and the sporting spirit of the race go hand in hand.' In all, eleven Parsis played Test cricket: the equivalent would be a town the size of Cambridge producing a Test XI in half a century.

Contractor, when I interviewed him in his late seventies, still had an excellent power of recall in spite of having his skull fractured on that tour of the West Indies by Charlie Griffith. This accident was the most serious in Test cricket in pre-helmet days and, I would venture, as much of a tragedy for Parsi cricket as the no-balling of Mody. Contractor was India's youngest captain when appointed at the age of 26, and he was only a few days past his 28th birthday when he ducked into Griffith's bouncer and was struck on the temple. His exceptional bravery had already been proven. In the Lord's Test of 1959 he had a rib cracked in the opening hour by Brian Statham, yet he batted on without a runner until tea and scored 81, the highest innings of the match. After his fractured skull, and more than one emergency operation, he returned to first-class cricket and played well into his thirties; but no more Tests.

Contractor was the first to captain India in a Test series victory against England, 2–0 in 1961–62. His counterpart, Ted Dexter, told me how he was batting out for a draw on the last day in Calcutta when the second new ball became due, and India's seamers loosened up to take it; but Contractor gave it instead to his spinners, and the left-armer Salim Durrani had Dexter leg-before to break England's resistance. If he had not been struck down in his prime, Contractor might have led India, skilfully, right through the 1960s and, owing to his bravery, become a famous role model.

When I rang Contractor, he said with a laugh that he was 'into the mandatory overs': that is, into the last hour of his life. I asked him why he had not played for Parsi Gymkhana but for the Cyclists instead.

'You had to be very affluent [to join the Gymkhana],' he said. 'As schoolboys and college boys we couldn't afford it. The entry fee itself we couldn't afford, let alone the monthly fee. For Parsi Cyclists the monthly fee was six rupees, and that covered everything, including the match fee. You had to take your own lunch but tea and snacks were provided.

'Playing on the [Parsi] Gymkhana would be more enjoyable because the outfield at Cyclists was terrible. In the rainy season [when the Kanga Shield was staged] the grass is knee-high. But the pitches were always pretty good, almost as good as the Gymkhana, and we had a lot of fun on the Maidan with all the other players. Rusi, Polly, Farokh, we all played there. When we went to the West Indies in 1961, four of us came from one club, Parsi Cyclists.'

Gradually they faded away. Every Parsi female who marries outside her faith is deemed to be no longer a Parsi, and the same applies to her children. The community died away in other cities, in Pakistan as well as India, and found it increasingly difficult to maintain their religious practices: cremation came to be a substitute for exposing their dead to vultures in Towers of Silence. Young men, heeding half of Framji Patel's hope, devoted themselves to education but not sport.

I saw Nari Contractor's son opening the bowling against England on their 1981–82 tour in a warm-up game. On the same tour, in the nets in Bombay, England faced the left-arm wrist-spin of Diana Edulji, who captained the Indian women's team. When I asked the late Graham Dilley to rate her bowling, he said it was of county second XI standard. As an opening batsman, Zubin Bharucha played for Mumbai in the first half of the 1990s, without losing a game. But that seems to be that; on the field, the Parsis' last hour has expired.

The Parsi Gymkhana is now the most discreet of the gymkhanas along the Queen's Necklace or Esplanade. The Hindu Gymkhana has an enormous clubhouse, dated 1894. Next door a sign on the main road proclaims 'Islam Gymkhana'. But the Parsis' clubhouse hides behind a petrol station, without any sign, and it is tucked almost underneath the flyover which turns from the sea into the city centre.

Bombay's maidans are still crammed with cricketers, but they are office workers rather than the next generation of Gavaskars and Tendulkars. Bombay's new heartland has moved north, out of the narrow peninsula, to Dadar and Shivaji Park, Tendulkar's club. This is not cosmopolitan old Bombay, but Marathi-speaking Mumbai. When the founder of the Hindu right-wing party Shiv Sena died, Bal Thackeray's funeral took place in Shivaji Park.

While cricket was centred in old Bombay, the cricketers were liable to be upper or affluent middle class. Dadar and Shivaji Park are where 'the Maharashtrian middle and lower middle class reside', according to Richard Cashman. 'The change has occurred because the more affluent youth of Bombay central often chose to pursue other diversions such as social tennis, swimming and the cinema, unlike the inhabitants of Dadar and Shivaji Park who have fewer recreational alternatives.' Dadar Union and Shivaji Park also charge nominal fees or waive them for promising youngsters. Further north come the lower-class suburbs and slums, without any space for a cricket ground, like Bangladesh.

When I last visited the Parsi Gymkhana, their display cupboard was still stacked with trophies, but not of recent manufacture. Their cricket team was competing in Division F of the Times of India Shield. The Gymkhana was home to training camps in the school holidays for Parsi boys from several western Indian cities; and the community, not far short of its heyday population of 100,000, still contains some of the biggest names in Indian business. But not a single adult Parsi was playing for the Gymkhana. Their community is a hot spot of cricket no more.

Over on the Maidan, Parsi Cyclists claimed to have 'six or seven' Parsi adult players. In the match that I saw, though, on their strip of bare reddish earth, the only Parsi was the smallest boy there, wearing very thick spectacles, sitting beside the scoreboard and doing the tins.

Everyone else in India seems to be playing cricket: every religion, every caste, and increasingly both genders. But of all the hot spots on earth, none is so hot as Bombay. They have won the Ranji Trophy 36 times since it was launched in 1934–35 – even more dominant than New South Wales or Yorkshire. In 1979, precisely one-quarter of India's Test players had been born in Bombay: 32 out of 128, leaving Madras languishing in second place with seven. Merchant still comes second only to Don Bradman for the highest first-class average, 72; Gavaskar was the first to equal and overtake Bradman's record of 29 Test centuries; and Tendulkar was the first, and maybe last, to score 100 international hundreds. These three have led the Bombay School of Batting, which specialises in an insatiable appetite for runs; and the Hindu practice of deification has done nothing to diminish their fame.

The locals proudly tell you that land, selling at US$50,000 per square foot, is now more expensive than in Manhattan. Yet the maidans and gymkhanas along the Queen's Necklace are still given over to cricketers. It is as if London not only gave Hyde Park and Regent's Park over to cricket, but Pall Mall too, so that Anglicans, Catholics, Methodists and Muslims could all play the game.

5
HOT LIKE FIRE

Emancipate yourselves from mental slavery.
None but ourselves can free our minds.

Bob Marley, 'Redemption Song'

EARTH AT DAWN has few places more delicious than the Garrison in Barbados. In the dewy freshness, jockeys canter their horses around the rails or lead them down to the beach for a splash in the calm Caribbean, where they look like Loch Ness Monsters in miniature. Old stone buildings surround the race-track, leaving green savannah in between, and are terracotta, two-storeyed, unmilitary. The house where George Washington stayed on a visit to his brother is older still. Quite a few Barbadian civilians start their day with a walk or jog around the Garrison, before the sun consumes the shade.

Cricket in the West Indies was born in these auspicious surroundings. Here the British West Indies Regiment was quartered, to keep its eyes and cannons trained on French designs on other sugar plantations in the West Indies. British officers and their men brought bats and balls from home. Nothing is recorded of scores and results until 1860, when Barbados played British Guiana at the Garrison in the first inter-colonial match. But we know that cricketers in Barbados, of every colour, have always had one supreme advantage – beyond the heat and the trade winds to temper it.

David Holford scored a century for West Indies in the Lord's Test of 1966 in a partnership of 274 with his cousin, Garfield Sobers. In the days when touring teams and media were officially entertained together, I met Holford at a reception at the start of an England tour of the West Indies. He had graduated from the University of the West Indies with a knowledge of the region's geology and geography. 'Barbados is made of coral limestone,' Holford said. 'No other West Indian island is, except for Antigua, which is partly coral.'

It is by nature's favour, therefore, that Barbados has produced more fine cricketers per capita than anywhere else on earth. Look at the all-time teams that each of the main West Indian territories could turn out: every one is stocked with brilliant cricketers, but Barbados above all. From a population that has only recently reached 250,000, an XI of all the talents can be selected: not only have they collectively scored more than 40,000 Test runs and taken a thousand Test wickets, but they can bat deep, bowl everything except off-breaks, unleash a four-man pace attack to terrify, and include the greatest all-rounder ever. As Holford explained, the Windward Islands, such as St Vincent, Dominica and St Lucia, are volcanic, with black sand, high rainfall, very little flat land, slow pitches; Trinidad and Guyana have alluvial soil, and slow pitches again. The coral of Barbados, on the other hand, allows rain to drain through the soil into the underground aquifers, and the turf has only to be tended for a cricket ball to bounce consistently and speed through to the wicketkeeper.

WEST INDIES TERRITORIES – ALL-TIME XIs

Note: Players born in the West Indies who have played for other Test countries are excluded.

Antigua
Enoch Lewis
Richie Richardson
Viv Richards*
Ralston Otto
Danny Livingstone
Ridley Jacobs†
Eldine Baptiste
Winston Benjamin
Curtly Ambrose
Andy Roberts
Kenneth Benjamin

12th man: George Ferris

Barbados
Desmond Haynes
Gordon Greenidge
Seymour Nurse
Frank Worrell*
Everton Weekes
Clyde Walcott†
Garfield Sobers
Malcolm Marshall
Wes Hall
Sylvester Clarke
Joel Garner

12th man: Conrad Hunte

Guyana
Roy Fredericks
Ramnaresh Sarwan
Alvin Kallicharran
Clive Lloyd*
Basil Butcher
Shiv Chanderpaul

Carl Hooper
Robert Christiani†
Roger Harper
Colin Croft
Lance Gibbs

12th man: Faoud Bacchus

Jamaica
Chris Gayle
Allan Rae
Lawrence Rowe
George Headley*
Jeff Dujon
Collie Smith
Gerry Alexander†
Michael Holding
Courtney Walsh
Patrick Patterson
Alf Valentine

12th man: Jimmy Adams

Trinidad
Jeff Stollmeyer
Darren Bravo
Brian Lara
Larry Gomes
Gus Logie
Gerry Gomez
Dwayne Bravo
Learie Constantine
Deryck Murray†
Ian Bishop*
Sonny Ramadhin

12th man: Mervyn Dillon

Back in 1860 it was a white man's game. Almost every black person in Barbados worked on the sugar plantations, free in name, not in reality. They – or those lucky enough to have survived deportation from Africa – were still ranked below the 'savages' of the British Empire such as Australia's Aborigines. The established churches did not think they were human enough to have souls and refused to marry them. The emancipation of black West Indians took far longer than the British conscience might like to admit. Capitalism was clever enough to make sure that the Emancipation Act of 1834 was only the beginning of a very prolonged and gradual process.

In the sheds where they were penned at night, black people sang: they remembered African rhythms, even if the words of their native languages had been obliterated, along with anything else they had ever owned. Their other active form of self-expression came to be cricket, once they were allowed to pick up a ball and bowl it with the muscles magnified by manual labour in the plantations. Another world was opened up: one in which white master and black servant could compete on a level playing field, until the game was over and the established order restored.

'We alone, of all people in human history, had to invent ourselves as a people, as a nation,' wrote Tim Hector, a polymath and senator in Antigua's parliament, an academic and cricket administrator, in *A Spirit of Dominance*. 'We had to put our own stamp on their language, their economic and political structures, their literature, their fashions, their cricket, and make them our own and distinctly so. The distinction is the thing.'

Tommy Burton was one of the first black Barbadian cricketers. He joined the Pickwick club, the lowest on the island's social ladder, in the late 1890s. Clearly he could bowl: in a first-class career of ten matches he took 57 wickets at 15.03 runs each, and bowled

W.G. Grace more than once. He was selected for the first West Indian tour of England in 1900 – a group of white players had toured North America in 1886, but this was the first tour of England – and he took 78 wickets at 21 each. These games were not granted first-class status, but they were against first-class counties in the main, and hard going for a team that had never seen English conditions. As their opening bowler, Burton lacked support. When Gloucestershire ran riot – Gilbert Jessop smote 157 – and totalled 619 at five runs per over, Burton alone kept control, with five for 68. When Nottinghamshire scored 501, Burton bowled 73.2 six-ball overs and took five for 159.

On their second tour of England, in 1906, West Indies were granted first-class status, and Burton was again selected, but he did not see the tour through. In the eyes of the white management, he had an attitude problem. In addition to playing, and doing most of the bowling, the handful of black members of the first two West Indian touring parties were expected to transport the team luggage: to load all the suitcases into cabs and trains, then unload them at hotels and grounds. Imagine bowling 73 overs in one innings, then carrying the team luggage. Burton dared to put his foot down.

He was sent home immediately. He was blackballed in Barbados. When he went to British Guiana, Burton could not get a game there either. He was banned from cricket for life in the whole region. He was gone. He emigrated to Panama to find work and spent the rest of his life there, only returning to Barbados to die.

One day in 1998, I found his son sitting in a stand at Kensington Oval, one of the many grounds from which Burton had been black-balled. The son told me this story. He had watched every single Test match at Kensington from the first in 1930, except for one when he had been studying in North America; and he had become Sir Carlisle Burton, head of the Civil Service in Barbados.

Emancipation, on and off the cricket field, was an incremental process from generation to generation. Simply playing the game as well as white cricketers was not enough; words and statements, as well as actions, were needed to break down the barriers. Clifford Roach was a dark-skinned Trinidadian. When West Indies played their inaugural Test series, in England in 1928, they could not make enough runs: they were weekend amateur players who did not know how to build a long innings. They scored only three half-centuries in the three Tests, and Roach made two of them. Back in the West Indies for the return series of 1929–30, Roach scored their first Test century and, later in the series, their first double century, setting up West Indies' first victory.

In 1980 I tracked him down to a house outside Port-of-Spain, where he lived with his daughter. Roach sat in a chair with a blanket over his legs, except that he had none: owing to diabetes, they had been amputated. He had trained to become a lawyer and practised in Trinidad, one of the first to break the barrier between non-whites and the professional classes. But the pain of not being heard or recognised also seemed to nag. When Michael Manley, Jamaica's former prime minister, published *A History of West Indies Cricket* a few years later, Roach was given the most cursory mention. He made 'the first-ever century for West Indies in a Test match' and 'a fine double century': that was about it for recognition, for being the first to do what only batsmen of England, Australia and South Africa had done before.

The first Afro-Caribbean cricketer to 'put his stamp' on cricket, as Tim Hector phrased it, *and* to be recognised for doing so, was Learie Constantine. He was the first to embody what we came to consider all the attributes of West Indian cricket. The son of Lebrun Constantine, the only black batsman picked for the 1906 West Indian tour of England, he was low-slung, long-armed and the most dynamic all-round fielder the world had seen. He bowled fast when he wanted to, and plenty of bouncers, as only Harold Larwood was doing. He was not so much a batsman as a hitter: if he made a century it would not take much more than an hour. 'To all of this he added an exuberant, dramatic good humour in the field, characteristics that can be traced directly to his African roots,' wrote Manley. And Constantine had someone to blow his trumpet, so that people not only saw but listened, until he was eventually ennobled by the British establishment as Lord Constantine of Maraval and Nelson.

When C.L.R. James wrote *Cricket and I* for Constantine in the 1930s, the first book by a black cricketer, the pair formulated a creed: 'They are no better than we.' Further, if black West Indians were allowed full self-expression and to captain their own teams, 'we' could become better than 'they' – and distinctly so. James began to lay the groundwork with his journalism and more books, like his history of the revolution that made Haiti the first western country governed by black people, and *Beyond a Boundary*. In the course of his essay about the beautiful strokeplayer Wilton St Hill, 'The Most Unkindest Cut', James relates how he walked past a shoemaker's shop in central Trinidad and a man ran up to him, awl in hand, to ask James if he was Wilton St Hill. James said no, regretfully, but stayed to talk with the men in this shop.

> Their enthusiasm boiled over. One said weightily: 'You know what I waitin' for? When he go to Lord's and the Oval and make his century there! That's what I want to see!' I have to repeat: It took me years to understand. To paraphrase a famous sentence: It was the instinct of an oppressed man that spoke. If further proof of this were needed it is the hostility with which anti-nationalists and luke-warm supporters respond to this now so obvious truism. As for those who believe that all this harms cricket, they should produce ways and means of keeping it out. They are blind to the grandeur of a game which, in lands far from that which gave it birth, could encompass so much of social reality and still remain a game.

To that first West Indian Test victory, which had been set up by Roach, Constantine contributed nine wickets. When West Indies won their first Test series, against England in 1934–35, Constantine, Manny Martindale and Leslie Hylton bowled quick and often short to take 47 wickets at only 15 runs each in the four Tests. England's batting line-up of Wally Hammond, Patsy Hendren, Les Ames, Bob Wyatt and Maurice Leyland would eventually score over 600 first-class centuries, but in this series no England batsman averaged as much as 30, while Headley averaged 97. Larwood had been forced out of Test cricket by Bodyline politics and a foot injury; Australia and South Africa had nobody outright quick. In fast bowling, the one area of the game where they were selected on merit and allowed to express themselves fully, 'we' were already better than 'they'.

Not for another generation did West Indian cricketers, and Afro-Caribbean people, take the next incremental step. Movements towards independence and self-government surfaced around the Caribbean in the 1930s, under leaders of light skin. Captain Cipriani in Trinidad and Alexander Bustamante in Jamaica, together with the teachings of Marcus Garvey, inspired mass demonstrations. But the masses prioritised the needs of Great Britain in the Second World War, and stifled their own cause until the 1950s. It would have been so much quicker, easier, to have broken free when Britain turned its back to face Germany. Generously, they did not.

Not until the end of the 1950s did political emancipation arrive. The attempt at a Federation of the West Indies failed when Jamaicans voted in a referendum to pull out, but independence followed, island by island. Another Jamaican of light skin, Gerry Alexander, declared that he should no longer be captain of the West Indies, but the black Barbadian Frank Worrell should. What is even more, when Worrell was appointed, Alexander served as his vice-captain and wicketkeeper. Their working together helped to make the Australia v West Indies series of 1960–61 the most exciting there had been, outside the Ashes at any rate, energising the whole of cricket after its dullest decade.

The nearest I came to meeting Worrell, who died of leukaemia in 1967, was in the archives of *The Observer*. He started writing for the newspaper in 1961, on England's home series against Australia, the summer after he had become a world figure. While I was researching among back copies of *The Observer* in a basement in Battersea, out of the dust emerged a photograph of Worrell. It had been taken by Jane Bown, short, slight and known as 'the Gentle Eye', but steely. She would disappear in the room where her subject was sitting, like a bird perching in the branches. Only when the subject had relaxed into being his natural self would she click her shutter.

Bown's black-and-white photograph of Worrell is as insightful as a portrait in oils. He has a moustache, a thin and discreet one, clipped well above the upper lip: he is differing from clean-shaven convention, but ever so slightly. He has high cheekbones, and eyelashes which curl up and around: when his grandmother brought him up in Barbados, he must have been the apple of her eye. After West Indies had won their first Test series in England in 1950, and Worrell had been chosen as one of *Wisden's* Five Cricketers of the Year, the editor Hubert Preston alluded to a 'dreamy casualness', before concluding: 'For beauty of stroke no one in the history of the game can have excelled Worrell.'

Bown has captured the inner strength, of unblinking conviction, beneath the calm. If Worrell's captaincy was anything like his writing, it had the quiet firmness of an authority you would not think to question. There was no more informed observer of one of the most historic days in English cricket, and probably the most traumatic: the last day of the Ashes Test of 1961 at Old Trafford, when England sailed to 150 for one in pursuit of 256 and a 2–1 lead, then collapsed. In his *Observer* column the following Sunday, Worrell observed that Peter May, England's captain, had been at fault for taking off David Allen after Alan Davidson had hit his off-spin for 20 from one over; but May was not at fault for trying to sweep Richie Benaud when he was bowling round the wicket. Worrell wrote that he had never seen Benaud bowl better; that Fred Trueman's running down the pitch had disadvantaged England because they had more left-handed batsmen than any other country; and that Brian Close's innings was the turning point. 'A more unorthodox exhibition will surely never again be seen in Test cricket': a prophecy that has not been obviously overtaken more than half a century later.

It was only when I interviewed his wife, Velda, Lady Worrell, that I found out that Worrell had first been selected for Barbados as a left-arm spinner, and had batted at number 11. Even in the 1940s, it was so much easier for a black cricketer to be selected as a bowler than a batsman – even a player whose beauty of stroke would not be excelled. Like the other two Ws, Sir Everton Weekes and Sir Clyde Walcott, he had been born within a mile or so of Kensington Oval, and had sunshine and space in which to learn the game. The difference between them was that Worrell had a rebellious streak, and no parents to crush it, because like so many people in the West Indies they had to emigrate to find a job. Worrell, too, had to emigrate, not a prophet in his own land.

An iron fist in a velvet glove: this was the verdict of more than one of Worrell's contemporaries. A pivotal decision was to drop the white Barbadian wicketkeeper David Allan for the 1963 series in England and replace him with the 20-year-old Trinidadian Deryck Murray. It could be argued, and was argued by some of Worrell's Barbadian contemporaries, that this decision was racist; and no doubt Allan in 1963 was the better wicketkeeper. On the other hand, Murray was always going to be a better batsman, and he held his end up in 1963, and he set a record for the most dismissals in a series by a West Indian wicketkeeper. And Murray is predominantly Indian.

West Indian cricket flowered under Worrell's captaincy as never before: 'exuberance' and 'flair' became the conventional epithets. The 1950s had been the slowest-scoring decade in Test cricket – Len

Hutton the pioneer of slow over-rates, it has to be admitted – and West Indies, before Worrell took over, followed suit. In the 1959–60 series at home to England, West Indies scored at 2.3 runs per over: not much self-expression by Rohan Kanhai or Garfield Sobers or Worrell himself. In the Bridgetown Test, Sobers and Worrell batted together for two whole days, like no pair before or since, and they added 'only' 399 runs. Once Worrell was captain, 'Calypso Cricket' took over.

Sobers was inspired by Worrell to become the finest all-round cricketer ever. The numbers are merely a confirmation: his Test batting average was 23 points higher than his bowling average, 57 to 34; and if you add the two series in which he captained the Rest of the World in England and Australia, Sobers scored 8961 runs at 58.18 and took 265 wickets at 33.53. Jacques Kallis of South Africa would come next in many estimations, but he would have had to bowl off-spin and wrist-spin, in addition to his other accomplishments, to match Sobers.

Worrell not only batted, but bowled left-arm pace and finger-spin – yet Sobers was still more versatile. Cricket's Bob Beamon moment has not been sufficiently recognised: it came after Sobers had been signed by Sir Donald Bradman to play for South Australia. In ten first-class matches in 1962–63, he did the double of 1000 runs and 50 wickets, and repeated it in only nine matches in 1963–64. Nobody else has come close to accomplishing this double in Australia, even all these years later, with the number of matches increased. After starting as an orthodox left-arm spinner like Worrell, then taking up pace bowling to get a job in Lancashire's leagues, Sobers chose wrist-spin in Adelaide, consistently the truest batting surface in the game worldwide.

Although Worrell anointed him as his successor, Sobers was human when it came to captaincy. Worrell could not have foreseen that English county cricket would be opened to overseas players in 1968, so they no longer had to qualify by residence, and that Sobers would start to play all year round and lose his enthusiasm. When

West Indies lost 3–1 in Australia under Sobers in 1968–69, the captain spent his spare time on the golf course.

Bown photographed him too, and while the two Barbadians had so many features in common, an inner strength of conviction was not one. Sobers had pride in his people: when South Australia played the South Africans in 1963–64, he put on his West Indian cap and marked apartheid's first encounter with a black West Indian by scoring a century. He announced in the dressing room that he wanted the South Africans to have 'a nice long look' at his maroon cap. But Sobers was no politician, and was gullible enough to play in Southern Rhodesia, unaware he would be condemned by people and governments back home.

The next and final incremental step in West Indian cricket would have to come from elsewhere. Not from Barbados, where the three Cs – Christianity, conservatism and cricket – lived together in a comfort zone. But from an island where the coral was mixed with something no less elemental.

Viv Richards was the most charismatic cricketer I have seen.

He was the most charismatic because he had the greatest sense of mission or purpose. His mission was to change the perception of, and attitude to, West Indians in general and Afro-Caribbeans in particular. Nobody in cricket has effected more change, for the better, than Richards. The one person to approach him is Basil D'Oliveira, of South Africa by birth and upbringing and England by adoption. Both fundamentally altered the mentality of white people, especially in Britain, towards non-white people: very few have done it to the same extent in any walk of life. Richards brought about this change intentionally; D'Oliveira accidentally, although when he became the central figure in the fight against apartheid in South Africa, he was not found wanting.

THE LONG STROLL TO FREEDOM

Basil D'Oliveira was unknown outside the Cape Coloured community when he left South Africa in early 1960 to become a professional cricketer in England. He had written to John Arlott, who had fixed him up with the job of pro at Middleton in the Central Lancashire League.

He made a bad start. Cold, lonely, and exposed to grassy pitches after having learned a back-foot game on matting, D'Oliveira was on the verge of despair after failing in his early games for Middleton. But he fought and persevered, the runs flowed, and he secured the highest batting average among the professionals in his league, higher than Garfield Sobers, and won himself a contract for two more seasons.

So when he returned home in September 1960, he was not a star in the eyes of Dr Verwoerd's government, which had just perpetrated the Sharpeville Massacre – quite the opposite. But in the eyes of many people in his native Cape Town he had, by proving himself through sport, done something quite heroic.

After his ship had docked, there was 'a tremendous reception on his arrival and [D'Oliveira] was driven in an open car headed by a pipe band to the city Hall,' according to the *Cape Argus* on 22 September 1960. There, he was received by the mayor, Mrs J. Newton Thompson, the first female mayor of Cape Town. She was 'one of the most publicised mayors in Cape Town's history – and one of the best', according to 'The Wanderer' in the newspaper's diary of 23 September.

D'Oliveira declared modestly on his return: 'I did not expect to get as far as I did in my first season and despite my success I still have a long way to go before I master the English playing conditions.'

Unlike many a professional sportsman, he thought not only of himself. He had recommended another member of his community, Cecil Abrahams, to another club in the Central Lancashire League, Milnrow, and Abrahams had been accepted for the season of 1961. 'But he will have to get his wickets in the first six or seven overs when the shine is still on the ball,' added D'Oliveira the cricketer.

What there was by way of a politician in him, after being brought up to have no such thoughts, then gave the pot a little stir. 'What I would like to see is a series of matches played in South Africa between White and non-White Springbok teams,' D'Oliveira was quoted in the *Cape Argus* as saying. The language of apartheid said it all: 'white' had to have a capital letter.

'Or, better still, to improve our cricket standard, a series of matches between mixed White and non-White Springbok teams,' D'Oliveira went on. 'Whether there is any possibility of this I can't say.'

He was not without support in some higher places. The president of the Western Province Board of Control, Mr J. van Harte, gave a welcoming speech in which he said that D'Oliveira 'had set a stirring example not only to Western Province cricketers but to sportsmen throughout South Africa . . . I hope the time is not too distant when all non-White cricketers in the Union will have a chance to get to the top.'

In reply, D'Oliveira said: 'I must warn them [i.e. future players who go to England] that it is not an easy task to adjust oneself to English conditions and to the fact that there is no colour bar.' The most pointed of his stories was about the time he got on a train in England for the first time and, search and search though he did, could not find a carriage for non-whites.

The biggest privilege in my journalistic career was to accompany D'Oliveira on his first visit to Cape Town after the end of apartheid. He had initially done a deal with the *Daily Mirror*, to go back to his native city and give them his reminiscences for £1,500 – enough to cover his flight and some hotel nights. They pulled out, and the *Sunday Telegraph* stepped in to pay his costs. He might have raked in millions of dollars if someone had been alive to the wonderful film to be made of his life.

We walked around the streets of Bo-Kaap on the steep hillside overlooking Green Point; it was on the more horizontal ones that D'Oliveira had started to play cricket with other boys labouring under the same disadvantages. The Cape Coloured community had been ordered to live there. 'Best place to live in Cape Town,' he said, not burning at the injustices inflicted by apartheid, but amused at how its authorities could be so stupid. (It was alchohol that made him burn with injustice.)

I did not think it right to trouble him with questions as he walked along the street of his childhood home, which he had not seen for decades – the same measured, immensely dignified walk, virtually a stroll, that had taken him out to the middle at Lord's in 1966, when he had become the first non-white South African to represent England, and had been applauded to the echo.

But I could not help asking him about how old he really was. He had always given his date of birth as 1931. He would not have been selected for Middleton, let alone Worcestershire and England, if he had been known to be older.

He said his actual age was more than two years more than the official one. I pressed, but he would not go further, and my final impression was that it was somewhere between three and five years more. If so, among his achievements, it is noteworthy that he was skilled enough to represent England in 1972 in his mid-forties, and Worcestershire until 1979, when he would have been over 50.

Alzheimer's and Parkinson's ultimately claimed him. He ended up in a nursing home in Worcester, speaking his first language of Afrikaans, recognising nobody except his wife, Naomi. But, by then, millions of people had recognised 'Dolly' as the pivotal figure in the fight for humanity in South Africa and the boycott which brought apartheid to an official end.

When Richards walked out to bat, his head told much of the story. His eyes did not look at the ground; if he deigned to look at an opponent, it was down his aquiline nose. He would wear his maroon West Indies cap, or bat bare-headed. Never did he wear a helmet, as all other of his contemporaries stooped to do. Either the cap or his bare head: one or other was his crown.

After winning the preliminary skirmish of eye contact by staring the bowler down, nonchalantly chewing his gum, Richards squared up. He would take on, for preference, the most threatening bowler. After his front leg had advanced down the pitch – before the first ball had landed – the ball did not seem to be alone in being whipped through midwicket.

As a fellow Antiguan, Tim Hector saw the beginning of Richards's career. Hector, indeed, contributed significantly to it. Before the combined Leeward and Windward Islands were given first-class status in the late sixties, Antigua's cricketers had no platform other than club games and an annual tournament, lasting a week, of two-day matches against Montserrat, Nevis and St Kitts. Hector expanded these into four-day matches, giving Richards and his contemporaries the chance to 'bat time' and make big hundreds, so they were prepared for the transition to first-class cricket. The Combined Islands had no formal coach, no money to sign an experienced batsman, just a tradition of being neglected by the West Indies Cricket Board; they had to use their own resources and learn for themselves.

'Something of the passion and intensity with which Viv Richards played cricket was entirely a Leewards phenomenon,' Hector wrote before his death in 2002. 'It was the same with Andy Roberts, only that Andy Roberts, like Richie Richardson, was more shaped by the Puritan tradition, which masks passionate intensity beneath what the French would call *sang froid*.' Hector went on to claim that Richards, as captain of the West Indies, never lost a Test series 'because the Afro/Indian people of the English-speaking Caribbean needed these triumphs to negate their marginalization in global history, trade and politics. To Viv Richards more so, cricket and anti-apartheid struggle were inseparable. West Indies against all comers, particularly England and Australia was, to him, an extension of the struggle against apartheid. It was a consciously held view by Isaac Vivian Alexander Richards, and it was consciously executed. Therein lies his immortality. Not the first man of pan-African views to lead the West Indies. Worrell was. But the first West Indian captain to see cricket and to play cricket with the view uppermost that cricket played by West Indians was part and parcel of the global struggle against racism and, in particular, apartheid. This was Viv Richards.'

But while I could see where Richards was heading, I did not know – even with Hector's help – where he came from. I saw Antigua taken over by mass celebrations when the island staged its first Test match in 1981 and Richards his wedding a couple of days before. I saw that Antigua, one big sugar plantation until after the Second World War, no longer grew a single cane – whereas neighbouring Francophone islands like Marie-Galante still happily grew sugar and drank its rum. I heard that Antiguan men were renowned, even among fellow West Indians, as the prickliest in the Caribbean. But for a long time I did not understand.

Richards himself never met Papa Sammy, who died at the age of 105 in 1982. But he knew and liked Papa Sammy's grandson, Keithlyn Smith, who listened to the stories about Antigua that his grandfather told him, memorised them and later wrote them down for the book *To Shoot Hard Labour*. Keithlyn Smith worked in Antigua's trades union movement and opposed the dynasty of Vere and Lester Bird that channelled arms to apartheid South Africa. After the Bird dynasty had gone, to be followed by their notorious business partner Allen Stanford, Keithlyn Smith became Antigua's ambassador at large and was knighted, without forgetting his roots. He was still living in his bungalow in Freeman's Village, after retiring as an ambassador, when I last met him.

What happened in Antigua after the Emancipation Act of 1834 happened, in effect, behind closed doors. If, in Barbados, women and children lent some kind of civilising influence to the sugar plantations as resident members of the planters' families, the planters who lived in Antigua were very few, and they usually appointed an overseer to crack the whip while they enjoyed the profits back in Britain. Nobody acted as a conscience when the gibbets around the island swayed with 'strange fruit'.

Papa Sammy did not recount his memories to his grandson in a spirit of bitterness. He kept on working on the plantations far longer than he had to, until he was 85, and claimed he did not take a single day off sick in 72 years. He simply told it how it was: how conditions did not perceptibly improve after the Emancipation Act until well into the twentieth century. The branding of slaves ceased in 1828, but that did not mean a black Antiguan was allowed his own identity.

Using the term 'bakkra' for plantation owners, 'nega' for people like himself, and 'picknee' for children, Papa Sammy recalled: 'Back then nega picknee carry the name of the estate owner. That practice live on a long time after slavery end. People seriously had the feeling that the child belong to the bakkra and the mother would usually take the child to the massa. In most cases, it would be massa that name the baby. The man that was the rightful father couldn't have nothing to do with the child.' So Papa Sammy recounted to his grandson.

Why did these ex-slaves not leave a brutal plantation and

transfer to another? 'Things was not as easy as that. A nega-house man could not live on another estate if he offend even one planter. If one planter tell him to leave, the others would usually refuse to let him work and live on their plantation, and that poor fellow wouldn't have had a place to turn to for a long, long time. Dog better than he when that happen.

'The conditions of the houses rapidly run down after the Emancipation even though they were strongly built. The normal size house was about sixty feet long by forty feet wide . . . Nothing to separate one family from the other. We use to live together like a flock of cattle, like goats or sheep in a pen. The truth is, there was no difference to speak of between the life of the animals and ours . . . Rats, mice, spiders, centipedes, scorpions and other crea-tures also lived in the houses.'

We British pride ourselves on having liberated slaves before the French or Spanish. We like to think that ending the slave trade was tantamount to ending slavery; we give ourselves a pat on the back while singing 'Amazing Grace'. But emancipation was as much a matter of economics as conscience. Paying a wage to the plantation workers cost the owner less than feeding, clothing and housing slaves – especially if they started a company store where the work-ers had to spend their wages.

Why didn't these 'emancipated' slaves fight back? According to the census of 1844, Antigua had 36,178 inhabitants, of whom 323 had the vote, which suggests the ratio of black to white was about a hundred to one. 'No way for us to fight back – it was like worm going against nest of ants – for the bakkra was the militia and the magistrates and the jail-house and the government. Whatever happen to us, we must grunt and bear it. If you didn't have manners, them give you the cat-o-nine and them hang you in jail. Nothing for it. You dead and gone. Them give you coffin and that's that.'

In that case, why didn't these 'emancipated' slaves simply leave the estates? Some did. They set up villages, like Liberta and Freeman's Village, but how do you build a house when neither you nor anybody you know has got a nail – a house that is not blown away in hurricanes? But hunger was the main deterrent from leaving the estates. 'There was widespread hunger, there was starvation. I am not lying: there was not a single one of us that did not suffer terrible hunger.' Slaves had not been taught how to swim so, once freed, they could fish only from the shore. The soil in the West Indies was never so fertile as Columbus made out, as he omitted to mention wind erosion in his reports to venture capitalists in Europe; and drought was frequent in Antigua after the native forest had been cut down to make way for cane.

Papa Sammy got his first job on the sugar estate at North Sound, where the Sir Vivian Richards Stadium was opened for the World Cup in 2007. It was a cricket ground Antiguans were loath to attend, and which seemed cursed when the 2009 Test match against England had to be called off after ten balls because of the unfit outfield. Never had it been happy place. 'One of the first things I learnt at North Sound was that we could not talk to each other at work. As soon as you reach the estate's works all talk must stop. In fact, gathering together was strictly not allowed. If massa would see us talking, we have to say what the talk was about.' So much for free speech after 1834.

'One morning after the roll call, we have to wait for orders from the planter in charge of the gang. While we were there waiting, Massa Hinds youngest boy, Ralph, starts to imitate his father and goes calling our names. Everybody answer like usual, until he gets to Harty Bab. At least she didn't answer, "Yes, Massa." Now Massa Hinds was close by, and he tell her that she was marked absent for not answering. He say she disrespect his son and she was not going to get pay for that day. Then he further accuse her of grumbling bad words at him. In the end he so annoyed he decide to lash her with a cart whip. When he try this, she resist him, but that didn't last for too long for she was over-powered and he beat her mercilessly. Then he forced her into the estate cellar where he leave her locked up for some days.

'When he give the order to release her, she was dead. Rats had bitten off her lips and nose . . . I was at that cellar and saw the body. I'll never forget that day. I was fifteen years old and still in the small gang, doing a man's job for a boy's pay.' Papa Sammy later heard the magistrate's verdict: Harty Bab had died of 'misadventure'. So much for the system of justice after 1834.

The established Church did not offer much consolation. When the North Sound planters went to St George's, they often used their workers not their horses to pull the buggy. On arrival, the workers were not allowed to wait near the church, let alone in it. Having cleansed his soul, the master would ring a bell when ready to go home. This was happening no less than six decades after the Emancipation Act.

Even after the First World War, living conditions for plantation workers did not improve noticeably. It was as late as 1918 that black Antiguans held their first meeting. 'This was the first of that kind of meeting to happen in the island in my time. Except for church service, you couldn't hold any meeting in this island.' The issue was that 'house-negas' who farmed a piece of land on an estate did not receive full payment for the sugar they grew: the factory paid the estate owner instead, and he took a sizable cut before passing on the rest to his workers. The reprisals for holding this meeting were savage. The Riot Act was read. People were shot by the militia. Well into the twentieth century, the system had not even begun to relent.

Governors of Antigua who did not side with the plantocracy

tended to be recalled, after lobbying in London. One who did care about the people managed to stay from 1921 to 1929: Eustace Fiennes, according to Papa Sammy, was the best governor Antigua had in his lifetime. Not his successor, though: 'Under Governor St Johnson there was no work. Everything crash. People min a dead for hungry [people died from starvation]. Nineteen thirty-four came, the one hundredth anniversary of the end of slavery. It should have been a time for cele-bration, a time for joy, but there was nothing to jump for. Most of the people were still living in misery on the estates and one hundred years after slavery the living conditions on the estates was no better than during slavery time. The bakkra neglect our people except when they go to jail. When that happen, the bakkra always make sure them wasn't neglected by the full weight of the law.'

Not until the Second World War, when the first trade union was organised, did workers on the estates get paid in full for what they grew. And even then a worker still could not move from one estate to another without the owner's permission: a woman who tried was given six days' hard labour.

The leader of the white planters, Alexander Moody-Stuart, with-drew recognition of the trade union in 1951. 'The union hit back by calling a general strike. It was head on strike between the planters and the union. War between Moody-Stuart and the union. Antigua hot like fire. The people was behind the union. Moody-Stuart said he was going to starve out the people. The fight was on. There were violence here and there. Some buildings in St John's was set ablaze. Governor Blackburne got afraid the thing would get out of hand and he called in the British fleet from Jamaica.'

Into this crucible, in the following year of 1952, Vivian Richards was born. No wonder he was, to borrow the phrase of Papa Sammy, 'hot like fire'.

Like most of the great West Indian cricketers, Richards came from
what could be called the lower middle class; only the occasional
fast bowler has come from the masses. His father was a warder at
the prison in St John's, next to the Recreation Ground. His elder
brother Donald tried politics and was a founder of the Afro-
Caribbean Movement in Antigua. The music industry in Antigua
was tiny, so Viv Richards chose the only other viable, non-violent
means of effecting change.

'The body belonging to the oppressed is a powerful means of
communication,' wrote Professor Rex Nettleford, artistic director
of the National Dance Theatre in Jamaica, for another essay in *A
Spirit of Dominance*, 'and personal control over it places it beyond
the reach of the oppressor. Cricketers and dancers without a
command of the scribal language can nonetheless communicate.'
As he grew up, Richards communicated.

Richards's younger brother Mervin has explained the origin of
the stroke that must have demoralised more bowlers than any
other. 'We used to play in a park where straight shots were not
advised. There used to be a fisherman who used to stand behind
the bowler's arm and every time you hit it to him he used to cut the
ball in half and throw it back. So we needed to hit it to midwicket.
And Viv mastered it.' What is implied here is no less significant: Viv
Richards had no formal coaching. He learned for himself to take a
pace forward and whip the ball with a vertical bat through
midwicket. Given a blank sheet of paper, he stamped on it his
indelible mark.

Some cricketers have been labelled great without making a side
stronger than when they first played in it. Richards's mission
was to exalt those of low degree, and he transformed five sides:
for the sixth that he represented, Queensland, he played only a

handful of games. No other cricketer, by my reckoning, has transformed so many teams. Perceptions, social attitudes, and teams.

Combined Islands was the first team that Richards exalted, in conjunction with Andy Roberts, whose fast bowling ensured that Richards's runs were not wasted. When Richards made his first-class debut for Combined Islands, the new team had played a dozen games in the Shell Shield as the poor relation of Barbados, Guyana, Jamaica and Trinidad. The impact of Richards was immediate, although he was only 19. He top-scored in one innings or the other of his first and second first-class matches for Combined Islands.

As he began to play for West Indies, Richards played less for the Combined Islands, but in 1980–81 he captained them to their first Shell Shield. His habit was to make his first innings of a competition or series a statement of his intent; and here he scored 168 out of his team's 317 in Trinidad, who fielded three international spinners. In the second match he contributed a century, and Roberts seven for 30, to an innings win over Jamaica. Even when he did not score runs, Richards competed and contributed, whether bowling flat off-spin, or clapping his hands at second slip, or swooping at midwicket, where he ran out three Australians in the 1975 World Cup final. Yet some modern batsmen have been labelled great even though they have disappeared for hours at a time in the field.

West Indies were the second team transformed by Richards. After Worrell had retired, they had gone up and down under Sobers and Rohan Kanhai, but they were never so down as in 1975–76 when they lost 5–1 in Australia under Clive Lloyd. Amidst this wreckage Richards stood up to fight. 'Overall there was a distinct lack of effort by their players . . . Richards was the exception,' *Wisden* reported. 'After losing so disappointingly in Sydney all the fight had gone out of the West Indies.' Richards got himself promoted from number five, too low for a great batsman to shape events, to open the batting. He began with two centuries in a first-class game against Tasmania, top-scored in three of his next four Test innings with 30, 101, 50 and 98, and went on to score more Test runs in the calendar year of 1976 than anyone ever before. Never again would a West Indian team containing Richards fail to fight.

This fight was nearly literal on one tour of Australia. The worst feature of Australian cricket has been the racist abuse by their players, which came to a height in the 1980s. Richards confronted it head-on during a game in Sydney while he was batting. He challenged any opponent who made another racist remark to a fight outside the ground at the end of play. Nobody cared to enter the ring with a young Joe Frazier. The attitude of Australian players to non-white opponents was forced to change.

Richards formed, if not transformed, another team when World Series Cricket was promoted by Kerry Packer from 1977 to 1979. When WSC West Indies played Supertests against WSC Australia, he top-scored in the first three innings and propelled his team to victory in the first two matches; and top-scored with a century in the third. The world's best fast bowlers queued up to be paid properly for the first time, and tore in on untried surfaces such as VFL Park in Melbourne, when cricket switched on flood-lights for the first time. Everyone bowed his head to wear a helmet, except Richards.

Taking over from Lloyd for the 1985–86 home series against England, Richards captained West Indies in 50 Tests without losing a series. True, he was blessed with great fast bowlers – one way in which the past had worked in his favour – and he may have been too much of a martinet at times. The Antiguan all-rounder Eldine Baptiste told me he had been reduced to tears in the captain's room one day, then pumped with pride in himself and Antigua and West Indies. Baptiste played only ten Tests yet won every one, uniquely.

Richards rounded off his first series as captain with the fastest Test century recorded in terms of balls received.* West Indies were 4–0 up and they were not going to ease off at the Antigua Recreation Ground. To set up a second-innings declaration, against a presentable if not powerful England attack, Richards hit a century off 56 balls, treating them like net bowlers. Once he had set this world record, he declared and sauntered back towards the pavilion. He could not claim, like Jack with his house, that he had built the Recreation Ground, although his father used to prepare its pitches with the aid of prisoners. But he, along with Roberts, had put Antigua on the map.

Some batsmen, in those days before big money, used to run the last few yards back into the pavilion after a century: they were amateurs modestly representing their country. Richards did the opposite. Halfway to the pavilion he halted, for a moment, and looked ahead. The crowd was going wild with adulation. Antiguans were no longer oppressed, as they had been only a generation before. West Indies were about to win 5–0, only the third time England had been whitewashed, and their own Viv Richards was captain. He had beaten the former masters, conclusively, at their own game. He had put his own distinctive stamp on West Indian cricket. He had proved not only that 'we' were as good as 'they'. Richards made West Indies the world champions of cricket for more than a decade.

All this Richards seemed to drink in while pausing. His saunter

* Pakistan's captain, Misbah-ul-Haq, equalled it against Australia at Abu Dhabi in November 2014.

was then resumed towards the pavilion and its celebrations. No man, of his time and place, could really have achieved more. He had put the words of his Jamaican contemporary Bob Marley into action. He had emancipated his people from mental slavery and freed their minds.

At the same time as he was transforming West Indies into world champions, Richards proved he was no racist by doing something similar to the small, white, conservative, agricultural backwater of Somerset. The county had never won a thing: third in the Championship was the best their limited resources and mindsets had ever attained. Richards could not win Somerset the Championship, which has remained elusive to this day, but he did win their first trophies. He dragged them through one-day knock-out matches at Taunton's rickety ground – the West Country equivalent of the Antigua Recreation Ground – and into the final at Lord's, where a century by Richards was almost as much a formality as it had been in the World Cup final of 1979.

The fifth and last team he transformed was Glamorgan. Before he arrived, the Welsh county was the laughing stock of English cricket for in-fighting and bad signings. When Glamorgan reached Canterbury in September 1993, they had been through what *Wisden* called '23 seasons of often abject failure'. They faced Kent in what was effectively the final of the Sunday League competition: Glamorgan went into this last game in second place, Kent in first, and the title would go to the team that won in front of the television cameras and a 12,000 crowd inundating the old ground. Chasing 200, Glamorgan were 98 for three when Richards went in. In a triumph of will as much as skill (he was 41), he scored an unbeaten 46 and led them over the line.

Almost as noteworthy was an incident in the County

Championship game into which this Sunday League match was sandwiched. Glamorgan fell 380 runs behind on first innings after a double century by Carl Hooper, yet Kent chose to bat a second time instead of enforcing the follow-on. Richards went mad on the balcony: this was not the way to play the game, he shouted at Kent's players. He had been brought up to respect and conform, by Bible-reading parents, not only to change and reform.

The very last time I saw Richards bat was in an exhibition of beach cricket organised by Antigua's tourist board. Most of us do not age gracefully; greatness can, even in a pair of shorts and T-shirt. Against a tennis ball, he obviously batted without gloves or helmet, and I saw this extraordinary sight. As the bowler ran in over the sands, Richards flexed his fingers on the bat handle like a concert pianist about to embark on a concerto, and he kept on flexing them until the ball had been bowled – and whipped through midwicket. I checked afterwards, and he said he had always done it, only these movements had never been visible inside his batting gloves. He was no bully or bruiser, except if fools needed to be bruised. Under the surface, Viv Richards was full of feeling.

|||

At Kensington Oval in Barbados in the 1980s, it was my observation that a higher proportion of the Test crowd was female than anywhere else. In Asia, from the time the Parsis faded until the Indian Premier League, females in the stands outside the VIP enclosure were scarce, if any. In England, a few women have always tagged along. Australian women and girls used to flock to a one-day international, especially a day-nighter, when cricket was cool, but not to a Test match.

No research was done about West Indian crowds until the history department of the University of the West Indies interviewed Barbadians after they had staged a mass boycott of the inaugural West Indies v South Africa Test at Bridgetown in 1991. (They found that the primary reason was political – South Africa had been restored to Test status too soon after apartheid – and that the omission of the Barbadian Anderson Cummins was secondary.) So I can only guess why Barbadian women in such large numbers used to line the wooden benches of the Kensington Stand and watch West Indies play.

They came by bus from the countryside to the main bus station in Bridgetown, and maybe did some shopping at the central market before walking on to the Oval. Saturday was their day out. Some must have been single mothers, after the father of their children had left home, perhaps to find work in North America or Britain. The magnetic line of the St Lucian poet Derek Walcott – 'There is too much nothing here' – can be taken to mean 'There is no lawful work to be had in the West Indies outside manual labour in the tourist industry.' Half of the West Indian population lives in diaspora.

These women came not merely to see West Indies win, but to watch these cricketers – their menfolk – walk, saunter, run, strut, throw, bat and bowl. Nettleford again, rhapsodically: 'The early West Indian cricketers, even when they were losing, were brashly and defiantly beautiful to behold! The celebration of the male body as hot-blooded power and authority in itself, as icon of athleticism, line and form, became a psychic threat to opponents in colder climes but a source of visual joy for West Indians, and especially for the tens of thousands of West Indian women whose love for, and expertise in the understanding of, this chauvinistically manly sport is nothing if not astounding.'

By the start of the twenty-first century, however, West Indian cricket was set in long-term decline. No infrastructure had been installed by the West Indies Cricket Board to cater for the drying-up

of the stream of great players. Two board members from each territory continued to represent the interests of each territory, at a
considerable cost in travel expenses and per diem allowances.
Together they allowed the pitches of the region to become slow; in
fact, for commercial reasons, they encouraged groundsmen to slow
down the Test pitches from the late 1980s, to make the games last
five days. So Courtney Walsh told me, and he had to bowl on them
for more than a decade before he broke the world record for Test
wickets.* For short-term gain, the West Indian board sowed the
seeds of their sport's decline. The finest features of Caribbean
cricket were now discouraged: the fast bowlers and the batsmen
who would take them on.

In 2004 in Jamaica, on a fast yet true pitch at Sabina Park, West
Indies were dismissed by England for 47. Steve Harmison blew
away seven wickets for 12 runs as emphatically as if he had been
Curtly Ambrose or Malcolm Marshall in their prime. The second
Test, in Port-of-Spain, was attended by the Rolling Stone Mick
Jagger. He visited the Trini Posse Stand and sang for them during
play. Other spectators in the small, desultory crowd joined in singing the lyric 'Can't get no satisfaction.' West Indian cricket was
playing to its own rhythms no longer.

Society in the West Indies was unravelling, as it was globally,
yet perhaps faster. The street was no longer the place for a piece
of wood and a taped tennis ball, but for hanging around, unemployed. Cricket had been cool when a player could have himself
a good time in county or league cricket in England and make
some decent money. Not any more. Cricket became another
sport, not the medium of West Indian self-expression. The
physical body was no longer 'oppressed'; no cricketer was 'hot

* An interview at Lord's, September 2011, before the Lord's Taverners dinner for the
Greatest Fast Bowlers.

like fire'. The message, if not fully enacted, had been articulated and delivered.

Small is weak in the global economy, but even its one advantage was wasted. In an island where everyone knows everyone or his or her cousin, mentoring should be easy – whether the system is official or not, whether the former greats are paid to keep an eye on youngsters or not. The first professional coach in the West Indies that I know of was employed by a sugar company in British Guiana in the 1950s. To all intents, West Indies became world champions in the 1960s without any coaching, and again in the 1980s. The mentoring of junior players by senior players was sufficient. Pakistan in the 1980s was similar: the two regions of the world that played the most exciting cricket effectively had no coaching.

Yet while there was 'too much nothing' in the Caribbean in general, what West Indian cricket had in abundance was wasted. In the Kolkata Test of November 2011, the West Indian fast bowler Kemar Roach had India's captain Mahendra Singh Dhoni caught behind off a no-ball when he had scored nine, and again when he had scored 16 off another no-ball. Dhoni not only went on to make a century but to trash the bowling. India passed 600 before declaring and winning by an innings.

Andy Roberts told me that earlier in the year, when West Indies had played in Antigua, he had asked permission from the team management to speak to Roach. The young Barbadian had pace, real pace, but Roberts thought his delivery stride was too long and wanted to talk to him about it. Roberts, the father of modern West Indian fast bowling, was refused permission. A few months after that Kolkata Test, in the Trent Bridge Test of May 2012, Roach again overstepped and had England's opening batsman Alastair Cook caught behind off a no-ball, twice.

West Indies in effect went back to where they started. They

settled in as eighth and last of the traditional nations in the Test rankings, ahead of only Bangladesh and Zimbabwe. In these extreme circumstances, their cricket fell back on their redoubt of Barbados, there to watch, wait and, let us hope, re-group with a new generation. Barbados had the same role to play as Yorkshire when England were in trouble, and Sydney when Australia were.

Ultimately, however, we should not wonder at West Indian cricket becoming so moderate, but at its once having been so magnificent.

This distinction was the thing.

6

HE BABBLED
OF GREEN FIELDS

*What was exquisite and memorable was the lyric move-
ment of the artist in action.*

Denzil Batchelor, on the England batsman C.B. Fry

He bowled like the devil.

Mike Selvey, on the West Indies fast bowler Patrick Patterson

GRAHAM GOOCH EMERGES from England's dressing room at the bottom of the George Headley Stand in Kingston at 10.20 a.m. on Friday, 21 February 1986, and walks up to the raised platform where players can see the field. He puts down his white helmet, bat and gloves to listen to music on his earphones before England open the Test series against West Indies.

Dire Straits would be appropriate.

England's captain, David Gower, on winning the toss, has decided to bat first because he feels he *has* to bat rather than because he wants to. Like most pitches, the one at Sabina Park is expected to get worse as the game goes on. Unlike most Test pitches, this one does not look sound at the start.

In the previous Test England played in Jamaica, in 1981, Gooch and Gower both hit centuries of 150-plus on an old-style belter. It was so shiny the batsman could see his shadow.

This time, one of the England batsmen in Gower's squad looks as though he is wearing dark glasses to combat the shine. But the pitch has changed a lot. The darkness on Mike Gatting's face has been caused by something more immediate.

At 10.28 a.m. Gooch hands his earphones and cassette recorder to Peter Willey, who is down to bat at number seven. He walks out alongside his partner, Tim Robinson, then ahead to the far end, to receive the first ball of the series from Malcolm Marshall. Nobody disputes that Marshall is the best bowler in the world at the moment. Has there ever been a better fast bowler?

The omens for this series have not been encouraging for England. The third ball of their tour hit Gooch on the helmet and rocketed skywards. It was delivered by the left-arm medium-pacer Desmond Collymore of the Windward Islands on a pitch in St Vincent that had started damp. It had been prepared by prisoners at the gaol in Arnos Vale, and they were said to be getting their own back with a spot of grievous bodily harm.

Gooch's helmet has no metal bars or plastic visor: he has rejected both options on grounds of weight. His teammate Allan Lamb, another renowned for his bravery against fast bowling, had also brought a helmet without visor or bars, but after being pounded by Jamaica's Courtney Walsh in the third and last warm-up game, Lamb added the bars. Gooch and Gatting went into the internationals with the helmets they had.

Before this tour, Gooch had carefully reassessed the rest of his equipment, to prepare for an attack by four outright fast bowlers. From the start of the 1985 season, he had worn special pads made for him by his former Essex teammate Rodney Cass, which were half the normal weight. To his batting gloves Gooch had added an extra layer of protection, coloured green, to the index and middle fingers of his right hand – the two most vulnerable. On his left forearm he wore a protector held in place by two sweatbands.

In that first warm-up game, to make up for the pitch, Arnos Vale had offered the most beautiful backdrop of any first-class ground I had seen: the island of Bequia across the sparkling waters of the Caribbean. But when Gooch had faced up to the bowling from the Bequia end, he saw a tramp steamer anchored behind the sightscreen. There would have been some delay if the umpires had suspended play while ordering the ship's captain to get steam up and move. Here was the second omen.

Three days before the first Test at Sabina Park, in the first one-day international on the same ground, came the third. Gatting – no visor, no bars – had his nose broken by a ball that kicked off the uneven surface. Marshall, the unwitting perpetrator, had wheeled away in horror. Gordon Greenidge had scratched at the pitch like a frantic chicken to remove the blood. A piece of bone or cartilage was reported to have been found in the ball. Gatting had been advised to fly back to London for surgery, but first he had to wait for the bruising to subside. Hence the England player in what appeared to be dark glasses.

Before the series, the West Indian selectors had been looking for a fourth fast bowler to partner Marshall, Joel Garner and Michael Holding. They had an embarrassment of riches, even though Sylvester Clarke, Colin Croft, Ezra Moseley and several others had been banned for going on a rebel tour of apartheid South Africa. Other candidates were queuing up in a plenitude that no Test team has enjoyed before or since. Walsh had given England a taste of the refined threat of short-pitched fast bowling from round the wicket; Trinidad had Tony Gray; St Vincent had Winston Davis; tiny Antigua alone boasted Winston Benjamin and George Ferris. All were straining at the leash to win a place in the West Indies team or, at least, a contract with an English county. All had been over-looked in favour of someone still more fearsome.

In what had been scheduled as a four-day game at Sabina Park a month before the first Test, Patrick Patterson had blown away Guyana in a single spell of seven wickets for 24 runs. Guyana had been dismissed for 41, the lowest total ever recorded in the Shell Shield. Holding, Jamaica's captain, did not even get a bowl.

Patterson, aged 24, was not from the conventional mould of Jamaican cricketers – not from Kingston or Spanish Town, not from the middle or lower-middle classes. He was from the east coast of Jamaica, 'the real Jamaaaica', far removed from the capital and the tourist beaches of the north-west coast. It was no coincidence he had sprung from the same background as Roy Gilchrist, who had terrified batsmen in the 1950s with his bouncers and beamers until he had been banned from Test cricket.

Patterson had been born and schooled in Happy Grove, ten miles north of Morant Bay. In the 1980s, the courthouse in Morant Bay looked exactly as it had when it had been the focus of the British Empire. Riots had broken out in 1865 on a scale unknown in Jamaica. Paul Bogle, a black Baptist minister, had called for an improvement in working conditions for the masses. Governor Eyre had retaliated by having Bogle tried and hanged in that very courthouse. More than a century later, judges in antiquated robes still sat in judgment over young men with incomprehension in their sullen eyes.

After being selected in the West Indies squad for the first one-day international and first Test, Patterson stayed with his elder brother in downtown Kingston. From the team hotel in the des-res suburbs in the foothills of the Blue Mountains, the sports photographer for *The Observer*, Adrian Murrell, and I shared a taxi. We figured we would be safe as soon as we reached the area where the Pattersons lived. Nobody would mess with them.

Patrick, taciturn yet amenable, posed for a photograph – first with his shirt on, then without a shirt, exhibiting the upper body of a heavyweight boxer like Joe Frazier or Sonny Liston. In the first one-day international Patterson took a wicket with his fourth and eighth balls for West Indies. England, in 46 overs of the heaviest going, scored 145 for the loss of eight batsmen – long-term in the case of Gatting. It had not been a match-winning total.

║

Gooch takes guard from the Barbadian umpire David Archer, who is standing at the Headley Stand end. Archer is relatively experienced for the period before professional umpires outside England: this is his 15th Test. His colleague Johnny Gayle is in his third and has never officiated in a Test outside Jamaica. When it comes to intimidation, England can realistically look only to Archer for protection. The current Laws allow any number of bouncers in an over, up to six if so desired.

It is quiet before the cyclone.

But warning signs are instantly apparent, like palm trees beginning to bend.

Marshall opens the attack, sprinting in, pigeon-toed, to four slips and Garner in the gully, and his first ball lifts sharply to beat Gooch.

The pitch is grassy. Clippings have been rolled in – it is not natural grass binding the surface. The second ball is short. Gooch fends it down to Desmond Haynes hovering at short-leg.

Already Gooch has seen enough to judge the amount of new-ball bounce. He lets Marshall's third ball, pitching on the short side before cutting back, pass over his stumps. He gets off the mark when Marshall pitches up his sixth ball, with a single pushed wide of mid-on.

Garner, the fastest bowler over six and a half feet there had been, aims a fuller length and is perceptibly slower. Garner is on-driven for four by Gooch with the full face of his bat.

Marshall eases into his work, athlete that he is: bowling fast never seems to take much out of him. In his third over Gooch, after fending down another bouncer, turns a four behind square, and at the end of it wipes his head with the white towel he has tucked into his trousers. Kingston is already hot, and he has faced 23 of the 31 balls, as a senior partner should.

Marshall switches to round the wicket for his fourth over: cue an all-out bouncer assault. Gooch, the non-striker, ironically raises his arm for Robinson's benefit, as if the sightscreen could be adjusted to suit the batsman. But the screen at the Headley Stand end is a permanent one, and permanently too low. The hand of tall bowlers comes over the top of the screen, out of the background of spectators in the stand – and they are not wearing white clothes. England's management had complained after the match against Jamaica and the pounding by Walsh. The response of the Jamaican authorities was that nothing could be done because the seats above the screen had been sold.

To roars from his home crowd, Patterson replaces Marshall for the ninth over. It is time for 'Pattoo', their Pattoo.

The stomach upset Patterson had before the game has cleared up. What he has to do is find some rhythm before working up to full pace. Unlike Marshall, the physical effort he puts into bowling is manifest.

Off a long straight run, he storms towards the batsman, pumping every piston, like Sonny Liston, and hurls himself at the crease.

On reaching it, he heaves his left foot so high the batsman has a full view of Patterson's studs. The look on Patterson's face adds to the impression he gives the batsman.

Patterson wants to crush him.

Gooch, unperturbed outwardly, takes a two and a single off Patterson's first over in Test cricket. The drinks break is close at hand, after almost an hour's play, England unscathed.

But Patterson has time for a second over before the break. The first ball lifts and leaves Robinson. His sixth ball angles in at Robinson and follows him like a mugger. He is forced to steer it to first slip, where Greenidge traps his fingers in catching it low.

The eruption would make a seismometer spike. It is a weekday, money is tight as always in Kingston, the ground is little more than half-full, but throats roar and umbrellas, serving as parasols, wave like palms in a cyclone. When the roar starts to subside, conch shells reinforce it. England are on the ropes and it is Pattoo, their Pattoo, who is pinning them.

Speedometers to gauge Patterson's pace have yet to be invented. For *The Guardian*, the former England swing bowler Mike Selvey writes that Patterson 'bowled like the devil in front of his home crowd'.

As negative evidence, Gooch does not try to hook Patterson, not after Gatting had been skulled by Marshall in the one-dayer. Because Patterson is not swinging or seaming the ball, he is reminiscent of the first English express bowler, Charles Kortright of Essex, Gooch's county, back in the 1890s. A contemporary batsman, asked whether Kortright swung the ball, replied: 'No, there was no time for anything else.'

When two England subs trot out at the break, Gooch gulps two glasses of Gatorade supplied by Bruce French and takes a fresh left glove from Neil Foster. He pours water down the back of his neck while he waits for Gower, at number three, to join him. Gooch has scored 25 of England's 32 runs.

West Indies had begun with the all-Barbadian attack of Marshall and Garner, to be succeeded by the all-Jamaican attack of Holding and Patterson. The background behind Holding consists of the Blue Mountains and a popular stand where he is relished like the curried goat served in some stalls. The four West Indian fast bowlers are not only competing individually. Inter-island rivalry also spurs them.

Gower drops Patterson's first ball at his feet. He follows by upper-cutting him for six and four. Although Sabina's straight boundaries are short, here is further evidence of Patterson's mounting pace.

Holding at the other end hits Gower on the shoulder: not exactly head-hunting, but West Indies have developed a tactic of targeting the opposing captain. At second slip, Viv Richards, Gower's counterpart, claps his hands to stoke the boilers of his bowlers and make them even hotter.

Holding's next ball is full, swift, straight: Gower gone, lbw for 16, in a flurry of ten balls.

Gooch's new partner is the left-hander David Smith, very tall for a batsman, almost big enough to be a West Indian fast bowler. It is Smith's Test debut, and he cannot do anything beyond get off the mark before being caught by the wicketkeeper, Jamaica's Jeffrey Dujon.

Gooch's next partner is Lamb. By now, even on the few occasions when the ball is fuller, Gooch is reluctant to push forward, as the bounce is becoming inconsistent. In the 18th over, his score 30, he edges Holding short of second slip.*

At 12.10 p.m., by when he has reached 42, Gooch calls for another fresh left glove from French. If nothing else, the delay takes him a minute closer to the 12.30 interval. Until then, he keeps ducking under the short ball and, with Lamb, survives.

In the dressing room Gooch consumes ice cream, cold water and energy drinks, along with salt tablets. He returns to the platform for another quarter of an hour of music, before having to face it. By the time he goes to the middle, the sponge inside the rim of his helmet has dried in the midday sun to the point of merely damp.

---

* Of this passage of play Gooch later wrote in his autobiography: 'At that point, for the first and, I think, only time, I began saying to myself "Graham, it might be doing yourself a favour if you got out, this boy Patterson is really firing and it could get very nasty indeed. If you don't watch it, you could get hit very badly." It was the only time I thought I might be hurt at the crease. Now I found that I was crouching very low, knees really bent, even before Patterson was into his delivery stride. Not a good feeling at all.'

Marshall resumes his attack from the Headley Stand end in place of Patterson, and is pushed straight for two runs by Gooch. This takes him to 51, as brave a fifty as ever made for England, out of 83 for three.

In my notebook I list the visiting batsmen who have subdued the West Indian fast bowlers in their own backyard in the 1980s: Allan Border, the hardest-boiled Australian who ever batted; Mohinder Amarnath of India; and Gooch. Amarnath had hooked everything with almost masochistic glee to total 598 runs in nine Test innings in 1982–83. A few months later, back in India for the return series, he had six more Test innings against West Indies – and scored one run. I interviewed him after this extreme reverse – six innings for a single run, against the same attack – and Amarnath's explanation was that he had a virus. But, though English was not his first language, he sounded as if he had something akin to shell-shock.

Sooner or later on this pitch a ball is bound to come along with Gooch's name on it. In Marshall's second over after lunch it arrives, lifting off a length around off-stump, and Gooch can only fend it to Garner in the gully. Although the bowler is not Patterson, the crowd celebrates as much as the players at the departure of their chief adversary.

Back in England, E.W. Swanton, the doyen of cricket correspondents, opines that a line should be drawn halfway down the pitch. Anything short of this line, he writes in the *Daily Telegraph*, should in future be called a no-ball.

But this match is not being televised at all. It is the last Test match that England played without any film footage. It is only being broadcast to Britain on radio. In Trinidad, where there is oil and money, a Test is sometimes televised, but not in the rest of the West Indies. And the essential point is that these balls are rearing at the ribcage from a length, or barely short of a length. They are not halfway bouncers.

Marshall is yet more threatening in his second spell than his first. He scents a rival to his status as West Indies' fastest bowler. He soon switches to round the wicket again and dares the batsman to hook. Ian Botham tries and is caught at deep backward square-leg.

Lamb, meanwhile, hooks Holding for six and sees him off. Or, rather, Holding walks off nursing the hamstring that had limited him to a dozen overs when England faced Jamaica. Garner replaces him and bowls Lamb with a shooter that goes under his bat. The correspondent for *Wisden*, John Thicknesse, estimates the ball hit Lamb's stumps 'no more than six inches above the base'. Shortly afterwards England, after opting to bat, are dismissed in only 45.3 overs for 159.

Haynes and Greenidge are almost as demoralising as the West Indian fast bowlers have been. England hope for a few quick wickets to get them back in the game. Greg Thomas, on his Test debut, is almost as fast as some of the West Indians, but two hard chances are missed in his first two overs, in the slips and gully. Haynes and Greenidge counter-attack to take West Indies to 29 without loss from four overs.

Greenidge begins limping, as he often does when in the mood, after being hit on the knee by Richard Ellison. He goes off after being struck again, this time over the left eye by Botham's bouncer, but already West Indies have responded with 79 for no loss.

On the second day, a Saturday, the home side's total mounts, if not so rapidly as the tourists' sense of foreboding. The West Indian batsmen are ever more troubled by the inconsistent bounce while adding 183 runs in the day from 75 overs (there are no penalties, however slow the over-rate). Quickly as Thomas bowls, he is on his own, not hunting in a pack.

On Sunday morning, West Indies take their first innings to 307. In my notebook I jot: '*Sabina packed and buzzing. Ten years since*

India reached 97 for six here and declared, because no one else was left in one piece to bat.'

By lunch, Gooch and Robinson are gone for ducks, the pitch even more unpredictable now the new ball is in West Indian hands. Gooch inside-edges a tentative push at Marshall, then sits on the platform with a book, perhaps reading it, perhaps not. Robinson is castled by a shooter from Garner, before picking up his earphones. Beside them on the platform, two England batsmen wait padded up. When West Indies had batted, only one man had been padded up on their platform.

Patterson, more settled and rhythmic than in England's first innings, dismisses Gower with his third ball after lunch. Richards had posted a fielder on the third-man boundary for the England captain's upper-cut. But Gower could consider himself unlucky that such a shot against Patterson had not flown over third man and out of Sabina Park, if not into the Blue Mountains.

The crowd, packed because it is the weekend, seems to be in a similar mood to the Colosseum on a Roman holiday. One after another, England's batsmen enter the arena and depart, vanquished.

'*Patterson pitching 3/5ths of way down the pitch & Dujon either taking it above his head or Lamb, ducking, taking it on the shoulder or arm*': so I note. Soon Lamb is no longer prepared to be a sitting duck. He dares a hook at Patterson and is, inevitably, late. The top edge spirals and is caught by Roger Harper, substituting for Greenidge, running back from first slip.

When Botham tries to hook Patterson, the top edge flies straight over the wicketkeeper for six. Another indicator of Patterson's pace is the ball that rockets over the head of Peter Willey the batsman and of Dujon the keeper, and pitches once – about ten yards inside the boundary – before going for four byes.

The press box is at the opposite end to the Headley Stand. It is open, without any windows and air-conditioning to shut out the atmosphere. When Patterson is not hurtling towards us, I look to the right, over the old pavilion of Kingston Cricket Club, to their reserve ground alongside Sabina. Another game is going on, from another era. For Jamaica Colts a left-arm spinner and right-arm medium-pacer are bowling at batsmen who push safely forwards. This scene is closer to Hambledon than to what is happening in the Test.

Patterson is rested. 'Gone back to his cage for raw meat,' quips *The Sun*.

A motivated Marshall replaces him. Almost behind his arm, on England's platform, while Gooch reads and Robinson listens, a game of chess is being played by John Emburey, not in the XI, and Thomas, the last man.

England's physiotherapist is also on the platform, ready to run on at any moment. *'Too much like an executioner's platform, waiting for the end, while ever-helpful Laurie Brown offers the next man a final drink.'*

At the peak of his manhood, Botham takes on Marshall. No shirking, no ducking. Seeing Botham hook his first ball for six provokes Marshall into going round the wicket, not to deliver half-volleys.

Botham hooks the second ball too, but though it flies to the fielder stationed halfway between the square-leg umpire and the boundary, Botham has no time to run a single, such is the speed of the action. So rapidly does the ball reach the fielder, a 17-year-old schoolboy called Jimmy Adams acting as sub, and so rapidly does he fire it back to Dujon, there is no run.

Botham hooks the third ball of this same Marshall over, above Adams's head, for four. The fourth is too high to hook. Sensing the fifth ball might also be on the short side, Botham is again waiting on the back foot, and he middles it, and I swear the ball would have killed Haynes at forward short-leg if it had hit him over the heart. Instead, it flashes past his unturned, unhelmeted head. The cricket hereabouts is as incandescent as the light away over Kingston harbour towards Port Royal.

Marshall's sixth ball whistles past Botham's swish and off-stump. So five balls, the first five of the over, have all been bouncers – and about as fast as any bouncers ever delivered. Yet umpire Gayle, now standing at the Headley Stand end from which Marshall and Patterson are bowling, passes no obvious comment.

Botham attempts to hook the first ball of Marshall's next over as well, but it keeps much lower than he had expected. The death rattle is loud, never mind the roars.

Willey had been promoted to number four, because Smith suffered sunstroke while fielding on the second day. Willey has mostly been at the other end, coping with Garner and the slightly hamstrung Holding. Willey's bottom-handed cuts and off-side slashes are far more suited to these circumstances than the ortho-doxy of staying in line and playing straight with a raised left elbow.

Off one of the few balls from Patterson that he faces before tea, Willey is dropped by Richie Richardson. When he reaches his fifty, the press box breaks with convention and applauds his bravery.

At the interval I ask Tony Cozier, who has covered West Indies on radio and in print since the 1960s, how he rates the pace in this match of Marshall and Patterson. 'I can't honestly say I've seen faster bowling than today,' says *the* West Indian commentator.

I ask John Woodcock of *The Times* to rank Marshall and Patterson among the fast bowlers he has seen over three decades. He cites Frank Tyson, of the immense shoulders, bowling down-wind at Sydney in 1954–55, reflects and says: 'There's nothing in it.' But he adds the point that Tyson pitched the ball up as regularly as Marshall and Patterson are pitching short, and therefore it was a completely different game. I wonder if someone bowling at 90 mph in the 1950s would have appeared faster, because of the novelty, than someone of the same speed in the 1980s.

Another consideration is that amateur and semi-professional bowlers were allowed to be inconsistent, and bowl flat out only when they felt like it, without speedometers and analysts and bowling coaches measuring them. Fast bowlers now bowl the same pace consistently – without peak or trough.

In any event, in *The Times*, Woodcock writes: 'I have never felt it more likely that we should see someone killed.'

After tea only the last rites remain. Willey upper-cuts Patterson for six, before stepping away once too often and seeing his stumps demolished by Garner. Bouncers and snorting lifters from Marshall and Patterson at one end, shooters and yorkers from Garner at the other. *'No way to build an innings against such bowling because no knowing what the pitch would do,'* I superfluously note.

Even when Patterson does not use the pitch, he is lethal, or even more so.

He hits Phil Edmonds in the ribs with a full toss – a beamer from the same parish as Roy Gilchrist. Edmonds is wearing a chest-protector made of foam that is designed to protect a fallen jockey from horses' hooves. Even so, Patterson brings out such a bruise, as if caused by a kicking horse, that the photograph of Edmonds's torso makes the back page of the *Today* newspaper. And they say cricket is a non-contact sport . . .

Willey's 71 makes West Indies bat a second time, before they win by ten wickets. The Test is over by the third evening, though West Indies have averaged only 11 overs per hour and England 12.

The tourists head off to the north-west coast with wives and girl-friends to drown their sorrows and fears. My final note: *'The assignment of going to the West Indies for 3 months to beat them at cricket must be the hardest, most taxing in all sport.'*

A camera crew flies to Trinidad for the second Test on behalf of Independent Television News, and some footage of the remaining matches is shot. But Patterson does not touch quite the same heights away from home and Sabina's broken pitch. He does not need to: several of England's players are scarred if not scared. West Indies win the series 5–0. No England player bats for two sessions.

The second of those omens in St Vincent is therefore clear long before the end. The signature tune for England's 1985–86 tour under Gower – the unofficial one, of course, sung by local fans – rings around the Caribbean. 'Captain, the ship is sinking!' they sing. 'Captain, the sea is rough.'

‖

Because the Kingston Test was not filmed or televised, readers who were not there – without images to cloud their memories – can judge the extent to which words can convey the reality of it. I would say, but then I would as a cricket correspondent, that words can go a considerable way towards conveying the reality of a match. Following the game on radio, or the ball-by-ball commentary on Cricinfo, we can picture the action in part and feel all of the tension being ratcheted up as a close finish approaches.

From the objectivity of ringside, it is easier for a reporter or spectator to see which team is winning than it is for a player. What a reporter cannot convey is what it is like to be out in the middle of the match he is covering. What we miss if we are not playing, or umpiring, is not the detail of the action – the slow-motion television camera, and Spidercam, can now see more than any human being – so much as the essential character of the protagonists. I learned more about James Anderson in one net session, where the England media were allowed to participate, than in watching him from a distance for a decade. Even though it was in an indoor school in Hobart, where he had been hanging around like an unemployed teenager on a street corner, the moment Anderson took hold of a ball and mooched back to his mark, a wild energy came over him. It propelled him on to the prairies, the wind in his mane, making one mettlesome colt into a stallion.

When we babble of green fields, language cannot answer our questions about how many runs have been scored or wickets taken, or how much time has been lost to rain, without the aid of numbers. But the written or spoken word can still tell us to a large extent about what happened in a cricket match, and how it happened, and why.

The language of cricket, I have come to realise, is predicated on batting being a very difficult act of survival.

When our terminology was first shaped, by James Love in his report of the Kent v England match in 1744, none of the four totals neared 100. Scoring 18 runs in one innings, as 'Great Newland' did, was almost a match-winning feat. For everybody in the world except W.G. Grace, batting remained difficult until the 1890s. The first Test between West Indies and England in 1986 was, in this respect, a return to the sport's infancy, when bowlers were ascendant.

From the beginning, therefore, the language of cricket sympathised with the batsman as the underdog. And our sympathy towards him, based on batting being so difficult, is reinforced by the fact that he is outnumbered. He has eleven opponents pitted against him, and only one ally – and even then his partner is an ally only when the ball is dead. Once the bowler begins his run-up, it is eleven* men against one – or even twelve against one, as the partner

---

* When Australia recruited their first fielding coach, Michael Young, from American baseball, he made much of the need – in an interview he gave me in Amsterdam in August 2004 – for fielders to 'hunt in a pack' and keep the batsman penned in. The ultimate exhibition of in-fielding I have seen came in the Sydney Test of 2006–07 when Kevin Pietersen was in imperious driving form but could not breach the offside field of Michael Clarke, Andrew Symonds and Mike Hussey. The batsman piercing the field can, I suppose, be viewed as the enemy escaping.

becomes a potential enemy who can run the striker out. Darwinians would say it is the same with every underdog: we identify with the batsman, and want him to survive, because the time might come when we find ourselves in his position.

The language of cricket has thus evolved to present the batsman as being positive, even creative, in the most arduous circumstances. No cricket team is on record as having been dismissed in ten balls, but in theory it could happen, and then the game would be terminated most abruptly. It would not be much of a day for anyone except the winners – certainly not spectators, including reporters. Anyone who is not a rabid supporter of the fielding side wants the game to go on for a certain length of time, and is therefore prepared to view batting – for prolonging the game – in a positive light.

The bowler, on the other hand, is portrayed as destructive, sometimes to the point where the language implies that he is morally reprehensible. In this dualistic world, as in no other English sport, one group of players on each side is cast as 'goodies', i.e. the batsmen, and the other group as 'baddies', i.e. the bowlers. If they are too effective, bowlers can ruin the game by ending it prematurely.

When Marshall opened the attack at Sabina Park, Gooch tried to 'build' not only an innings of his own but a partnership with Robinson. In the process, he tried to 'construct' or 'create' a platform for his side, a metaphorical version of the one outside England's dressing room. When Gooch 'made' runs, the implication again was that he was being creative. 'Make' is the verb the Bible uses to describe what God did to the world: what, in the eye of believers, could be more creative? 'Make' has become a synonym for 'score', for the basic function of a batsman.

When a batsman hits the ball skilfully and often, he becomes a 'stroke-maker'. When the ball hits the meat of his bat, he hits it 'cleanly' – a healthy act in itself. A batsman who makes runs quickly can also be described as scoring 'freely'. In the words of the song commissioned by Frederick, Prince of Wales: 'Britons never, never, never shall be slaves!' We have always treasured freedom, for ourselves.

A batsman has to defend his wicket, stumps or 'castle', unlike Tim Robinson in the Sabina Park Test, who was 'castled by a shooter from Garner'. As an Englishman's home is his castle, what could be more precious to defend? If the batsman can defend his castle for a prolonged period, the implication must be that he is worthy of our approval, even admiration.

Some words of Sir Henry Newbolt's poem 'Vitaï Lampada' must have crept into the brain of every cricketer in England:

> There's a breathless hush in the Close to-night—
> Ten to make and the match to win—
> A bumping pitch and a blinding light,
> An hour to play and the last man in.
> And it's not for the sake of a ribboned coat,
> Or the selfish hope of a season's fame,
> But his Captain's hand on his shoulder smote—
> 'Play up! play up! and play the game!'

Here the boy, on Clifton College Close, is instructed to hold up his end until the last ten runs are made for victory. Once he has grown into a man and joined the army, and his regiment is on the verge of defeat – when 'the sand of the desert is sodden red' – he is again instructed to 'Play up! play up! and play the game!' The boy who defends his wicket is as courageous as the soldier who defends the last ditch; or at least the father of the man.

The area inside the creases* has to be used just as much by

---

* I am indebted to Professor Adrian Poole of Trinity College, Cambridge, for pointing out that the white line of the cricket crease was once called the 'scratch'. The word, more commonly used in pugilism, led to the phrase 'coming up to scratch' for two boxers coming up to the mark to fight.

bowlers as batsmen, for every ball. Yet the Laws of Cricket, officially unbiased, term this area 'the batsman's ground'. They do not
call it the bowler's ground, although the crease is pivotal to a pace
bowler's physical well-being, even his whole career: he has to bring
his front foot down somewhere inside the crease without twisting
his ankle in a worn patch or tearing his Achilles. So the Laws award
the crease to the batsman: he is defending *his* ground, as well as his
wicket, against eleven aggressors.

Radio and television commentators reinforce our perception
that the crease is the batsman's, and his alone, by saying the batsman, having completed a run, has 'got home safely' – never that he
has reached the bowler's crease in time. We are reassured when we
hear that a person has got home safely, as a child from school. We
infer that he is worthy of our interest and support.

The sympathies of the neutral observer are enlisted again if he is
told that a player is brave or courageous. Graham Gooch was
described as both, most deservedly. But not Michael Holding,
although he braved the risk of further injury by returning to the
field with a hamstring strain to bowl West Indies to victory.

A batsman like David Gower can, in addition, be showered
with praise normally reserved for the fairest of the female sex. His
batting can be described as 'dazzling' or 'beautiful', or even
'divine'. Nobody in cricket is more romantic than the free-spirited
stroke-maker who plays the occasional brilliant innings – especially if he is left-handed or dies young. (Archie Jackson,
Bradman's contemporary and equal until Jackson died aged 21,
could be regarded as the Keats of cricket.) 'Brave' and 'beautiful',
these batsmen are called, combining the most desirable of male
and female qualities.

Even he whose batting is the opposite of beautiful normally
escapes any linguistic censure. He might make 'ugly runs' but he
himself is not called an ugly batsman: functional or efficient or

workmanlike, but not ugly. If he 'carts the ball to cow corner', or 'mows to leg', or 'scythes', the analogy is derived from farming, that valuable work upon which our existence depends; and if he 'farms the strike', he is being thoroughly responsible, a fellow of yeoman qualities. Such a batsman might go on to 'nurse the tail' – and how gallant is one who follows in the footsteps of Florence Nightingale!

Even batsmen who do not make a run for their side are treated very differently from bowlers who do not take a wicket. Negatives are heaped on the bowler who toils 'in vain', 'fails' to make an impression and is 'ineffective' or even 'impotent'. Aspersions can be cast on his very manhood.

On the other hand, the batsman who scores zero 'makes' a duck. This has creative, even humorous connotations. If he does so twice in one game, he 'makes' a pair of spectacles. If he is out first ball in both innings, he 'makes' a king pair; and if he is dismissed in both innings without facing a ball, he 'makes' an emperor pair, more regal still! The more a batsman fails, the grander the language to describe – and excuse – his failure. When he scores nothing, he is deemed to be polite and considerate too, because 'he does not trouble the scorers'.

When the bowler fulfils his role – or, in professional cricket, does his job – the language used to describe his achievement is often, at best, negative. It can even be pejorative, to the point where Patterson in Kingston was reported – by a former professional bowler – to have 'bowled like the devil'. (The bowler with a suspect action is also 'diabolical', or so the batsman mutters to enlist our sympathies after his dismissal.)

Various attributes are used to describe an effective pace bowler, not a single one complimentary: hostile/nasty/destructive/ dangerous/threatening/mean/menacing/vicious/explosive. They have connotations of such immoral and violent aggression that the pace bowler, as he wreaks havoc and mayhem, is no better than Genghis Khan.

What is actually being described here is the bowler as seen from the viewpoint of the batsman – and therefore of the reporter, too, with his conditioned sympathy for the batsman. An effective ball is 'hostile' or 'vicious' or 'threatening' – both to the batsman's wicket and, as at Sabina Park, to his physical well-being. But the adjective is transferred by the reporter or commentator to the bowler himself, who is thereby made to sound morally reprehensible.

It is the same whether he is a 'shock bowler' in traditional parlance, or 'a strike bowler' in modern: he is still one of the 'baddies'. And this is not just the modern English press failing to give the opposition's fast bowlers their due. Sir Frederick Hervey-Bathurst of Hampshire, the swiftest bowler of his day, was described in 1851 as 'if in the vein, very destructive'.

A pace bowler will, of course, learn from experience that these epithets are actually compliments. He will come to appreciate – he has no alternative – labels like 'hostile' and 'menacing'. After striving flat out all day, he has to be content with being compared to the devil, while his teammate up the order is said to bat 'like an angel'. The nearest to a consolation for the bowler is that football's multi-million-pound strikers can also have some of these epithets, like 'dangerous', 'menacing' and 'penetrative', thrust upon them.

Such language must predispose the newcomer or neutral observer against bowlers, albeit subconsciously. At any rate, in England and most Test-playing countries, batsmen have always been more admired than bowlers; and if it cannot be proved that language has played a part in shaping this perception, it cannot be disproved. In England, the big money – from sponsorships, benefit matches, books, newspaper contracts and endorsements – has traditionally gone to batsmen, and more lately all-rounders, notably Ian Botham and Andrew Flintoff. Of the seven highest benefits between the First and Second World Wars, not one went to a specialist bowler. Knighthoods too. The ones awarded to British citizens for cricket have gone to batsmen or administrators, with two exceptions: the all-rounder Sir Ian Botham, and the bowler Sir Alec Bedser, who made much play of being the first bowler to be knighted since Francis Drake (Sir Frederick Hervey-Bathurst was an hereditary baronet). If language has shaped our perception of cricketers, the consequences have sometimes been lucrative – for batsmen.

While batsmen can be compared to the deity, pace bowlers for their pains are likened to animals. The less threatening ones are mere beasts of burden: they 'do the donkey work' or act as the 'workhorse' of their team. The more threatening ones bowl 'a brute of a delivery' and 'hunt in a pack', no better than wolves, preying on hapless batsmen.* The implication is that the fast bowler, even Sir Frederick, contains an element of the primitive or savage.

A batsman 'makes', constructively. A bowler 'breaks', destructively. The law uses the neutral phrase 'put down' to describe the bails being removed from the stumps; the rest of us do not. If a bowler bowls a batsman out, we say he 'breaks' the wicket. If he takes several wickets early in an innings, he 'breaks' through and wrecks the opposition's top order. If he ends a long stand, he 'breaks' the partnership. (Breakback, off-break and leg-break are

---

* I much regret that I saw Imran Khan bowling in a Test in Pakistan only once (he never played at home against England), when a piece of magnificent theatre in Faisalabad in 1982 made me think of a predatory animal. Australia's number seven, Peter Sleep, came to the wicket after Pakistan had made a huge total. Imran, Pakistan's captain, was bowling what is called reverse-swing now, but he was swinging it a far greater distance than recent norms. Sleep at the crease was as helpless as a tethered goat as Imran ran in. The ball, delivered from wide of the crease, went a few inches wider still until it was almost on the line of the return crease, before boomeranging and pinning Sleep leg-before first ball. Yes, why not? It was Imran's own favourite image: he could have been a tiger.

derived from another meaning of 'break' and do not, or should not, have this connotation of destructiveness.)

In dismissing a batsman, a bowler makes a wicket 'fall', either factually, by dislodging the bails, or figuratively. This word adds to the impression of wanton destruction. Batsmen making and creating on the one hand, bowlers taking and breaking on the other, or causing things to fall: they could be good children and bad children, given toys to play with, if not actual representatives of good and evil.

A spin bowler is also viewed in a negative light, linguistically. He is cunning/wily/tricky/deceptive – no better than Eve tempting Adam to fall from Paradise. Like a cruel hunter, he traps, snares and deceives poor batsmen. Sometimes he too uses 'bait' in his deception. No wonder no spinner has been awarded any honour approaching a knighthood. He is no better than an animal – if he bowls 'donkey drops'. As for bowling 'under-arm', this is being 'under-hand', a condemnation in itself, or else he is bowling 'sneaks', beneath contempt.*

Even accuracy is not an admirable quality in a bowler, according to the vocabulary we have inherited. At best, the accurate bowler is 'economical', like a civil servant with the truth; more often, he is labelled 'tight' or even 'miserly'. 'Keeping it tight' sounds mean-spirited. Even if he 'makes the batsman play', this is not 'make' in the creative sense: the bowler is forcing the batsman to play the ball, coercing him unkindly.

All bowlers, whether fast or slow, are portrayed as bloodthirsty.

---

* The scandal of the 1890s, in England, was the relationship between Oscar Wilde and Lord Alfred Douglas, nickname 'Bosie'. When Bernard Bosanquet unveiled the googly in first-class cricket in 1900, the ball could therefore not be termed a 'Bosie' after him. A schoolmaster telling a boy 'Show me your Bosie' could have been misconstrued. Besides, cricket – male cricket – has always feigned that homosexuality does not exist. In Australia, however, there was no such barrier to calling the googly a 'Bosie' after two match-winning spells by Bosanquet, in the Ashes of 1903–04 and 1905.

The batsman who falls prey to a bowler is a 'victim', like one who has suffered at the hands of a heartless criminal. The successful bowler either 'takes' wickets, or 'snares' them, like an illegal trapper, or 'grabs' them, like a burglar. A 'yorker' was not only the speciality of bowlers from Yorkshire, according to Michael Rundell in *The Dictionary of Cricket*: to 'york', or 'put Yorkshire on someone', originally meant to trick or cheat a person.

The balance between bat and ball has fundamentally shifted since 1744. The process was started by Grace, and the hand-mower, and the roller. Starting with the 1996 World Cup, when Sanath Jayasuriya of Sri Lanka attacked like no opening batsman before in international cricket, batsmen have done more and more of the attacking: they can now 'destroy' or even 'murder' bowling with their power-packed bats. Especially in the Twenty20 format on a flat pitch, bowlers have become the defenders. But the language has yet to evolve sufficiently to encompass this new reality: it is still predicated in favour of the batsman. The nearest he can come to being condemned as immoral is to be called 'a flat-track bully'.* Cricket is renowned as a batsman's game, and it is linguistically too.

Suppose we are in a train that stops beside a village ground while a game is going on and we know nothing about either team. Almost all of us, I suspect, would instinctively support the batsmen.

|||

Batting, however, can still be difficult – heaven knows! – in certain circumstances. On a rough pitch, or against very fast bowling, or both as at Kingston, it can still be perceived as an act of survival in

---

* The once-common phrase in which a hard-hitting batsman 'flogs' the bowling has gone out of fashion since corporal punishment was made illegal in British schools. I wonder if it was used in an approbatory sense, suggesting that the feeble bowlers were given their due when a batsman flogged them. Calling on their experiences of disciplining a dormitory, C.B. Fry or Douglas Jardine might have approved of flogging . . .

itself, a matter of life and death. When facing fast bowlers on a pitch of variable bounce, or spinners on a turner, the batsman sooner or later will get a 'ball with his name on it', as Gooch did. The metaphor is taken from warfare, from the First World War if not before, where situations were so hopeless that a soldier was doomed to be hit by a bullet.

When Desmond Haynes was dropped early in his innings at Sabina Park, he was 'given a life' by England's slip-fielders. It is an extraordinarily potent phrase. We are saying that a batsman is alive when he is at the wicket. When he is out, therefore, he is dead, killed by the bowler, perhaps aided and abetted by fielders. If the batsman makes a false stroke, it can be a 'fatal' mistake. Thus a dismissal in cricket can be equated to death. We must empathise and sympathise with the batsman all the more.

This perception is reinforced by the phrase often employed at funerals. As people gather to reminisce about the departed, they may well say that Old So-and-So 'had a good innings'. A person's life is equated to a batsman's innings, never to a bowler's spell; or indeed anything else. If a person survives a major operation or accident, he can be said to have had a second innings.

I take this as an amazing compliment to cricket. The sport has had such a profound place in English, or British, life for so long that one of its phrases has been taken by the public and used as a metaphor for life itself: he, or she, had a good innings. Another famous saying – 'it's not cricket' – is now seldom used;* while

---

* Of the saying 'it's not cricket', Lord Harris claimed in *A Few Short Runs*: 'The bright-est gem ever won by any pursuit: in constant use on the platform, in the pulpit, Parliament, and the Press, to dub something as being not fair, not honourable, not noble. What a tribute for a game to have won, but what a responsibility on those who play and manage it!' Ironically, as we have seen, the phrase seems to have been first used to describe bowling which was not under-arm: the Reverend James Pycroft in 1851 claimed that round-arm was 'not cricket'.

'keep a straight bat' is well on the way to being an anachronism in the era of 20-over cricket (much better to heave across the line). But 'he had a good innings' remains part of our daily discourse.

We can say that a dead person has 'had a good run' – a phrase that can be used to describe a batsman who has played a succession of large innings, without being derived from cricket – but it does not extend to his whole lifetime. At a funeral, for example, it might be said that somebody, following a major operation, had a good or decent run. But 'to have a good innings' is borrowed from cricket alone. And I can think of no other phrase which is used as a metaphor for a life or lifetime – the single most important thing in our existence.

Samuel Maunder composed a poem called 'The Game of Life' in the 1820s. Maunder opens with his observation that people philosophise about life and its ups and downs; and he himself thinks that life is like a game of cricket; and that 'a steady Player' (i.e. person) may 'have a good long Innings'. Cricket was therefore used as an analogy for life two centuries ago.

Death then intervenes – and, according to Maunder, Death is the bowler. Death can bowl out some people 'before they've got a notch': infants, as I interpret. Or else, being so cunning, Death can throw a person off guard with some easy balls 'till presently a rattler stops his breath'. This metaphor persists today: a batsman who is bowled is sometimes said to hear 'the death rattle', like Ian Botham at Sabina Park. So the most devastating and destructive force in human existence has been likened to a bowler.

And while Death bowls, according to Maunder, Time keeps wicket. A batsman/person may go through life virtuously and carefully, and block Death out, but Time will prevail in the end. In the words of his poem, Time watched the popping-crease 'until the wish'd-for opportunity arriv'd', then stumped the batsman out. One or the other will get you in the end: if not Death the bowler, then Time the wicketkeeper.

On first reading this poem, I was shocked. I had thought of bowling as an activity full of vitality; wicketkeeping might be a pretty dumb thing to do, except if you want to break a finger, but bowling! If a spell goes well, it ranks among the happiest times of my life. Yet Maunder equates bowling, not with joy and animation, but death and destruction.

Maunder, mercifully, concludes on an optimistic note:

> And yet, although old Messieurs DEATH and TIME
> Are sure to come off winners *in the end,*
> There's something in this 'Game of Life' that's pleasant;
> For though 'to die!' in verse may sound sublime—
> (*Blank* verse I mean, of course—not doggerel rhyme),
> Such is the love I bear for Life and Cricket,
> Either at single or at double wicket,
> I'd rather play a good long game, and spend
> My time agreeably with some kind friend,
> Than throw my bat and ball up—*just at present!*

Apart from the fact that I would much prefer to play eleven-a-side, because of the camaraderie, this is my philosophy too.

Words can add up to fine writing, and fine writing makes an additional source of pleasure for those who follow the game, almost a reason in itself. This applies not only to English but to the sport's second language. Several dozen Bengali newspapers are published in Kolkata and Dhaka, and several cricket books containing fine writing have been written in Bengali.

If we argue that Mary Mitford's subject in *Our Village* was village life in the 1820s rather than cricket, the first cricket book in prose is also the first to contain some fine writing. The first half of it, *The Young Cricketer's Tutor*, was written – or more likely dictated – by John Nyren in the 1830s. He teaches us basic principles of the game, some of which have not changed in two hundred years. Among these eternal verities, the role of the leading elbow in the biomechanics of batting: 'If you do keep that [leading] elbow well up, and your bat also upright (in stopping a length-ball), you will not fail to keep the balls down; and, vice versa, lower your elbow, and your balls will infallibly mount when you strike them.'

Nyren instructs us that every fielder should be alert to the wicketkeeper's directions, for he is 'the General, and is deputed to direct all the movements of the fieldsmen: not, however, by word of command, like the military commander, but by the simple motion of his hand.' Although the hand now wears a glove, here is another eternal verity. So is Nyren's instruction that the bowler should practise bowling over and round the wicket, though this was neglected in the twentieth century before one-day cricket. Also, the best cricketers seldom become the best coaches: Nyren says of one Harry Hall that 'like many of inferior merit in performance, he made nevertheless an excellent tutor.' Nyren's definition of the qualities required of the fielder at point and midwicket – or the middle wicket, as he called it – still applies to a Twenty20 specialist.

The second half of Nyren's book, *The Cricketers of My Time*, moves from the didactic to such fine writing in some places that they make our first sample of cricket literature in prose. He fondly recalls the players of his day, and what they used to drink after the matches at Hambledon, though without declaring his interest: the landlord of the Bat and Ball Inn was his father Richard Nyren. The punch was 'good, unsophisticated, John Bull stuff—stark!—that would stand on end—punch that would make a cat speak! Sixpence a bottle! We had not sixty millions of interest to pay in those days [a reference to the crippling national debt after the Napoleonic wars]. The ale, too!—not the modern horror under the same name, that drives as many men melancholy-mad as the hypocrites do;—not the beastliness of these days, that will make a fellow's inside like a shaking bog—and as rotten; but barley-corn, such as would put the souls of three butchers into one weaver. Ale that would flare like turpentine . . .'

In his dotage, Nyren also waxes lyrical about some of his team-mates: how they were honest men, above all, who did not engage in match-fixing or spot-fixing, or 'trickery' and 'crossing', as he termed them. He testifies to the character of John Small junior: 'The legs at Mary-le-bone never produced the least change in him; but, on the contrary, he was thoroughly disgusted at some of the manoeuvres that took place there from time to time.'

Nyren launches cricket nostalgia: he was the first, of many, to write that the cricketers of his day were much superior to those of the present. No bowler since Hambledon, he says, has been so quick as Thomas Brett, who 'was, beyond all comparison, the fastest as well as straightest bowler that was ever known'. William Beldham was 'the finest batter of his own, or perhaps of any age' – or at least 'the finest player that has appeared within the latitude of more than half a century'. Tom Sueter was not only the first batsman to use his feet to leave his crease and get to the pitch of the ball, according to Nyren, he was also the finest of all wicketkeepers: 'Nothing went by him; and for coolness and nerve in this trying and responsible post, I never saw his equal.'

While some of Nyren's passages are fine writing, they do not, however, amount to a work of literature. Internal inconsistency, for a start: the page after saying of Sueter that 'nothing went by him', Nyren tells us in detail about his long-stop, George Lear, and how accomplished he was. It may be that in the Hambledon era the wicketkeeper was allowed to ignore any ball going down the leg-side, and to confine himself to balls on the stumps and wide of off-stump. In that case, though, Nyren should have clarified or qualified that phrase about Sueter.

While we concede that Nyren is looking at the human condition from a new angle, which is necessary for a book to be regarded as literature, too many of the other alchemic ingredients required to turn fine writing into literature are missing. Firstly, while the language is at times elevated (probably where the literary figure of the 1830s, Charles Cowden Clarke, embellished Nyren's dictation), the didactic parts of *The Young Cricketer's Tutor* are mundanely prosaic, and rightly so in the interests of clarity. Thus the instruction for an outfielder: 'When the ball does not come to his hand with a fair bound, he must go down on his right knee with his hands before him; then, in case these should miss it, his body will form a bulwark.'

Secondly, it follows that the author's imagination is not, or should not be, at work in these passages of instruction. As one of very few images he employs, Nyren gives us a picture of Lear's attributes as a long-stop: 'The ball seemed to go into him, and he was as sure of it as if he had been a sand-bank.' Nyren does let play a little with his imagination in *The Cricketers of My Time* when he describes how John Small senior saved his skin, by using his violin, after being confronted by a vicious bull while walking across a field: Small 'with the characteristic coolness and presence of mind of a good cricketer, began playing upon his bass, to the admiration and perfect satisfaction of the mischievous beast.' Most of his book, though, is a combination of didacticism and straightforward recollection.

Ⅲ

Several pieces of cricket poetry deserve to be ranked as literature. They give us an insight into the human condition and are flavoured by the imagination. Their language synergises with the content, thus opening them to literary appreciation.

Francis Thompson's poem 'At Lord's' should still be accorded the highest place in cricket's contribution to English literature. It consists of four stanzas, but generally only the first – which is repeated as the last – is quoted. The second and third stanzas tell of Gloucestershire, driven by the 'resistless Graces', going north to play Lancashire in 1878, 'long ago' when Thompson was aged eighteen. But the poem has stood the test of time.

The first, and fourth, stanza looks at the human condition from a new angle. Most of us find solace in trying to recreate the happy moments of our youth. Not Thompson in his middle age, when he thinks of going to watch Lancashire again, playing at Lord's. Not now he is down and out on the streets of London: 'The field is full of shades as I near the shadowy coast'. Already he has premonitions of his death, which occurred at the age of 47.

Thompson finds little or no consolation in seeing the successors of Hornby and Barlow playing at Lord's. The single most poignant word in the poem, I feel, is 'my': 'O my Hornby and my Barlow long ago!' Thompson is telling us that he used to be so physically and emotionally close to these two Lancashire batsmen of his child-hood that they were, in effect, his. But now they have retired and are no more than ghosts flickering to and fro, to and fro. Time has separated them, for ever, from him.

It is usually when cricket and time interface that the game's fine writing transcends into literature. Dannie Abse pursues the same theme in a poem called 'Cricket Ball', which deserves to be ranked as English, and Anglo-Welsh, literature.

Among poems about cricket and the evocation of lost youth, I would place it second only to 'At Lord's'. But whereas Thompson, a drug addict on the streets of late Victorian London, did not want to go to Lord's to see Lancashire play again, because it would be too poignant, this poem is life-affirming.

As a boy, Abse watched Cyril Smart of Glamorgan, or 'slogger Smart', hitting the ball out of the ground at Cardiff in 1935. But so many years have passed since then that he refers to himself as 'I, a pre-war boy, or someone with my name'.

Abse is captivated by one of Smart's hits, in particular. In reality, the ball disappears through the window of a hotel outside the ground, but in his imagination it soars away, over the roofs and the River Taff, into the Caerphilly mountains. Such is the flight path of a boy's aspirations.

Now, in his old age – it is late, Abse says, and 'the sky is failing' – he recalls this golden moment of his childhood, a time of inno-cence, for him especially as a Jewish boy in the mid-1930s, before the Holocaust. Yet the Taff is still running. And a particular smell comes to him which evokes his past. All is not lost, not yet.

> I smell cut grass.
> I shine an apple on my thigh.

No book of prose specifically about cricket has been accepted unequivocally as literature. The two authors who have come closest wrote in much the same time and place: Edmund Blunden in *Cricket Country* and Hugh de Selincourt in *The Cricket Match*, published in 1924, set in his Sussex village. Literary figures like Mary Mitford, Thomas Hughes, Siegfried Sassoon and L.P. Hartley have devoted part of a book to cricket. So too Sir Neville Cardus in *Autobiography*, a work of such impeccable prose that barely a punc-tuation mark is out of place.

C.L.R. James wrote some brilliant chapters in *Beyond a Boundary*, not so much the Victorian history as his profiles of the West Indian cricketers of his time, such as Headley and Constantine. Cricket serves as the backdrop in *Netherland* as a Dutchman comes to know the immigrant underclass of New York, and the novel deserves to be ranked as American literature. But it is not specifically about cricket; it is more of an update of *The Great Gatsby*, as its author Joseph O'Neill agreed.

The cricket writer and critic Stephen Chalke, in a lecture about cricket writing at Lord's in 2010, observed that no book had been devoted to a single non-fictional match except for Alan Ross's *West Indies at Lord's*, and regretted this failure to make use of the dramatic possibilities. But, fine writing though it is about the 1963 series in England (not simply the Lord's Test), Ross's book cannot be ranked as literature, because factual reportage – or 'run of play' – cannot be turned by the author's imagination into literature without violating the truth, as recorded by television and/or reporters at the match. I do not see how Rahul Bhattacharya's description of a one-day international between Pakistan and India in *Pundits from Pakistan* could be improved upon; but again his imagination was perforce circumscribed by a mass of data.

I take this to be partly the result of the nature of the sport itself. Cricket is easier to describe, or more reportable, than most if not all other sports. The bowling of a single ball is a distinct, or discrete, event; so is the batsman's stroke; so is the fielding of that ball. A bouncer from Marshall, bowling round the wicket to Botham, which is hooked to Adams, can take several words, or sentences, to describe in detail. James Love takes twelve lines of verse to describe Thomas Waymark's attempt to make the decisive catch in 1744. (The zenith was reached when A.G. Macdonell in *England, Their England* took several pages of side-splitting humour to describe a ball slogged high in the air and all the palaver that occurs during its descent.) But that which makes cricket so reportable prevents it being taken over by the imagination and transformed. When a ball is actually bowled and a shot played, there is – or should be – little that the imagination can do to embellish these facts.

A pass in football, hockey or rugby is more difficult to isolate and describe than a cricket stroke or a ball bowled, because it is one part of a larger on-going movement. Furthermore, several people may be involved in the passing move, rather than the two cricketers who bowl and hit the ball, thus blurring the picture. The time between deliveries helps the cricket reporter to make notes; but there is time too after a free kick or penalty has been awarded. It is the less distinct nature of the action leading up to the free kick which makes it harder to analyse in detail and describe in words.

An actual cricket match leaves little scope for the writer's imagination. The action is too easily anchored by words and numbers to be thus exploited. Nevertheless, on a winter's evening when no match is being played at home or broadcast from overseas, plenty of fine writing about cricket can supplement the warmth of the fire; and the pick of it is literature.

7

NUMBERS

I always teach young players that cricket is not about averages even if it is a stats-based game. It is about how and when you score runs and take wickets.

Shane Warne

Make it 400.

Dr W.G. Grace's instruction to the scorer, after he had scored 399

YOU HAVE BEEN invited to umpire a game of cricket in the remote highlands of Papua New Guinea. A few of the local tribesmen have gone down to Port Moresby, seen the sport played there and brought a couple of bats and balls back to their village. Enough rainforest has been cleared for a match to be staged on the fringe of it, beyond the huts, and a challenge issued to the neighbouring village.

Shortly after the match starts, a problem arises. In these highlands, as in a few other uncolonised parts of the world such as the Amazon basin, the numbering system is simple – extremely simple. The villagers count 'one, two, three, plenty'. That is it. Without the perceived needs of materialist western societies, they do not need to go above three. If they have trapped more than three fishes or three birds, they have plenty to eat.

When a batsman hits a ball into the rainforest, the game comes to a halt, and not because the ball is lost. The problem is that you, as the umpire, signal 'six' but nobody knows what six means. It is all right when a batsman is bowled without scoring: you can shake your head in sympathy and tell him he has scored a bird of paradise, rather than a duck. But there is this little local difficulty when a batsman hits a boundary. The scorer has no idea what to write down in his scorebook other than 'plenty'.

This match, in the absence of more than three numbers, quickly dissolves into being a middle practice that goes on and on and on. One batsman stays in for most of the day and hits some superlative shots, but he never has the satisfaction of reaching a fifty or a century, or of acknowledging the applause which normally greets these landmarks. When this batsman is out, the scorer records his name, the manner of dismissal and 'plenty' – exactly the same as for the slogger who middled one big hit into the tropical undergrowth before being bowled. In the folk memory of this village, this batsman will be long remembered for his strokeplay, but its value cannot be measured and recounted to posterity.

When the turn of the visiting village comes to bat, it is again rather unsatisfactory. They do not know their target – how many runs to chase off how many overs. In the end, as a gorgeous sun sets over the rainforest, everyone gets bored and drifts home for supper, leaving you to pull up stumps. The match is a test, but of little more than stamina, and the result is never decided.

Numbers help us to capture the details of a cricket match, very concisely too, and determine the result. They can only go so far: they cannot tell us about the state of the pitch, the weather and overhead conditions, the quality of fielding or standard of umpiring or the mindset of any of the players. Nevertheless, if you wanted to know what had happened in a game of cricket and, in addition to being given the names of the players, you had to choose between thirty words or thirty numbers, you would discover a lot more from thirty numbers.

Numbers convey the basic value of a cricketer. An outstanding batsman may be dismissed for nought in one game, but over the course of his career the numbers that he has compiled will give an approximate indication of his worth. He might not always score his runs when they are most needed, or quickly enough, but still: sooner or later, the fine cricketer scores runs or takes wickets, and these numbers are recorded once and for all. Only the fine ground-fielder, without any statistics to measure his contribution, can feel neglected.

Like chess notation, numbers enable us to pin down every move in a game. Right, this ball coming up will be the first ball of England's second innings in the third Test. Now, and if needs be in future, we can focus on this single ball, and tell others about it. (We may also deduce that the ball was new and maybe swinging, and therefore batting was relatively difficult at this stage.)

From here it is an easy step to betting. Thanks to Love's poem, we know that at the precise moment when England had scored three for five wickets in 1744, the odds on Kent winning were ten to four. Correspondents on England's tours to the West Indies in the 1950s reported that spectators would bet on almost every ball, in an entirely innocent way: I bet you a few pence or cents that Rohan Kanhai or Clyde Walcott will hit a four in the next over. It is this fact that every significant moment in a cricket match – every ball – is numbered and identifiable which makes the sport so inviting to punters and bookmakers, and those with less innocent intentions.

Numbers also go a long way towards grounding the cricketer in reality. The player in another team sport who goes home and tells his family he has played brilliantly is not easily disproved. The bowler who has taken nought for plenty can call himself unlucky one day, but he cannot go on taking nought for plenty and expect to be considered much good. Numbers, being objective measurements, contradict him.

As long ago as the 1940s, baseball employed the first analyst to examine numbers and statistics, but baseball is almost binary: the ball is hit for a run or it is not. Analysts became fashionable in cricket after the publication of Michael Lewis's *Moneyball* in 2003, but cricket did not prove quite so susceptible to analysis and clear-cut conclusions. In the limited-overs game, the strike-rate of batsmen and economy-rate of bowlers came to be studied much more closely. In all formats, the strengths and weaknesses of batsmen were analysed and quantified, so that Kevin Pietersen was found to average much less against left-arm spin, or Andrew Strauss and Mike Hussey much less against left-arm pace. Bowlers, captains and coaches could be informed by analysts on how to target batsmen.

But cricket was not revolutionised by the study of numbers as baseball was. The most highly trained eye – if only that – could detect these technical weaknesses just as well, and temperamental ones. Cricket is too complicated, and has too many variables, starting with the pitch, to be broken down neatly into numbers. Even a simple statistic like the percentage of matches that a player has won can be very misleading: he can be the finest wicketkeeper/batsman the world has seen, more Gilchristian than Adam Gilchrist, but if his team has no bowling to speak of, he will come bottom of the table.

The shorter the format, the easier a game is to analyse and a formula to be devised. Test cricket is too much of an ocean for anyone to have trawled all its depths, and thank goodness. Well over two thousand Tests have been played, and still the plot of every one is different.

I am not numerate, but numbers held sufficient attraction for me at about the age of ten to type out the scorecard of a match. It was a very high-scoring one: the first-class game between Cambridge University and the West Indians at Fenner's in 1950, which was the highest-scoring match ever in terms of runs per wicket. Cambridge batted first and declared at 594 for four wickets, and the West Indians totalled 730 for three wickets by the end. I had yet to realise that a game in which seven wickets fall in three days is no sort of contest. It must have been the magnitude of the numbers which attracted me, and their natural progression: not only that of the two totals, but John Dewes scoring a hundred and David Sheppard 227 for Cambridge, then Everton Weekes 304 not out.

Ever-increasing numbers give us vicarious pleasure in the case of a favourite batsman compiling ever bigger scores. They can also give us the illusion that mankind is improving: that ascending numbers lead to the Ascent of Man. We watched mountaineers climbing ever higher peaks until they reached the summit of Mount Everest; we do not have to be mountaineers to want to see how high cricketers can go.

Headingley was packed with 25,000 on Saturday, 7 June 1952. It was the first Test of the series between England and India and of the career of the local lad, Fred Trueman, a promising fast bowler.

Running in from the Kirkstall Lane end, down the slope, Trueman dismissed Pankaj Roy with his second ball of India's second innings, a top-edged hook to Denis Compton at slip. He bowled Madhav Mantri with his seventh ball, again for nought. At Trueman's next ball, Vijay Manjrekar aimed a loose drive, and he too was bowled.

As Alec Bedser had dismissed another of India's batsmen without scoring, the scoreboard stood at nought for four wickets. 'Take a good look at it,' England's captain Len Hutton told his players. 'You'll never see another like it in a Test.'

The irony was probably lost on most of India's players and supporters at the time. Their countrymen, about a millennium before, had invented zero.

The figure '0' has a void in the middle, like no other digit, not even 6, 8 or 9. Into a void a batsman might wish to disappear after scoring nought in front of a capacity crowd.

The footballer or hockey or rugby player, if he has not scored, does not leave the field with 0 against his name. True, if the bowler has not taken a wicket, he has to contend with a zero on the scoreboard, but his shame is dissipated through having been spread over several hours of fruitless endeavour: he has come gradually to the dreaded cipher. Posting a duck on the scoreboard or television screen – a zero being the shape of a duck's egg – goes only so far in softening the blow to the batsman who has made nought. Hence the preoccupation of all batsmen with getting off the mark.

Three is a magic number in cricket. Number three has been the most glamorous position in the batting order, and viewed as the most important, since Don Bradman made it his own. He had a hard act to follow – Charlie Macartney averaged 59 at a dashing rate for Australia at number three – but follow it he did. Simultaneously, Wally Hammond averaged 74 for England at number three. Since Bradman, Ricky Ponting has averaged 56 there in Tests; Brian Lara averaged 60 at number three, against 51 at four; Kumar Sangakkara 62; while Rahul Dravid, alone, has scored 10,000 Test runs in this position.

Three wickets in successive balls is a feat that has been celebrated since the game's dawn, and used to be marked by the presentation of a hat. Even a bowler in the remote highlands of Papua New Guinea can take a hat-trick. Simon Barnes speculated in *The Times* that a hat-trick has achieved such prestige because, in part, it has religious associations, with the Holy Trinity.[*]

The first hat-trick in Test cricket was taken in the second Test at Melbourne in 1882–83, by the off-spinner Willie Bates of Lascelles Hall. Everyone knew the significance of the moment after Bates had taken two wickets in consecutive balls. England's fielders crept closer – and for a hat-trick ball to this day, even in a Test match, reason goes out of the window and fielders take up positions the captain and coach have never visualised, usually based on standing an equal distance apart. The batsman facing Bates's hat-trick ball was Australia's finest hitter, George Bonnor, a Flintoff-like colossus of six feet six – only he seldom used his physique to hit the ball. England's close fielders gambled on his tendency to block, not bash, and inched closer. Sure enough, Bonnor pushed forward to Bates, the ball bounced up and he was caught in front of the wicket close in on the leg-side. Bates was later presented with a hat made of silver by his grateful skipper, Ivo Bligh, because his trick materially helped to win the Test and level the series.

It is irrational that the achievement of taking four wickets in four balls is less prestigious. It is so much rarer that, while more than 30 hat-tricks have been taken in Tests, no instance of four wickets in four balls has to date occurred. In purely numerical terms, the feat is 33 per cent more valuable again than a hat-trick. Yet the bowler and everyone else on the fielding side appear satisfied once a hat-trick has been taken. Only as an afterthought do they think about the new batsman, still hastily putting his kit on as he comes to the crease. Ambition has been

---

[*] Things were done differently, of course, at Eton College. According to John Murray of the publishing firm: 'When I first went to Eton in 1863, the getting of three wickets with successive balls was called "bowling a gallon", and the bowler was supposed to be awarded a gallon of beer.'

fulfilled; individual glory has been achieved. The name of the bowler, if he has taken his hat-trick in an Ashes test, is immortal. Four is not magical.

Thirteen is perceived to be the unlucky number in cricket, in England and elsewhere, if not Australia, and in ordinary life. And this superstition has a rational basis in that a first-class player through the ages has been more likely to be dismissed for 13 than for 12 – but only just.

Here are the scores, up to 20, for which batsmen have been dismissed in first-class cricket as a percentage of all dismissed innings (65,680 of them before October 2014):

Score	Number	Percentage
0	8106	12.34
1	3120	4.75
2	2486	3.79
3	1961	2.99
4	2637	4.01
5	2107	3.21
6	1901	2.89
7	1669	2.54
8	1715	2.61
9	1510	2.30
10	1399	2.13
11	1337	2.04
12	1322	2.01
13	1334	2.03
14	1170	1.78
15	1056	1.61
16	1088	1.66
17	1084	1.65
18	921	1.40
19	937	1.43
20	851	1.30

Compiled by Benedict Bermange, Sky Sports statistician

It was a relatively innocuous bouncer, of no great speed, and the bounce was true: this was, after all, a first-day pitch at the Sydney Cricket Ground. In fact, the ball arrived more slowly than Phillip Hughes had calculated, so that he had completed his hook too soon. The ball hit the left side of his neck, below the helmet, with fatal consequences.

Cricket had little or no experience to fall back on when deciding how to react to the death of Hughes two days later from a catastrophic haemorrhage. It was so shocking because it was so unprecedented – the first death of a professional batsman from a direct hit by a cricket ball since George Summers of Nottinghamshire at Lord's in 1870, at the same tragically early age of 25.

Two numbers were seized on to become a focus of the grieving process. The next time Australian batsmen reached 63, Hughes's score when he died, they raised their bat and helmet and looked to heaven. In the case of his teammate David Warner, in the first Test at the SCG after the accident, he put his bat and helmet down in the crease when he reached 63, and knelt to kiss the spot where Hughes had fallen.

The first Test of Australia's series against India, which had to be rescheduled after Hughes's funeral, had been at Adelaide. When Australia won, they gathered at the large '408' which had been painted on the outfield, as Hughes had been Australia's 408th Test cricketer, and returned there shortly afterwards to sing their team song.

Lord John Sackville was no great batsman, for all Love's flattery, yet he had a more than tenuous link with cricket's first individual century. Sackville's son became the Third Duke of Dorset and fielded teams on the family estate at Sevenoaks. One of his regular players was John Minshull, also known as Minchin, and the Duke's household accounts record the match he played against Wrotham in 1769. John Nyren wrote that Minshull was 'as conceited as a wagtail', but then if we had climbed cricket's Mount Everest by scoring the first century, it might have gone to our head. A century means you have dominated your opponents. You personally have bettered the best they have to offer, even if your team goes on to lose. You can score a fifty while one of the opposition's main bowlers is resting, but if you make a century, you have overcome all that has been thrown and bowled at you.

Something literally goes to a batsman's head on reaching a century: the sound waves of clapping. Such occasions tell us that, in the eyes of spectators at least, cricket is more of an individual game than a team game. A crowd applauds far more loudly when a batsman reaches a landmark such as 50 or 100 or 200 than when a team does. Indeed, one of the curiosities of cricket is that the moment a team wins is often greeted with no applause at all. The winning run is scored, players shake hands, spectators pack up and leave. No wonder Minshull was conceited!

I can barely recall my only hat-trick, but until I lose consciousness for ever I will remember my only century – and my emotional, utterly irrational, response after waiting for 48 years. Having reached 99, against Warminster Sunday 'A', I pushed a ball on the off-side, ran a single, and kissed the umpire at the bowler's end . . . All I can say is that I have never had occasion to kiss an umpire since.

Nobody has better described the anguish of falling short of a century than the late Peter Roebuck who, in his schooldays, had scored a hundred on the same ground where I scored mine, Hinton Charterhouse near Bath. When playing for Somerset in his mid-twenties, he passed 50 thirty times in a row, by his own account, without going on to a hundred. 'Unless you score 100 you haven't really asserted your mastery, the innings is not fully matured,' Roebuck wrote in *It Never Rains*. 'If you reach 100 years of age, the Queen sends you a telegram; if you hit 100 runs, opponents congratulate you and headlines proclaim you.'

When Roebuck next reached 99, in a Championship game against Kent at Maidstone, he sought a quick single, only for his partner Joel Garner to send him back.

> I could feel a surging despair at that moment, a premonition of failure. Kent's captain Chris Cowdrey woke up, brought in the field and denied me a single which I'd regarded as my right after six hours' gruelling work under a blistering sun. Suddenly scoring a run became an impossibility. I was panic-stricken as I could see my hopes sliding away. I tried to tell myself to take my time but suddenly my body was ill at ease and my mind jumpy. Somehow it seemed inevitable I'd be out. From the moment Garner refused that single a barrier arose in my mind, a paralysis affected my judgement and my nerve. It was all so absurd. How could it happen?

All this mental torment the author would never have experienced if he had been batting in the highlands of Papua New Guinea; or if Britain had not dispensed with the Roman numeral system in the early Middle Ages. The process of converting 99 into a century might then have seemed easier. A part of scoring a hundred is to turn two digits into three, that magical number. But turning XCIX into C might be less satisfying – as scaling down – and the failure to do so less galling.

Or suppose we used the Babylonian numeral system in cricket, as in other walks of our life. For telling the time, we still have sixty seconds in a minute and sixty seconds in an hour. This sexagesimal system extends to our geometry and a circle of 360 degrees. The people of ancient Mesopotamia, who wanted to buy land that had been desert but was now irrigated by the Tigris or the Euphrates, found it a most convenient system: sixty is the lowest number which can be divided by 1, 2, 3, 4, 5 and 6. If you wanted to buy or rent some of this land from the royal treasury, the calculations would have been relatively simple.

Had this numeral system been extended to cricket, 'the nervous nineties' that so consumed Roebuck and many others would never have existed. Instead, the batsman's landmarks would have been 60, 120, 180 and so forth. On a batting pitch, an individual score of sixty would not have been a major landmark – a fifty with knobs on – because the batsman could not claim to have dominated all the bowlers. Charles Bannerman would still be remembered, but for scoring the first 120 in Test cricket rather than the first century. Len Hutton's 364 against Australia at the Oval in 1938 would be even more famous than it is, as he was the first to the landmark of 60 multiplied by six.

But cricket would have been a lesser game, I think, under the Babylonian numeral system. On a dull day, when batsmen are too much on top, spectators lean forward in their seats and fielders move closer simply because a batsman has entered the nineties. Will he follow Graham Gooch's precept of continuing to bat in exactly the same manner as has so far served him so well? Or will he be tempted to get it over and done with as soon as he can? Paul Collingwood missed out on his maiden Test hundred when, on 96, he tried to hook a six and holed out to long-leg in Lahore in 2005–06; he missed another hundred in Brisbane in 2006–07 when, on 96 again, he decided to run down the pitch at Shane Warne for the first time in his innings, and missed; but he did reach 100 in an Edgbaston Test by striking a six over long-on, against South Africa in 2008. Having batted like a corporal, disciplined and unglamorous, Collingwood wanted to bring up three figures in cavalier style; to swop the hair shirt for robes of glory. There would have been no such flourish, in his nineties at any rate, if he had batted for Babylon.

The best individual example I have seen of how a number can form a barrier was when it impeded Sir Richard Hadlee.* He was a commoner then, but a most uncommon bowler, a supreme exponent of swing and seam, the nearest to a fast-medium automaton.

Give him a juicy pitch, a new ball, choice of ends, and Hadlee was guaranteed to make the most of them. Except that on 12 February 1988, the first day of the first Test between New Zealand and England at Christchurch, when he was given these conditions, he did not strike.

Hadlee entered the match with the same number of Test wickets as Ian Botham, 373, and therefore a share of the world record. The build-up focused on how soon he would take the record-breaking wicket, and how appropriate that he would do it on his home ground, and how far ahead he would extend his lead over his rival.

Hadlee, however, did not become the world record-holder on that day. Or in that game. Or in that series. Striving too hard, he bowled for 18 overs without taking a wicket. He was bowling against English batsmen whose foibles he knew well from his time with Nottinghamshire, and on a similar pitch to Trent Bridge as it was then, and could have been expected to finish with a Michelle, or 'five-for'; but either the expectation or cricket's perversity was too much. Then he pulled a calf muscle and went off.

It was not until nine months later, in India, that Hadlee's 374th wicket arrived, and with it sole ownership of the world record for most Test wickets. He was also first to reach 400 Test wickets – in his native Christchurch.

---

* Number one had an inhibiting effect on England when they reached the top of the ICC Test Rankings in 2011. They focussed on retaining that position, instead of keeping their eye on the ball and winning.

Numbers have cemented the reputations of the two most famous cricketers: W.G. Grace and Don Bradman. They show that Grace was far and away the best batsman of his time, especially considering that Arthur Shrewsbury only appeared towards the end of this period, when pitches were much improved.

Most first-class runs, as at the end of the 1895 English summer

	Matches	Inns	NO	Runs	HS	Avge	100	50
W.G. Grace	669	1141	84	43265	344	40.93	105	193
W.W. Read	428	692	44	21212	338	32.73	37	107
G. Ulyett	537	928	40	20823	199*	23.44	18	101
A. Shrewsbury	365	600	63	18959	267	35.30	43	73
W. Gunn	366	597	49	16589	228	30.27	26	74
A.N. Hornby	400	665	33	15504	188	24.53	16	72

Most first-class wickets, as at the end of the 1895 English summer

	Matches	Balls	Runs	Wkts	Avge	BB	5I	10M
W.G. Grace	669	104887	42116	2465	17.08	10–49	215	61
A. Shaw	403	101597	24455	2024	12.10	10–73	177	44
J. Southerton	286	68774	24286	1682	14.43	9–30	192	59
G.A. Lohmann	261	66112	23010	1667	13.80	9–67	161	52
J. Briggs	398	68123	23409	1619	14.45	9–29	150	41
W. Attewell	341	86970	23165	1612	14.37	9–23	117	25

Most catches in the field over the same period

	Matches	Catches
W.G. Grace	669	784
R. Abel	355	473
G. Ulyett	537	369
A. Shaw	403	368
E.M. Grace	312	367
W.W. Read	412	346

Compiled by Benedict Bermange, Sky Sports statistician

But Grace enjoyed one purple patch that nobody has equalled, not even Bradman. From 11 to 18 August 1876, Grace raised the numerical bar to new heights by scoring 839 runs in three first-class innings. Two of them were the first triple centuries.

After Minshull it had taken almost half a century for the first double century to be scored, at any level: William Ward's 278 for MCC against Norfolk at Lord's in 1820, in a fixture that could be called first-class except that matches of the time were not awarded any such status. To raise the bar, Ward had pioneered his own method of practice: in the nets at Lord's he had the groundstaff bowling at him from 18 or 19 yards, so that batting in the middle felt easier. Ward also practised by batting with a walking stick, as Bradman would do, to condition his reflexes. One difference from modern practice was that in scoring his 278, he used a bat which weighed four pounds and lasted him for 50 years. After Ward, more than half a century elapsed without anyone reaching 300 at first-class level.

In July 1876, Grace warmed up by being credited with, if not actually scoring, the first 400 by an adult. It was against XXII of Grimsby, when every one of his opponents fielded. As Grace came off the field, after his United South of England XI had been dismissed for 681 off 340.1 four-ball overs, he asked the scorer how many he had got and was told 399. 'Make it 400,' Grace said. The only surprise, I suppose, is that he did not order the scorer to make it 405, for then he would have made the highest innings at any level, beating the 404 made by a schoolboy, Edward Tylecote, at Clifton College in Bristol.

Like many batsmen who enjoy a purple patch, Grace was in his prime at the age of 28, blending youthful energy and experience to maximum effect. Grace no longer did athletics in his off-seasons – he had won 70 trophies, mainly running races, so he claimed – and it was only by playing cricket that he became match-fit and was able to make light of his 15 stone. At Canterbury, representing MCC, Grace had to bowl and field while Kent scored 473. MCC buckled in the heat in their first innings and had to follow on. By the close of the second day they had scored 217 for four wickets and Grace was 133 not out. *The Times* reported on Monday, 14 August, after the three-day match had ended on the Saturday:

> No one attempted to forecast the result, and few, if any, dreamt that Mr Grace would rub out the debt of arrears himself, but he did. This feat puts into the shade that of Mr Ward in 1820, whose score of 278 has till now been regarded as the most wonderful of its kind on record. The enormous total of 344 completed by Mr Grace on Saturday occupied six hours and a quarter, this giving an average of 57 runs per hour. He had to contend against all the Kent bowlers save one. Three of them went on three times and three twice. In one instance Mr Yardley bowled from the right arm and then from the left. Never was a more striking exhibition of endurance against exhaustion manifested. To explain the progress it may be well to say that play began at 12 o'clock on Saturday, and in 90 minutes the overnight total of 217 advanced to 323, and ten minutes later the arrears were pulled off. At 4.35 Mr Grace had scored just 300, and at 5 o'clock the figures 500 appeared on the telegraph . . . Now came the close of Mr Grace's career – caught at mid-off, and great was the joy thereat. His score of 344 contained 51 fours, eight threes, 20 twos, and 76 singles. Half an hour remained for play.

When Grace wrote, or rather dictated, his memoirs, he added a few details. 'Saturday was one of the hottest days of a very hot month, and I thought I might as well put my best foot forward.' On the Friday, when opening MCC's second innings, Grace had decided to hit out or get out: if the latter, he could get home by train on the Saturday, to rest on Sunday before Gloucestershire's match against Nottinghamshire at Clifton College on Monday. Grace also recalled that he broke his bat during the first part of his 344 and had to borrow another, but its handle was too thin. 'However, during the luncheon-hour the Hon. Spencer Ponsonby Fane very kindly got hold of some thick twine, which he wrapped round it and brought it up to the right size. Tired nature began to tell its tale during the afternoon: but relief came from the officers' tent in the form of champagne and seltzer.' Alcohol seems to have made an effective substitute for tea, there being no such interval then.

The start of Gloucestershire's match on Monday at Clifton College was put back until 1 p.m. after Nottinghamshire's players had been delayed on the train. Grace set off like one, driving the second ball of the match from Alfred Shaw, the best bowler in England, for four and cutting the third for four more. But not every side of the College ground had a fixed boundary. According to the *Bristol Times and Mirror*, Grace ran seven after one hit: 'The champion drove the bowler tremendously to square-leg, right to the Pembroke-road end of the field for 7, which were run amidst great cheering.' Professional batsmen of today are doubt-less fitter but they never have to run 140 yards without stopping.

After luncheon Grace hit a six 'right over the trees into College-road'. When he lofted a ball towards the grandstand, a lady was about to be hit by 'a rather hot one' until the champion's younger brother Fred intervened 'to jump high up and catch it'. Grace pretended he had been caught out, and took a few paces towards the pavilion 'but returned amidst loud cheers'.

The crowd evidently expected him to go on to surpass his 344 of two days before, but after Grace had been batting for three hours, Nottinghamshire tried an occasional bowler in John Selby, soon to keep wicket in the first of all Tests. Fred Grace pulled Selby's first ball for seven, 'for there was no boundary on the sloping side of the College Ground in those days,' as W.G. recalled. The champion then helped himself by pulling Selby for six. But the Nottinghamshire fielder William Barnes then moved himself to deep square-leg. When Grace tried another pull against Selby, he 'got under the ball' and was caught by Barnes for 177. Grace had to be content with taking eight wickets in Nottinghamshire's second innings and leading his team to the double over a county they had never beaten before. If Gloucestershire avoided defeat against Yorkshire in their next game, they would be county champions for the first time, so proclaimed the newspapers of the day.*

Next morning, Grace was in Cheltenham to face Yorkshire. The old story is that the Yorkshiremen had bumped into the Nottinghamshire players at a station and been told what happened at Bristol. Yorkshire's Tom Emmett had replied: 'The big 'un has exhausted himself, and cannot do the century trick thrice in succession. If he does, I mean to shoot him, in the interests of the game; and I know there will be general rejoicing, amongst the professionals at least!'

The new story is that Grace seems to have placed a bet on himself to score 300 against Yorkshire. The *Bristol Times and Mirror* reported: 'It was rumoured on the ground, and was probably only a rumour, that Mr W.G. Grace had offered to back himself (before starting) that he would make 300. The wicket is in splendid condition, and it is not at all improbable, barring accidents that he will do it.' It is unlikely that a reporter on a daily provincial newspaper, in the respectable mid-Victorian era, would have reported a rumour without any substance.

On another hot day, Grace opened the batting with his elder brother, Edward or 'E.M.' Just as the previous game had attracted the largest crowd yet recorded at a match in Bristol, so did this

---

* The County Championship started 'officially' in 1890, but it was real enough for cricket followers well before then.

game in Cheltenham, such was the excitement the champion was generating. E.M. was soon 'neatly caught' by mid-on, who, in those chivalrous days before a county took a twelfth man to away games, was a Gloucestershire player. Yorkshire, in need of a substitute, had been lent R.E. Bush, down to bat at number seven. The champion would not have been amused if he had been caught by one of his own players, but he might well have chortled behind his beard when this fate befell his elder brother, with whom he competed all his life.

Yorkshire's side contained three bowlers soon to represent England. None could stem the champion's flow. 'Twice in succession did he drive the bowler out of bounds for four,' reported the *Bristol Times and Mirror*: the victim was Allen Hill of Lascelles Hall. Next to be taken apart was George Ulyett. 'The score having run up to 114, Ulyett changed his bowling from slow underhand to fast round hand, but without any immediate effect.' Immediately after lunch, by when he had made 94 out of Gloucestershire's 139 for one wicket, Grace cut the first ball from Tom Emmett – the third England bowler in the making – for two, and on-drove the next for four. In the game at Clifton College, Grace had been restrained after the interval, as if he had lunched too well, but not here.

Grace hit another seven, on this occasion off Robert Clayton: 'The champion opened his shoulders and cut him right away to the entrance gate, for which he ran seven, amidst great cheering.' At 168 for four, Gloucestershire were by no means on top in this crucial match but, whether assisted by champagne and seltzer or not, 'the champion knocked the balls where he liked' and reached 216 by the close of the opening day. Yorkshire's bowlers were demoralised by run-scoring on a scale never seen before. Hill was reduced to the point where he refused point-blank to bowl at Grace. His captain Ephraim Lockwood also hailed from Lascelles Hall, but Hill would not be persuaded; at which point, according to another anecdote, Emmett* criticised Lockwood for letting Hill get away with it.

August's heatwave then broke, and rain made batting difficult – for mortals. Simon Rae's biography of Grace has Gloucestershire's last man, James Bush, coming to the wicket when the champion was 'a few runs short of 300' and assuring Grace that he would stay in 'until you get your runs' – and until Grace had won the money he had bet on himself, one might conjecture. The champion's own account of this innings at Cheltenham was extraordinarily brief, given that it was by far the highest score ever made in Championship cricket. He confined himself to saying that he never played on a better wicket than this one at Cheltenham and that Mr Moberly batted in 'his very best form for 103' in their fifth-wicket stand of 261. (William Moberly, having attended Rugby School, played rugby for England, as did James Bush.) 'Our total was 528, and my score 318 not out. Yorkshire

---

* On behalf of Tom Emmett, I would like to claim that he was the father of reverse-swing. For a start, he was quick enough to bowl it. W.G. Grace's innings of 66 against Yorkshire at Lord's in 1870 was called the best innings ever seen because it was made against Emmett and George Freeman on a fiery pitch. 'Every third or fourth ball kicked badly, and we were hit all over the body, and had to dodge an occasional one with our heads,' as Grace remembered.

Secondly, Emmett had the slingy action required: he bowled 'fast round-arm left hand', according to Grace in his book *Cricket*. Emmett's particular delivery which sounds like reverse-swing had its own name, too, suggesting it was rare or unique: 'the sostenutor'. No such word exists; it may have been derived from *sostenuto*, a musical term, from the Italian word 'to sustain'; most likely, the sound was the attraction. As Grace described it: 'His best ball was one pitching between the legs and the wicket, with sufficient break and rise to hit the off bail.' In other words it moved away from the right-handed batsman by an abnormal distance. 'More than once he bowled me with that ball when I was well set and had scored heavily, and I left the wicket believing a similar ball would always beat me or anyone.'

After retiring, Emmett was the coach at Rugby, where any descendants of Tom Brown and Arthur would have been told, when playing forward, to 'smell her'. He ended his days in Marlborough, like George Smith, with Grace's tribute as an epitaph: 'No finer professional cricketer has ever appeared.'

made 127 for seven wickets.' Such is Grace's complete account; and, I would venture, a suspiciously bare one.

The Graphic was a weekly periodical which used large illustrations to tell its readers about the benefits that British soldiers around the world were bringing to mankind: a double-page sketch in August 1876 depicts 'Bashi-bazouks attacking women and children' in Serbia. After Grace's 318, which would surely have gone on to exceed his 344 if only a teammate had stayed with him, *The Graphic* opined with some foresight: 'The gigantic scores of this wonderful batsman and "all-round" cricketer, obtained against first-class bowling, fairly astonish the present generation, and will probably remain the wonder of many generations to come.'

As a professional historian, and an eminent one, C.L.R. James wondered rhetorically about Grace in *Beyond a Boundary*: 'What manner of man was he? The answer can be given in a single sentence. He was in every respect that mattered a typical representative of the pre-Victorian Age . . . His humours, his combativeness, his unashamed wish to have it his own way on the field of play, his manoeuvres to encompass this, his delight when he did, his complaints when he didn't, are the rubs and knots of an oak that was sound through and through.'

Grace left a less favourable impression on Australians after he captained the English tour of 1873–74, before Tests had been invented. An amateur, Grace negotiated a fee ten times that of the professionals, and insisted on taking his newly wedded wife, Agnes, for free, and on free food and drink. Betting by Grace and his players on the matches was prevalent, even rampant. 'Those who have strenuously opposed any attempt to introduce the betting element into cricket had a specimen on Saturday of how a game may be marred when the players are pecuniarily interested in the result,' the *Sydney Mail* reported after Grace and his team had been booed from the field. A commentator in the same newspaper is quoted by Rae: 'The play of Grace and his team is looked upon with the utmost distrust.' Such eyewitness accounts do not square with James's verdict on Grace's oaken soundness: 'All who played with him testify that he had a heart of gold.'

Grace was unquestionably popular and the most famous sportsman in Britain, perhaps second only to the Queen as a recognised figure in the Victorian era. He was the first sportsman to be depicted by the cartoonist 'Spy' in *Punch*. The *Daily Telegraph* launched a National Shilling Testimonial during his annus mirabilis of 1895, when he not only became the first to score 1000 first-class runs in May (only two batsmen since have done it *in* May), but also reached his 100th first-class century. It raised £5,281 9s 1d, while another appeal by MCC raised more than £2,000. But what was he like, and what made him so good, apart from his technique? His contemporary Allan Steel noticed that Grace, by the 1880s, was one of only a small handful of batsmen who had adopted the revolutionary method of playing forward with bat and front pad together.

On the 150th anniversary of Grace's birth I visited Downend. The house, with the orchard where his mother had bowled to him and taught him to play off the back foot, had disappeared long before 1998. But still standing was the house to which his family moved, across the road from Downend's cricket ground. There I met two men past 70, cricketers in their day, who had lived all their lives in Downend; as had their parents, who had observed the Graces at close quarters.

I had been inclined towards the heart-of-oak interpretation, because James was eminent, and persuasive. Yet, talking to this pair of ancients, I realised that Grace and his family were ruled by hugely acquisitive appetites. Whatever was going – runs, wickets, food, drink, money – W.G. insatiably grabbed.

I asked the pair directly: 'What were the Graces like?' Both men replied with the same word at the same moment. I did not think I had heard correctly, so I asked again. No mistake. The single word they uttered was: 'pigs'.

‖

Archie MacLaren, benefiting from the infrastructure of cricket at Harrow, was the first to scale 400 in a first-class match. As Somerset had only recently been granted first-class status, *The Times* did not have its own reporter at Taunton in 1895, but relied on this agency report, replete with commas:

> Dr W.G. Grace's record for a first-class match of 344 for MCC v Kent, at Canterbury, in 1876, after standing for 19 years, has at last been beaten, and to Mr A.C. MacLaren, the old Harrovian, belongs the honour. Mr MacLaren yesterday, at Taunton, after batting all Monday and well into Tuesday, made 424, so that he exceeds Dr Grace's figures by 80 . . . Mr MacLaren was seventh to leave at 792, when a catch in the long-field disposed of him. He played splendidly from the time he went in, and his success, following on his fine feats in the colonies with Mr Stoddart's team, will be universally esteemed. The highest individual score ever made in any match was the 485 by Mr A.E. Stoddart for Hampstead v Stoics in 1886. In the present match Mr MacLaren was batting seven hours and threequarters, and his best hits were one six, 62 fours, 11 threes and 37 twos. After Mr MacLaren had gone the Lancashire innings was rapidly finished.

Not until the 1920s was the numerical bar raised again, fuelled by the rivalry between Victoria and New South Wales. The Victorian Bill Ponsford scored 429 against Tasmania, who had first-class status but were not considered up to the Sheffield Shield, then 437 against Queensland, who had just been admitted to the Shield.

For NSW, Bradman responded by scoring 452 not out against Queensland, establishing his reputation as the greatest of run machines. The news spread, if not so quickly as today. Eventually, it reached the ears of a family who clung to cricket after being caught up in the mass slaughter of Partition.

Hanif Mohammad told me in an interview in Karachi how he came to break Bradman's first-class record of 452 not out, and to reach 499, and fall four feet short of becoming the first to score 500 runs in one innings. He had retired from other work but still oversaw the preparation of pitches at the National Stadium in Karachi. One afternoon on England's 1987 tour of Pakistan, he motioned to one of the groundstaff to bring a couple of wicker chairs on to the outfield, and lit a cigarette in a holder. Like Len Hutton, like most traditional opening batsmen, Hanif did everything cautiously and carefully.

By 1958 he was Pakistan's most famous sportsman. Radio had spread his reputation among the masses, as television was to spread Imran Khan's, and had served to unite the young nation. When Hanif had scored 337 against West Indies, in the Bridgetown Test of 1957–58, Pakistan's government had granted him 337 square yards of land in Karachi on which to build a new home. He and his four brothers had been born in Porbandar, in a well-to-do family (his mother had been liberated enough to play badminton), then lost everything in Partition's terrifying turmoil. They had washed up in a deserted Hindu temple in Karachi, bringing to the newest country nothing save their skills. Wazir, Hanif, Mushtaq and Sadiq Mohammad went on to score 29 Test centuries between them, in a period when Pakistan sometimes played only one or two Tests a year. Along with Raees, the five brothers scored 190 first-class centuries and took more than 1200 first-class wickets.

Most batting records are set against weak or weakened teams. Norfolk in 1820 had lost three men absent injured by the time they had their second innings, after Ward's 278. The Kent side against which Grace scored his 344 contained twelve players, but the bowling was mostly in the hands of amateurs. Somerset in 1895 were on their last legs because they had been hit for more than 600 by Essex the day before MacLaren's 424. When Brian Lara trumped Hanif and scored 501 not out in a four-day Championship match against Durham in 1994, it was a literally pointless exercise after Warwickshire had reached 350 and their fourth batting point, because the match was condemned to a draw.

Hanif's feat of mountaineering came in the semi-final of the Quaid-e-Azam Trophy in January 1959 between Karachi and Bahawalpur. Bahawalpur were weak in batting but had a Test off-spinner in Zulfiqar Ahmed, who had been prominent in Pakistan's first Test victory over England at the Oval in 1954; and they were, according to Hanif, a decent fielding side.

On the first day, Bahawalpur were rolled over for 185. Their home ground, the Dring Stadium, built according to the instructions of Colonel Dring, adviser to the Mir of Bahawalpur, had a turf pitch.* This semi-final venue, the Karachi Parsi Institute ground, had a pitch made of coir matting, like all pitches in the city then. It was not unknown, whether in India, Pakistan, South Africa or Trinidad, for coir matting to be drawn tight, before being nailed

---

* My chief memory of England's match in Bahawalpur on their 1977–78 tour of Pakistan does not, however, concern the pitch but the captain, Mike Brearley, coming round to the press tent with a list his players had been compiling – a list of the fifty greatest batsmen to have represented England. We weighed in, though probably only John Woodcock of *The Times*, and the nicest judgement, had valid points. It is hard to believe the England players of today would have such an interest in their predecessors.

down, when the home side batted; and to be loosened when the visitors' turn came, so the ball would bounce unevenly.

In any event, the KPI pitch must have been sound when Karachi batted, for Hanif said that during this innings he learnt to drive on the up off the back foot. The outfield was like glass on the bare side of the ground where hockey was played, and by the end of the second day he had scored 255.

Over the family dinner table that evening, Hanif's elder brother Wazir issued the challenge. Wazir, another member of the victorious Pakistan team in the Oval Test, and good enough to have hit 189 against West Indies, was now the Karachi captain and nicknamed 'Wisden' because he knew records by heart. He was conscious, furthermore, of the prestige that would accrue to the newest nation if Bradman's 30-year-old record was broken by a Pakistani.

'Now you must go for the world record of 452 by Bradman,' Wazir told Hanif over dinner on this second evening. 'You can have good rest tonight and go for it tomorrow.' The key to Hanif's batting, so he himself said, was concentration; and the key to concentration was sleep. During a match, Hanif said, he would sleep for nine hours a night.

Next morning Hanif cruised onwards to 451. He hit a two to overtake Bradman and set a new world record. 'I waved to Wazir and naturally everyone was clapping, including the fielders, though they were tired.' But Wazir did not declare. So Hanif kept batting until the shadows of the trees came over the KPI ground, and when the final over of the third day began, the telegraph scoreboard showed that Hanif's score was 496.

'One of the medium-pacers was bowling and I thought I needed four runs from the last two balls,' Hanif remembered. 'So when I hit the fifth ball to extra-cover – who was quite deep and misfielded – I thought I could get back for a second, and score two more runs off the last ball.

'Then the next thing I saw was the ball going towards the keeper's end and into his gloves, and I was run out by four feet, and I thought "Bad luck!" But as I was walking off, the boys on the scoreboard put up 499. They said the score had been going so fast that the scorers hadn't been sure about what I'd made. Then I was very annoyed.' If Hanif had known he had been on 498, with two balls to go, he would have played the situation differently.

Hanif did not sound annoyed as he sat in his wicker chair at the National Stadium, where Pakistan had never lost a Test match to that point. He even asked politely for my help. He said that when he had scored his 337 against West Indies, the time of his innings had been recorded as 999 minutes. *Wisden*, however, had marked him down for 970 minutes: still the longest Test innings to this day, but almost half an hour short of what Hanif had thought it had been, and one minute short of one thousand. The next time I was in Barbados I forgot to look in the newspaper section of the Bridgetown library. But thanks to Cozier *père et fils*, Tony and Craig, I can cite the archive of the *Barbados Advocate*: Hanif batted 'for 16 hours, 13 minutes' or 973 minutes in all.

The first recorded innings of 300, and 400, and 500, and 600, were all scored at Clifton College in Bristol.

When Edward Tylecote made his unbeaten 404 in a house match in 1868, it was between Classical and Modern or, roughly translated, Swots v Oiks. The Close was bedding in then, as the College had not been founded until 1862, but it should have been a well-drained ground, being situated above the Avon Gorge. W.G. Grace might not have chosen Clifton College to be his son's school in the 1890s had the pitches not been sound.

Tylecote was a renowned sprinter, and such were the rules then on the Close that only one of his strokes was a boundary: all of his other 400 runs had to be run. I would like to know if Tylecote was one of those batsmen who kept his own score, as he went on to take a first in maths at Oxford, and to become a maths tutor there, in addition to being the first Test wicketkeeper to score a fifty.

A generation later, in 1899, Arthur Collins became the first to scale 500 and 600. A reproduced scorecard hangs on the wall of the junior house called North Town, against whom Collins scored his 628 not out. The junior house for whom he played, Clarke's, exists no longer. The ground is only a hundred yards down the road from the junior houses, so the 13-year-old would not have had to lug his bag far after his innings – nothing like Tommy Burton, at any rate. Collins also took 11 wickets in the game, which can be viewed as a more valuable contribution than his batting, because Clarke's won by an innings and 688 runs.

Unromantic truth be told, the ground on which Collins scored his runs is very small, tucked around a corner of the main buildings from the Close where Tylecote and Grace scored their runs. On three sides a stone wall runs sometimes only 30 yards or so from the central pitch. The one smaller cricket ground I have seen is that at Banket School in Zimbabwe, where Graeme Hick scored his first century at the age of five.

The entrance to Clifton College is no mere gate. High-arched, it is more of a mausoleum, and through it pupils to this day have to walk in silence. On the internal walls are the names of pupils killed in the two World Wars, column after column after column. In the First World War alone, 578 of Clifton's pupils died, including Collins himself, killed in action while serving with the Royal Engineers at the First Battle of Ypres.

A statue of Field Marshal Douglas Haig, who as commander of the British Expeditionary Force for most of the war decided on the strategy of trench warfare, and another Clifton College alumnus, stands close by. Five hundred and seventy-eight deaths: that is only fifty short of one death for every run Collins scored. At this scene, of the breathless hush, 578 is the number I recall.

॥

Numbers, and the awe that their natural progression can inspire, kick-started my career. In the records section of *Wisden*, no doubt for ever more, is the match in Pakistan in 1964 when Railways (910 for six declared) defeated Dera Ismail Khan not by the mere margin of 851 runs, but by an innings and 851 runs. Beyond these huge numbers, however, what was the human face of this story?

On my first England tour, in 1977–78, I went ahead of the players to travel for a couple of weeks in Pakistan. I could not get to Mohenjo-daro, which is one of the world's wonders as the great city of Indus Valley civilisation, on that visit; but I flew to Chitral, rode on the back of a jeep over Lowarai Pass to Swat, and ended up in Dera Ismail Khan, or D.I. Khan as the locals abbreviated it, on the west bank of the Indus.

The match had happened exactly 13 years earlier, to the week, which seemed a highly appropriate time span. After this single match, D.I. Khan's inaugural first-class game, the Pakistan board expelled them from the Ayub Trophy. Subsequently, most of their players had left town, but with the aid of an interpreter I tracked down one of their opening bowlers, Inayat Ullah, whose figures had been 59–2–279–1 (hell, I could relate to them).

Inayat lived in a mud-brick hut, without electricity, on the outskirts of town. Through the interpreter, as we sat on his floor, he told me his wife was ill. I asked him about the match and he seemed a little awkward at first, although he should not have been. D.I. Khan were a collection of club cricketers assembled for the first time and packed off to Lahore to face Railways, who were a professional outfit: in the early 1960s they and Pakistan

International Airlines were the two teams that employed cricketers.

Inayat recalled his opening partner, Anwar, who was in the army and bowled a touch quicker than his own medium pace. Anwar had not been so economical, but he had been more penetrative, slightly: 46–3–295–3. As the Railways' total mounted, Inayat recalled, Anwar had walked back to his mark, then past it, and kept walking until he hid behind the sightscreen. I warmed to this sense of humour, and proportion.

My father had possessed one autograph: that of Wally Hammond. Too shy himself, he had pressed his twin sister Rosemary to go and ask Hammond, with a piece of paper torn from a notebook. The only cricketer whose autograph I have asked for comes at the opposite end of the spectrum, but I thought Inayat Ullah's perseverance was admirable. In the absence of back-up bowling, he could have thrown in the towel, yet he kept going for almost 60 overs, taking quite a few hits for his team. Only later did the realisation dawn that Inayat's sadness might not have been entirely due to his wife being ill, but a legacy of his one first-class match. As D.I. Khan travelled on that train to Lahore, he must have nursed some slim hopes of making the grade as a professional cricketer, which would have set him up for life, but they died in the dust of Punjab.

In the short term, young and heedless, I took the overnight Khyber Mail, wrote up my story – an exclusive, of an historical kind – and filed it at the telex office in Rawalpindi. Satisfied, I went to dine in old Raj style at Flashman's Hotel. Waiters in dinner jackets lined the walls, though I was the only person in the dining room. Travelling to new places, in countries that I would not otherwise have been able to visit, and dining at someone else's expense – *and* paid to do so. This was the life!

Having ordered the consommé, and a beer from the local

Murree brewery, I sat back and savoured. In a couple of days the England team would arrive. They were to bring a copy of *The Observer*. Some, like the captain Mike Brearley, were amused by my story of what was the biggest defeat ever, for in reply to Railways' total of 910, D.I. Khan had scored only 32 and 27. As the soup and beer slipped down, I felt something itchy under my sweater – and out fell a cockroach. It landed on the carpet, in the middle of the dining room, and walked away in front of all those dinner-jacketed waiters. That's cricket: however big the numbers, it never misses any opportunity to cut you down to size.

8

THE SPIRIT OF CRICKET

What a noble game it is, too!

The young master in *Tom Brown's Schooldays*

That's very sharp practice, W.G.

Billy Murdoch, Australia's captain

IT WAS THE *Sunday Telegraph* sports desk on the phone. Delhi Police had released the transcript of a conversation between South Africa's captain Hansie Cronje and an Indian bookmaker which they had allegedly taped.

> CRONJE: Ok, and financially the guys want 25. They want 25 each.
>
> CHAWLA: Alright, ok.
>
> CRONJE: So that's 75 for those three, and what can you pay me? I do not know how much you pay me.
>
> CHAWLA: You say.
>
> CRONJE: If you give me 140 for everybody.
>
> CHAWLA: 140 altogether?
>
> CRONJE: Yeah.
>
> CHAWLA: Ok, that's fine.
>
> CRONJE: Alright. So we are definitely on.

As soon as this transcript had been read out, I was persuaded it was authentic. Cronje had been caught in the act.

Modern fixing, if it ever had been, was no longer an Asian preserve.

Next morning, Saturday, 8 April 2000, I went to London. It was the first time I spent the whole day in the office.

Not all the other Sunday newspapers were persuaded of the transcript's authenticity; at least one ridiculed it as a fake. I had an advantage in having done a one-on-one interview with Cronje five years before. Although it had been the strangest and most unsatisfactory interview of my career, it had made me more familiar with his speech patterns, not to say his unusual personality.

He had played a full season for Leicestershire in 1995, when the county was a power in the land. I was already an admirer of Cronje's cricket. He was establishing himself as one of South Africa's finest batsmen ever against spin, using his long arms to slog-sweep Shane Warne. But his biggest single contribution to making South Africa a power in the world after apartheid had been as a fielder. It was one of the feats of fielding that I shall always remember, even though I only saw it on television.

When Australia needed only 117 to win the second Test at Sydney in 1993–94, and had reached 75 for seven, Damien Martyn drove a ball through the covers. Cronje, from extra, ran back – or loped and lolloped, arms pumping – then picked up, turned and threw down the stumps at the bowler's end without spending a second lining up his target. Warne, who had taken 12 cheap wickets in the game, was run out.

Cronje was captaining the side, too. Although the youngest player in the team, he was officially South Africa's vice-captain, destined for the top since being the boy-hero at Grey College in his native Bloemfontein, and he had coolly taken charge after Kepler Wessels had broken a finger. Confronted with the pressure orchestrated by Cronje, Australia seized up and lost by five runs. This was South Africa's first tour of Australia for a generation, and they had won in Sydney. I thought that as West Indies were declining, South Africa were all the more welcome back at the top table.

Before the start of a Championship match at Grace Road, when Leicestershire took the field, we agreed to meet at lunchtime. At lunchtime, Cronje said he would do the interview at teatime. Not really long enough, twenty minutes at most, to get inside someone's head or skin – and then only if he did not answer calls from nature or anybody else.

I talked to the Leicestershire coaching staff in the meanwhile. 'I've never seen anyone train so hard,' said one of them. 'He wants it so much.' At this time – five years before the Qayyum Report into match-fixing in Pakistan, or the report by the Central Bureau of Investigation in India, or his conversation with Chawla – we assumed that 'it' meant success.

When Cronje came off at the tea interval, to the interview room, he said he would be back in a minute and went upstairs. Not satisfactory at all. The clock ticked away. We were halfway through tea by the time he came back.

Subsequently, I have wondered what he was up to during that lunch and tea break. He certainly did not spend the time eating: he was lean, fit as a butcher's. The coach had been spot-on about the intensity of Cronje's training.

He was not busy socialising either. He was popular at Grace Road, married to the sister of the Leicestershire bowler Gordon Parsons before he arrived there, but the life and soul of the party? No. In the ten-minute interview, Cronje was polite but distant, cold, unapproachable – more so than any other interviewee I have met. 'Hansie' did not suit; his baptismal names of Wessel Johannes were more appropriate.

Was he already fixing in 1995? For certain, he had toured India twice, so he would have been open to illegal approaches there. But even if he had not engaged with bookmakers before 1995, his personality by then would have made him a useful contact.

A batsman's Test record is not a bad lie-detector. It is almost impossible to make a Test century without a clear mind. Cronje hit five Test centuries in his first 38 Test innings, before 1995. In his last 73 innings, when he was at the physical peak for a batsman, he scored one.

Four days after the story had broken in 2000, Cronje admitted his guilt. He confessed later, at the King Commission, to spot-fixing but not match-fixing: he had always tried to win for his country. But if you engage some of your players to underperform, the inevitable consequence is that you reduce your chances of winning. It was an ingenious way to salve his conscience.

I followed Cronje's trail to places I had never been before. The Taj Palace in New Delhi was already part of the beat: a hotel en route to the airport, remote from the warmth of India, convenient for meeting contacts, or for hiring a large locker behind the reception desk in which wads of cash could be passed on. Room 346, where Cronje had talked on the phone to Chawla, looked sterile when I put my head round the door as it was being cleaned.

Less familiar was the headquarters of Delhi Police where the commissioner announced: 'From the conversation between Sanjay Chawla and Cronje, it emerges the one-day matches between India and South Africa played recently in India were fixed in exchange for money. We will seek the help of Interpol as a huge international crime has been committed.'

I came to subscribe to the version of events which had the Delhi Police spilling the beans and exposing Cronje because some of them had lost money on the one-day international in Cochin earlier in the 1999–2000 series between India and South Africa. Well, I guess we all have our price; whatever walk of life we are in, to be human is to be tempted. But not all of us, if captain, would have bullied the inexperienced players into spot-fixing, usually the non-white ones.

I would never otherwise have gone to downtown Johannesburg and a shop that sold nuts, cashews and biltong. The owner, Hamid 'Banjo' Cassim, had befriended Cronje and acted as his go-between. Or to the bar in Cape Town where I had arranged to meet a senior member of the Scorpions, the South African government agency that investigated organised crime and corruption. He told me Cronje had approximately 20 overseas bank accounts, half of them joint accounts. At the time you needed US$5000 merely to open an account in the Cayman or Virgin Islands.

In the most expensive suburb of Cape Town, I interviewed Mervyn King, who chaired the commission that questioned Cronje and sentenced him to a ban for life. We talked in an amiable atmosphere in his sitting room before King protested, and protested, that there had been no political interference in the winding-up of his commission. The government had *not* ordered him to stop any more skeletons tumbling out of the cupboard – such as those players with whom Cronje had shared an overseas account – and a national disgrace.

As with all official inquiries, the King Commission opened the lid a little – just enough to catch a few wrongdoers, mostly at the bottom of the food chain – then slammed it shut. The timescale is always a giveaway. We shall investigate from this date until that date, and no more, lest more embarrassment be unearthed. The King Commission had the narrowest of windows, from 1 November 1999 to 17 April 2000, less than six months, apart from a South African tour of India. The lid of Pandora's Box could never be closed; that of an official inquiry always can.

Cronje's death, aged 32, was announced during the second Test between England and Sri Lanka at Edgbaston in 2002. He was still wheeler-dealing: even a man of his means was unwilling to pay for ordinary air tickets. He had made a contra-deal so he could fly from his palatial south coast resort to Johannesburg on cargo planes. One of them crashed in stormy weather, at an airfield which had never seen a major accident before, which prompted conspiracy theories.

Sitting in the press box on the opposite side of Edgbaston, I saw Cronje's face again, behind the window of the visitors' dressing room. Back in 1999, South Africa had been knocked out of the World Cup when the Edgbaston semi-final – still a strong candidate to be ranked the best one-day international of all time – ended in a tie. Ordinary humans would have expressed their emotions. He just sat there silently, haunted – and haunted by something else, apart from the defeat?

Cronje trained so hard as a form of penance, to expiate what he had done.

Three young men sitting on the boundary's edge are engaged in earnest conversation – so earnest that their eyes and thoughts sometimes turn away from the game which is reaching its climax in front of them.

One of the trio is Tom Brown, who is playing for Rugby School in this match against MCC. He has already batted twice but, as captain, still has to oversee the school's fourth-innings run-chase. He will break into this conversation – slightly lowering its high moral tone – to debate whether the batting order should be rearranged and a hitter promoted.

The second member of this group is the sickly and saintly Arthur, who almost died of illness earlier in his school career and now prays for his enemies. Arthur has yet to bat, if he can drag himself away from the moral high ground.

The third member is a young master, who is not playing in this match. Thomas Hughes, author of *Tom Brown's Schooldays*, does not name the master but his function is to be the mouthpiece of the creed Hughes is trying to impress upon the reader. This young master is even less worldly than Arthur, and so academic that he knows nothing of sport, having to be instructed by Tom and Arthur in what they are watching.

The match boils down to Rugby needing 20 or 30 more runs to win in the few minutes remaining before stumps are drawn. MCC's players have to catch the last train back to London. At this point the young master exclaims:

'What a noble game it is, too!'

'Isn't it? But it's more than a game. It's an institution,' said Tom.

'Yes,' said Arthur – 'the birthright of British boys old and young, as habeas corpus and trial by jury are of British men.'

'The discipline and reliance on one another which it teaches is so invaluable, I think,' went on the master, 'it ought to be such an unselfish game. It merges the individual in the eleven; he doesn't play that he may win, but that his side may.'

Hughes was writing in the 1850s about his time at Rugby in the 1830s, after the school had undergone regime change. 'Flogger' Keate at Eton had set the tone of the British public school, but the new headmaster of Rugby, Dr Thomas Arnold, preached what came to be known as Muscular Christianity: duty and service – with plenty of flogging thrown in. The boy schooled at Rugby could thus be trusted to execute the orders of the imperial government when he found himself in charge of an African colony or a regiment in Rajputana. He would be disciplined, self-reliant and unselfish, just as the Doctor had ordered, subsuming his individuality in the greater cause of ruling the heathen. He would play up and play the game, as Sir Henry Newbolt phrased it, not to win fame and fortune for himself, but hearts and minds for his country.

A finer exemplar of this creed than Sir George Grey could hardly be found. He was the Governor of New Zealand, then of South Africa, where a statue to him was raised in Cape Town in his life-time and dedicated to 'a governor who by his high character as a Christian, a statesman, and a gentleman, had endeared himself to all classes of the community, and who by his zealous devotion to the best interests of South Africa and his able and just administration, has secured the approbation and gratitude of all Her Majesty's subjects in this part of her dominions'. In 1855 Grey founded the school in Bloemfontein named after him. The motto of Grey College is *Nihil stabile quod infidum*: 'Nothing is steadfast if not true'. One of their star pupils could be said to have exemplified this ethos, if only in the breach.

The new code of football devised at Rugby, and described by Hughes, was the opposite of cricket. The bullying and fighting – not to mention the toasting of backsides in front of a fire – which went on in the school corridors were forbidden on the cricket field. But, on the rugby field, boys could be boys and vent their pent-up aggression.

In the cricket match, as Rugby chase down their target, Tom Brown decides to promote Jack Raggles, alias 'the swiper'. He hits one ball for five runs but, lacking the self-discipline of Muscular Christianity, swipes a slower ball skywards, which the bowler himself catches. Young Raggles is unfit, as yet, to serve the cause of empire.

Having caught the ball, the bowler – a member of MCC, who has come to show the boys how the game should be played – 'playfully pitches it on to the back of the stalwart Jack, who is departing with a rueful countenance'. The belief in cricket as an ethical system is not extinct: some like to think that playing cricket helps us to distinguish between right and wrong. But if an England bowler were now to playfully pitch a ball at the back of a departing batsman, all hell would break loose, illustrating how much cricket's customs, laws and regulations have changed.

The laws of a sport are designed to ensure that the outcome of a contest is the result of skill and performance, not deceit and manipulation. To this end, cricket's Laws have grown many times over in size. The original code of 1744 was embroidered on a large handkerchief, equivalent to two pages of paper at the most. By the revised Code of 2011, they had expanded to 52 pages of *Wisden*, catering for a growing number of situations, closing loopholes, turning grey areas into black and white.

'The earliest laws of cricket, like their counterparts in baseball, are nowhere near sufficient to play the game from scratch,' according to Beth Hise, an American academic who researched the origins of the two sports. Cricket's original Laws of 1744, she observed, 'simply prescribe a few elements (probably the most disputed) of an otherwise known custom of play'.

It would have been so much simpler if the legislators of 1744 – members of the Pall Mall Club – had given omnipotent powers to the umpire, like the referee in football, hockey or rugby. Instead, we have the apple in the Garden of Eden: a clause that has led to dispute ever since. 'They are not to order any Man out unless appealed to by any one of ye Players.' The exact phrasing has altered, but not the vacuum thus created. It led to the expectation – on the part of spectators if not all players – that the batsman would give himself out after an appeal of 'How's that?' if he knew he was out, even if the umpire did not think so.

Subsequently, the inconsistencies and contradictions have accumulated. A batsman is applauded for giving himself out and 'walking' when he alone knows that he has edged a ball to the wicketkeeper. Yet he is simultaneously committing a cardinal offence: he is not respecting the umpire's decision. If Hughes and Newbolt were banging on about anything, it was about respecting the umpire's decision, as if it were the will of God or the British government.

Another inconsistency, of many: the batsman is expected, by some spectators if not all players, to give himself out if he edges a ball to the wicketkeeper. Yet if the batsman is run out when a couple of feet short of the line, he is not expected to 'walk', even though he is perfectly placed to see what has happened and knows he is out.

The Laws instruct the umpires to intervene in all sorts of minor matters, such as when the bowler oversteps: 'If he delivers ye Ball with his hinder foot over ye bowling Crease, ye Umpire shall call No Ball, though she be struck or ye Player is bowled out, which he shall do without being asked,' according to the Laws of 1744. The same in the case of wides: the umpire has to call them without being appealed to. In addition, he has to intervene if a fielder impedes a batsman when running between wickets and order 'a Notch' to be scored: the first penalty run. (It had been a contact sport originally: under the first code of 1727 a batsman could prevent a fielder taking a catch by getting in his way.) 'Each Umpire is ye sole judge of all Nips and Catches, Ins and Outs, good or bad runs, at his own Wicket, and his determination shall be absolute,' decreed the code of 1744.

The umpire's authority, however, is not absolute. He cannot adjudicate on the major matter of dismissals unless a player has appealed to him.

I deduce that the context of the time was influential. Magna Carta had long since established that the English king could not behave like an absolute monarch and levy taxes whenever he wanted: he was not to be omnipotent like a French king or Russian tsar. Almost a century after Oliver Cromwell's revolution, by the 1740s, both Parliament and the British people were even keener to rein in George II and stop him spending taxpayers' money on the wars in Europe he was conducting in his other role as Elector of Hanover.

As I see it, this hierarchical order was replicated on the contemporary cricket field. The umpire was appointed to be king, but a constitutional one, bound by the Laws. Imagine if he had been empowered to raise his finger and dismiss a batsman whenever he liked, without any appeal by the fielding side. It might have been logical if cricket's founding fathers had granted the umpire this absolute power – cricket's equivalent of life and death – and banished any chance of controversy over walking. But it would have been in the spirit of totalitarian France before the Revolution, not of Georgian Britain.

Only twice in the first 2000 Test matches was a day's play lost because of a dispute over unfair play. On both occasions it occurred in a match between England and Pakistan. In the first instance, England not only refused to tour Pakistan for the next 13 years, but the fallout spread from sport into society: after the Faisalabad Affair, some of the friction between indigenous Britons and Pakistani immigrants turned nasty.

Though the England players took the field on the third morning of the second Test in Faisalabad in 1987, Pakistan's batsmen and the Pakistani umpires did not. The *casus belli* was that England's captain, Mike Gatting, had moved a fielder behind the batsman's back on the previous evening, and the umpire Shakoor Rana had stepped in to prevent him. In itself the charge was emotive: someone did something behind somebody's back.

The convention in Pakistan then was that a fielder should not be moved behind the batsman's back without the fielding captain informing the batsman. This used to be the convention in England too. In *Forty Years of English Cricket*, another stocky Middlesex and England batsman, Harry Lee, gives an illuminating example of a fielder being moved behind the batsman's back. It happened in a county match in 1920 when both captains were grandees. One was Pelham Warner of Middlesex, to be knighted; the other Lionel Tennyson of Hampshire, to be ennobled:

> H.K. Longman was batting against Hampshire, and I was at the other end. The bowler had begun his run up when I saw two fielders move from the slips to the leg side. This practice of moving behind the batsman's back is a fairly common one, and is, to my mind, grossly unfair, for the batsman naturally aims to place his shots with a strength and direction intended to avoid the field as he has studied it. I called, 'Look out, Mr Longman,' and he walked away from his wicket and refused to accept the ball. I was told by the Hampshire captain, the Honourable L.H. Tennyson, and by the umpire that I had no right to attract Mr Longman's attention, that the move was quite legitimate; in fact, I was made to feel even smaller than Nature has decreed that I should be.
>
> When I returned to the Pavilion, Mr Warner asked what had happened, and I made my report. He assured me that I was quite right in my action. I do not know what happened behind the scenes, but I received a very handsome apology later in the day from Mr Tennyson – and there was thereafter at least one umpire on the first-class list who showed me an almost embarrassing friendliness until the end of his career.

Maybe it was as a direct result of this incident that county captains in England ceased for several decades to move fielders behind the batsman's back without informing him. One of the journalists present in Faisalabad, Jack Bannister, had bowled for

Warwickshire from 1950 to 1968 (and his grandfather, a police detective, had taught him how to memorise). Bannister could not recall any captain moving a fielder behind the batsman's back without informing him. But soon after he had retired, the Sunday League was introduced in 1969 and limited-overs cricket became common fare. Thereafter, a captain would sometimes change his field several times an over; amid this hustle and bustle, the responsibility for telling the striker about movements behind his back fell to the non-striker, à la Lee. Not so in other parts of the cricket world, such as Pakistan, which took to limited-overs cricket far more slowly. There, it was still considered unsporting to move a fielder without telling the striker. So here we had a clash not only of personalities, between Mike Gatting and Shakoor Rana, but of cultures.

The Pakistani umpires thought they were in the right in this specific instance. Overall, England's players thought they had been wronged, grievously wronged, in the series to this point. In the previous Test in Lahore, and up to that point in the Faisalabad Test, the umpires had given a succession of decisions which could not be excused as unintentional human error. Gatting had not been alone in being given out lbw when Abdul Qadir's leg-break had pitched outside his off-stump; and more than one England batsman had been given out caught when his bat had manifestly not come near the ball. Too many decisions had gone in favour of Pakistan for the umpiring to have been at all times impartial.

A former Pakistan batsman of some distinction, Wasim Raja, who died in 2006, told me at the time, in confidence: 'The [Pakistan] Board puts pressure on its umpires. It says to them that Pakistan have to win a particular match and that if Pakistan don't, they won't be umpiring any more Test matches.' At the end of this series I calculated that 196 visiting batsmen had been given out lbw in Tests in Pakistan, against 101 Pakistan batsmen. After an especially rough tour in 1958–59, Garfield Sobers vowed never to return, and did not.

In addition to this general rule was the current state of affairs in Pakistan: martial law. I concluded that an order had gone out from some higher authority than the board for the umpires to ensure that Pakistan won this Test series. They had lost the semi-final of the 1987 World Cup in Lahore, a shattering disappointment, as the Australians were little more than fit and workmanlike, and had been defeated 3–0 by England in the subsequent one-day series; and it has since emerged that General Zia ul-Haq, the military dictator, gave this order himself. The British High Commission in Islamabad had heard and alerted England's management of trouble ahead.

On the second day at Faisalabad, after fine batting by Chris Broad and Gatting himself had taken England to a total of 292 that was considered formidable as the pitch was expected to deteriorate, Salim Malik went to pull an off-break. He thought there was a fielder at square-leg, Broad, saving the single; so he hit it in the air into the deep. Malik was almost caught by Broad, who had been moved back to deep square-leg. Malik had not been informed, either by Gatting, in accordance with current Pakistani and old English custom, or by his partner at the non-striker's end, in accordance with new English custom. Malik complained to the umpire at the bowler's end, Shakoor Rana.

Come the final over of the second day, Rana was standing at square-leg when he saw Gatting wave to David Capel at backward square-leg, behind Malik's back, while the bowler was running in. Rana did not hear Gatting warning Malik that he was doing so, as Gatting later said he did. Rana walked in waving his hands and shouting, leaving it to his partner Khizer Hayat to signal 'dead ball'. England's captain thought he was in the right, having being wronged so often in the series; Pakistan's umpire also thought he was in the right, by stopping England from taking an unfair advantage. Their conversation immediately degenerated into shouted abuse and accusations of cheating.

Gatting was accustomed to leaving harsh words and hard feelings on the field. Rana demanded an apology, and informed the press that evening that he would not take the field again until Gatting had apologised. It was not irrelevant that Pakistan had lost five wickets cheaply and, with three days to go on a pitch expected to wear and tear, were liable to lose. Gatting was prepared to apologise to Rana for swearing, provided he did so in return. Then, as the third day passed without any cricket, top-brass diplomats and administrators went to work and forced Gatting to apologise, alone. The game had to go on, irrespective of the spirit of cricket.

The Faisalabad Affair taught me that a cricket match begins with a social contract between all concerned. Primarily this contract is between players and umpires, and between the players of one side and those of the other. But it can go further. The government, for example, is expected not to intervene and dictate the result in advance. Spectators are expected not to invade the pitch and damage it. The scorer is expected to keep the score honestly. The groundsman is expected not to favour the home side excessively, by making the pitch dangerous for batting; the tea lady is expected not to poison the visitors, and so forth.

The players of one side also enter into a social contract with their opponents, whatever the level. The home side expect the visitors to turn up, in time, with eleven players. In return, they will give the visitors acceptable hospitality; a dressing room not much inferior to their own; fluid, if only water, during the game; food of some kind if the game is longer than 20 overs per side;

and somewhere, if only the outfield, to warm up and practise. During the game, the players of the two sides might not exchange a word, but everyone expects the norms to be observed: for the batsman to walk after being given out by the umpire; for the fielder to signal four if the ball has gone over the boundary (and television cameras are not present); for the sight-screen to be moved; for opponents to 'try it on' perhaps, but not to cheat outright. Afterwards, some social interaction is part of this contract: if not the traditional western custom of having a beer together, then the modern custom, derived from rugby and foot-ball, of forming a line outside the pavilion and shaking hands.

Captains enter into an even more detailed form of social contract. The first known set of Laws of 1727, governing the game between the Duke of Richmond and Mr Brodrick, specified that the captains were to have the final decision in the event of dispute; and even though this responsibility had devolved upon the umpires by 1744, the captains were still being held responsible for the conduct of the game when MCC promulgated the Spirit of Cricket in 2000. If the captains exchange team lists before the toss, they expect the names to be of real people, not aliases, and no twin to be replaced during the game by another twin, which has happened. The captains have to agree on local playing conditions, if a tree sits inside the boundary; and on a revised time, if the start is delayed by rain and no official umpires are present. When the home captain tosses, he is expected to use a coin which is not ambiguous; and the visiting captain not to pick it up before his counterpart can see it, as in the India v Pakistan Test at Calcutta in 1979–80. When the two captains shake hands before or after the toss, they signify that they are going to work together to make a game of it, over and above the loyalty to their team. They have established a channel of communication which will remain open until the end of the game.

This social contract extends to the relationship between the players and umpires, assuming they are independent officials, not members of the batting side taking a turn with the white coat. A bowler trusts the umpire to stand where the bowler asks, provided the umpire has a good view, and to stand still; also, to hold his sweater, cap or sun hat while he bowls. He expects the umpire to count up to six correctly.

Khizer Hayat and Shakoor Rana, who had stood in the Faisalabad Test, later officiated a game between the Indian and Pakistani media. Suresh Menon, a respected journalist captaining the Indian team, recalled in *Bishan*, his biography of Bishan Bedi:

> As we were winning the limited-over game, chasing, I noticed that Hayat was giving the bowlers four- and five-ball overs. I was the non-striker when I mentioned this to the umpire: 'Khizer *bhai*,' I said, 'do you know that you umpires are calling "over" after four balls?' 'Yes,' said Hayat, in a tone that has always remained with me. 'But what can you do about it?'

A batsman's relationship with the umpires begins with his request to be given the right guard. Nothing is written in the Laws that the umpire should correctly give the batsman the guard he requests. It is simply expected as part of this social contract.

All players trust the umpires to tell the time honestly and call for an interval at the right moment. They expect the umpires to help if a player gets something in his eye, or if the ball needs its leather trimming or loose stitching cut. Above all, they trust the umpires to administer the Laws and regulations impartially. It is symbolic that when a bowler has mud in his studs, he leans on the umpire while digging it out with a bail.

In return, the umpires expect players, after they appeal for a verdict, to accept it. The exceptions are those cases when the field-ing side can appeal to the square-leg umpire after the umpire at the bowler's end has turned down their appeal; and when a third or television umpire is officiating. These are considerable expectations. Acrimony begins, and accusations of cheating, when they are not met; when the social contract breaks down; and when someone tries to take an unethical advantage.

||

No guesses are required to identify the first person in international cricket to be accused of violating the spirit of the game. The single Test of 1882 was a low-scoring dogfight at the Oval in a damp late August. After being dismissed for 63, the lowest total of their tour, Australia had bowled England out for 101. In Australia's second innings, on the cut-up turf, Hugh Massie hit 55 at a run a minute to give the tourists a lead and the prospect of setting a defendable target. Then Billy Murdoch, Australia's captain, pushed a ball on the leg-side and ran a single with his partner Sammy Jones. Jones grounded his bat, then walked down the pitch to pat down the turf where the ball had pitched.

'How's that?'

It was W.G. Grace. He had grabbed the ball and removed the bails. Jones was out of his crease. The umpire, Bob Thoms, had not called 'Over'. Thoms gave Jones out – run out for 6.

'That's very sharp practice, W.G.'

These were Murdoch's words as remembered by the umpire at the other end, Luke Greenwood, who had travelled down from Lascelles Hall. Greenwood had got on well with Australian teams when he had umpired them, and his sympathy was with them here. 'Had I been appealed to I should not have given Jones out, for the ball was to all intents and purposes dead, and there had been no intent to make a second run,' so Greenwood told 'Old Ebor'.

After Australia had been dismissed in their second innings for 122, Fred Spofforth went into the England dressing room to confront Grace. Spofforth's speech seems to have contained more vernacular than that of Murdoch, a lawyer. Highly strung, and known as 'The Demon', Spofforth returned to his dressing room and announced that Australia could defend a target of 85 on a pitch that was even more cut up than he was: 'This thing can be done.' In spite of Grace scoring 32, Australia won by seven runs, and their first Test victory in England prompted newspapers to proclaim the death of English cricket, and launch the myth of the Ashes.

The law about 'dead ball' in 1882 was too vague: 'After the delivery of four balls the Umpire must call "Over," but not until the ball be finally settled in the Wicketkeeper's or Bowler's hand; the ball shall then be considered dead.' As it stood, therefore, this law prescribed what should happen *at the end of an over* but not during it. In 1884, MCC amended this law to read: 'After the ball shall have been finally settled in the wicketkeeper's or bowler's hand, it shall be "dead".' Another loophole tightened, and less scope in future for Grace's gamesmanship.

Bodyline caused the Australia v England series of 1932–33 to be the most acrimonious of all Test series, even more so than England's in Pakistan in 1987–88, if only because it went on longer. As the cricket administrators of Australia and England publicly accused each other of the grave offence of being unsporting, politicians became involved, as they were to be on England's tour of Pakistan.

Before 1932–33, it was considered unethical for a pace bowler to bowl more than occasionally at the batsman's body or head, as a test of his courage. Larwood began to bowl several short balls or bouncers in an over to a packed leg-side field. Surviving footage of Bodyline suggests that Larwood had two sorts of bouncer. Len Hutton swore to me that Larwood did not throw, so pure was his action; and Don Bradman showed footage of Larwood on his film-projector at home and swore that he did. I deduce Larwood bowled one sort of bouncer, not very fast or threatening, that looped through to England's wicketkeeper, Les Ames, who caught it with his fingers pointing down; and he delivered a second sort of bouncer that hurtled through, was caught by Ames at head-height with his gloves pointing up and made Bodyline a threat to life and limb.

As a result of Bodyline, MCC in 1934 issued a 'special instruction' – not a law – that ruled 'direct attack' to be unfair. It was thereafter up to the umpires to decide whether the bowler was attacking the batsman directly with persistent short-pitched bowling. The convention that bowlers should be sporting and aim at the stumps no longer sufficed.*

When Dennis Lillee and Jeff Thomson, Andy Roberts and Michael Holding, gave batsmen – still unhelmeted – their first taste of 90 mph bowling at both ends, umpires were not inclined to intervene. 'The persistent bowling of short-pitched balls at the batsman is unfair if in the opinion of the umpire at the bowler's end, it constitutes a systematic attempt at intimidation,' said the Notes to the Law on Unfair Play in the 1970s. Many batsmen were visibly intimidated; I recall more than one England tailender backing away from Colin Croft in the Antigua Test of 1981. But the ethos of cricket has always erred on the liberal side of laissez-faire rather than the legalistic. Had an umpire done much more than talk to an intimidating bowler, he would have been branded as officious, or autocratic, like a tsar.

In the 1980s, more and more teams contained more and more outright-fast bowlers, until West Indies could field four of the

* It is a myth that MCC, as an antidote to Bodyline, limited the number of fielders on the legside to five, with only two behind square-leg. This was done, initially in England, as an Experimental Law, in 1957. The intention was to curb defensive inswing bowling – and off-spin to a lesser extent – to a packed legside field, which was reducing scoring rates and killing the county game as a spectacle.

all-time best. By now they were bowling short at batsmen who were wearing helmets and extensive padding, whose lives were not therefore endangered as they had been during Bodyline. But this generation of batsmen was the last to grow up without being exposed to extreme pace as part of their training, because the mechanised bowling machine was not commonplace until the 1990s. Some attempts to fend off these West Indian bouncers made an amusing spectacle for the unsympathetic.

Viv Richards had his mission, to prove the worth of West Indians in general and Afro-Caribbeans especially. Most of the West Indian bowlers did what they did in order to win as quickly as they could within the Laws. The film *Fire in Babylon* made good drama, but the prosaic truth is that the West Indian fast bowlers, as professionals, were intent on earning the substantial bonuses that came from winning, to enhance basic pay that was unworthy of world champions. Allegations were made that they were racist; yet the most intimidating attack I saw, outside the Kingston Test of 1986, was the one by Courtney Walsh on Devon Malcolm in the first Test of 1993–94. Walsh, of West Indies, went round the wicket and pounded the life out of Malcolm, of England, as well as the Sabina Park pitch. They were of the same race, same colour, and born in the same island of Jamaica.

∭

Aap ke sa he! As-salaam alaikum, Mullahji!

Please come and sit and take some rest. You bless this house with your presence, Mullahji.

Here is some chai, please make yourself comfortable. There! Our friend told me you were the man I had to speak to. He has lost his child and found Allah, the Merciful and Compassionate.

Mullahji, I have decided the time has come. There is a Sura that says: 'For him that gives charity and guards against evil and believes in goodness, We shall smooth the path of salvation.' This is the path I want to take, Mullahji, the path of salvation, because maybe the end is coming for me.

I want to tell you my story. Allah the Generous will not judge me harshly and, inshallah, you will not judge me harshly. I have not told anyone these things, but now is the time, so I will tell you the truth as I remember it.

Bismillah ar-Rahman ar-Rahim, I remember the first part of my life very clearly. I was not born in a rich part of this city but in a poor area with no schools, no hospital, no cricket clubs. It was not a badmaash area then – we were a simple people. We did not have guns everywhere, killing, killing.

I had only little education. Instead of school I went to the stadium and bowled at the players when they went for practice. They gave me a T-shirt and after some time I was bowling good spin in the nets and one of the players gave me a bat he did not want. One day they were short, and they took me to a club match in the park. I batted number ten and though I did not play big shots because I was small-small, I did not get out.

To cut the long story, after a few weeks they gave me another game, at the Gymkhana club, and I scored a half-century. The Gymkhana people asked me to join them – no membership fee, no match fee, we give you money for tuk-tuk to come and practise here every evening. Gymkhana was very good for me. I got selected for national under-17 team, then national under-19. When there were some problems with senior players I made my international debut and – to Allah the praise – I did well.

After one-two years in the national team, I got a contract in England with a county. After three seasons, when I came back, I had the money to buy this house where you are sitting, Mullahji. Second thing: I joined a regional bank as international cricketer. I did not have to work in their office; I went to receptions and presentations when I was not playing and did little-little coaching.

Everything was good for me. Soon I got married, to a local girl, except her mother was from Germany – she had come to work here for international company and met local businessman. This was big marriage for a boy with no matriculation.

Then one day I was batting at the Gymkhana when two black cars drove into the ground and stopped behind the pavilion. I forgot about it because I was nearing my century, but after my inning, when I went back to the dressing room and before I had taken my shower, the captain said there was a big man to see me – a VVIP.

When I walked out of the back door of the pavilion, some goondas pushed me into a car, front seat. In the back seat was the son of one of the big ministers. He said he was not happy. He said the regional bank I worked for had gone bust and he had lost a lot of money. He was holding me responsible. He wanted his money back after one month. If he did not get his money back after one month, I have to find new wife.

What to do? Why didn't these goondas trouble other people who had worked in that bank? How could I tell my wife about this thing? She would have been very scared, run away to her mother in Germany, never come back. So many badmaash peoples now.

Then I remembered. Two seasons before, we had played one-day match at a major international venue, and we had stayed at this big hotel. In the lobby it had a jewellery shop and the owner had seen me and given me a present – Rolex watch, free gift, he said. He gave me his card and said he had very nice restaurant too, and many players had been his guests.

I kept this card. I kept it in my cricket bag, or coffin as we say, Mullahji. Yes, a cricket bag is now a coffin. One day the player next to me in the dressing room saw the card and smiled. 'You know him? He is very rich man. I didn't know he was your friend.'

So I rang the number on this card, hoping he might lend me the money so I could pay off that bastard minister's son with his goondas.

I was never going to get the money by playing cricket, not if I won man-of-the-match in the World Cup final. No problem, my friend, he said. How much do you want? Any time, no problem, if you want big loan. Pay me back when you like, my friend.

After two days only, the money arrived by hawala at Gymkhana club early one morning when nobody there – better than coming to this house when my wife is here. Next home game, the goondas came and asked me how things going, and I tell them I can pay the money. Next day I gave them money for bastard minister's son. He says he is very happy with me, no more problem.

After one month we are going to play home Test match, Mullahji, and the phone rings in my hotel room – this is before everyone has cellphone. It is my friend who has given me the loan. He says the loan is no problem, pay me back as you like, my friend, but he wants to know little-little thing about the Test starting day after tomorrow. Is it flat wicket and will we be playing second spinner?

We have just had team meeting and it's hush-hush we are going to play second spinner because the wicket has been made to turn. Why should I tell him this thing?

I say sorry my friend, this is very important match, we are behind in this series and must win, I cannot tell you. He puts down the phone. I think he is angry with me, but little bit angry only. Next day I practise with everyone. In the evening we have another team meeting to finalise everything, then when I get back to my room the phone rings again. Are we going to play second spinner or not? And this time, if I do not tell him, he wants his money back straight, right now.

All my money had gone on buying this house. I was not playing county cricket any more because I was playing so much for my country and we did not get big money – two thousand dollar for Test match, one thousand dollar for one-dayer. What to do?

I am sitting in my hotel room, thinking, thinking. I have told this man to ring me back after one hour. Then I remember when I was

The Scoring Table

Coming out

Going in

General view of the Match

A Parsee Cricketer

More than a flavour of Kipling's 'Gunga Din' about these sketches of a match between the British military and the Parsis in 1878. But the most remarkable point is that ruler and subject were playing with and against each other on a level field.

J.M. Framji Patel, who captained the Parsis against George Vernon's XI, sits in the centre of the middle row. Also in a striped blazer, to his right, sits the man of that match, M.E. Pavri.

Tom Brown, captain of Rugby's cricket team, talks to the young master instead of watching his side's run-chase against MCC. Arthur looks on, instead of visualising his innings.

Learie Constantine walks out to bat.

No Uncle Tom: Tommy Burton, third from right in the back row of the West Indian team to tour England in 1906.

Right: Dreamy eyes – and the vision of a dreamer: Sir Frank Worrell.

Below: Ironically, the sculptor Robert Hannaford has captured Sir Donald Bradman playing a front-foot off-drive in Adelaide, a shot he did not favour.

Fred Trueman, full-on, and side-on.

His bouncer was known as 'the throat-cutter': Patrick Patterson in the first Test against England at Sabina Park in 1985–86, as Ian Botham backs up, a bit.

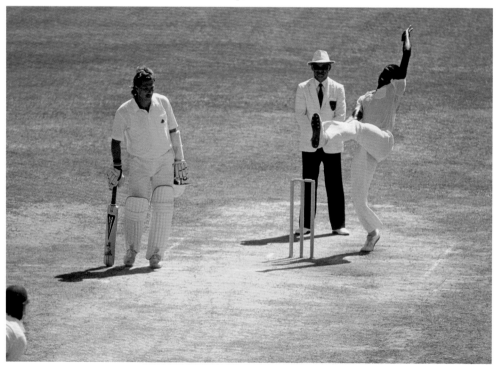

Sir Isaac Vivian Alexander Richards, head unhelmeted and unbowed.

Clockwise from top left: Donatello's David, in the *contrapposto* position; Bernini's David, exuding more power; Ted McDonald, bowling at Leicester at the start of the 1921 Australians' tour; Castagno's David.

Perfection: Wally Hammond at the Sydney Cricket Ground in 1928–29, with Bert Oldfield keeping wicket.

Ian Bell: more powerful, more sponsored, less beautiful.

Above: More Yorkshire than Yorkshire: Len Hutton, personification of the county's cricket, came from the Moravian community in Pudsey.

Right: Alastair Cook at the end of England's 2013–14 tour of Australia: uneasy lies the head that wears a crown.

Below: Cheerleaders at an IPL match in Pune.

playing for my county in England, we were doing very well in Sunday League one season and very bad in County Championship. On Sunday morning, our captain talked with the other captain and came back and said: 'Boys, this is the deal. We are going to win this game today, and they are going to win the match tomorrow.' In England in those days they played this Sunday League in the middle of a County Championship game. Mad people! Anyway, they make sure we win today, and we make sure they win tomorrow. 'Anyone disagree?' the captain asked. I remember one player, young player, put his hand up – that was it. You see, Mullahji, people were doing it in England, with their Spirit of Cricket and all.

Another time, early in my career, I was playing for Rest of the World team in three-match one-day series. Organisers say it had to be 1–1 after two games, then everyone interested and odds very equal, then we make sure home team win the third. During the third game, when Rest of the World were fielding, one of our players came back on the field after drinks break, and said: 'Hey, boys, there is envelope in dressing room for all of you, two thousand dollar each, just make sure we lose this game.' We lost it but I did not take the envelope, I swear, Mullahji. Some of my teammates took it, but not me.

So I am sitting, thinking these things. And what about my neighbour here, Mullahji? He has big parties in his house, big politicians, lots of girls, so many presents. Why should cricketers miss out? Politicians spend whole lifetime making money – we have five, ten years only. When this man rang back, I told him we are playing second spinner.

It is difficult to remember the second half of my career so clearly, Mullahji. It became very difficult, trying to win sometimes, trying to lose sometimes, trying to score runs, trying to get out, telling so many lies.

Things became more difficult when another syndicate started fixing in our team. One of us, when we were playing in Sharjah and staying in Dubai, he was trapped by Uzbek or Ukrainian woman, all same-same. She was working for the boss, Mullahji, the big boss, Mullahji. This player have no chance of escaping after he was secretly filmed in his room. His life finished with shame if he doesn't do what he is told.

Now we all have cells and things very difficult. We have one team, two syndicates, and who knows what is going on. The player who was trapped in Dubai bowls first ball down leg-side to give four wides – and this is the first I've heard of it! People walking in and out of dressing rooms, sending messages, who's bookie, who's punter, who's boss, it make my head hurt. Do we all put caps on after drinks break to say the deal is on, or only one player put cap on backwards? Do we have to give away total in 220–240 bracket or 240–260? And sometimes the other team is trying to lose the same time we are trying to lose. When you can't trust other team to try and win, it is very difficult.

Sometimes it worked beautifully. One bowler, he agree not to bowl me certain ball and I made a lot of runs. Umpire at his end cut into deal, so no chance he give me lbw. Win-win, boss very pleased. Another time we play World Cup game against small country and the deal is extras will be top-scorer. One of them played county cricket and scored some runs, but we still gave enough byes and wides to beat him. My friend so pleased he say you never have to give back the money, it is free gift for life, and one day a new four-wheel-drive is parked outside my house, all tax paid.

Only one problem. Some players get greedy and get found out. That South African captain get caught by Delhi police bugging his phone.

But now I want to change, Mullahji, I want to take the path to salvation. My wife, she has been visiting her mother in Germany for seven years now. I pray the five prayers every day and want to do Haj, if only government give me back passport.

To have no son must be Allah's punishment for what I have done,
Mullahji. But now I have done punishment, so please help me find
His mercy. The Sura says: 'Does he now know that when the dead are
thrown out from their graves and men's hidden thoughts are laid
open, Allah on that day will know all that they have done.' I have
opened my thoughts to you, Mullahji, and I ask forgiveness in the
name of the Merciful and the Compassionate.

Match-fixing was born in the decadent Regency period in England.
It resurfaced there in the 1970s when the county schedule became
too packed, and temptation too easy.

Nothing so crude as money was involved, old boy – not most
of the time, at any rate. This was England: nothing tacky like cash
changed hands. A nudge was as good as a wink when one county
played another not only in a Championship match but in a
Sunday League game in between. As a season drew to a close, if
one county was going well in the Championship and the other in
the Sunday League, it was tempting to rest your older players and
give a few youngsters a game in the competition you were not
going to win.

Was it ethical if a captain made these selections of his own
accord, but unethical if he came to such an arrangement after a
verbal agreement with the opposing captain? And what if the
agreement between them was a tacit understanding, without even
a nudge or wink, and simply done in the expectation that the other
side would follow suit? The main point is that the players should
never have been exposed to such temptation in the first place: to
intercalate, and play one match during another, is wrong.

And the law facilitates the fixer. It resembles a number eleven
who blocks every ball in an old-fashioned game, without any overs
limitation. Block, block, block: every delivery – every attempt at

variation – he kills with his dead bat. The libel law in the United Kingdom makes it impossible to name any names unless you have cast-iron evidence such as bank statements or secretly shot footage – and then only if it has been done in the public interest. Only the dead, like the late Cronje, can be mentioned, let alone exposed. Thus the fixers have lived to fight, and deceive, another day, often in the guise of coach or commentator.

||||

Ball-tampering is normally done behind the back of the umpire standing at the bowler's end. As the bowler returns to his mark, he can pick the seam to make it prouder, or change the condition of the ball without the batsmen or umpires seeing his coin or bottle top, suncream or lip salve, sweets or zipper. He is not allowing the ball to age naturally, therefore he is thought to be taking an unfair advantage. But officialdom's view has varied from country to country, and period to period, about whether changing the condition of the ball intentionally is ethical or not. In England, bowlers were once permitted to rub a ball into the ground, not so that pace bowlers could reverse-swing it, but so that spinners could grip it.

When two neutral umpires, Darrell Hair of Australia and Billy Doctrove of West Indies, suspected Pakistan's bowlers of changing the ball's condition during the Oval Test of 2006, they replaced it with a new one. The Pakistan team, under Inzamam-ul-Haq, felt they had been accused of cheating and refused to play on after the tea interval, conceding the game. For the second time, a day of Test cricket was lost, and Pakistan's board was billed for compensation of half a million pounds.

||||

Throwing, I would say, has generated more righteous indignation – more heat under the collars and caps of cricketers – than any other single issue, even more than moving a fielder behind a bats-man's back, or ball-tampering, or Mankading.*

The failure to keep a straight arm, or rather the act of straighten-ing the arm in delivery, is widely seen to be unethical. Which is strange, because often the pace bowler with a hyper-extended elbow is not trying to take an unfair advantage. Rather than making a conscious choice between right and wrong, he is merely bowling in the style that comes most easily to him. But I believe that a few have gone wide of the crease and speared in the bouncers, knowing that thereby they have increased the likelihood of their delivery being a throw.

Cricket was not originally associated with the concept of straight-ness. It was not until the late eighteenth century that bats became straight, no longer curved like a hockey stick. Only when bats were straight, and round-arm then over-arm bowling required a straight elbow, did the sport become synonymous with this concept. The honest person thereafter kept 'a straight bat'. If he was not playing straight, it wasn't cricket.

So, while a bowler may not be aware of bending his elbow to an unacceptable extent, as soon as his opponents think he does, the whispered accusations of cheating begin. Bending an elbow is perceived to be taking an unfair advantage because it can add extra speed or extra spin to the ball. As Ranjitsinhji observed: 'Mere physical or brute strength ought not to gain an advantage over the real subtleties of the art of bowling.'

---

* If there has been an exception to this rule about throwing generating the most heated indignation, it was when Trevor Chappell, on the instructions of his captain and older brother Greg, bowled an under-arm delivery for the last ball of the one-day international between Australia and New Zealand at Melbourne in 1981 when New Zealand needed six to win. New Zealand's prime minister Robert Muldoon weighed in by saying, 'It was the most disgusting incident I can recall in the history of cricket,' and he now understood why the Australian team's uniform was yellow. The loophole allowing under-arm was swiftly closed.

Ranji had raised uproar in Australia when he accused the South Australian Ernest Jones of throwing on England's 1897–98 tour. Jones was also accused by an umpire and became the first to be no-balled in a Test for throwing. Matters were brought to this head by James Phillips, who was a century ahead of his time in being a professional umpire all year round. Alternating between seasons in the northern and southern hemisphere, he fearlessly no-balled several bowlers in England and Australia. Some were banned or phased out, and the issue of throwing did not resurface as a major issue until the 1950s.

Whereas the majority of bowlers suspected of throwing used to be pace bowlers, now they are more likely to be spinners: spinners of various kinds except leg-break and chinaman bowlers. The first cause célèbre involving a spinner centred on Tony Lock in the 1950s. He had started as a normal left-arm orthodox spinner, until Surrey practised one winter in an indoor school with a low ceiling and he altered his action. Lock was no-balled in a Test match in 1953–54 in the West Indies, and would surely not have got away with throwing as long as he did if he had not enjoyed MCC's backing. But again he knew not what he did. Ted Dexter told me that during England's 1958–59 tour of New Zealand, Lock was filmed by a cine-camera while bowling.* At a party at the house of the former New Zealand captain Geoff Rabone, this film was shown, and Lock was stunned, mortified. He went home and worked to restore his action to what it had been before the indoor school.

The received wisdom is that the International Cricket Council changed its regulations to allow Muttiah Muralitharan of Sri Lanka to continue bowling. When I first saw him in the one-off Test in Colombo in 1993, I thought he threw; and was told that

---

* Private conversation during the third Test between England and India in Kolkata, December 2012.

on Sri Lanka's tour of England in 1991 the first-class umpires had given the tourists an unofficial warning that he should not play in the one-off Test at Lord's. After the Australian off-spinner Bruce Yardley became Sri Lanka's coach, Muralitharan became much less chest-on, more side-on in delivery; and I thought his wrist and fingers put almost all the energy into the ball, to the point where his elbow was almost irrelevant. When the ICC allowed bowlers to have a hyper-extension of their elbow up to 15 degrees of flexion, Muralitharan's off-break appeared to me to be just about within the law.

The doosra – or 'the other one', as opposed to the off-break – complicated matters again, by demanding far more of a bend in the elbow than the off-break. Maybe it is not a coincidence that Lahore, by my reading at any rate, has been the birthplace both of the doosra and of reverse swing of the now-accepted kind.* On England's last tour of Pakistan in 2005–06, I was told that a cousin of Majid Khan used to bowl a doosra in the Bagh-i-Jinnah long before Saqlain Mushtaq was hailed as the pioneer. Spinner and swinger were reacting to the same circumstance: pitches so conducive to batting, like concrete, that a bowler had to devise a new way to deceive his opponent.

For all the definitions in the Laws and the ICC regulations, throwing is partly in the eye of the beholder. If a bowler is in our team, his action is not so questionable as that of an opponent, even though their actions are identical; there seems to have been this subjective element ever since R.E. Mody. Our opinion can depend on the literal perspective too: an action that seems fine from one end of the ground can look 'diabolical' from the other.

---

* Reverse-swing produced by soaking one side with sweat was common in Barbadian club cricket from the 1950s, or even before, so I was told on England's tour of the West Indies in 1989–90 by Richard ('Prof') Edwards, who represented West Indies in the 1960s in five Tests.

|||

'Come,' says Muttiah Muralitharan, asking for a volunteer. We are sitting in the reception room of his villa – a fairly modest one, not suspiciously expensive – on the outskirts of Colombo.

The world record-holder for Test wickets goes to his sideboard and kneels. But he is not asking for mercy from the assembled journalists, for once. He is giving us the readings from his last testing by the ICC on his right elbow.

Palm upwards, the record-holder extends his right arm along the sideboard. It is not straight. According to Murali, his elbow rises at an angle of 27 degrees above the horizontal – even when the volunteer pushes down on Murali's right forearm as hard as he can.

Murali's right elbow simply does not straighten. Nor does his left elbow, which rises 24 degrees above the horizontal, so he says, credibly. It is a condition, he says, which he inherited from his grandfather.

Thus a lot of cricket history is explained. In releasing one of his fizzing off-breaks, Murali's elbow went from an angle of 27 degrees to 38 degrees. According to the new lasers which can make precise measurements, his elbow bent 10.5 degrees in delivery, well within the 15 degrees now permitted.

Some more biology. It was Murali's bent arm – his naturally, unavoidably bent arm – that allowed his wrist and fingers to spin the ball like a top. 'When you really straighten your arm, according to science, the movement of the wrist is less,' Murali said. 'When you're bent, it's more. So I have an advantage with a bent arm!' Some advantage: he finished with 800 Test wickets, a record that will never be surpassed, given the popularity and commercial success of Twenty20.

|||

Another son of Jamnagar stirred controversy in Australia exactly half a century after Ranjitsinhji. When Vinoo Mankad was bowling his left-arm spin for the touring Indians against an Australian XI in 1947–48, he warned the non-striker Bill Brown not to leave his crease before he had bowled. The second time Brown did it, Mankad ran him out. Public opinion, and Brown himself, thought this action justified: the non-striker was taking unfair advantage, after he had been warned.

In the subsequent Test at Sydney, when Brown backed up again as the non-striker, Mankad ran him out again – without a warning. Majority opinion this time was against Mankad. Disproportionality seems to me to be the key here: the punishment of Mankading is not proportionate to the crime. The crime is to get a head start in running between wickets (for the sake of the striker and the team, without any direct benefit for the non-striker); the punishment is for the non-striker to be run out. Natural justice says that someone should not lose his life for a minor offence, especially if he has not been warned.

Of the two finest examples of ethical action in English cricket in my time, the first was the boycotting of South Africa. MCC, still in charge of the professional game at the end of the 1960s, would have been all too happy to continue playing apartheid South Africa; the conscience of two of its younger members, Michael Brearley and the then Bishop of Woolwich, David Sheppard, was not at first shared by the vast majority. Basil D'Oliveira, however, was the man for this moment.

The second example came in the World Cup of 2003 in South Africa – or rather in South Africa, Kenya and Zimbabwe. If it had been held in South Africa alone, there would have been no such moral dilemma. It boiled down to the England team being left to decide, by themselves, whether or not they should play their match against Zimbabwe in Harare. At first it was a security issue: could England withdraw from the fixture on these grounds, just as New Zealand withdrew from their match in Nairobi, thus conceding the points to the home team?

But once England's security concerns had been more or less satisfied, and the players realised they would be perfectly safe if they visited Harare, it became an ethical issue – one the players were left to answer on their own. The England and Wales Cricket Board, and even more so the British government, were in a far more informed position to pass this judgement. But, depending on your point of view, they either liberally left grown men to make their minds up, or washed their hands.

England's players, stuck in this impasse and a downtown hotel in Cape Town, went through several days of increasing anguish. Andy Flower and Henry Olonga had just alerted the cricket world by wearing black armbands during Zimbabwe's first match in the World Cup. England's players were then given a presentation, by a Channel Four producer, on the country ruled by Robert Mugabe: the repression, the malnutrition, the arrests, the torture. Several dozen spectators who had attended the World Cup match in Bulawayo had been detained and beaten by police; so how much more likely was it that violence would be perpetrated on a greater scale in Harare, where Zanu-PF did as Mugabe liked? The venue for the Zimbabwe v England match, the Harare Sports Club, was next door to the president's residence.

Here was the chance of a lifetime for most of England's cricketers to achieve something memorable in a global tournament. Those who had survived the Ashes tour – directly before the World Cup – had been toughened, if tired. If they beat Zimbabwe, they were going to qualify for the Super Six stage, with the semi-finals in sight. Refusing to play Zimbabwe, whatever the grounds, would likely lead to an early exit from the World Cup – and few of the players would be around for the next one four years later.

In the end, England's players decided not to go to Harare, by a majority verdict, and mainly on ethical grounds. Nasser Hussain, the captain, went through something close to hell before coming out the other side. As I was ghosting him at the time, I knew the anguish was not feigned. 'We couldn't have lived with ourselves if we had played that game and spectators or people outside the ground had been arrested and beaten up,' Hussain said.

Fruitless, perhaps. Yet it was one of England's finest performances.

It is very rare now for the Spirit of Cricket to be applied on the field. In more than 400 Tests I have seen, the only time it has happened was at Trent Bridge in 2011, when Ian Bell was invited to resume his innings after being run out off the last ball before tea. And it was as a result of pressure being exerted upon India's captain, M.S. Dhoni, by India's board president, Narayanaswami Srinivasan, in a phone call during the interval. The political need to maintain good relations between the two boards and countries was the deciding factor as much as sportsmanship.

The Spirit of Cricket has been applied off the field. After Australia had announced their team before the Edgbaston Test in 2009, their wicketkeeper Brad Haddin hurt a finger in practice. They asked England to allow Australia to replace Haddin with their reserve wicketkeeper, Graham Manou, and Andrew Strauss agreed. According to the Laws, he had the right to refuse. It was common sense, Strauss said, that a specialist should keep wicket and none of the other members of the Australian XI could do so. In the next Test at Headingley, England's generosity was repaid when Australia's captain Ricky Ponting allowed Matt Prior extra time to recover from a back spasm before the revised start.

Otherwise, the Spirit of Cricket is applied in little more than gestures. A fielder who bends down and ties a batsman's bootlace for him is considered sporting, or rather he would be called unsporting if he was seen to refuse. In-coming batsmen are no longer applauded, except in a Sunday friendly on the village green or if a great player is retiring, after the fashion of an actor or musician going on stage; but the Spirit of Cricket dictates that fielders, though not the bowler, should applaud his century and clap him off the field at the close of a day. The Spirit of Cricket dictates that the fielders shall wait for the batsmen to leave the field first at an interval, except if they are lagging too far behind, in which case they should wave the fielders off first. If a batsman drops his bat while running between wickets, a fielder will be considered a good sport if he picks it up and returns it. Similarly, if a ball comes to rest in or near the crease, the batsman is considered polite if he picks it up and passes it to a fielder. That was until the Australian team around the turn of the millennium told the batsman not to bloody touch it.

These are not actions, however, that affect the outcome of the match. The result is the same whether or not a fielder picks up the bat that the batsman has dropped. If Arthur, Tom and the young master were to be reincarnated in their blazers and boaters, they would be pleased to see the fielder pick the bat up for the batsman: they might see it as a vestige of Muscular Christianity, of doing unto others what we would have done unto ourselves. But it is no more than a gesture.

Cricket is more likely now to teach the young player practicalities than ethics. It can teach the eight-year-old to fasten his laces or pads properly so he does not trip over. It can teach him how to switch his concentration on and off while fielding. He will learn how to be alert, whether anticipating the need to back up a loose throw in the field, or keeping an eye on his captain between deliveries, or when looking for a quick single while batting. He will learn how to concentrate on one ball at a time, even if this is ever less useful in a world of multi-tasking.

The Laws, overall, have done their job. If a youngster from the North-West Frontier – perhaps where Tom Brown was sent to serve as a district officer – takes up cricket, he may have a lot to learn about the Laws, if he so wishes, but not much about the Spirit of Cricket. On the field of play, he will seldom have to make a judgement based on good and evil, right and wrong.

The young master at Rugby, the disciple of Dr Arnold, would be disappointed. But then the war on terror, starting in the early twenty-first century, led to the erosion of individual liberties in Britain. So habeas corpus and trial by jury are not what they used to be either.

I know my place. The boarding pass reminds me. My seat on the plane is usually 64B or 76C. Apart from my solitary century, the nearest I get to a hundred is when I fly.

From the back, however, I can see who comes and goes – 'who's in, who's out', as King Lear said. In *Beyond a Boundary*, C.L.R. James said the Ancient Greeks divided people into those who act on the stage, those who sit in the audience and applaud, and those who sit in the wings and write about those who act on the stage. He did not cite his Classical source, but I agree: mankind is divided almost exactly into those three categories.

But I should have got out of my seat at the back of the plane – or in the wings of the theatre – and acted upon the stage in the question of Sri Lanka.

Should it have been in 1984, during Sri Lanka's inaugural Test in England, when Tamil demonstrators ran on to the ground at Lord's to demonstrate against the civil war? Some people laughed: who are these funny chaps waving flags and banners sporting the name of 'Eelam'? Plays for Kent, doesn't he? Alan Ealham! Haw, haw.

At least I did not do that. But I was guilty of the sin of omission. I did not take the trouble then to find out about the Tamil minority, and how events set in train by the British divided the country. The educated Tamil elite ran the bureaucracy, using the English language; on Ceylon's Independence in 1948 the Sinhalese majority began pushing the pendulum back their way by making Sinhala the language of government and education, squeezing Tamils out.

Tamil culture is highly advanced, and very conservative, so that the caste system had endured in their northern and eastern areas of Sri Lanka. A member of a low-caste fishing community, Velupillai Prabhakaran, assassinated rival leaders, before taking control of all the Tamil protest movements in the name of his organisation, the Liberation Tigers of Tamil Eelam.

It may be difficult to sympathise with people in a country that is just a name on the map. But I visited Sri Lanka for the first time in 1993. Should I have protested then on behalf of press freedom in Sri Lanka? The army was forbidding journalists to go to the north and east to see what was happening – for 'their safety'. Or perhaps for the safety of the Sri Lankan army's reputation.

I could agree, at a push, with the reasoning that the only way to end the civil war was for the Sri Lankan army to win it by military means. Prabhakaran was too much of a psychopath ever to submit, ever to do what was best for the people he nominally represented. In the event, I closed my eyes and ears, until an official in the British High Commission in Colombo told me the lie behind the official statistics.

About 70,000 people, according to the Sri Lankan government, had died during the civil war as it approached its end after 30 years. This number, however, excluded all those who had disappeared and were presumed dead, or who lay in mass graves unearthed. Only corpses were officially counted. This made a very different equation. Seventy thousand dead over 30 years was a terrible tragedy, but it was a civil war, and it was 'only' two thousand or so people killed per year. Whereas, in reality, that number had to be multiplied several times over.

Or was the best time to protest after the Sri Lankan army won, killing not only Prabhakaran, but many unarmed and innocent Tamil civilians in the process? As the months passed, it became apparent that the government of Mahinda Rajapaksa, no matter what it said, was not using the peace wisely. Tamil civilians were held in concentration camps; army abuses denied; journalists and United Nations officials still forbidden from investigating in war-torn areas; everything sanitised. And foreign governments carried on happily negotiating with the Sri Lankan government for all the minerals with which the island is enriched, including uranium.

Cricket was the only possible lever. The government would have been shaken if the cricket world had boycotted Sri Lanka when the country was about to stage a major tournament. Nothing might have made the government change its repressive ways, but cricket could have come closer than anything to forcing it to do so. And, as a member of the cricket media, I could have tried to kick-start the process.

Had the cricket community threatened a boycott of the World Cup in Sri Lanka in 2011, or of the World Twenty20 finals in 2012, the government might have been forced to allow a proper Truth and Reconciliation commission, instead of the official whitewash, to investigate military abuses; to allow Tamils a meaningful role, not only in economic regeneration, but in political life; and to pay some compensation to the families of those who 'disappeared', including dozens of brave Sri Lankan journalists.

Instead, too many Tamil resentments were buried in the bloody earth. Unlike the corpses, they may rise again, if not initially in Sri Lanka, then in Tamil communities in India, Canada, Australia or Britain.

Mea maxima culpa.

9

A THING OF BEAUTY

For poise, grace, symmetry, composition and power it might be a picture of a statue by Pheidias.

Ronald Mason, on the batsman Wally Hammond

Pheidias would certainly have taken him for a model.

John Nyren, on the bowler David Harris

CRICKET BECOMES BIGGER and better as more and more money enters it. Nobody, not even the most nostalgic of old-timers, would dispute that the standard of fielding has gone up as boundary fielders leap to flick the ball back to a converging colleague to complete the catch. The range of shots increases, and the thickness of bats, and the number of sixes. The different types of delivery increase, too, as spinners devise doosras and carrom balls, and pace bowlers do anything not to be slogged at the death. The size of the global television audience grows, if only because India's population does; and we can suspect an increase in the amounts of money gambled on the game.

In one major respect, however, cricket is reduced. It is a less beautiful game than it used to be – and while its beauty could be recaptured, the forces which spoiled it are not going to recede in the foreseeable future.

The apex of beauty in batting was captured in Sydney in November 1928. A freelance photographer, Herbert Fishwick, who normally specialised in travelling to the Australian outback and photographing Merino sheep for wealthy graziers, decided to go instead to the Sydney Cricket Ground, as the MCC tourists were in town to play New South Wales. He went equipped with his 'Long Tom'. This new type of camera, between four and six feet long, had been developed for aerial reconnaissance during the First World War. When peace prevailed in the 1920s, it allowed, for the first time, action photographs of cricket matches to be taken from the boundary. Along with his Long Tom – of which only a handful existed in Australia – Fishwick would have carried between one and two dozen fragile plates on which to capture the day's events. Given so few, his timing had to be as precise as a batsman's.

Two prodigies, one on each side, were in action at the SCG in this build-up to the Ashes series. Don Bradman, a boy from Bowral, had just slipped into the New South Wales team. The English side contained a batsman a bit older, in Wally Hammond. The previous year, 1927, Hammond had scored 1000 first-class runs in May, which only W.G. Grace had done. It was Hammond's first tour of Australia, but whenever he walked to the wicket at number three (four in this game), he had either Jack Hobbs or Herbert Sutcliffe to talk him through those early overs when English batsmen must adjust to Australia's sharper light and sharper bounce.

MCC batted first after their overtly cheerful captain, Percy Chapman, won the toss. The pitch had been rolled and rolled into the consistency of iron; and Australia's nationwide lack of bowling was reflected in the state side. Since 1912 England had won a solitary Test in Australia. Now they had some fine bowlers who could win this series – provided their batsmen could bat as well as Australia's (Bill Ponsford had twice gone past Archie MacLaren's world-record first-class innings of 424). MCC set about amassing a total over 700.

Fishwick's index finger must have hovered over the shutter of his Long Tom several times in the course of every ball. At some moment after midday, needing to use up at least one plate on England's prodigy before Hammond was dismissed, Fishwick took the plunge. Cricketers were not so docile or predictable as sheep. As one of the state's spinners happened to be bowling, Bert Oldfield was standing up to the stumps, and he was Australia's wicketkeeper. On one plate, Fishwick could capture two major cricketers.

He pressed.

Later that day, when the plate reached the dark room of the *Sydney Mail* and was developed, what emerged was nothing less than cricket's most beautiful photograph.

The first to appreciate it in detail was Ronald Mason in *Batsman's Paradise*. This photograph, Mason wrote in the 1950s, was:

> . . . the most striking action picture of a batsman that has ever been put on record. For poise, grace, symmetry, composition and power it might be a picture of a statue by Pheidias; there is a flawless balance in the distribution of every line and every mass in the field of vision, and moreover it conveys an infinite potentiality of strength . . . Compositionally the picture has built itself up most happily in the form of a pyramid; the wicket-keeper, who is Oldfield and therefore adds an instinctive grace of his own, is bent alertly in such a way that the line of his back and the transverse [sic] one of his arms and outstretched gloves exactly lead into and answer the corresponding lines of the batsman's figure. All these lines point to the centre; to the great shoulders and whipcord sinews at the hub of this explosive activity.

All true. It is the most beautifully composed photograph of the most beautiful cricket stroke. But Mason devoted only one paragraph to his analysis of this superlative illustration, albeit one page in length. The author was a dear, self-effacing man whose quiet nature allowed him to make invaluable observations about the passage of time in cricket; but the fanfare for this prime example of aesthetics should be blown longer and louder.

I would go so far as to claim that the combination of this photograph and this stroke attains perfection. Change any signifi- cant detail of this composition and it would tumble back to earth. And by studying it, we can not only comprehend the elements of its beauty, we can also see what the sport has subse- quently lost.

The first point to note is the most basic: the bails remain in their grooves. The whole edifice would crumble if everything were the same except a bail had fallen and Hammond had been bowled or stumped. The batsman would have failed in his primary purpose, that of defending his wicket. The first point, therefore, is that the batsman has fulfilled his primary function.

The second point is Hammond's posture. As Mason observed, 'the left toe, giving direction to the stroke, is pointed as lightly and as weightlessly as a ballet dancer's.' No less essential is the fact that Hammond is not playing off the back foot. Suppose that the bowler had pitched short and Hammond had driven him in exactly the same direction but off the back foot, he would not have given the same overriding impression of mastery. Instinctively, we protect our head and reproductive organs before any other parts of our body: this is one reason to play off the back foot. If, therefore, a man is ready to commit his head to the combat by pushing it ahead of his body, and to play off the front foot, he signals that he wishes to get as close to his opponent as he can, without hesitation or fear. Given a big swing of his weapon into the bargain, his intent is predatory. Hammond, in the course of his innings, is taking the attack to the bowlers.

Not every stroke played off the back foot is a defensive one, of course. Nonetheless, 'on the back foot' has become part of English speech, as a metaphor for being on the defensive. To be on the front foot is to display the will to dominate; and with it, if the posture is correct, comes the most beautiful representation of the male human form.

Let us go back, in order to move forward, to classical Greek sculpture. Take a statue in the British Museum, of the hunter who has raised his right arm to throw his spear. He is a beautiful young man, and strong, as his musculature bespeaks, especially in his thighs and calves. But he is not a threatening figure, or a particularly aggressive one, considering that he is a hunter; and this is because most of his weight is on his back leg.

If we move on to Donatello's statue of David as a second example, we see the victor, sword in hand, shortly after he has slain and decapitated Goliath. David stands in the *contrapposto* position: his weight is more on his back leg than his front, but it is spread over both. The impression that David gives us is one of grace and elegance – and, if his smile is anything to go by, a degree of self-satisfaction at his own clever skill with a sling. But, being in the almost upright *contrapposto* position, David does not radiate strength and menace. He does not need to, having slain Goliath.

For the next picture in this sequence, we should consider an athlete in a half-forward position: again it is David, this one sculpted by Bernini. We can see from the side view that David has begun to transfer his weight on to his right and leading foot, in the direction of his opponent. By so doing he adds to the velocity and accuracy of his sling. Bernini's David is tense, braced for action, intent on being as brave and effective as he can in this mortal combat. But we cannot feel convinced about his prospects for success, as we do for Hammond after looking at Fishwick's photograph (Hammond went on to score 225). David does not inspire us with the absolute confidence that would have been conveyed if he had committed himself fully to his front foot and a posture of outright aggression towards his opponent. He has set aside his armour, which leans beside his right leg. We cannot be sure he will not need it.

Modern coaches use the term 'power position' to describe the pose in which an athlete leans forward with his head over a bent, leading leg: the position of Hammond at the end of his off-drive. This position achieves the most explosive power, whether in shot-putting, sprinting, throwing, batting or bowling. It captures the essence of masculine strength and beauty.

We can all recognise these qualities when we see them in action, even if we do not have Fishwick's gift for capturing the moment. We can also recognise them when they are absent. Nobody called the batting of England's Alastair Cook 'beautiful' in the Ashes series of 2010–11: prodigiously effective, and second in productivity only to Hammond in 1928–29 among England batsmen in any series (766 v 905), but neither beautiful nor handsome. The reason lay in the uprightness and stiffness of the position in which Cook played his shots – characteristic of the subjects in early Greek sculpture of the Archaic period, before the concepts of movement and elegance evolved.

Because the power position is most aesthetically pleasing, the cricket strokes which involve it are considered to be beautiful; those which do not involve it are deemed less so, if at all. That is why strokes on the off-side can provoke the praise of 'beautiful', but seldom shots on the leg-side. Cricket is thus distinguished from baseball, in which all hits are cross-batted and mostly to what cricket would call the leg-side.

The drive, when well executed from the power position, normally directs the ball to the off-side; only the drive through mid-on goes to leg. In the Kolkata Test between India and South Africa in 2010–11, the master technician Jacques Kallis drove through midwicket a ball from Zaheer Khan, bowling left-arm over the wicket, which pitched outside his leg-stump. This is the squarest angle on the leg-side that I have seen a ball driven from the power position. If a batsman aims any squarer than that, he has to play round a braced rather than bent front leg.

The late cut involves the power position in reverse. The batsman's head, instead of pointing towards the bowler, is pointed in the opposite direction towards the wicketkeeper. A late cut is deemed beautiful if the batsman bends into the stroke in this way, whereas an attempt at a cut from a stiff and upright position is merely a 'dab'. But while the late cut can be beautiful – Frank Worrell the supreme exponent – it does not convey power and aggression.

Even the man who is still held to be the paragon of batting style cannot be an exception to these principles. Victor Trumper striding down the pitch towards the bowler was cricket's first famous action photograph; and he makes a majestic sight as he sets himself to drive the ball straight. But this stroke is not so beautiful as Hammond's front-foot off-drive because Trumper is playing with both legs braced and his torso upright.

Runs scored on the leg-side are more likely to stem from 'shots' than 'strokes': the nomenclature tells us that more power than beauty is involved in the pull and the pick-up, or the flick over square-leg, if not the leg-glance. Whether the batsman concerned is Hammond or David Gower, Frank Woolley or V.V.S. Laxman, no pull shot is deemed beautiful. It is the most primitive shot, the nearest to natural. It may even be termed 'savage'.

When a batsman hooks a ball above shoulder-height, he makes a concession to the bowler's speed and bounce, either by moving on to the back foot or by keeping his weight spread on both feet. In either event, he does not go down the pitch with his head leading his assault upon the ball and bowler. Brave, yes; effective, yes, and extremely so if the ball is hooked for four or six. But not absolute mastery from the moment the ball leaves the bowler's hand, because of that initial concession.

Hammond's physicality is the third most significant feature of this photograph; or, as Mason called it, 'an infinite potentiality of strength'. A man's cricket – the style in which he bats, the method he bowls – is shaped, like his character, by his physical characteristics. Oldfield is neatness; Hammond is strength.

Although not naked like the subjects of classical Greek and Renaissance sculpture, we can sense the musculature rippling beneath the white flannels. In particular, as Mason observed, the breadth of Hammond's shoulders, before tapering to his waist, illustrate the power: a power no less than that of David as sculpted by either Bernini or Michelangelo. By comparison the latent strength of Donatello's David seems feeble.

Yet all this power embodied in Hammond is perfectly balanced. He does not need to use his heels, like lesser mortals, as a platform for his body weight. He is sufficiently lithe to need only his right toes and the ball of his left foot. He is almost as light as Mercury, as in the study by Giovanni Bologna: his Mercury is a god who cannot be held down by the bonds of earth and gravity, and is almost taking off from the toes of his left foot. Hammond embodies lightness and strength, power and balance, in a perfect equipoise.

Mason calls the composition of this photograph 'a pyramid'. This is the only point where I would disagree, and it may be the result of his looking at a picture of Hammond alone, without Oldfield (in a footnote, Mason says the only surviving print omits the wicket-keeper, which has subsequently proved incorrect, thankfully). The overall form captured by Fishwick is that of a scalene triangle, one without equal sides or equal angles such as a pyramid has.

This triangle begins at Oldfield's left heel. One line runs up Oldfield's back, then along Hammond's back to his head. The second line runs from Oldfield's feet and through his gloves to Hammond's left foot. The triangle is completed by the third line, a vertical running down from Hammond's hands to the toe of his left foot: a line which exists because Hammond has moved his head and front foot into the technically correct position. This triangle would have been broken if Oldfield had not crouched so low, to the point where his eyes are level with the bails, or if he had stood up too soon, as ordinary wicketkeepers do.

Other details heighten the effect, especially if the person studying this photograph is hibernating in Britain. The light and shade speak of sunshine and heat. Both batsman and wicketkeeper are wearing caps, and the shade that covers their eyes keeps out the sun which warms the rest of their bodies. Neither figure is wearing a sweater; both men have their sleeves rolled up to slightly below the elbow. The time told by the shadows is past midday but not far past. It makes for a not inappropriate symbolism, for some would say the 1928–29 series saw the high noon of the battle between Australia and England for the Ashes, before Bodyline in the following series in Australia foreshadowed the modern era.

Hammond, as a 25-year-old professional sportsman, is unlikely to have been aware of Michelangelo's technique of polishing marble to increase the effect of light and texture. But we know from the playwright Ben Travers, in a monograph he wrote about this tour, that Hammond spent some of his spare time in the Ladies' Pavilion at the Sydney Cricket Ground, while his teammates were in the main pavilion, and would sign autographs for female admirers. So we are dealing here with an individual human being, with strengths and weaknesses; we are not dealing with idealised form, as in classical Greek sculpture. The handkerchief in Hammond's right pocket was a mannerism, perhaps affectation, that he copied from his Gloucestershire captain, Bev Lyon; and he wore silk shirts, like very few cricketers of his day, especially cash-strapped professionals. Hammond's pride, his polishing of his image, are manifested here, and not without reason.

Note also the creases, and the simplicity of their white lines, by comparison not only with all the lines which now mark a cricket pitch but also the ones that criss-cross an American football field and give gridiron its name. Because we have only two white lines – in a pleasant parallel – they do not distract from the human activity. Indeed, I would argue the straightness of the two lines serves as a counterpoint to the curves of which the two cricketers are composed. Hammond and Oldfield have no straight lines, no sharp angles, no jagged edges: the nearest to a straight line is Hammond's back or right leg, in conformity with orthodox technique. For Hammond, like other elite athletes in cricket such as Ranjitsinhji and Sobers, the conventional epithet was that 'he had no bones'.

The simplicity of these two white creases allows us to feel that cricket *au fond* is a simple game of bat and ball, almost a natural one, with few artificial additions. Or so it was then. Subsequently, from 1963 in England, the front or popping crease became the marker for no-balls, not the back or bowling crease (which had not deterred fast bowlers from dragging their back heel over the line). To accompany this change in the law, the return crease had to be lengthened from a couple of inches to two or three yards.

It might be argued that the equipment, being artificial or man-made, detracts from this composition: the pads of both batsman and keeper, and Oldfield's gloves, and Hammond's bat (his gloves seem part of his white clothing). I would argue the pads are not an impediment to the movement of the two players or, therefore, to our enjoyment of this scene; while Hammond's bat is a simple extension of his arms, less intrusive than the sling wielded by Bernini's David, or the spear brandished by classical Greek warriors. The bat at the end of Hammond's follow-through could even be said to lend an uplifting quality, akin to the torch that carries the Olympic flame. It is not an axe or a sword or a spear coming down upon an opponent; the bat has been raised in a positive or life-enhancing act, not a destructive one.

Above all, as Mason says, we have at the centre of this composition this 'infinite potentiality of strength'. I think of a rowing boat when the crew find their rhythm and suddenly synchronise; of Taiaroa Head near Dunedin, and an albatross, which hangs motionless in the wind then achieves, with no more than a twitch of its vast wingspan on a thermal, surging acceleration; or passages of Beethoven when he goes full steam ahead yet seems to have nuclear power stations of energy in reserve. At such moments we forget that mankind is fallible and, even if it is illusion, sense we are capable of something grander.

Left-handed batsmen, ever since 'Great Newland', have been perceived to be more graceful than right-handed ones.

My theory is that this is a function of width. Until limited-overs cricket took off, and especially Twenty20, most right-arm pace bowlers bowled over the wicket. Therefore their line was not at the stumps – because then they would have pitched outside the batsman's legs too often – but across the left-handed batsman. He was therefore able to 'free his arms': to get into the power position and drive the ball through the off-side.

Take a mirror if need be. When a right-handed batsman faces a left-arm pace bowler who is bowling over the wicket, the angles are reproduced, and the effect is the same: if this bowler is not swinging the ball into the batsman, he gives him width and therefore scope to play aesthetically pleasing strokes.

The gracefulness of the left-hander evaporates once the right-arm pace bowler goes round the wicket and angles the ball in. The left-hander who scores most of his runs leg-side is not considered beautiful. Thus the Kent amateur Gerry Weigall compared the two best left-handed batsmen of his day: Frank Woolley, of his own county, and Maurice Leyland of Yorkshire. Woolley flowed through the off-side; Leyland was 'a cross-batted village-greener, sir!'

My favourite left-hander? Even more than David Gower or Brian Lara, it has to be Pakistan's opening batsman of the late 1990s, Saeed Anwar. He added an extra dimension. Having reached the power position in which to cover-drive, Anwar would wait for the ball, and if it did not come to him, but was slanted to go further away, his wrists went after it with an amazing elasticity, and they kept on going, extending and extending, until they were on the line of the ball, however wide it was angled, then whipped it. No lazy flicking or wafting.

|||

No longer, however, can a photograph capture a perfect stroke in all its beauty unmarred. Cricket is not only an escape from reality, but an integral part of the commercial world. It might be hyperbole to claim that cricket sold its soul when Kerry Packer launched his World Series Cricket in 1977; but the sport did proceed to sell its broadcasting rights to the highest bidder, to deter the best cricketers from signing for a private promoter. The consequence was marketing, advertising and branding.

When Hammond played his off-drive in 1928, no bat stickers or logos obtruded into the purity of this prelapsarian world. By the time Ian Bell played an off-drive comparable to Hammond's, the distractions were numerous – and advertisements are meant to be distractions, if only noticed subliminally. Mammon insinuated itself, from the stumps and the batsmen's clothes and equipment to the outfield and advertising boards – and, in return, paid the money which allowed Bell to devote his whole career to the pursuit of excellence. Hammond was free to wear the white silk shirt he liked, pure and unsullied, because he was not contracted to wear official team kit – but he had to work for a car dealership in Bristol in the off-seasons when he was not touring, to pay the rent.

The photograph is party to this loss of innocence: the advertisements are now captured and passed on to all who look. From the boundary, only the spectator who is very short-sighted can fail to see the logos and lettering.

A second change has taken place since 1928, in addition to the sport's commercialisation. To hit the ball to the boundary, Hammond had to use his wrists and follow through with his bat in a full circle of 360 degrees. Sobers, into the 1970s, would follow through with his bat so far that, at the end of a back-foot drive, it would slap against his back. No modern batsman has to expend such effort any longer and propel his bat through so generous an arc. Bell's bat is almost twice as thick as Hammond's, but barely heavier because of technological advances in compressing the willow. Bell – or anyone else in international cricket, 'stylist' or not – has only to play a checked half-drive, little more than a defensive push, to send the ball past mid-off to the boundary, without anything like the same input from his wrists. If Bell did follow through as far as Hammond, he might be criticised for a needless flourish or affectation, for 'posing'.

A daring, albeit helmeted, batsman who slog-sweeps can get into much the same position as the front-foot driver. But, while using his strength and athleticism to hit a six, he will lack the element of poise and balance as he hits across the line – and perhaps falls over to the off-side, as the brilliant Guyanese Rohan Kanhai did when he began to sweep opponents aside from the late 1950s.

Today's batsman gets more value, in terms of runs, than his predecessor did for the effort he puts into his shots. As a rule of thumb, the proportion of boundaries in a side's innings has increased from one-third to almost half. Today's spectators, however, gets less value, in terms of aesthetic pleasure, for their entrance money.

Any technological advance has to be tried until the lawmakers reject it: it is incumbent upon the professional sportsman to take any advantage he can. But the time may have come for the thickness of the bat to be limited, as its width and length are. This would make the sport safer too, as well as more aesthetically pleasing, by reducing the risk of a ferocious straight drive felling the bowler in his follow-through, not to mention the non-striker or the umpire.

Thirdly, the proliferation of limited overs cricket has made batting less aesthetically pleasing. Its emphasis on scoring-rate has led to an ever higher proportion of runs scored on the leg side. When A.B. de Villiers hit the fastest 150 in one-day internationals off 64 balls, and went on to 162* off 66 balls against West Indies in the 2015 World Cup at Sydney, he hit twice as many runs to leg (53–109). Keeping a high leading elbow has gone; power is generated by clearing the front foot and swivelling the hips. Cricket is growing closer to its distant cousin, baseball.

In the countryside of northern Italy in the first half of the fifteenth century, a shepherd boy called Andrea doodled and drew graffiti on the walls of caves while tending his sheep. His talent was noticed and brought to the attention of the Medici family, who patronised Andrea del Castagno. It was the same rural pathway, from pastures to professional painting, followed by Giotto.

Castagno brought movement into his pictures – not so much in his *Last Supper*, or his fresco in St Mark's Basilica, but in the painting on a leather shield that was to be used in Medici processions around Florence. His subject, again, was David. On this occasion, however, Castagno depicted David as he points with his left arm towards Goliath. His extended right arm holds the sling – presumably with a stone inside – and starts its deadly swing.

No bowling coach could come up with a better model for a

right-arm medium-pacer. Cut off most of the hair, remove the orange tunic, add some trousers and boots, and it could be the Australian bowler of the 1980s Terry Alderman in his delivery stride. (There is even a passing facial resemblance between Goliath and Alderman's opening partner, Dennis Lillee.) David's left arm points in the fashion prescribed for side-on bowling actions, his head and feet just so. The stone might out-swing nicely, assuming Goliath is a right-hander.

If anyone has known how to get value for money, it was the Medicis. So Castagno would not have been on their books had he not been a fine painter; and here is one of his most celebrated works. The human form is displayed very pleasingly in two-dimensional form. Yet, I would say, there have been bowling actions more beautiful than David's slinging.

Ted McDonald was Australia's opening bowler on their tour of England in 1921 and, in company with Jack Gregory, hit batsmen as they had never been hit before. Not everyone in professional cricket wore two batting gloves before Gregory and McDonald, but they did by the end of the decade. Another of Herbert Fishwick's photographs captures what an extraordinary physical specimen Gregory was, all limbs. As well as for pace bowling, Gregory used those long arms to set two records which have not been equalled, let alone broken, almost a century later: the fastest Test century in terms of minutes, 70, and 15 catches in the 1920–21 Ashes series, mainly at slip.

McDonald had a gliding run-up of 18 yards, according to the best cricket historian between the world wars, Ray Robinson, 'and there was something ominous about the way he came up, his arm swinging with rhythmic menace, the wrist coiling like a cobra about to strike.' The book in which Robinson wrote about McDonald, *Between Wickets*, contained no photograph of McDonald (the author was based in Australia, whereas the bowler spent most of his career in England). But happily another photographer equipped with a Long Tom was present at the start of the Australians' tour in Leicester in 1921; and what he captured in black and white was, and remains in my eyes, the most beautiful bowling action.

It may be slightly unfair on Castagno and his David, but McDonald has his athleticism heightened by the passivity of the umpire, who stares at where McDonald's right or back foot is about to land, to monitor the no-ball law of the time. The umpire's trilby adds to this passivity: no hat would stay on McDonald's head, so fast is he running. In the complete photograph a fielder, probably at mid-off, looks impassive too, immobile. It was only later in the 1920s that the captain of New South Wales, Alan Kippax, initiated the practice of having fielders walk in as the bowler delivered.

Even if you airbrush away the umpire and mid-off fielder, the figure of McDonald in his delivery stride captures much the same 'infinite potentiality of strength'. Robinson's image of a cobra is apposite: McDonald snapped his wrist to strike with fatal effect. He can still be called the most valuable overseas signing made by any county, as he took Lancashire to the Championship title in four of his eight seasons – and in the following 80 years they won it outright only once. When McDonald ripped out Don Bradman's leg-stump in 1930, McDonald was 38, but still cutting the ball into right-handed batsmen at pace.

Michelangelo lengthened the arms of his David for additional effect, not least because the sculpture was originally to be placed high on a buttress on the side of the cathedral in Florence, and thus viewed from a distance. McDonald, by nature, had exceptionally long arms. He was six feet one inch tall and, according to Robinson, his arm-span from fingertip to fingertip was six feet four inches: even longer than the arm-span of the contemporary world heavyweight boxing champion Max Schmeling, who was the same height as McDonald. The bowler was double-jointed too: able to clasp his hands in front of himself, then pass them over his head and rest them on his backside.* Such a prime physical specimen could be turned by the anonymous photographer into a work of art.

Power is manifest in McDonald's shoulders and his overall athleticism. Yet poise, balance and lightness are evident, too. As McDonald has both feet in the air – and there is nothing to suggest he will get them tangled up and fall over – he is lighter than Mercury. If Nijinsky had run across a stage and coiled himself into a similar position, I do not see how he could have been more aesthetically pleasing.

Other bowlers have come close. Harold Larwood in one photograph is in the same pose as Castagno's David, only more muscular; and he too brought down an opposing champion, in Bradman. The Sussex and England bowler Maurice Tate, again side-on, exudes more energy than David with his sling. But if we are hyper-critical, Tate is a trifle too bulky for physical perfection; he has balance, but not poise.

Fred Trueman is the embodiment of power as he pauses in the split second before pounding his left leg down. The Australian fast bowlers Ray Lindwall and Dennis Lillee had most of these qualities. Michael Holding had the most graceful run and run-up. I remember him running round the boundary to his right at Sabina Park in the 1981 Test against England, picking the ball up and throwing in mid-air to the top of the stumps. The crowd – his crowd – groaned in ecstasy.

Only not any more.

To prevent back injuries, bowlers are now coached to keep their spines as straight as they can in the action of delivery. In consequence, they no longer bowl side-on like McDonald, Larwood and

---

* McDonald, Brian Statham, James Anderson: one adopted and two native Lancastrian bowlers renowned for being double-jointed.

Trueman, whose mantra was that 'cricket is a side-on game.' The torsos of their successors are more chest-on to the batsman, more stiff and upright: safer, so the medical research suggests, but less aesthetically pleasing. It is as well that Trueman did not live to commentate on T20.

Spin bowlers are still allowed to turn side-on. But their visual effect is not going to be the same as that of a fast bowler, because spinners do not strive for speed, so less power and strength are manifest. The photograph of India's left-arm spinner Bishan Bedi taken by Ken Kelly captures wristy artistry in action, or poetry in motion, but not awe-inspiring power. So too Rodin's statue *l'Age d'airain*: one of the statues cast in the original mould found its way to Leeds, where it could have served as inspiration for Wilfred Rhodes.

Rex Nettleford, as the artistic director of the National Dance Theatre Company of Jamaica, has observed the parallels between cricket and dance. 'The game of cricket is reminiscent of a choreographed dance work in which individual players are utilized by a captain to create a unified and technically adept instrument analogous to that by which the choreographer gives effect to his creative imagination. A well-captained team in the field often seems to move like a corps de ballet when it is doing well, as the fieldsmen crouch and/or move forward, as the bowler approaches and the players cover for one another. Similarly, when things are not going well or when the team is badly captained, the team often looks like nothing more than a group of novice students of the dance.'

But while certain exponents of batting and bowling are hailed as beautiful, no fielder is. Why not? Why isn't a slip-catcher who dives away to his right to catch an edge called beautiful? I think it is because his movement is spontaneous, in the sense that it is

governed by the ball and its trajectory. There is no scope for individual, or artistic, interpretation as there is in the act of batting and
bowling.

Some of Nettleford's points are specific to West Indian cricketers,
and those of Afro-Caribbean origin in particular. He quotes the
former prime minister of Jamaica, Michael Manley: 'West Indian
batsmen escaped the geometric rigidities of the best coached exem-
plars of the English and Australian game. Instead they moved in a
more poetic manner, the stroke seeming to begin with the toes and
to move in a supple, flowing line through the legs, arched back and
whiplike arms.' West Indian batsmen, says Nettleford, *dance* down
the pitch.

He ends with this observation: 'The dance is always "unfinished",
and is itself "dynamic and ceaseless" in its quest for excellence and
truth. The ephemeral nature of any performing art would not allow
it otherwise. One is, in any case, only as good as one's last work.
Yesterday's performance belongs to yesterday. One never quite
knows what tomorrow will bring.' Mundane as life itself most of the
time, cricket in the right hands, and with the right bodies, can burst
into more than one form of art.

Cricket's most aesthetically pleasing film has to be *Out of the Ashes*,
about the growth of the game in Afghanistan. The eagle that soars
against the background of that azure sky captures the ambition of
those who learned how to play in the refugee camps of Pakistan.
For a painting, it has to be Russell Drysdale's surrealist impression
of cricketers in a deserted town in Australia's outback. For the most
pleasing music in the realm of cricket, I am tempted by Roy
Harper's song 'When an Old Cricketer Leaves the Crease': the ghost
of Francis Thompson can be seen humming along.

For a complete experience, for a start, please give me St

George's Park in Port Elizabeth, on the top of a hill a mile from the Indian Ocean, and its band. The Eastern Province association has usually given the band members some lunch or help with the cost of a minibus, but they are not paid: they simply want to play their music at the cricket. And they have something to sing about: in Port Elizabeth, more than any other area of South Africa I have seen, indigenous Africans have been able to obtain decently paid jobs, perhaps in the car assembly plants in the industrial free zone. So when they go to St George's Park they can readily forget about daily existence, abandoning themselves to the sea breezes and joy of the moment.

Often two church bands come together, in the middle of the old wooden stand to the left of the pavilion, and begin their songs. They will not play all day long, not during a Test match against England, but after a warm-up during the morning session they will sing their hearts out in the afternoon. The state of the match is somewhat immaterial. Before apartheid they always supported the opposition; a newspaper report of England's 1888–89 tour observed: 'It is singular that the sympathies of the Native spectators were with the English.' Now they wave South African flags, but what they are celebrating is not so much an impending victory. When they sing 'Stand By Me' or 'Shosholoza', they celebrate being alive, and having a decent job, and the freedom to be part of humanity, and being at the cricket on a sunny day – and never have I heard music more joyful, not even Handel.

I would take this old wooden stand running along one side of St George's Park, along with its band, to create a composite version of the ideal setting for a cricket match. From grounds which have staged Tests, I would take the backdrop of Bequia, which graces St Vincent, to serve at one end; at the other, either Jamaica's Blue Mountains, which can be seen in the distance from Sabina Park, or else the closer hills behind Queen's Park Oval in Port-of-Spain.

Add the pavilion at the Sydney Cricket Ground, with its nine-teenth-century ironwork (no English pavilion is so open and inviting, because it has to keep out the cold). Plant Adelaide's scoreboard and cathedral on the side opposite to the old wooden stand and the band. Let the pitch be taken from Bramall Lane, one of those that had something for everyone in the 1960s. Let Michael Holding and Ted McDonald measure out their run-ups to bowl against Saeed Anwar and Wally Hammond, and let the band strike up!

10

THE ULTIMATE TEST
OF CHARACTER

It's a thinking game, is cricket.
Anonymous

'HAVE YOU BEEN to Brisbane?' asked Sir Leonard Hutton.

He would never dive straight in. First, he always cautiously surveyed, to pick up every relevant cue: it was part of his training as a Yorkshire opening batsman. I remember him pulling up in his car outside the offices of *The Observer* in Blackfriars. He did not know where to park, and I was on the other side of the road, stranded by a busy dual carriageway. Without haste or panic, he assessed the situation: no entrance to the office of any kind on his side of the building. I could only watch and, well, observe the only England captain who to that point had won a full Ashes series at home and away.

He and Denis Compton did not have much in common. Having to fend off Lindwall and Miller armed with a new ball every 55 overs (not 80 in the 1940s), Hutton was cast as the northern Roundhead, while the southern Cavalier was free to come in down the order and attack the spinners. But I noticed that they shared a trait: chatting to hotel porters and doormen. As well as the geographical lie of the land, or perhaps the bars in Compo's case, they wanted to know who was coming and going so that they were not caught unawares, as professionals in the society of amateurs.

Eventually a passer-by came along, Sir Len wound down his window, had a chat, then slowly pulled his car away from the kerb.

'Is there still a river in Brisbane?' he asked.

'Yes, there is.' As he well knew.

'In 1954, after I'd sent Australia in and we lost the first Test by an innings, I went for a walk beside the river in Brisbane.'

Pause.

'And I thought of throwing myself in.'

He widened his bright blue eyes. He was not joking.

The purpose of psychology in cricket is to minimise the pressure a player feels so that he can be in the right frame of mind to perform his best. All sport contains an element of cat and mouse; a cricketer tries to anticipate what his opponent is going to do next and stop him doing it. In the right frame of mind, he is tuned into everything of importance that is going on around him. His nerves are not disabling but enabling. He lives in the moment, completely. He does not think about the past, even the previous ball; he does not think about the future, beyond the next ball.

In cricket through the ages, no person has felt more pressure than the England captain in the first Test of an Ashes series in Brisbane. If India and Pakistan had played each other on a regular basis since 1952–53, and in five-Test series, the pressure their captains would have been under would undoubtedly have been greater: even more national prestige would have been at stake, especially at times of war between the two countries. But India and Pakistan have played each other irregularly, so no enormous caseload of history and tradition has built up, as with the Ashes, which began in 1882.

It had been stressful enough for Hutton at home. As the first professional to captain England in the twentieth century, he had

been trusted so little by the establishment that for the second Test
of the 1953 Ashes he had the chairman of selectors in his side,
Freddie Brown, watching his every move on the field and in the
dressing room. But this was nothing compared to the stress Hutton
felt after going to Brisbane in November 1954, defying all precedent by selecting an all-pace attack without a spinner, sending
Australia in, losing Compton with a broken hand, watching
England drop approximately twelve chances and Australia post 600
before declaring, and losing by an innings.

Into the Brisbane River, during his walk after the Test, Hutton
did not throw himself. Instead, he did exactly what Wally Hammond
had done eight years before, after he had captained England (as an
amateur, no longer a pro) and lost the opening Test at Brisbane.
Hammond got into a car and silently drove the many hours to
England's next venue, barely exchanging a word with his passen-
gers. Hutton was brooding over Alec Bedser, England's finest
bowler by a street since the war but losing his nip, and how to drop
him. Before the series was won 3–1, Hutton felt the pressure so
much that he lay in bed one morning shortly before the start of a
Test, staring at a wall, too depressed to get up. The manager and
senior players were needed to coax their captain to the ground.

Consolations of the flesh have been a traditional way for the
England cricketer on tour in Australia to mitigate the stress. But
Hutton could not afford to be caught with his trousers down, even
if he had been that way inclined. The establishment would have
hung him (not his trousers) out to dry.

The night before the Brisbane Test is nerve-racking for the rest
of England's cricketers too, but they only have to worry about their
own game. They can prepare in the pragmatic way that experience
has taught them. From what I have observed over four decades, the
batsmen are no different from soldiers on the eve of battle. They do
the equivalent of polishing swords, checking bowstrings and

sharpening arrows as they fiddle with their bats and new rubber grips. The combatants are visualising what will happen on the field of battle on the morrow, so they are not caught unprepared, and do their job.

In cricket's recorded annals, Richard Nyren was the first captain to be astute at psychology. In a big game between Hambledon and All England, in front of 'many thousands', Hambledon were set a large fourth-innings target and one of their players, Noah Mann, kept pestering Nyren to let him go in. Mann was a left-handed batsman and 'a most severe hitter', according to John Nyren, son of Richard, in *The Cricketers of My Time*. But Captain Nyren held him back, and back, until Mann went in at number eleven with ten runs still to make. Mann blocked a few balls then hit an over-pitched ball for six and soon finished off the game. 'Never shall I forget the roar that followed this hit', wrote John Nyren in his dotage.

Afterwards Mann said to his captain: 'If you had let me go in an hour ago I would have served them in the same way.' John Nyren, however, thought his father had made the correct move: 'The old tactician was right, for he knew Noah to be a man of such nerve and self-possession, that the thought of so much depending upon him would not have the paralysing effect that it would upon many others. He was sure of him, and Noah afterwards felt the compliment.'

Extrovert players will talk on the eve of battle; the introverts fall silent.* Whatever type of personality, the best will avoid this 'paralysing effect' and not waste their energy in fruitless anxiety. They will control their fear and the 'what ifs'. They will practise discipline

---

* My observation is that one who plays cricket for a living, male or female, is a restive person, more likely to chew fingernails than sit still with a book. It may be an extreme case, but C.B. Fry spoke for many when he wrote of K.S. Ranjitsinhji: 'He is very lithe, full of spirits and animation. He could no more think of standing still than could a young kitten.'

and self-reliance, as preached by the young master in *Tom Brown's Schooldays*. It is the teammate who distracts or needs help who is a menace, almost as dangerous as the enemy, reducing your chance of survival.

Uneasiest of all is the head that wears England's crown at the toss in Brisbane. The captain cannot bowl a spell then retire to fine-leg, or bat then do a crossword. The match, perhaps the series, hinges on him – and it may boil down to his single decision, whether to send his batsmen or bowlers into battle. It has to be one or the other, unless he loses the toss. Bat or bowl. Fight – but not flight – for if he resigns he will be remembered for a lifetime and beyond.

To switch to the nautical metaphor which has long been applied in cricket, I think the captain of an England team on a turbulent first day of an Ashes series must feel like the skipper of a sinking ship. If he is a batsman himself, he tries to save as many of his crew as he can by partnering them at the crease and helping them score runs; he also has to steel himself at the sight of players who are drowning, never to get into the series.

Doug Insole, Essex's captain of the 1950s, defined the captain's role as 'a public relations officer, agricultural consultant, psychiatrist, accountant, nursemaid and diplomat'. Michael Brearley wrote the definitive treatise in *The Art of Captaincy*, soon after he retired from playing and became a psychoanalyst; but when he captained England in Brisbane in 1978–79, Australia were a much reduced side because Kerry Packer had signed their best players for World Series Cricket. I recall the air of inevitability as what was in effect Australia's Second XI batted first, and so naively that they were rolled over within a couple of sessions. For other England captains like Hutton and Nasser Hussain, the decision to send Australia in after winning the toss in Brisbane went a long way towards defining their lives.

I doubt whether anybody in the world is subject to such intense scrutiny as the England Test captain in an Ashes series. A leading actor is exposed for as many hours, live, but not to millions watching on television. A politician can carefully stage-manage his relatively few public appearances before the nation: he does not have to spend the best part of 30 hours a week in front of television cameras, as the England captain has to do if he bats well. When Britain's prime minister goes to the House of Commons, Question Time is no longer than the press conferences an England captain has to do before and after a Test match; and the prime minister in Parliament does not have more than 20 television cameras ready to capture any false move, or more than 600 people who can boo.

Test batsmen have to walk along a tightrope suspended across Niagara Falls. They have to keep on doing it until their nerve fails and they know their time has come. The extreme risk they take – if they nick off cheaply three or four times, their international career may be over – makes for compulsive viewing; and if that batsman is also the captain, the fascination is even greater. The wonder is that so often they reach the other side.

Hussain, before the toss at the Gabba in 2002–03, was so consumed with tension that in the players' tunnel – not a long dark tunnel, as one might imagine – he went past Mike Atherton, his oldest friend in cricket, without noticing him. Atherton had retired from playing and had just arrived in Australia as a commentator, so they had not met for weeks. Hussain, haunted, walked straight past him.

Australia ended the first day, after being sent in, at 364 for two. On the third evening I had to ghostwrite Hussain's column for the *Sunday Telegraph*. Immediately and bravely he admitted his mistake, and did not seek to blame anybody else for his decision. But it took years of being ribbed in his retirement before he could begin to laugh it off. One evening, when he and Atherton were talking to each other at my dining table, I overheard them agreeing that what each of them would be most remembered for was their one big mistake. Which would be most unfair, were it true.

Tim Noakes, the professor of sports science at Cape Town University, who was employed by South Africa's cricket board for the 1996 World Cup and other occasions, told me in an interview on England's tour of South Africa in 2004–05 that no sport is more draining, mentally and physically, than a Test match for a top-order batsman. To perform his best, he has to be alert to every cue throughout the five days, or at least until he has batted twice, whereas the bowler can switch off when his side is batting. So how much more draining for the top-order batsman who is captain? When Andrew Strauss scored 110 at the Gabba in 2010–11, it was the first century on the ground by an England captain; and to get that far, after making nought in his first innings and seeing Australia rack up 481, and after losing so much sleep, Strauss for the first time in his career tried a well-advertised energy drink at lunch on the fourth day, just to keep going.

At the other end of the batting order, when Bob Willis led England in their 1982–83 Test in Melbourne – a match on a knife edge throughout until England won by three runs– he walked off the field one evening, through the dressing room and across Yarra Park to the team hotel, took the lift straight up to his room, lay down on his bed and fell asleep with his boots on.

Better than any press conference for getting inside the head of England's captain before the opening Test of an Ashes series in Brisbane is Henry V's speech on the eve of Agincourt.

|||

But at least the batsman who is paralysed by nerves, like one of Noah Mann's teammates, is not exposed to public humiliation for long; and the close fielder, dreading that the ball will come to him, may be moved away from the bat after he has dropped a sitter. For the bowler, especially in a one-day match in which he is depended upon to bowl his quota, there may be nowhere to hide save retirement.

The yips which can affect bowlers is more than nervousness. It is a psychological crisis, indeed a collapse. According to my research, bowlers of all types have completely lost their accuracy and self-confidence, to the embarrassment of everyone on the field, but left-arm spinners more than any other. India's Ravi Shastri – who went through the experience when playing for Glamorgan and came out the other side, not least because he had his Test-class batting to fall back on – was very clear about the best way to rehabilitate. It had to be step by step: firstly by bowling in the enclosed safety of the nets without a batsman; then in the nets with a batsman; then in the middle without a batsman, and so on. Once he is playing competitively again, the left-arm spinner should begin his spell over the wicket, and bowl a few economical, confidence-building overs, before switching to round. From what Shastri said, the umpire at the bowler's end can unwittingly form a roadblock: running between him and the stumps, or behind him, is one more hurdle at which the nervous left-armer can baulk. Hence, start over the wicket.

After his postgraduate research into the yips, Mark Bawden became the psychologist for the England team. He told me that a general rule applied to bowlers, of whatever type, who suffered the yips. Their sudden loss of accuracy and confidence stemmed from some traumatic event when young, perhaps not related to cricket or sport at all. Only if they dealt with this fundamental issue would they recover their bowling. Insole underestimated a captain's tasks: in addition, he has to be a psychologist and consultant psychiatrist.

The perfect psychological state for a batsman in a Test match is widely agreed to be what Michael Brearley defined as 'relaxed concentration'. A fast bowler might want to rouse himself from a state of lethargy by means of anger. Shane Warne, the master of spin-bowling psychology, would pick a verbal fight with an opponent if he wanted his competitive juices to flow. For Test match batting, relaxed concentration is ideal.

Brearley told me a story against himself to illustrate how he had been relaxed and concentrating, but not in the right way. We were waiting at Hyderabad airport in Sind, little more than a landing strip, the day after England's second Test against Pakistan in 1977–78.[*] He and Geoffrey Boycott had been skilfully batting out the last afternoon against Pakistan's spinners, notably Abdul Qadir, until a draw was assured: Imran Khan was not playing, so there was no chance of a late burst of reverse swing, not that anyone in England knew the term. The one issue remaining before the close was whether the two England batsmen could make their century.

Boycott, in order to reach his milestone, called for the extra half-hour. A loophole in the regulations, which was closed as a result of this incident, allowed a Test side to take an extra half-hour even when no definite result was obtainable. Thus Boycott sailed into port and was 100 not out at the close. With a different objective in mind, Brearley started blocking, and was eventually dismissed five minutes before the close for 74. He never made a Test hundred.

'I became obsessed,' Brearley admitted at Hyderabad airport. 'I became obsessed with the concept of purity in the not-out.' The unblemished, the unbeaten, the pure. But the muse of cricket does not like blocking: it is too negative for her taste. We must bat, and look for runs, even when aiming for a draw.

---

[*] I remember this Test fondly, even though it was a bore-draw. England had nobody to bowl wrist-spin in the nets before the game – except me!

By the time he retired, though, Brearley had taken captaincy to new heights. In 1981 he unbound Prometheus's batting at Headingley and Old Trafford. On the last afternoon at Edgbaston, as his last resort, Brearley inspired Ian Botham to pluck five Australian rabbits from his hat for one run. It was the force of Botham's liberated personality that swept Australia aside, not the intrinsic merit of his medium pace. If a self-effacing person had apologetically bowled exactly the same deliveries, Australia would have swept to victory and a 2–1 lead.

Brearley also pioneered the tactic of getting inside a batsman's head by standing in the crease of a new batsman as he walked out and took guard. Then he would tell one of his fielders to drop back to deep square-leg, because the batsman could not hook the ball down.

In *The Art of Captaincy*, Brearley observed how the professional game had become far more aggressive in his time, and how the aggression stemmed from several sources: from opponents, crowd, media, as well as from the players in his own team. And it is up to the captain – who else? – to deal with these changing social mores. 'He is responsible for the appropriateness of his team's degree of ruthlessness, including his own.' He also mentioned the letters he received from followers of the game who deplored the manifestations of this aggression.

But not all international cricket is riddled with aggression and sledging. Even a match between England and Australia can pass without a word of abuse. If the bowler is hit for four, she takes it out on herself. If her fielder drops a chance, she reacts with a sympathetic smile.

If or when men's international cricket begins to pall, through over-aggression or match-fixing, I look forward to going back to the old-fashioned virtues of the women's game. So do others, I suspect. When, as the editor of *Wisden*, I broke a taboo by selecting a woman as one of the Five Cricketers of the Year, I received the grand total of one irate letter: it was, perhaps predictably, from an MCC member in Manchester. If we reach the age when we no longer have a taste for the behaviour of alpha males, cricket can still offer a form of the game to suit us.

The mind filled with relaxed concentration enters, at its apogee, the trance-like state called 'the zone'. It is not for the bowler: he puts so much physical exertion into his pace or spin that his mental condition cannot remain untroubled for long hours. But the batsman who enters the zone feels he can go on for ever.

Mike Atherton entered this zone while he batted for 643 minutes against South Africa in Johannesburg and scored 185 not out to draw the second Test of 1995–96 for England. Owing to the dictates of work, as Atherton was then a columnist for the *Sunday Telegraph*, I was first to speak to him when he walked off, as soon as he had crossed the boundary line, because our sports editor wanted him to write about this historic innings.

Jack Russell, England's wicketkeeper and Atherton's partner for the last four and a half hours, was triumphantly celebrating their re-enactment of Rorke's Drift. Atherton was quiet and calm: not visibly tired at all, far from drained, just serenely calm. He spoke first, about the South Africans: 'They didn't seem to be trying very hard.' Save for the last few minutes, it had looked to everyone watching as though they had been busting a gut for almost two days to dismiss Atherton, so I think what he specifically meant was: 'They didn't try much by way of variation in their bowling or field-placings.' He looked as though he could have gone back out to the middle, taken guard again and batted until the animals in the safari park came home.

It is a state which neither the young nor the old batsman attains.

Atherton was aged 27 and a half, almost the same age as W.G. Grace when he had his purple patch. If he ever enters the zone, a player will do it when his surroundings are fairly familiar, when he is at or near his physical peak, before his end is in sight.

For a programme on television about 'the zone', Atherton later underwent some tests in an attempt to explain how his innings of a lifetime came about, but nothing much more scientific emerged. After he had retired, I had first-hand experience of his essential character. When he was playing, it was manifested not only when he was batting: simply to overcome his degenerative back condition and colitis, and get on the field, he had to take such strong painkillers that the day after his final Test he collapsed and had to be taken to hospital to have his stomach pumped out.* On this occasion, we played a game of chess for more than an hour, and he fought a rearguard action, ditch by ditch, without admitting defeat or resigning, and in that time he played one attacking shot. Stubbornness personified.

At a laughably lower level, at the opposite end of the spectrum in a friendly club game, I – just once – entered this zone. I went in at number seven with an hour and a half to go, and for the first half-hour we chased the runs until my partner was out, then, with nothing much to come and six wickets down, we had to aim for a draw. Looking back, I realised it never once occurred to me that I would get out, having spent the whole of my batting career being afraid of doing so. Losing a partner was no cause for disappointment, as Atherton had observed after the Johannesburg Test: he was too far above the battle to notice, too inwardly certain of success to think for one moment of failure. A blessed state, never to be recaptured – except perhaps by those like Hashim Amla and

---

* Touchingly, when his first child was about to be born shortly after his retirement, he and his partner had to tie each other's shoelaces as neither could bend down.

Mohammad Yousuf who have been able to call on religious practices to achieve this state of mind.

||||

The bravest cricketer, in my eyes, is the one who is not only physically brave. He is morally brave as well, in telling us the truths we need to know.

Of all those who have played cricket, nobody could have been more courageous than Siegfried Sassoon. In the First World War he fought at the front, and led his men from the front, and won the Military Cross. The citation read: 'For conspicuous gallantry during a raid on the enemy's trenches. He remained for 1½ hours under rifle and bomb fire collecting and bringing in our wounded.' Having been there and done it, he risked court martial and the firing squad by his public statement that it was a war that should not be fought.

It was many years after the Great War before Sassoon found solace, in marriage and male friendships, in writing prose and verse, and on the cricket field at Heytesbury in Wiltshire. Although he had bought the estate, he did not exercise his right as lord of the manor to captain the village team. Instead, tall and stiff with war-wounds, he fielded at mid-on or mid-off; and when the ball was hit in his direction, he put his feet together, as if standing to attention once again, and let the ball strike his legs. I would have thought the last person who deserved to be injured while playing cricket was Sassoon.

Of England cricketers, the bravest in my estimation has been Marcus Trescothick, and not so much when he was opening the batting for England and facing the first bowlers to clock 100 mph, such as Shoaib Akhtar and Brett Lee. Principally, having been there and done it, he risked ridicule when the stress became too much and he told us so.

Trescothick's predecessor as a Somerset and England opening batsman, Harold Gimblett, had set down on a tape-recorder the manic depression he had endured. He was brilliant enough to have had a long career as Hutton's opening partner, but only managed three Tests before the Second World War. He scored 67 not out on his Test debut, and finished with more first-class hundreds than anyone for Somerset to this day, including Trescothick. But the public scrutiny, even before television, was too much and he became ever more depressed. Gimblett recorded his thoughts on tapes and left them to the author David Foot to publish after his overdose.[*]

I have to admit a soft spot: from second slip I watched Trescothick in a game during the season when, aged 15, he scored 4000 runs, mostly for Keynsham. He was very quiet as he played his cover drives and scored about 27. Having performed for his country for six years at home and abroad, Trescothick went a stage further than Gimblett and publicly admitted his torment while still alive, while still a player. Like a peacetime Sassoon, he was brave enough to tell us what we needed to know about the professional's touring life, his anxieties and fears and panic attacks, alone in hotel rooms far from home. He thereby removed our rose-tinted spectacles.

---

[*] About the time Trescothick flew home at the start of England's 2006-07 tour of Australia, the Professional Cricketers Association expanded its welfare services with a helpline for members feeling suicidal. Thanks to this initiative and the PCA's pastoral care in general, there has been no reported case of a member committing suicide – with the exception of Peter Roebuck in still unexplained circumstances in Cape Town – since Mark Saxelby took his life in 2000 in a tragically gruesome case. Before this millennium the suicide rate among English professional cricketers was higher than that among the British population at large, according to David Frith in *Silence of the Heart*. The rate among cricketers in countries with substantial populations of Anglo-Saxon origin, like Australia, New Zealand and South Africa, was also remarkably high. The reporting of suicide in south Asia has been too limited for any comparison to be drawn there.

Professional cricketers tend to view luck as a powerful force, a divinity that can shape their ends. And if a batsman is facing up to a bowler, and in the split second before the ball hits the pitch an earthquake strikes, and the ball hits a crack which has opened up and shoots through to pin the batsman, let us call that luck – or, rather, sensationally bad luck. Or if a batsman cops a poor umpiring decision at a formative stage of his career, I would say he too is unlucky: he is a victim in spite of having made no mistake.*

But I would argue that luck is perceived to be far more prevalent than it is. If the average county batsman faces 50 balls of fine outswing and survives in spite of numerous play-and-misses, he is deemed to have enjoyed a lot of luck or 'arse'. In order to repeat his luck in his next innings, this batsman wears the same socks, perhaps unwashed, and puts on his equipment in the same order, in what can snowball into a host of superstitions. But I would say that if this batsman goes through exactly the same scenario one hundred times, there will be an occasion when he nicks the first ball and is caught, and another when he survives the whole spell of 50 balls, and dozens of outcomes in between. This is the nature of cricket. It is simply a verbal shorthand to say he was 'very unlucky' when he was dismissed first ball, and 'very lucky' when he survived.

From what John Nyren tells us about Hambledon, cricketers in the

---

* By this reckoning, the unluckiest batsman I have seen in international cricket was Clayton Lambert. He was brought into the West Indies team for the fifth Test against England in 1991, when their supply of great batsmen was running out. He scored 39 in his first innings, before a tremendous heave at Phil Tufnell. He had started all right in his second innings, too, when he missed a pull at a short ball from Ian Botham which, on a hard Oval pitch, was destined to go over the stumps. The umpire seemed to give Lambert out, for 14, on the strength of Botham's appeal – as was the case with a few of his latter-day England wickets. Lambert, 29 then, was dropped for the next six and a half years. By the time he was recalled, against England in 1998, he was 36, and still good enough to hit a Test hundred, but not young enough to smooth out the imperfections in his game. What could have been a substantial career was limited to five Tests.

Age of Enlightenment had no such belief in luck. And in the absence of verifiable scientific evidence, rare in cricket, I see no rational case for arguing that luck – as we define it in the case of an earthquake damaging the pitch – plays a significant part. In Test matches, for instance, no captain has been very lucky with the toss over a prolonged period, or very unlucky. Of those who have captained in 40 Tests or more, Peter May has won the highest percentage of tosses, 63 per cent; and the late Hansie Cronje won the lowest percentage, 41 per cent.

If a fielder drops a catch, I dislike hearing teammates say 'bad luck'. The ball has either been too fast for his reactions, in which case some other term of sympathy might be justified; or, more likely, his catching technique has been faulty. If the non-striker is run out while backing up, after the striker has hit a straight drive, I do not think him unlucky but wonder if he has ever practised sliding his bat back or diving for the crease. Ed Smith, who represented England in three Tests, wrote that he could be considered lucky to have attended Tonbridge School, which has produced numerous fine cricketers on its fine pitches; but I would call this circumstance, or happenstance.

Again, the professional batsman who is dismissed for 13 may want to read something into it; or the Australian batsman who is dismissed for 87; or the team that loses a wicket when the score is 111 or 222 or 333. But by the end of his career, almost every cricketer has been rewarded almost precisely in accordance with his skills and efforts – unless he has fallen victim to superstition.

Or to hubris. What I remember from the only occasion I interviewed Jacques Kallis was that he said, almost vehemently: 'Even a bowler from the fourth XI can bowl a ball that gets you out.' Anyone in cricket, however exalted, can be brought down by anyone, however lowly – not most of the time, true, but always in theory and very occasionally in practice.

The longer the contest between two teams, the greater the psychological element. The axiom is that a limited-overs match is won by 'the side that plays better on the day'. But in a series of three or more Tests, the principles of traditional Chinese warfare come into play, and a Test match is transformed into the sport's highest and most fascinating form.

Western military thought has paid relatively little attention to the psychological element; so, too, traditional cricket thinking. Clausewitz enunciated the theory of building up your forces at the decisive point until you outnumber your enemy, then victory will assuredly follow. When Douglas Jardine employed Harold Larwood to bowl bouncers at Australia's batsmen in 1932–33, Bodyline was Clausewitzian. The equivalent in modern cricket is to make a big first-innings total, pile on 'scoreboard pressure' and have a fresh bowler always available, or at least keep the batsmen tied down.

Sun Tzu by contrast, in *The Art of War*, stated that the objective of Chinese military strategy should be psychological mastery of the enemy. Once you have achieved this, success in battle is a fait accompli; and if success is achieved with no battle at all, so much the better, for China's resources are thereby preserved.

> The victorious army
> Is victorious first
> And seeks battle later;
> The defeated army
> Does battle first
> And seeks victory later.

The Chinese board game of wei qi encapsulates this way of thinking. The aim is to encircle or surround your opponent. Chess, the western board game, is Clausewitzian: you overwhelm your opponent by marshalling superior forces at the decisive point.

Unintentionally, the strongest Test teams have copied Chinese strategy and combined it with western military tactics. West Indies established such a psychological mastery through the 1980s and into the mid-1990s that they exuded the impression that, to win, they had only to turn up. England's coach, Micky Stewart, said in his retirement: 'In all my time in sport I'd never experienced top players, really top players [he implies Ian Botham], speaking in such awe of their opponents.' No wonder West Indies won 14 out of 15 Tests in a row against England, drawing the rain-affected other. In a five-Test series the psychological superiority was reinforced even further, game by game, defeat by defeat.

When I ghosted Hutton, I had not read *The Art of War*, and my guess is he had not either. Yet I believe he was one of the first captains, if not the first, to combine western and Chinese strategy. In the 1953 series against Australia, he avoided a showdown with their fast bowlers, Ray Lindwall and Keith Miller, as he had none of his own: thus did a weak Chinese emperor avert a decisive battle with barbarian hordes. In post-war Tests, Australia were 11–1 up against England. Hutton slowed the over-rate down, and wore his opponents down, month by month, until he caught them on a turning Oval pitch made for England's finger-spinners, of whom Australia had none.

When he arrived in Australia for the return series in the autumn of 1954, Hutton was as politely inscrutable as a Chinese diplomat in ceremonial robes and long moustaches. By then he had acquired some fast bowlers, while Lindwall and Miller had aged, so he could have been overtly aggressive. Yet he enacted Sun Tzu's dictum: 'Feign inability. When deploying troops, appear not to be.' The Australian press corps were predisposed to Hutton because he was the first non-amateur to captain an England tour of Australia since the 1880s, and they were further disarmed when he declared: 'We're here to learn a lot from you.' He added that his party contained no bowlers of real note and, for that matter, no batsmen of real note. Only when Frank Tyson bowled bouncers at their unhelmeted heads did the Australians realise what was hitting them, and their psychological mastery was lost.

To reach number one for the first time in the era of ICC rankings, England had to make a similar psychological leap to defeat Australia in 2010–11. They had lost their five previous Ashes series in Australia, and by huge margins, with three Test wins (all when the Ashes were not alive) to set against 18 defeats. And though he had not read *The Art of War*, Andrew Strauss used the same principles as Sun Tzu had advised and Hutton had used. If he did not feign inability, he made no public statements about the prowess of his team to alert the enemy. Instead, his side dominated the three warm-up games to such an extent that they generated apprehension in the Australian media and public; and when they scored 517 for one wicket declared in their second innings at Brisbane, England gave the impression of invulnerability and gained the psychological lead, even though the first Test was drawn.

In the second Test at Adelaide, in a chess-like conflict at the decisive point, England's spinner Graeme Swann out-bowled his opposite number – seven wickets for 161 runs against Xavier Doherty's one for 158 – to achieve victory by an innings. England lost the third Test in Perth. They were indeed overwhelmed, but in public Strauss shrugged off the defeat, and reaffirmed England's existing strategy: big individual centuries, unerringly accurate bowling with seam or swing movement on a fullish length, and occasional interventions by Swann, especially against left-handed batsmen. 'The highest form of warfare is to attack [the enemy's] strategy itself,' according to Sun Tzu. England, under pressure, adhered to the one they had devised.

So when England were beaten in Perth, Australia's players and public were still presented with a strongly united front. When

England's opening bowler Stuart Broad pulled a stomach muscle during the second Test and was ruled out of the series, three possible replacements bowled on the Adelaide Oval straight after the match. Whenever England lost a man, his successor seemed stronger; whenever Australia dropped a player, his replacement seemed weaker. In the only public act of indiscipline, Kevin Pietersen borrowed a Lamborghini in Melbourne and was fined for speeding. In Australia such an episode could be explained away as laddishness.

While England seemed to have no doubts, Australia appeared riddled. Should their captain Ricky Ponting be replaced by Michael Clarke? The Australian selectors did not sing from the same song-sheet and one, Greg Chappell, was ready to be quoted whenever he disagreed with his colleagues. The front page of *The Age* in Melbourne was bordered in black after Australia's defeat in the second Test, preparing readers for the worst. The inconsistencies of Australia's leading bowler, Mitchell Johnson, were seized on by England's supporters, who constituted half the crowd at times, and who mocked Johnson in a lyric which almost became the anthem for this series: 'He bowls to the left/ He bowls to the right/ That Mitchell Johnson/ His bowling is shite.' In addition to music, dance was another form of affirmation that the series would end in England's favour: the players began to dance 'the Sprinkler', not too soon because cricket hates hubris.* But it was there, rehearsed and waiting, as soon as the celebrations could begin.

By the end of this series in Sydney, England had convinced all concerned that every factor was working in their favour. Even the weather was abnormally cool and rainy – well, English – and allowed the tourists to get away with four specialist bowlers and no

---

* For proof, one has only to declare while fielding that one never drops a catch or has not dropped a catch all season. In being proudly complacent, one takes an eye off the ball.

all-rounder: the first time they had won an Ashes series in Australia since the First World War with such a limited attack. England's retention of the Ashes was perceived to be inevitable, a fait accompli. 'Shi' is the Chinese term for the understanding and exploitation of all factors, so that victory is like water flowing downhill on its swiftest course, along the path of least resistance.

The same happened *to* England, in reverse, a year and a half later. When South Africa toured in the summer of 2012, they did to the hosts exactly what England had done to Australia. It was a series of only three Tests, and one that most commentators – including the neutral Shane Warne – prophesied that England, as number one in the Test rankings, with home advantage, were going to win. But South Africa established psychological mastery in their first innings of the series, at the Oval: this speeded up a process which might otherwise have taken several Tests to unfold. Their innings was even more monumental than England's second in Brisbane had been. England's bowlers were exposed as impotent. Hashim Amla scored South Africa's first triple century, Graeme Smith and Jacques Kallis masterful centuries, in a total of 637 for two declared. England's batsmen were picked off by South Africa's attritional seamers and new-ball bursts at the decisive point by Dale Steyn.

In violation of Sun Tzu's principle, England discarded their strategy in the second Test at Headingley: the defeated army sought victory after losing the psychological mastery. England selected four pace bowlers, dropped Swann and sent South Africa in on a pitch that soon offered turn. England were playing chess, and chess alone. They were trying to attack South Africa at what they hoped would be the decisive point: the fullish length at which a ball would swing conventionally under cloud cover at Headingley.

England failed to win; the match was drawn; cracks widened and doubts deepened in the home side. Strauss, before the series, had contemplated that it might prove to be his last; and once self-doubt sets in, the decline accelerates. According to Chinese military theory, the emperor could help by offering baits to the leaders of barbarian hordes threatening China, pacifying and disarming them; it did not allow for his abdication.

England's façade of unity was shattered when Pietersen told a press conference at the end of the Headingley Test: 'It's hard being me in the England dressing room.' Achilles was sulking in his tent, announcing that he did not want to play for England again in limited-overs cricket. Instead of focusing on the third and final Test at Lord's, England were engaged in firefighting and crisis-management, dropping Pietersen and having to explain why. The South Africans concentrated on giving their tailenders a rare chance to bat, in a practice game in Derby. Vernon Philander, who had not made a fifty for many months, scored 68 not out. In the Lord's Test a few days later he scored 61 and 35, took seven wickets, and was player of the match. South Africa won by 51 runs and took the series 2–0. Strauss resigned and retired from all professional cricket a week later. The result seemed as inevitable as water pouring downhill – whereas at the start of the series, when South Africa had no psychological mastery, it had not.

‖

A wounded animal finds a place to lick its wounds. It takes time out from the fight, to die or recover. The England cricketer who is on a losing tour of Australia has nowhere to hide his vulnerability except an inner-city hotel room, air-conditioned, without windows that open, looking out on concrete and streets; nature is not available to console. Luxurious, yet a luxurious prison. If he escapes it to avoid 'hotel fever', the player returns to the hostile environment where taxi-drivers, front pages, golf club members and airline staff all point a finger and say, loudly or silently: 'You loser.' There is no hiding place unless he is given special permission to leave the city, an admission of weakness in itself. Tasmania used to perform that function, when a week across Bass Strait was relief, and a couple of friendly games against weekend amateurs in countryside reminiscent of home, at Launceston and Hobart, was part of England's schedule. Now, only one hiding place exists, or rather a semi-sanctuary.

England's Ashes series of 2013–14 was the complete opposite of their 2010–11 series. On their earlier visit, after the first four days in Brisbane, they had not appeared vulnerable save on two occasions: firstly, when they lost the third Test in Perth, but even then they shrugged off their defeat and reaffirmed their strategy; secondly, when Paul Collingwood announced his retirement, and then it was towards the end of the last Test in Sydney, when England were on top and no whiff of vulnerability was going to alter the outcome.

The first shot in the next series was fired by Australia's coach, Darren Lehmann. During the first Ashes Test of 2013 at Trent Bridge, Stuart Broad had edged a catch to Brad Haddin, who was standing up to the stumps, and who deflected it to slip. Broad did not 'walk' and was given not out. 'That was just blatant cheating,' Lehmann said in an interview with a Melbourne radio station, then added: 'I hope the Australian public give it to him right from the word go for the whole summer, and I hope he cries and goes home.' For orchestrating Australia's campaign in the return series, Lehmann was fined by the ICC: but those several thousand dollars he may have subsequently considered the best money he has ever spent.

Australia's media had been quiescent, almost defeatist, in 2010–11. This time they played their part in regaining the Ashes. England arrived in Brisbane to find the local daily newspaper, the *Courier-Mail*, taking the lead. Broad's name was blanked out of their reports. Even when he took six wickets in Australia's first innings, he was referred to as a '27-year-old English medium-pacer'. After the match the newspaper tried to laugh off their campaign, but it did not come across as fun at the time. Lehmann's psychology had identified the target for the media and crowds to aim at. I doubt whether the England players knew how few people were involved in such journalism. A couple of cricket correspondents, and a newspaper editor or sports editor who might know very little about cricket, can give the impression the whole country is against you. But this campaign served to rabble-rouse all right. When Broad made his first appearance of the series – and I was sitting in the crowd, not the sealed press box – I estimated at least one-quarter and maybe one-third of the Gabba's 40,000 spectators chanted: 'Broad is a wanker!' A section of every crowd continued to do so up to and including the very last day of England's tour.

Broad's spirit as a bowler was never broken: he was England's best and most successful bowler in the series, with 21 wickets. Whether his spirit as a batsman was affected, I am not so sure. His highest score was 42: not bad for a bowler-who-can-bat, but England needed their number eight to keep out Johnson, and to face more than 172 balls in the whole series. Nothing, except perhaps dropped catches, so gnaws away at dressing-room morale as the lower order being constantly blown away. Broad's batting might or might not have been affected by the hostility of the crowds and media; it was by the bombardment of Johnson, Ryan Harris and Peter Siddle. Kevin Pietersen, after seeing the rejuvenated Johnson go after Jonathan Trott in Brisbane, admitted to being 'petrified'.

Translate Sun Tzu's creed to Test cricket, and the quickest way to make your opponent betray vulnerability is to hit him. Sport, for men, is war by surrogate means. This is what Johnson, Harris and Siddle began to do. Even if the England batsman reacted with contemporary stoicism – not the traditional keeling-over and much rubbing, surrounded by sympathetic opponents – he knew that he had been hit and a gap in his defence had been found. Even if the ball had not hurt him because of his protective equipment, the batsman had become vulnerable because he knew he could be hit again, soon.

Cricket offered a test of courage long before Bodyline or the invention of the helmet in the late 1970s. Old Nyren tells us, in so many words, that David Harris obtained bounce like nobody else at Hambledon, and on the rough pitches of the late eighteenth century he was quick enough to draw blood: 'His balls were very little beholden to the ground when pitched; it was but a touch, and up again; and woe be to the man who did not get in to block them, for they had such a peculiar curl, that they would grind his fingers against the bat; many a time have I seen the blood drawn in this way from a batter who was not up to the trick' – who, in our terms, played with his hands too low.

Helmets made batting a different game, and even more of a bats-man's. He could be hit seriously, but not fatally like George Summers of Nottinghamshire in 1870, until the totally unexpected death of Phil Hughes. Helmets made for a fair compromise in the balance between danger and safety. But batsmen then took advantage to innovate shots like the scoop and the ramp, which the survival instinct would never have allowed without a helmet.

One after another England's batmen were hit during the first three Tests of the 2013–14 series, until the Ashes had been regained and Australia's fast bowlers could husband their energies. The exceptions were the captain, Alastair Cook, and Pietersen, and they were bombarded with verbal criticism instead. I had never before seen the full set of antagonism from every source. In the 1980s in the West Indies, England had faced all-out aggression from the bowlers and the crowd, but not the fielders, who remained silent, and the local media, which was too small to signify. On England's tour of Australia in 2006–07, they had faced all-out aggression from Australia's bowlers and fielders and crowd, but not quite to the same extent from the media, who had not been officially orchestrated as Lehmann had. By the time Trott flew home after the first Test in 2013–14, Australia's media had fired a quiver of arrows, surprising those who knew only its meekness of the previous tour.

Sports psychology makes much of visualisation: 'Never go somewhere your mind has not gone before.' Yet in addressing their horrible record in Brisbane, where England have won only twice since the Second World War, no priority has been given to playing a warm-up fixture in Brisbane or, at any rate Queensland, which has a time zone one hour earlier than Australia's other eastern states: dawn comes soon after 5 a.m. On the four occasions that England have won a Test in Brisbane, they have always played a preliminary game in Queensland. They have thereby adjusted to the different time zone, the greater heat and humidity, the more American way of life.[*]

Even though they did not play a game in Queensland before the opening Test of 2010–11, at least the bowlers missed England's last warm-up game in Hobart and flew ahead to Brisbane to acclimatise. In November 2013, it was back to the schedule of flying in on a Monday, albeit from the closest city, i.e. Sydney, visiting the Gabba

---

[*] The analysis of ten years of Major League Baseball data has illustrated a decline in performance following travel across multiple time zones. According to W.E. Leatherwood and J.L. Dragoo in the *British Journal of Sports Medicine* in 2013, 'teams competing in their home environment enjoy a home court/field advantage and travelling teams are met with a considerable task of overcoming such an advantage. This advantage is often hard to separate from detriments in performance related to travel.' But the evidence identifies sleep loss as a main consequence of flying between time zones, as England teams do, not only on arrival in Australia but in the course of their tour, especially when flying to or from Perth. 'Sleep loss is associated with sizeable effects on alertness, negative disturbances in mood, cognition and motivation and may have an affect on performance via these mechanisms. Additionally, each individual uniquely experiences vulnerabilities in their cognitive functioning as a result of sleep loss and may be more susceptible to the effects of sleep deprivation when performing one cognitive task over another.' Bob Willis told me during England's 1982–83 tour, which he captained, that he woke up at about 2.30 a.m. and never went back to sleep – and he did not normally go to bed straight after the close of play.

on the Tuesday – for the first time for some of the touring party – and trying to feel settled by the 9.30 start on Thursday morning. In 2006–07, England's players did not arrive until the Monday evening, to be greeted by jet-lagged wives and disoriented infants.

Whenever England's team bus has pulled up in Vulture Street outside the Gabba, only the toughest have been prepared for a five-day battle. Anecdotal evidence suggests the bus has usually been silent on the way to the ground. If sleep loss has not had an effect already, the subtropical humidity and heat soon will. It is an alien world, far from home. When five minutes remain before the start of the Ashes series, a bell does not ring; an alarm buzzes. Australia have not been defeated in a Test since 1988 to date at the Gabba, and England have seldom had any psychological mastery.

After the first Test of 2013–14, whenever Cook looked at his ranks of men, one or other dropped out of the firing line, unable to perform. If a senior player is exposed on a tour of Australia, he is mortally wounded and will never make a full recovery: he knows he is no longer good enough, if he ever was. A junior player who is seriously wounded can be withdrawn from the firing line and survive to fight another day.

England's strategy of bouncing out Australia with tall fast bowlers – of whom four were tall, though none so fast as Johnson or Harris – was shelved after the first Test. Defeats at the Gabba and the WACA in Perth were perhaps predictable, given England's record on those grounds, but not at Adelaide. It was a drop-in pitch, but its characteristics were the same as the traditional ones: essentially benign for batting.

If a touring batsman cannot score runs in Adelaide, he will not score runs anywhere in Australia – and England's didn't. Johnson dismissed Cook with a perfect away-swinger that hit his off-stump (Cook having been bowled in a smaller proportion of his dismissals than any top Test batsman), then with a perfect bouncer. Cook scored three and one, the lowest match total by an England captain in an Ashes Test in Australia since Willis, a specialist bowler; and Johnson finished with the best innings figures of any pace bowler in a Test at Adelaide, seven wickets for 40. He swung to the left/ He swung to the right/ That Mitchell Johnson/ His bowling was right – right up there with the all-time great fast bowlers.

In other sports the vanquished can bow out quickly if not gracefully. For an England captain who has lost the first three Tests in Australia, hell is far from finished. He can save face, as Hussain did by spurring on his men to win the fifth Test of 2002–03, or else make history and be remembered for ever as one who was whitewashed. But winning a dead-rubber Test in Australia is no longer as simple as it was. When England finally won their first Ashes Test after the Second World War, at Melbourne in 1950–51, the crowd was cheering England home, according to E.W. Swanton in *Elusive Victory*. By 2013–14, 'chivalrous' had been replaced by 'ruthless'.

If cricket was not such a psychological sport, I would not watch much. Results come and go, some won, some lost, but what is perennially fascinating is how elite performers react to the most demanding circumstances. Cricket was boring when Australia had an opening batsman called John Dyson, who wore a helmet that obscured his face like the man in the iron mask and blocked all day. No human or cricket interest there. We are fascinated by human reactions to extreme situations.

During that series of 2013–14, watching the England captain being eaten away was the most distressing – or nearest to distressing – experience I have had in journalism. The fresh face of a young Cook became a middle-aged mass of worry lines. He was torn in all directions, by each succeeding crisis, and had no time left for himself. His men could desert their posts; not he. England's captain has to go down with his ship, and the process takes a lot longer than for his naval compeers – around three months. Cricket is further from enjoyment than it can ever be. Cook's haunted eyes, instead of picking up the cues, looked straight ahead. After the tour, I reflected on whether I had projected my own feelings: boarding school is three months without a hiding place. But I think not.

Our response should be nothing less than admiration for those England captains who have led their country through the psychological minefield of a losing tour of Australia and yet succeeded in keeping their own game together. Since Willis, all England captains – losing or winning – have scored their share of runs in Australia. Of losing captains, before Cook averaged 24, only Andrew Flintoff had averaged below 35 in the Test series – and he, as an all-rounder, took 11 wickets in addition to averaging a presentable 28.*

Who have England's mentally toughest batsmen been? You could argue that those who scored heavily against West Indies in the 1980s, or in Asia in the last generation, should be ranked in this category. But the environment which has been extremely demanding through the ages, and has thus provided the same measuring stick for all, has been Australia. And a simple pattern emerges: of the ten England batsmen with the highest averages in Tests in Australia, seven have played for Surrey or Yorkshire, England's two most successful counties in terms of winning the County Championship: winning habits, tough environments and tough club cricket, into which the youngster has been thrown at the deep end against men, to sink or swim.

Should sport be allowed to cause an individual so much torment

---

* Here is empirical evidence to substantiate the thesis put forward in the *Journal of Science and Medicine in Sport* (2012): that mental toughness is more significant in Test match batting than other branches of international sport. 'Contrary to the research hypothesis, it was found that the highly skilled batsmen were only distinguishable from batsmen of lesser skill by their higher degree of global mental toughness. The skilled batsmen scored significantly higher on mental toughness dimensions relating to motivation (Personal Bests, Task Value and Commitment), coping skill (Perseverance) and self-belief (Potential).'

that he mentally disintegrates? The case for and against can be argued, but it is too late to change the schedules. Besides, if an Ashes series did not cause so much torment, it would not cause so much joy for the winning captain, players and supporters. The difference is that for an Australian captain losing in England there is somewhere to hide: he can play a practice game at a small county ground against modest opposition, or find a part of London where he is not recognised, and rain will normally ensure at least one draw somewhere. For his English counterpart in Australia there is no escape. The grim inevitability of Greek tragedy takes hold – except that in having to fall on his sword, out of a sense of honour, he is like an oriental emperor.

That semi-sanctuary? It is not much of one. But there is one place where an England player on a losing tour of Australia can retreat: behind sunglasses. Towards the end of their 2013–14 tour, a remarkable division occurred between the England players. The senior ones wore sunglasses in the field most of the time; the junior ones with nothing to hide, like Joe Root and Ben Stokes, did not.

A one-off Test, or a one-day series, does not allow time for all these psychological factors to interplay. Players can hide even in a three-Test series: a batsman can fail in all six innings and still live to fight another day in the next series, without being dropped. A five-Test series is make or break for the protagonists, and therefore the most fascinating drama. A proper Test series between two well-matched teams is a combination of chess and wei qi, of Clausewitz and Sun Tzu, of western and eastern strategy. Nothing less.

BODY LANGUAGE

STRAIGHT UP

Eng v WI, 5th Test, the Oval, 1984

Arms which are extended vertically to the full are a gesture of celebration (it is what the football supporter does when his team scores a goal), and this is what the fielder does when, anticipating the umpire's verdict, he confidently expects the batsman to be given out. When he raises his arms *without* extending them fully or vertically like the second slip here, the fielder is expressing doubt and asking the umpire. More often than not, in my observation, the umpire will share this doubt and say 'not out'.

Here the bowler, wicketkeeper and first slip are reinforcing the fully extended arms by leaping into the air as well in an act of celebration, before the verdict, such is their confidence. The first slip fielder, the West Indian captain Clive Lloyd, may even be conveying a subliminal message by making himself into a shape like a raised finger. Short-leg too is pointing his finger skywards, as he expects the umpire to do, so unanimous are the prosecutors. The case for the defence is not strong: Allan Lamb, the batsman, is halfway to bending the knee in a movement that could be interpreted as an act of submission.

THE GUILTY LOOK

Eng v Aus, 2nd Test, Lord's, 1981
Ian Botham, in his last match as England
captain, is given out lbw for 0 by umpire Ken
Palmer. By looking at the umpire for a verdict,
one way or the other, Botham is expressing his
belief that it is a close call, almost inviting the
verdict of 'out'. Botham has opened himself up, not
even using his bat in self-defence, and is doing
nothing visibly to protect himself, perhaps
knowing that the end is coming. Having made
a pair he resigned after this match, at the
same time that he was replaced as captain
by the England selectors.

Batsmen have since learned to look
away when an appeal is made against
them, or to re-mark their guard to show they are staying, or
even turn their back on the umpire (which may not be good
psychology as the umpire may feel he is being ignored and
decide to teach the batsman a lesson). Thereby they send
out the message: this appeal is to be disregarded, it is
inconceivable that I am out, and I dare you to say otherwise.

THE GRANDEST GESTURE

Eng v Aus, 2nd Test, Edgbaston, 2005
After Australia have lost by two runs, Andrew Flintoff bends down to speak to
the defeated – although personally unbeaten – batsman Brett Lee and places a
hand on his shoulder in consolation. By descending to the same level as his opponent, by this act of self-abasement, Flintoff has acknowledged Lee as a warrior of
equal valour. Or has he? Is the act of putting his left hand on Lee's shoulder
something more? Is Flintoff thereby saying,
after England have levelled the series at
one-all, that he and his team are on top
now, and have the upper hand, and
the power to offer solace in defeat to
the fallen?

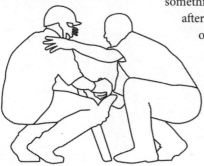

TOUCHING THE HEIGHTS

Eng v WI, 3rd Test, Old Trafford, 1988
High fives by Courtney Walsh, the tallest of these West Indian bowlers, and Curtly Ambrose, but not by the shortest, Malcolm Marshall. The gesture was popularised in American basketball and volleyball after a player had scored. In this context, it demonstrates to opponents and spectators the outstanding physical attribute that has made the West Indian fast bowlers of the 1980s so omnipotent: their height.

SOLIDARITY

Eng v SA, 4th Test, the Oval, 2008
Whereas the fist-bump was originally an American gesture of some flamboyance, punching gloves at the end of an over – or after hitting a boundary – has become an undemonstrative, very English style of gesture. It quietly sends the message: we are hereby reconnecting and reaffirming our partnership, we are here for each other, the bond is unbroken. I would date its introduction to the England team to around 2000, when central contracts were introduced.

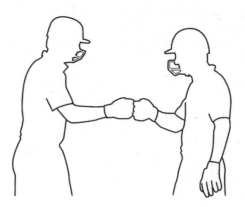

THE HUNTER FINISHES OFF HIS KILL

Aus v SL, World Cup SF, Port Elizabeth, 2003

This is the most primitive piece of body language seen in cricket. The gesture has been called 'the chainsaw', but the sawing of wood is meaningless in this context and to my mind it is a euphemism. The action is that of a hunter finishing off his opponent or prey with a spear or sword. It was pioneered by Brett Lee of Australia and Dale Steyn of South Africa, and its savagery no doubt added to the fear they generated. In this case Lee had another reason to celebrate: this wicket – that of Marvan Atapattu – was taken with a ball timed at 160.1 kph or 99.5 mph. Both fast bowlers gradually shelved the gesture, whether it was because they aged or because they joined the Indian Premier League, where they often bowled against their fellow-countrymen: after dismissing a national teammate, the gesture would have been too bloodthirsty.

THE CARMODY FIELD – OR LOOK BEHIND YOU!

Aus v NZ, 2nd Test, Eden Park, 1977

An expression of one team's complete psychological dominance over another: Dennis Lillee bowling at Auckland with nine slips. Lillee is telling the New Zealand batsman that he is not capable of hitting the ball in front of the wicket, and that he will be caught off one of his fast outswingers. Lillee ended up with match figures of 11 wickets for 123. The Carmody field was devised and used on a regular basis by Keith Carmody, the captain of Western Australia, in the 1940s, when even Australian batsmen from the eastern states were surprised by the bounce of the WACA in Perth.

11

THE TIME
OF MY LIFE

Such is the love I bear for Life and Cricket.
Samuel Maunder

IN ADDITION TO all the other reasons for playing and watching cricket, the sport offers a time frame by which we can measure our lives. It has also been known to create the happy illusion that we have lived longer than we actually have.

Thanks to cricket, rather than a photograph album, I can date an early family holiday in Scotland. We went out one afternoon, confident that England would knock off the runs they needed to win the fourth Test against Australia, came back to our seaside cottage, waited for the television to warm up, and watched in dismay as England were bowled out. I have only to look up *Wisden* to find the date: it was 1 August 1961. Sixteen years later, to the day, I was decorating a bedroom.

In the fifth Test of that series between England and Australia, England's opening batsman Raman Subba Row played his last Test innings before retiring at the age of 29. As he walked out to bat at the Oval, for the final time, I was probably affected more than he was. I came to know him when he managed England's tour of India in 1981–82, and he kindly wrote a foreword to my book about the tour, *Cricket Wallah*. He seemed to have enjoyed his career in business, and never expressed to me any regret about giving up the game so young. But for a seven-year-old watching black-and-white television, Subba Row's retirement – premature in terms of his cricket – was my first rite of passage, and one which moved me very close to tears. It was my first sense of loss, the first time I felt that time was passing, never to return.

We can measure so much of our lives by cricket's time frame because it occupies so many days of the calendar. I remember exactly where I was on the morning of 17 February 1971, to the very point on the stairs, on hearing that Ray Illingworth's team had regained the Ashes: it was the first occasion in my conscious life that England had held them. The afternoon of 21 July 1981? Why, I was pacing round the back of the press box at Headingley as if outside a maternity ward, while Bob Willis put the finishing touches to Ian Botham's 149 not out and the biggest turnaround in England's Test history. (Afterwards, as the nation celebrated, I caught a lift with Graham Gooch, who must have been the only person in England not euphoric: his Test place was in danger.) Many of us can recall where we were on Sunday, 7 August 2005, when England beat Australia at Edgbaston by two runs, to turn the wheel, at long last.

Other sports offer a similar service of escapism. But cricket has been going on longer, for the best part of three hundred years. It offers us this time frame, as well as a brace to stiffen us against the blows of Fate.

Cricket's interaction with time serves other uses. Together, as a pair, they can keep memory alive. This will become ever more relevant as more of us live to an older age. The last memory that Alzheimer's leaves us may be that of the first Test match we attended, or the shot that brought up our maiden century.

Dudley Carew survived the First World War, then suffered,

among countless others, a sense of purposelessness. He decided to spend the summer of 1926 watching cricket matches and writing about them. *England Over* contains some of the finest writing of any cricket book: at least two chapters deserve to be ranked as English literature. When he visited the Oval, his attention dwelt not only on the game between Surrey and Cambridge University but on spectators, who were coping with the start of the General Strike and Great Depression, as well as the effects of war. Carew met

an elderly man who will talk to you for so long as you care to listen of Abel and Richardson, Lohmann and Lockwood. While he is talking one has time to observe him carefully. One notices the square-toed, unpolished boots, the rucked waistcoat with the spot or two of grease on it, the clean, ill-fitting collar, and one wonders, if one has an inquisitive mind, what manner of life this man has led. What suffering has he been through, and what happiness? Who is his God, and what in life or in death does he most fear? One wonders what he has worked at, and whether his wife is alive, and whether he has children. One wants desperately to pierce to the reality behind the clothes and talk, and it is only after one has been listening to him for some time that one begins to realise that the reality may lie precisely in those words 'Abel,' 'boundary,' 'slow-bowler,' he is perpetually uttering. We are always so insolently certain that the accidents which over-shadow the world such as death and suffering and love are of immense importance to everyone. We do not allow for the curious filter of the individual mind which can rob such words of all significance and distil from such apparently trivial occurrences as a cricket match, a night at a theatre, an unexpected five-pound note, essences of strength and purity. Looking at the particular old man to whom I spoke, the conviction grew on me that *this* was reality for him, this ground, this scoreboard and these slim, yellow stumps, and that he would carry out with him into the darkness, not the recollection of a woman's lips against his own or of the laboured, weakening breath of a child, but rather of Richardson walking back to begin his run or of Hobbs lifting his cap after completing his century.

After this Oval game, Carew visited Lord's for the annual two-day fixture between Eton and Harrow, not that he had attended either school. He found this match to be still a highlight of the social calendar:

The Eton and Harrow match keeps up its ritual wonderfully well. Year after year coaches gather round the tavern, the popping of champagne corks is heard, salmon mayonnaise is handed round. Top hats glitter in the sun and gaitered legs perambulate backwards and forwards by the pavilion. The ground itself seems to become jolly and benevolent, like an old gentleman who puts his age and dignity by and exerts himself at a children's party. The parade at luncheon and between the innings somehow carries one back to the days when Dan Leno held the Empire in adoring silence and women stood on chairs to catch a sight of Lily Langtry. Immaculate old men, leaning on sticks as they walk, seem to have come out of Meredith's world.

The cricket itself is mundane as Eton score 312 in their first innings. Carew looks around, and in front of the Tavern he notices a woman whom he observes all the more closely as the first day wears on. And time, having offered an illusion of the early Victorian era of George Meredith, kicks in again with a reference to the eighteenth century: 'Her black dress, elaborately pleated, spoke of another age, and the white feather in her hat, a full voluminous feather, gave her, for all her ampleness, a faint but startling resemblance to the women that Gainsborough delighted to paint.'

This woman stirs to life when Harrow commence their innings on the first evening. In his curiosity, Carew approaches her, on the pretext of offering his scorecard, but she does not need it. She knows full well who Harrow's opening batsmen are: 'Crawley and Clover-Brown, we should see some good cricket now, Crawley is the best bat on either side.'

Carew, impressed by her knowledge, continues the conversation and asks if she watches Eton v Harrow every year. 'Oh! no, only since the war and the one year before it.' At this point she turns away. Their conversation has been terminated, at least for the day.

When Carew arrives a little late at Lord's on the second morning, this woman is in exactly the same seat. She informs him: 'Crawley is out, there is no chance of a Harrow win now.' She has no beauty of face or physique, but there is something of it in the way she speaks. 'Her actual voice was more perfect than the ghost of it my memory and imagination had created together in the night.'

The match is heading for a draw, as it is a four-innings match spread over only two days, and it resolves into a fight for first-innings lead and a modicum of honour. 'Excitement hung electrically in the air, and the shouts of "E-ton," "Har-row," which are supposed to be becoming fainter every year, took on the robust note of an earlier age.' Spurred on, Harrow take the first innings lead, and extend it to 64, before Eton comfortably bat out time.

> I turned to the woman beside me. 'Another draw, I wish Harrow could win, it would do them a lot of good.'
>
> Slowly, reluctantly, she turned her eyes from the cricket, and in her exquisite voice there was a faint note of rebuke. 'There are years to come,' she said slowly. 'Years and years, years and years.'

It seemed as though as she spoke she saw in her words a vision of those years to come which upheld and elated her.

Feebly I murmured, 'You like cricket, then?' She turned towards me and her vacant, slightly protruding eyes searched my face as though to discover an expression, a feature known to her. 'He said that,' she murmured at last, 'that Harrow would win, he was always so optimistic, so full of plans. The things he was going to do! He loved cricket so. He thought he might even play for Harrow if he stayed long enough. He always said they would win, though. In 1914 he said, "We shall win next year, mother." There was no match in 1915, you see, so he was wrong, he was wrong.'

Carew is horrified. Only at this instant does he realise why this woman comes annually to Lord's. He stammers that he is 'so terribly sorry'.

She replies: 'You are not old enough, young man, to know how easy it is to forget, not half old enough.' She continues, after a pause: 'When you are old it is difficult to remember, to remember clearly. Memory lives not in the brain but in places, young man. You must go out and find memory if you want her, she waits but does not come.'

She turns away, to absorb the scene she would not see again until her pilgrimage the same time next year. 'She stopped gazing at me, and took in, in a slow and comprehensive glance, the pavilion, the coaches, the stands, the scoreboard as though to illustrate to me how, in this ground at any rate, memory waited for her faithfully and enduringly.'

The result of the match being certain, Carew decides to leave Lord's. Before going, he asks the woman if she will stay till the end. 'Her voice, resonant, deep and beautiful, echoed my words. "Till the end."'

After walking away, Carew turns to see her, still in her seat, 'watching with a glowing intensity the last few overs of a dying game.'

> 'Memory waits,' she had said, and I know that I shall never enter Lord's again without finding her ghost there, tragically and pitifully evoking the memories of her dead son.

Those last three monosyllables are hammer blows. They nail the coffin.

Cricket can be used not only to keep memory alive and vivid in the present. Ronald Mason, in *Batsman's Paradise*, believed it can also serve to create the illusion that time has halted. This is what great painters do.

When Denis Compton made his first-class debut for Middlesex in 1936, Mason was avidly watching at Lord's. It was the Whitsun Bank Holiday Championship match against Sussex, and on a fresh morning Middlesex's batsmen had not coped with the seam bowling of Maurice Tate. At number eleven, a 17-year-old walked out to join Gubby Allen, the England captain. The boy, 'spruced up and looking new and nervous', played back to his first two balls from Tate and missed. After Allen had gestured to him, 'the boy shook his head as if the flies were at it; played desperately forward at the next ball and got it clearly in the middle.' Compton went on to score 14 before being given leg-before, after a half-hearted shout. Before the end of the following season he was batting at number five for England.

In 1953 Mason saw Compton bat again at Lord's. In the long interim 'the boy Compton had gone . . . The pinkness had left his features, his mischievous eyes had retreated behind contemplative wrinkles; he was soberer, firmer set, authoritative, assured.' Mason asked himself where the delightful urchin had gone. And gradually, while Compton battled against an Australian attack led by Ray Lindwall, the author 'glimpsed the touching struggle for re-emergence of my lost and charming urchin from the other side of the war, from the other side of a barrier of destructiveness, from the other end of a moving and unreturning band of Time.'

Mason's hypothesis was that the game itself – the way cricket was played, its style and method – did not fundamentally change. Neither did cricket grounds, like Lord's, change 'barring certain structural alterations which do not much matter'. Only the players change, Mason argued, from one generation to the next.

> Therefore we are presented with the illusion of a constant watcher of a constant background, marking dutifully off as they [i.e. the players] pass before his eyes the only elements in the scene which vary. If they did not vary, there would be no Time. Their variations are the only means of marking Time off, in the context of the game.

This hypothesis has not, however, stood the test of time. It worked for Mason, but not for us, his successors. Even on a ground which has not been structurally renovated, the game has changed, a lot. When Mason watched Compton batting at Lord's, all the attacking was done by the bowler, whether Tate in 1936 or Lindwall in 1953. The run-rate was seldom so high as three per over. Bats were light, and the ball was stroked along the ground, neither a helmet nor an advertisement in sight.

Since the 1990s – Sri Lanka's winning of the 1996 World Cup makes as definitive a starting point as any – the batsmen have done ever more of the attacking. Caution and the fear of getting out have disappeared, replaced by bravado and an obsession with strike-rate. A 17-year-old making his county debut now would be barely able to show his face in the dressing room if his innings of 14 did not include a four and a six.

On only one occasion in Mason's long experience of watching professional cricket did he glimpse this future which has become our present. It occurred in the end-of-season fixture of Champion County v The Rest at the Oval in September 1924. Frank Woolley and Percy Chapman, perhaps the two most attacking batsmen of the period, were facing Wilfred Rhodes and Roy Kilner, the Yorkshire left-arm spinners who were the two most economical bowlers of the period. They spent whole seasons conceding fewer than two runs an over.

Woolley and Chapman, both left-handers, took Rhodes and Kilner apart. Judging by Mason's description, they mostly drove or pull-drove, or slog-swept as we would say, over midwicket. The author, aged 12, was sitting amid a gaggle of schoolboys near the gasometers. In exactly seven minutes by his reckoning, perhaps three overs, they scored 50 runs.

Never again did Mason experience such joy:

> I felt, innocent and inexperienced as I was, a sense of tremendous exultation. It was elementary, charity-match stuff; but it affected me as no incident at any cricket match has ever affected me, before or since . . . Whenever I woke up in the night visited by such fears as often plague our humanity for very little cause, I would find my palpitations quietened almost inevitably by a handhold out of the past from that bright little incident of my boyhood. The sunny Oval, and Chapman, all red-faced and laughing, dancing out to drive, and the ball soaring and the crowd rising and cheering, made a living light-giving cameo that very many times in the lonely night-watches of real or imaginary distress cooled and soothed my agitation and eased me into a quieter mood of resignation or sleep. It is a part of the past that is bodily of the present still.

Since the 1990s, and especially the growth of 20-over cricket, a 12-year-old going to the Oval has not been surprised by the sight of 50 runs being struck off three overs. Indeed, he has probably gone there expecting to see such a scoring rate. In many a training session, no doubt, Surrey's batsmen have rehearsed '50 off 18'.

The gasometers outside the Oval have not changed. Inside, almost everything has.

It is partly because the element of time is right that the Test match is widely considered to be cricket's highest form. In most cases, five days allow for a fight to the finish. The contestants are not mindful of time until the fifth day approaches. It has long been axiomatic that a team which sets out to draw a Test match usually fails. A Test is a 15-round boxing match; a one-day international a bout of three rounds, and a Twenty20 of one.

The duration of a Test match has not always been five days, but it has for the last half-century; and the proportion of draws has diminished from a third in the 1960s to the point where a draw has become a rarity in some countries in the absence of rain. Five days: any less, and some players would be tempted to enter the match with the aim of achieving a draw, a stalemate. Any more, and the intensity of each day would be diluted, and the focus could wander.

A span of five days allows for an almost infinite number of variations to unfold; and, having seen almost a fifth of all Tests, I cannot think of two the same. The physicist Professor Brian Cox equated cricket with the universe – except that the former has far more laws governing it than the latter. 'When you get so many variables [of pitch, ball, weather, human characteristics etc], the number of possibilities becomes enormous,' Cox said. 'Cricket is more complicated than the Universe.' Preserve the Test match and cricket will carry on creating novel possibilities.

It is a coincidence that the most epic battle in the western world lasted for six days: five days of fighting and a rest day, such as Test cricket had until the 1980s. Or maybe it is not a coincidence at all. Maybe the ideal time span for any epic contest is five days.* When Homer composed *The Iliad*, his time span allowed the action to breathe, to have light and shade, quiet and tumult. The final showdown between the Greeks and Troy after the ten-year siege had time for the revelation of human character, but not too much time, so the action was sufficiently compressed to generate tension.

Suppose the fall of Troy had occurred in the same time frame as a one-day international. Achilles would either have sulked in his tent throughout and missed the action, or he would have come out to fight before the tension became unbearable. Either way, we would have been deprived of the 'will he, won't he' come to the aid of the Greeks. We would not have had time for more than one duel between Achilles and Hector, no time for Achilles to chase Hector around the walls of Troy three times. Once round the block would have been somewhat less dramatic.

The lengthier time span of five days of fighting allows the advantage to swing from one side to the other and back. Each evening, everyone can look back and take stock: has the Greek position improved since the day before? Everyone has to endure an anxious night before finding out what happens next. Homer could have been describing an England captain who had sent Australia in at Brisbane, not King Agamemnon wondering how to win without Achilles: 'Groan after groan came up from the depths of his being, and his heart was shot through by fear.'

Other similarities between the Siege of Troy and a Test match

---

* In another ancient narrative, we are told God created the world in six days, followed by a rest day.

suggest themselves. The fighting begins when Paris and Menelaus draw lots to see who will throw the first spear; the equivalent in cricket, of course, is the tossing of a coin. Duels simplify the action, whether between Greek and Trojan, or Shane Warne and Andrew Flintoff, England's Achilles in 2005. The team game of cricket has thrown up individual champions since 'Great Newland' challenged Hodsoll in 1744, and such duels are easier to describe and follow than amorphous meleés.

Some Homeric descriptions of death are brief and conventional, like a spear through the shoulder blade, whereas more spectacular demises are recounted in the goriest detail. The downfall of a batsman in a Test match is analogous. We can be given a stock phrase – 'he was trapped lbw' – or treated to a blow-by-blow account, like his being set up by a bowler before he is caught at deep-square off a bouncer, which heightens the drama.

Homer's time span of five or six days allows for soliloquies by men and gods, and conversations between the two; the parallel is the press conference or television interview. The speech of both warrior and cricketer is filled with conventional epithets and pious aspirations, infused with sufficient modesty to offset the accusation of hubris. Hector declares to Achilles: 'I know that you are a great fighter, and I am much your inferior. But these things [i.e. the outcome] lie in the laps of the gods.' Ditto the Test captain in his eve-of-match conference.

Some consider it a defect when Homer warns us of what is to happen because it lessens the drama: he tells us that Athene has lobbied Zeus to ensure victory for Achilles before his final duel with Hector. Others say this foreknowledge allows us to concentrate on how the protagonists develop in the face of their impending fate. Does not the spectator of a close cricket match enjoy the best of both worlds? He does not know the outcome, unless he has paid for the result to be fixed, *and* he can see the players reacting *in extremis.* Only on its first night does a play in a theatre hold so much glorious uncertainty.

Homer uses time in another way familiar to followers of cricket. He tells us that Nestor's squadron numbered 90 ships, Diomedes commanded '80 black ships', and the Athenians had 50 ships, many more than the Greeks of Homer's day could muster – and they were crewed by virtual giants and commanded by demi-gods. Ever since John Nyren insisted in *The Cricketers of My Time* that bowlers were quicker in his day, as well as the beer being so much stronger than in the effeminate 1830s, cricket has shared this tendency to aggrandise the past – more so than other sports or human activities, I would observe. Cricketers are never so good as they used to be. The selectiveness of memory is at work here: we have forgotten the mistakes and mundane passages, and remember only the outstanding moments. In addition, we have the narrator at work. He wants his listeners or readers to be awed by the past, to stay tuned.

We also have in *The Iliad* the first account of sport in western culture. Achilles organises funerary games in memory of his friend Patroclus: a chariot race, boxing, wrestling, discus-throwing, archery, throwing the javelin and duelling until blood is drawn. These sports keep the Greeks fighting fit during the truce, and nourish competitiveness, but they also present Achilles in a far more attractive light. He had been the spoilt brat in his tent, then savage in his treatment of Hector's body, letting each of his men stab the corpse in front of the walls of Troy and Hector's parents. But he is redeemed in our eyes by staging these games, and chivalrously adding an extra prize for a contestant who had been unfairly impeded in the chariot race. His sportsmanship proves Achilles has a generous side, and a sense of fairness, in peace if not war.

The place where time has come closest to standing still for me is Hinton Charterhouse, outside Bath. For well over 30 years I have played there and the ground has not changed. The air is fresh and the light clear as Hinton is reputed to be the second highest settlement in Somerset, and the westerlies blow the rain clouds down the valley below. Every community is more settled, more knitted together, for having a cricket team.

The manor house through the trees, blessed with an orangery, is Georgian architecture in Bath stone at its most handsome, not austere and symmetrical. The elder brother of Raymond Robertson-Glasgow, cricket correspondent of *The Observer* in the 1950s, used to live here and laid out the ground. The tradition is that he had the soil for the square brought from Lord's, and the pitches have always been good for batting, except for an hour after rain. Every tree in the grounds of the manor house is different, creating an arboretum.

In my devotion I am not alone. Our head groundsman, Ed, is over 90, artificial hips and all. Old Al has been mowing the outfield since the 1970s; and for over 30 years several of us have put the 'creak' back into cricket. We cannot bring ourselves to retire, even when the ball trickles past our ankles, or between. Hinton players tend to move to another area for work, or die on partially active service. Alan, our second-team wicketkeeper, was hit on the head by a top edge, diagnosed with cancer when he went to hospital, and died within the six-month, leaving a wife and three young children. In January, we huddled in the cold of the churchyard beside the manor. 'Can't be a god, can there?' asked our first-team keeper.

Old Shardy took hundreds or rather thousands of wickets with his unerringly accurate medium pace, nibbling away around off-stump, creating so many chances that one afternoon I held three catches at second slip. He kept on playing friendlies into his seventies. His shoulder had long since stopped him bowling, he hid in the field at 45 degrees, and wanted to bat no higher than eleven; but he could not give up playing cricket at Hinton.

On a Sunday in spring and summer, playing at Hinton is for us as much a ritual as attending church. We are like Hindus or Jews in worshipping our way of life, only in the English countryside.

Going up the drive, I look first to see if the stumps are up: if not, Ed might think the ground is too wet for a game.* Then I look for a few cars parked behind the pavilion: too few and it might mean the opposition will not turn up, and the afternoon is lost.

If the visitors are warming up with nets and drills, if they are aged between 20 and 30, or if they have a cricketer of note, I am confident we will play our best. When the opposition look a shambles of too old and too young, we will relax and probably lose. We are lucky to have entertained some of the finest cricketers at Hinton Charterhouse. When he was the professional for Imperial in Bristol, Shane Warne was not yet the master of spin-bowling psychology. (He took 200 Test wickets when he ripped his leg-break, and 500 wickets after he damaged his shoulder but mastered mind games.) At Hinton, he left the field for a fag and a pint after his brief spell: 4–0–15–1 in our scorebook.[†]

Viv Richards graced our stage before my time when qualifying for Somerset in 1973 by playing for Lansdown; so did Ian Botham

---

* As with everything to do with life and death, Tolstoy summed it up: 'He had that feeling of concentrated excitement that every sportsman experiences as he approaches the scene of action.' (Of Levin, when he goes shooting, in *Anna Karenina*.)

† This match, a Sunday friendly in 1991, ended prematurely because the life of one of the Imperial players nearly did. I was at the non-striker's end when my partner, surrounded by close fielders without helmets, swung a ball to leg and hit a fielder, who swallowed his tongue. He had about two minutes left to live – except that the sister of one of our players had just qualified as a doctor and happened to be on the ground. She extricated his tongue and got him breathing again, long before the ambulance arrived. For some years afterwards, when Warne visited Bristol, he either met or checked up on his former and so nearly departed team mate.

and the rest of the Somerset team when they played a couple of benefit games at Hinton in the late 1970s (one of the rare occasions when Botham kept wicket). Colin Croft once became bored with off-breaks and rolled back some of his years; Jon Lewis[*] bowled a lot here, then for Gloucestershire; and Marcus Trescothick, a Keynsham teenager, slog-swept spinners into the arboretum.

To avoid the tendency to aggrandise the past, we have had our lean seasons, very lean in the early 1980s. The only new members who joined would say: 'I haven't played since school but . . .' When posted to mid-on, they would not walk in, but bend forward, hands on knees.

Whatever the game, I prefer to field first. My teammates who have played a league game on Saturday, and obviously socialised until late, want to bat first on Sundays, but I am nearly as keen to take the field as I was in my childhood. I like fielding for an hour or so, catching up with news and banter, before a bowl. A batsman stumped when charging a leg-break or gated by a googly: these are my favourite dismissals, and not so familiar that they breed contempt. A buzzard has taken to flying over Hinton in recent seasons, but it never seems to spot easy prey when I am bowling.

Sharing a meal with fellow-believers is a part of most rituals. Home-made tea, in the pavilion or on the verandah, is another of Hinton's delights. Ivo Bligh, unwittingly, set a long-term trend by visiting Rupertswood. All cricketers now worship the urn.

I don't mind a bit of umpiring afterwards: anything but scoring, because that still evokes the frustration of my childhood. When the bowling is from the other end, I like to alternate between square-leg and cover, to take in the views. My favourite umpiring moment comes in April, in the first game of our season, before a leaf on the

* Another press box witicism: 'Jon Lewis, never knowingly under-bowled' – Mike Walters, *Daily Mirror*

trees. It is an insight into how God must have felt at the launch of creation when I drop my arm and joyfully shout: 'Play!'

If it happens to be a perfect afternoon, I will go in about number seven or eight with 30 runs to win off the last few overs and help knock them off. Very seldom, if ever, is life perfect. Whatever runs I have scored or wickets taken, I will replay them in my head when I wake up during the night, stiff, and content if we have won our league match and I have done my bit by taking a few wickets and dragging the rate back. If I bowl well in April, the pleasure is flooded with relief: I have one more season, at any rate. Does anyone who plays sport have to go through the self-doubt of the ageing club cricketer? He has to wait seven whole months before he knows whether he can perform again or not.

The ritual after the game is to shake hands with the opposition, and for us to clear the field while they cluster in their dressing room and maybe shut the door to review their performance. The clunk when carrying the stumps back to the pavilion contrasts with the clink of the metal poles when we take them out to rope off the square. We share a drink or two, pay our match fee and set off home, when the tops of the trees are tall enough to catch the lingering light. It is only on driving back that I realise the outside world has not intruded all afternoon, not even the sound of traffic through the trees.

Sunday evenings are best. After the game I drive into the sun setting in the west, along lanes where the followers of the Duke of Monmouth straggled before the last battle on English soil, at Sedgemoor; but I only identify with them if Hinton have lost. When my wife awaits at home, and one or two of our children, and some of my wife's cooking, and a bottle of wine, and I have taken a few wickets, I cannot think of anything to make me happier.

I hate September when leaves from the lime tree that towers above the pavilion scud into the nets and across the square: yellows and auburns are inadequate compensation. The far side of the ground sloping towards the manor is damp from dew when I get slogged over there. Only a few packets of peanuts are left for sale on the wall of the bar. I want to play on and on, as some trees are still fully leafed. How about a friendly on the last Sunday of September, Ed? Or a 20-over game in early October starting at noon? Please, please? But we have to reseed the square and 'put the club to bed', tenderly, as if it were a baby.

The next time I go to Hinton I will be another year older, and even less capable of stopping the ball that swirls past my left ankle, even with my boot. The gap between knowing what to do, and being able to do it, grows larger and larger. An injury takes longer to heal, not days but months. Next year I shall be even more racked with self-doubt: have I lost what little I had? Only one thing is to be said for old age as a spinner: the ball is less likely to bounce over the bails. The silver lining in Shardy's death was that he had never quite reached the stage of saying: 'This is my last ever match for Hinton.' For me, knowing I was playing my last game of cricket would be as poignant as knowing I was making love for the final time.

All too soon I will resemble that old man Carew met at the Oval. Except that on my final bed, before going into the dark, I will not remember Richardson walking back to his mark or Hobbs raising his cap on reaching his century. It will be my wife and children, and my few proud moments on the field for Hinton. Until this time, 'such is the love I bear for Life and Cricket', I hope to watch and play.

▯

To know ourselves, Chekhov said, we should find out our desires. Our actions are to a large extent imposed upon us. It is by our desires that we can know ourselves.

So deep was the sense of rejection I felt when invited not to play in that school match, but to score instead, that I used an opportunity that presented itself 40 years later when I became editor of *Wisden Cricketers' Almanack*. I had started an after-school cricket club at the primary school that my son attended in Bristol, where the children whacked plastic balls and whizzed around the playground even on the wettest afternoon in January: if you cannot play, the next best thing is to see kids enjoying themselves at cricket.* One year we had four pupils in Gloucestershire's junior teams: not much by the standards of Lascelles Hall primary, or Wolmer's, but not bad for a school which had never had a cricket team.

As *Wisden*'s editor, I was able to use the name and start the Wisden City Cup for lads aged 16 and over who lived in inner cities and did not have access to cricket grounds, let alone proper pitches. The competition grew steadily from its base in Middlesex, where the director of cricket, Angus Fraser, and the chief development officer, Phil Knappett, trialled it – until it spread to eight cities, then twelve, too big to be a labour of love, and the England and Wales Cricket Board adopted it. The competition evolved into the Lord's Taverners City Cup, in association with the ECB, MCC (who contracted the most promising player as a Young Cricketer) and *Wisden*. Inner-city, then inter-city in the knockout stages, it became established as a pathway to the top for those outside the traditional club and county structures. The games had to be played on midweek evenings, because clubs with decent pitches used them at weekends: so 20-over matches they had to be.

---

* Even at this level, cricket does not lose its capacity to be a great leveller. On returning from England's victorious tour of Australia in 2010–11, I went to the school for our Thursday afternoon session – and the rain was lashing down, absolutely pelting. The coach put it to the kids: 'Do you want to go outside and play in the rain, or do you want to listen to Mr Berry telling you about the Ashes?' Nineteen out of twenty squealed: 'Play outside!' One girl, about eight, bless her, tentatively suggested we could do both – listen, *for a bit*, then go outside.

The competition spread to cities like Wolverhampton, which had never produced an England Test cricketer. The difference now is that England's inner cities are populated in large part by British Asians, for whom cricket has always been the number one sport, and always will be – until role-model footballers come along and lead them away from cricket, as was the case with Britain's Afro-Caribbeans. I want to see, in parallel, a semi-hard-ball competition for girls, because the south Asian female population has to be the biggest potential growth area for cricket in Britain. If they play cricket, the sport's future is guaranteed; if they do not, it will likely shrink into a middle-class niche.

Outside inner cities, in towns and villages and suburbs, the future of amateur cricket is fairly healthy, in spite of the sport being removed from terrestrial television at the end of 2005. It is governed by people who care for it: those who volunteer to organise, help, coach and play. A single match can include all manner of physiques, temperaments, personalities and age groups, and both genders, unlike most sports.

Every English county, whether first-class or minor, should have not only its current team but also a Veterans XI and Rookies XI, who play each other. The seniors will have crafty spinners, such as the juniors would never meet if they bat against only their contemporaries. In my retirement I would pay to watch a county's past players playing against the future ones at a scenic out-ground, no longer used by the county side. To extend this intermingling of the generations – at which Anglo-Saxon society, unlike Mediterranean, is bad – I would like to see each county's Over-50 team play against their Under-15s in an annual fixture or best-of-three; and their Over-60 team play against their Under-13s, and their Over-70s against their Under-11s. Fathers v sons is traditional, so why not – given greater longevity – grandfathers v grandsons? There is no better motive to play on.

Amateur cricket has social responsibilities yet to be fulfilled. It is said to be the ideal sport for those with Down's Syndrome, because it can be broken down into comprehensible units, one over at a time, whereas a football match can appear an overwhelming mass. So why not an inter-city competition for them too? But it is, overall, on the right lines.

Professional cricket around the world is mostly governed by businessmen and politicians who are skilful at committees, and some use cricket for their own advancement. Kerry Packer was able to buy up the best cricketers for World Series Cricket because administrators before 1980 were unworldly paternalists, who had played themselves. Not any more; nobody can accuse their successors of being unmaterialistic. And until the boards of the International Cricket Council and the Test-playing countries follow New Zealand's example in creating an executive board of independent directors who are 'great and good', without conflicts of interests, and some of whom have played at first-class level, professional cricket will be ever more infected by its rulers' values.

Each of the last four centuries has witnessed a match which has been a turning point for the sport. Kent v England in 1744; the inaugural Test match, between Australia and England, in 1877; the World Cup final between India and West Indies in 1983, which engaged Asia's interest in 50-over cricket. In this century the turning point was the World Twenty20 final between India and Pakistan in Johannesburg in 2007, which prompted India to launch their own domestic T20 league.

The time is coming when the majority of professional cricket matches will be T20; and if they are televised, there is a distinct possibility they will be corrupted, especially if they are part of a domestic league. The 'legs' at Lord's, whom Mary Mitford and John Nyren deplored, have spread around the world. In 1827, the Sussex v England game at Brighton was fixed; in 2011, it was the 40-over game between Sussex and Kent. Once bookmakers and punters began to make significant sums in the 1980s, the mafia bosses moved in, including the biggest in south Asia. Such forces above the law are never going to disappear, even supposing that governments wanted them to.

The cricketer who represented his country, or his county or state, used to have a tie of local loyalty to overcome before he was tempted to fix; the T20 mercenary has none. George Smith held the franchise for the Artillery Ground and made a few profits; the T20 franchise-holder, who owns his cricketers, can make enormous profits through dishonest means.

International cricket has become too cosy, in that it is in the interest of almost all the stakeholders to let fixing continue under the table. I was told by a most senior official of the ICC's Anti-Corruption and Security Unit that one of the most famous of all cricketers would be exposed as soon as he retired; but I am still waiting, my breath no longer held. It is more alarming for the authorities if fixers are exposed, because then broadcasters could be scared away, taking the basic revenue with them. The very occasional player who confesses is sufficient – and, by definition, he is low down the food chain, because the major fixers have a mafia behind them.

Even when a 20-over match is not corrupted, it lacks an essential ingredient which longer formats have. The finish may be exciting – indeed, through being shorter, it is more likely to be exciting than the end of a first-class match – and the skills on parade are certain to be spectacular. But the human interest has dwindled. The batsman is not presented with a range of options, as he is in a longer format; decision-making has been simplified for him. He has been reduced to a hitting machine. After a few balls to play himself in, perhaps, his aim is to hit the ball to or over the boundary: one or the other.

Such a game is all action, no drama, and sometimes not much action either: the bowler runs in, bang, the ball sails out of the ring, and nobody moves. Does a crowd assemble to watch a golfer in a driving range hitting every ball as far as he can? When big hitting is routine, it is less of a spectacle, not more: the spice of variety has gone.

A 50-over game has time for batting *and* hitting, for the agony of indecision *and* the revelation of human character. In the titanic World Cup semi-final of 1999 between Australia and South Africa at Edgbaston, Shane Warne rose to the occasion, to turn and tie the match, so that Australia went through to the final, while some of his opponents wilted.

Ultimately it is this revelation of human character, and how it develops under duress, that is the fascination of cricket, or fiction, or theatre. Had W.G. Grace been born not in 1848 but 1990, his appetites would have led him to be a full-time, round-the-world T20 specialist. He would have channelled his energies into earning as much as he could. In the process, his personality would have been submerged, like the beard beneath his helmet.

Scott Fitzgerald suggested that life is best observed through a single window. It is not true. Life is best observed through several windows, but there is nothing wrong if cricket is one of them.

As the world subsides into lawlessness and violence, largely through un- and under-employment, some would argue that cricket should take a back seat. I would argue the opposite: if people cannot obtain a decently paid job, they should be offered all the more encouragement to play sport.

Limitless greed, and the new tribalism, are the twin evils of our time. The greed of a few individuals, and of unregulated multi-nationals, has concentrated the world's wealth in a few hands.

How else are rich and poor ever going to meet now except on the sports ground? The old tribal structures have broken down, to be replaced by a new tribalism, like that of extremist religious sects. Sport, especially cricket,* promotes the contrary value of inclusiveness.

I am conscious that international cricket depends on the rivalry between countries; and that the brutal conflicts around the world, especially the Middle East, are predicated on national boundaries. It would be a far happier world if they were dissolved and countries were replaced by city-states. We would simply vote in and pay taxes to the city in which we live, or else the nearest. But in this utopia, if so it is, let national boundaries be retained for sport: we have seen enough of franchises to know that the highest form of cricket will always be England v Australia, or India v Pakistan, not Warriors v Raiders.

In the film *Out of the Ashes*, the opening scene is of the visionary Taj Malik driving through the devastated streets of Kabul, having launched the Afghan game on a concrete strip in a refugee camp in Pakistan. 'As you know, there is a lot of problem in the world today, no?' he says with half a laugh. 'The solution of all the problem is cricket.' In Afghanistan, it has become the best way to promote peace and integration. In some Taliban areas, schoolgirls play the game.

Cricket is so flexible that it can play a positive role in any society. In the Negev Desert, an Arab and a Jewish village played each other at cricket in their first social interaction, as chronicled by

---

* Amateur cricket, that is. The takeover of the International Cricket Council in 2014, by the chairmen of Australia, England and India, was obscenely similar to the way in which modern capitalism operates.

Tom Rodwell in *Third Man in Havana*. Had it been football, there would have been physical contact, and the chance to misinterpret and take offence, but cricket orders its players to maintain a respectful distance.

In Rwanda, cricket has become the sport to heal the wounds of genocide. When its people fled to neighbouring countries like Kenya and Uganda in the 1990s, they saw cricket being played, and brought it home after the civil war, for fun, and therapeutic comfort.

In some countries, like the Netherlands, cricket is the elite sport. In Cuba it is the sport of the lowest sector of society: people of West Indian origin who left Barbados and Jamaica between the World Wars to work on the sugar plantations and the American naval base at Guantanamo. Cricket represents everything that Guantanamo does not: fairness, nobody above the law, a level playing field, respect for those who are other.

Nothing makes me count my blessings like the sight of visually impaired people playing cricket. I heard the captain of England's first V.I. women's team before they toured Nepal and she scarcely contained her joy. Hundreds upon hundreds of women in Bangladesh have had acid thrown in their faces by the most contemptible cowards: please let them have the chance to play cricket, and go on tour, and represent their country, and alert the world to stop this tragedy.

This game can bring together so many sections of society to play and watch, whether people do so for the camaraderie; or for the gratification of physical sensations; or to make a statement about themselves, or their ethnic group, or their country; whether they enjoy the game's language or literature; whether or not they are intrigued by the numbers the game generates; whether they admire the game's ethics, or enjoy its aesthetics; whether or not they are fascinated by the game's psychology; whether they use the game's time frame like a Zimmer frame, as something to cling to in the face of eternity. This sport can support us all. Cricket is the game of life.

James Love, first of all cricket reporters, was right. All that has to be done is to extend his vision, from male to female, from country to country, to all social groups and ages:

Hail CRICKET! Glorious, human, *global* Game!
First of all Sports! be first alike in Fame!

SELECTED DATES IN CRICKET HISTORY

1727	Articles of Agreement drawn up for the conduct of matches between the teams of the Duke of Richmond and Mr Alan Brodrick.
1730	First recorded match at the Artillery Ground in London, home of the Honourable Artillery Company.
1744	George Smith charges spectators to see Kent v an All England XI at the Artillery Ground.
	First known version of the Laws of Cricket, in which the length of the pitch is set at 22 yards, there are two stumps and an over consists of four balls.
1745	Publication of James Love's *Cricket: An Heroic Poem.*
1769	First individual century, by John Minshull for the Duke of Dorset's XI v Wrotham.
1771	Width of bat limited to 4¼ inches, still the official maximum.
1774	The lbw law introduced.
1775	Three-stump wicket introduced (though not specified in the Laws until 1838).
1780	Cricket ball manufactured by Duke's of Penshurst, Kent, presented to the Prince of Wales.
1787	Formation of Marylebone Cricket Club.
1788	First revision of the Laws of Cricket by MCC.
1806	First Gentlemen v Players match at Lord's.
1807	First mention of round-arm bowling, by John Willes of Kent.

1820	First individual double century (278), by William Ward for MCC v Norfolk at Lord's.
1828	Bowlers authorised by MCC to raise their hands level with their elbows.
1833	Publication of John Nyren's *The Young Cricketer's Tutor* and *The Cricketers of My Time*.
1841	General Lord Hill issues a General Order that every military barracks should have a cricket ground.
1844	First official international match: Canada v United States.
c. **1850**	First use of wicketkeeping gloves.
1851	In *The Cricket Field*, James Pycroft uses the phrase 'not cricket'.
1864	MCC authorises 'overhand bowling'.
1868	Tour of England by an Australian Aboriginal team.
1873	W.G. Grace becomes the first player to record 1000 runs and 100 wickets in a first-class season.
1876	W.G. Grace makes the first two triple centuries in the course of scoring 839 runs in three consecutive innings, against Kent, Nottinghamshire and Yorkshire.
1876–77	First Test match: Australia defeat England by 45 runs at Melbourne.
1878	An Australian touring XI beats MCC by 9 wickets at Lord's.
1880	First Test in England: England beat Australia by 5 wickets at the Oval.
1882	England's first Test defeat in England – by Australia at the Oval – prompts an 'obituary notice' for English cricket in the *Sporting Times*.
1882–83	Ivo Bligh leads an England team on a tour of Australia, during which the tradition of the Ashes begins, and Willie Bates of England takes the first Test hat-trick.

1888–89   South Africa's first Test match, v England at Port Elizabeth.

1889   In England, five-ball overs introduced.

1889–90   Parsis beat G.F. Vernon's XI by 4 wickets at Bombay.

1890   County Championship officially constituted.

1895   W.G. Grace scores 1000 runs in May, and reaches his 100th hundred.

Archie MacLaren makes 424 for Lancashire v Somerset at Taunton.

1896   K.S. Ranjitsinhji plays his first Test for England, v Australia at Old Trafford.

1900   In England, six-ball overs become the norm.

First West Indian tour of England (not first-class).

1906   Second West Indian tour of England, from which Tommy Burton is sent home.

1909   Formation of the Imperial Cricket Conference (ICC – now the International Cricket Council), with England, Australia and South Africa the original members.

1910   Six runs awarded for any hit over the boundary, rather than only for a hit out of the ground.

1922–23   Bill Ponsford makes 429 for Victoria v Tasmania at Melbourne.

1927–28   Bill Ponsford makes 437 for Victoria v Queensland at Melbourne.

1928   West Indies' first Test match, v England at Lord's.

1928–29   Herbert Fishwick photographs Wally Hammond batting for MCC v NSW.

1929–30   Donald Bradman makes 452* for NSW v Queensland at Sydney.

New Zealand's first Test match, v England at Christchurch.

1930   On his first tour of England, Don Bradman scores 974 runs in the five Ashes Tests, still a record for any Test series.

1932   India's first Test match, v England at Lord's.

1932–33 The Bodyline Ashes series in Australia.

1948   First five-day Tests in England.

1950   Cambridge University v West Indies, highest-scoring first-class match in terms of runs per wicket.

1952–53 Pakistan's first Test match, v India at Delhi.

1953   Under Len Hutton, England win the final Test at the Oval to take the series 1–0, regaining the Ashes after 19 years.

1954–55 After losing the 1st Test at Brisbane, Len Hutton leads England to a 3–1 Ashes victory in Australia.

1958–59 Hanif Mohammad makes 499, for Karachi v Bahawalpur at Karachi.

1963   Publication of C.L.R. James's *Beyond a Boundary*.

1964–65 In Lahore, Railways defeat D.I. Khan by an innings and 851 runs.

1966   Basil D'Oliveira plays his first Test for England, v West Indies at Lord's.

1970   South Africa have their tour of England cancelled, and are excluded from international cricket because of their government's apartheid policies.

1970–71 Under Ray Illingworth, England regain the Ashes in Australia, winning the final Test at Sydney to take the series 2–0.

         First one-day international: Australia v England at Melbourne.

1973   Final cricket match at Bramall Lane, Sheffield.

1974–75 Viv Richards plays first Test for West Indies, v India at Bangalore.

1975   First World Cup: West Indies beat Australia in the final at Lord's by 17 runs.

1977–78 Kerry Packer launches World Series Cricket.

Australia's Graham Yallop becomes the first batsman to wear a helmet in a Test, v West Indies at Barbados.

1981   Ian Botham's 149* and Bob Willis's 8–43 help Mike Brearley's England to an unlikely victory over Australia in the Headingley Test, after following on.

1981–82   Sri Lanka's first Test match, v England at Colombo.

1985–86   Under David Gower, England lose all 5 Tests in the West Indies.

Viv Richards scores fastest Test hundred by balls faced (56), v England at St John's, Antigua.

1987–88   England captain Mike Gatting and umpire Shakoor Rana clash in 2nd Test at Faisalabad.

1992–93   Zimbabwe's first Test match, v India at Harare.

1993   The ICC becomes an independent organisation, no longer administered by MCC.

1995–96   Captain Mike Atherton scores 185* to help England draw the 2nd Test v South Africa at Johannesburg.

2000   Revised Laws of Cricket include a definition of the Spirit of Cricket.

South Africa's captain Hansie Cronje banned from cricket by the ICC after admitting receiving bribes from bookmakers.

2000–01   Bangladesh's first Test match, v India at Dhaka.

2003   Twenty20 Cup inaugurated in England.

2002–03   Under Nasser Hussain, England lose the Ashes in Australia 4–1.

England refuse to play in Zimbabwe, leading to an early exit from the World Cup.

2005   Under Michael Vaughan, England regain the Ashes in England after 16 years.

2006   Pakistan become the first team to forfeit a Test, for refusing to resume at the Oval.

2006–07 Under Andrew Flintoff, England lose the Ashes in Australia 5–0.

2008 Indian Premier League launched.

2010 Three Pakistan players are banned by the ICC for bowling deliberate no-balls in the 4th Test at Lord's.

2010–11 Under Andrew Strauss, England complete a 3–1 Ashes win in Australia.

2011 England beat India 4–0 to go top of the ICC Test rankings for the first time.

2012 After England lose the home Test series v South Africa 2–0, Andrew Strauss retires from professional cricket.

2013 Under Alastair Cook, England win the Ashes series in England 3–0.

2013–14 England lose the Ashes series in Australia 5–0.

2014 Changes to the governance of the ICC are pushed through by Australia, England and India.

2015 Australia beat New Zealand in the eleventh World Cup final in Melbourne.

SELECT BIBLIOGRAPHY

Bailey, Philip, Philip Thorn & Peter Wynne-Thomas, *Who's Who of Cricketers* (Hamlyn, 1993).

Beckles, Hilary McD. (ed), *A Spirit of Dominance: Cricket and Nationalism in the West Indies* (Canoe Press, 1998).

Berry, Scyld, *Cricket Wallah: With England in India 1981–2* (Hodder & Stoughton, 1982).

Bhattacharya, Rahul, *Pundits from Pakistan* (Picador, 2005).

Blunden, Edmund, *Cricket Country* (Collins, 1944).

Brearley, Mike, *The Art of Captaincy* (Hodder & Stoughton, 1985).

Cardus, Neville, *Autobiography* (Collins, 1947).

Carew, Dudley, *England Over* (Martin Secker, 1927).

Cashman, Richard, *Patrons, Players and the Crowd: The Phenomenon of Indian Cricket* (Orient Longman, 1980).

Clark, Manning, *A Short History of Australia* (Mentor, 1963).

Constantine, Learie, *Cricket and I* (Philip Allan, 1933).

de Saussure, César, *A Foreign View of England in the Reigns of George I and George II* (John Murray, 1902).

de Selincourt, Hugh, *The Cricket Match* (Jonathan Cape, 1924).

Fire in Babylon, directed by Stevan Riley, 2010.

Framji Patel, J.M., *Stray Thoughts on Indian Cricket* (Times Press, 1905).

Gibson, Alan, *Growing Up With Cricket: Some Memories of a Sporting Education* (Allen & Unwin, 1985).

Gooch, Graham, *Gooch: My Autobiography* (Collins Willow, 1995).

Grace, W.G., *Cricketing Reminiscences and Personal Recollections* (J. Bowden, 1899).

Guha, Ramachandra, *A Corner of a Foreign Field: The Indian History of a British Sport* (Picador, 2002).

Harris, Lord, *A Few Short Runs* (John Murray, 1921).

Hise, Beth, *Swinging Away: How Cricket and Baseball Connect* (Scala, 2010).

Hughes, Thomas, *Tom Brown's Schooldays* (1857).

James, C.L.R., *Beyond a Boundary* (Hutchinson, 1963).

Kulke, Eckehard, *The Parsees in India: A Minority as Agent of Social Change* (Weltforum, 1974).

Lee, Harry, *Forty Years of English Cricket* (Clerke & Cockeran, 1948).

Lewis, Michael, *Moneyball: The Art of Winning an Unfair Game* (Norton, 2003).

Love, James (James Dance), *Cricket: An Heroic Poem* (1745; facs. edn ECCO, 2014).

Macdonell, A.G., *England, Their England* (1933; Picador, 1983).

Manley, Michael, *A History of West Indies Cricket* (André Deutsch, 1988).

Mason, Ronald, *Batsman's Paradise: An Anatomy of Cricketomania* (Hollis & Carter, 1955).

Menon, Suresh, *Bishan* (Penguin, 2011).

Mitford, Mary Russell, *Our Village* (1832).

Nyren, John, *The Young Cricketer's Tutor/The Cricketers of My Time* (1833; David Nutt, 1893).

O'Neill, Joseph, *Netherland* (4th Estate, 2008).

Out of the Ashes, directed by Tim Albone, Lucy Martens & Leslie Knott, 2010.

Pavri, Mehallasha, *Parsee Cricket* (J.B. Marzban, 1901).

Pullin, Alfred ('Old Ebor'), *Talks With Old Yorkshire Cricketers* (Yorkshire Evening Post, 1898).

Pycroft, James, *The Cricket Field* (1851; St James's Press, 1922).

Robinson, Ray, *Between Wickets* (Collins, 1946).

Rodwell, Tom, *Third Man in Havana* (Corinthian, 2012).

Roebuck, Peter, *It Never Rains: A Cricketer's Lot* (Allen & Unwin, 1984).

Ross, Alan, *West Indies at Lord's* (Eyre & Spottiswoode, 1963).

Rundell, Michael, *The Dictionary of Cricket* (Allen & Unwin, 1985).

Scott, Jas, *Early Cricket in Sydney*, ed. by Richard Cashman and Stephen Gibbs (New South Wales Cricket Association, 1991).

Smith, Keithlyn B., *To Shoot Hard Labour: The Life and Times of Samuel Smith, an Antiguan workingman* (Karia Press, 1985).

Strudwick, Herbert, *Twenty-five Years Behind the Stumps* (Hutchinson, 1926).

Sun Tzu, *The Art of War*, tr. John Minford (Penguin, 2008).

Swanton, E.W., *Elusive Victory: With F.R. Brown's M.C.C. Team, 1950–51* (Hodder & Stoughton, 1951).

Trevor, Captain Philip, *The Lighter Side of Cricket* (Methuen, 1901).

Underdown, David, *Start of Play: Cricket and Culture in Eighteenth-Century England* (Allen Lane, 2000).

ACKNOWLEDGEMENTS

My thanks, first of all, to the editors and sports editors who have sent me on assignment and thereby allowed me to see and do what I wanted. Thereafter, in alphabetical order, my thanks to: Benedict Bermange for the tables he supplied; Ankush Berry for his technical skills; Freya Berry for calling on her double-starred first in English to supply the quotation for chapter one; Sceaf Berry for his advice on music and the sounds made by bat on ball, though not for his fielding; Roddy Bloomfield for taking on the book and being everything I could have wanted a publisher to be; Ian Chappell, who taught me to see the game through un-biased eyes and much else besides; Robert Craddock for his advice on the Australian chapter and friendship; John Curran for the coffee breaks and humour; Sam Dewes for his advice on the Artillery Ground and playing there; Andy Flower for his advice on the chapters about psychology and aesthetics; David Foot for his general encouragement and advice on Siegfried Sassoon; Ramachandra Guha for his friendship and advice on the Indian chapter; Steve James for his comradeship and advice on all matters relating to batting; Susan Kay for her literary advice on the draft; Jane Kentish, my cousin, for her instruction on classical and Renaissance art; Dr Prashant Kidambi for identifying Parsi players in nineteenth century photographs; Jack Lewars for his tuition on the subject of Homer; David Luxton for being everything I could have wanted from an agent; Emma and Peter Mitchell for their reading of the original draft and all their suggestions for improvement; Professor Adrian Poole for his advice on eighteenth-century matters; Susan Richardson for her professional counsel on literature; David Smith for his invaluable input in the second chapter and for the use of the best cricket library in the west country; Madeleine Riley, my godmother, who has been my sounding-board throughout; Fiona Rose for her efficiency in correcting the proofs; Sir Keithlyn Smith for permission to quote from his wonderful book *To Shoot Hard Labour*; Fraser Stewart of MCC for reading and commenting on the chapter about the Spirit of Cricket; Tim Waller, for being outstandingly brilliant at copy-editing; Simon Wilde for all the talk and tennis, or rather for all the talk and some of the tennis; all the other journalists with whom I have shared a press box, for the helping, laughing and learning; all the cricketers who have given me one-on-one interviews and opened up to tell me about their world; and, finally, the England captains I have had the great privilege to ghost and from whom I have learnt so much, in chronological order: the late Sir Leonard Hutton, Mike Atherton, Nasser Hussain, Michael Vaughan and Andrew Strauss.

PHOTOGRAPHIC ACKNOWLEDGEMENTS

The author and publisher would like to thank the following for permission to reproduce photographs:

akg-images/Album/Oronoz, Alfieri/Mirrorpix, Jane Bown/The Observer, Gareth Copley/Getty Images, Adam Davy, Mark Dozier/Corbis, Patrick Eagar, Patrick Eagar Collection/Getty Images, Mark Eklid, Empics Sport/Press Association Images, Mary Evans Picture Library, Excel Media/Rex Features, David Hares, High Level Photography/Rex Features, Hulton Archive/Getty Images, Leemarge/Corbis, MCC Library & Archives, Melbourne Cricket Club Archives, Mirrorpix, David Munden/Popperfoto/Getty Images, National Museum of Australia, Gianni Dagli Orti/Corbis, PA Archives/Press Association Images, Popperfoto/Getty Images, Ben Radford/Visionhaus/Corbis, Rooth Robertson, Transcendental Graphics/Getty Images, Trustees of the Goodwood Collection/Bridgeman Images.

INDEX

An invitation from the publisher

Join us at www.hodder.co.uk, or follow us
on Twitter @hodderbooks to be a part of
our community of people who love the very
best in books and reading.

Whether you want to discover more about a book
or an author, watch trailers and interviews, have the
chance to win early limited editions, or simply browse
our expert readers' selection of the very best books,
we think you'll find what you're looking for.

And if you don't, that's the place to tell us what's missing.

We love what we do, and we'd love you to be a part of it.

www.hodder.co.uk

 @hodderbooks

HodderBooks

 HodderBooks